Psychology in Black and White

The Project of a Theory-Driven Science

A Volume in
Advances in Cultural Psychology:
Constructing Human Development

Series Editor
Jaan Valsiner, *Aalborg University*

Advances in Cultural Psychology:
Constructing Human Development
Jaan Valsiner, Series Editor

Psychology in Black and White

The Project of a Theory-Driven Science

by

Sergio Salvatore
University of Salento

INFORMATION AGE PUBLISHING, INC.
Charlotte, NC • www.infoagepub.com

Library of Congress Cataloging-in-Publication Data

Salvatore, Sergio,
Psychology in black and white : the project of a theory-driven science /
by Sergio Salvatore.
pages cm. -- (Advances in cultural psychology: constructing human
development)
ISBN 978-1-68123-116-7 (paperback) -- ISBN 978-1-68123-117-4 (hardcover) --
ISBN 978-1-68123-118-1 (ebook) 1. Psychology--Philosophy. 2. Psychology.
I. Title.
BF38.S2236 2015
150--dc23

                                                                    2015017079

Cover page by Giovanni Salvatore

Printed in the United States of America

To Carlo, Gio, Ely, and Monica,
aware of the time and the desire
this book has taken away from you.

To Luisa and Michele
I wish you were here

CONTENTS

PART III: A NEW METHODOLOGICAL APPROACH

NEW SYNTHESIS

A Dynamic Theory of Sensemaking

This book is long awaited within the contemporarily creative field of cultural psychologies. It is a theoretical synthesis that is at the level of innovations that Sigmund Freud, James Mark Baldwin, William Stern, Kurt Lewin, Jean Piaget, Lev Vygotsky and Jan Smedslund have brought into psychology over the past century. All these classic thinkers have had the courage to go against the prevailing belief systems that governed the common sense in the societies of their lifetimes. They had to fight against being misunderstood by their contemporaries, and were—at times—even stigmatized for their standing out on their own.

Psychologists of recent times usually pride themselves for "standing on the shoulders of giants" of the past. This nice phrasing may create a theoretical myopia of our contemporaries who rush to follow established theoretical systems, rather than understand the limitations in the thought of the "classics" and attempt to develop their ideas further.

However—nothing is more dangerous in science for the fate of the ideas of our predecessors than efforts to follow them. "Being" a "Vygotskian" (or "Piagetan" or "Wernerian") is a loyalty pledge, rather than an identity marker that indicates that the given person might expand the ideas of the declared guru figure of the past. Honoring the important thinkers of the past without trying to solve their unsolved problems in new ways is actually disservice to their ideas.

Sergio Salvatore is not standing "on the shoulder of giants" of the past—he is a giant himself, of today. Over the past decade he has

Psychology in Black and White: The Project of a Theory-Driven Science, pp. xvii–xx

systematically, thoroughly and with great constructive arrogance[1], built up
a new perspective of cultural psychology that has relevance for the rest of
psychology. He is perhaps the most creative younger generation theoretical
thinker in cultural psychology of our beginning of the 21st century
who has enormous practical experience in clinical psychology and who
simultaneously is well versed in abstract theoretical discourses. He builds
on ideas of the most creative intellectual tendencies of the 20th century—
yet his resulting synthesis is a major breakthrough of his own making. In
the present book he creates an elaborate theory of sensemaking dynamics.
Here we can observe a creative solution to integrating cultural psychology
with the rich traditions of psychodynamic perspectives, without repeating
the conceptual impasses in which many psychoanalytic perspectives have
become caught. In a previous volume in our series (Salvatore & Zittoun,
2012) different new perspectives from psychoanalysis have been analyzed
by him and his colleagues.

In principle, it is all very simple. Human development can be conceived
of as the *increase of the variability* of meanings through the sensemaking
dynamics. Such variability is produced by persons who make and use
signs that allow for generalization beyond the here-and-now setting. Such
generalization is produced by *abductive* inference—which allows *qualitative
leaps* in the human sensemaking process. From the logic of abductive
inference one can draw a specific form of generalization—*abstractive
generalization*. That notion—emphasized by Karl Bühler (1934/1965) in
his *Sprachtheorie*—gains a new meaning in Salvatore's hands. It is a part
of constant sensemaking—we make signs, and as these signs are made,
they generalize. Cultural psychology in the thinking of Sergio Salvatore
is semiotic psychology. Furthermore—it is idiographic in its nature. This
is its particular strength—all psychological phenomena emerge at first
as single cases with their own organization. The normative frequency
of psychological phenomena is 1. Any accumulation of the numbers of
similar phenomena (from $N > 1$ to $N =$ "large sample") adds specimens to
our collections, but do not alter the reality of the very first case. The efforts
of the Wright Brothers to break out of the gravity of the Earth in their first
aeroplane operated on the same principles that our "dreamliners" of the
21st century.

Much of this book is dedicated to methodology in cultural psychology—
and psychology in general. As the author points out—methodology is the
discourse on method. It is the theoretical domain designed to define the model
of knowledge bridging the general theory to the practices of investigation.
This would allow the interaction between thought and action required
for the construction of scientific knowledge. Psychology in general is in
dire need for building up a new, phenomena-bound methodology that
takes the whole < > parts relations as its central focus, and open-systemic

axiomatics as its starting point. The tyranny of the statistical method that has governed psychology for a century is an unfortunate impasse of a young science looking for its focus, and finding it in places where the phenomena become lost (Cairns, 1986). In the 21st century we are in the process of repairing this epistemological rupture (Rudolph, 2013).

Sensemaking happens in the *directional* communication process. Paraphrasing the author (see p. [156] ff in the book), a statement

You are the Reader

implies the unity of opposites *at the same time*. While designating "you" as "the Reader" I simultaneously imply that you are not in the high variety of actors' roles you could be in, in relation to the book, but in which you are not (e.g., book buyer, collector, paper re-cyclerer, janitor, censor, etc.). It also creates systemic oppositions with tensions—a suggestion (*"I am the Reader"*) can be seen to evoke the resistance (*"but I do not want to read"*). Thus, statements that seem to be those of ontology ("S is P") are actually—in the open-systemic relations between statement-maker and statement-consumer—imperatives of general and future-oriented kind. Thus, claims "you are our son" or "you are a soldier" are not classificatory but performance-bound statements for the future. The theory of cultural psychology of sensemaking is an original perspective that transcends the limits of ontological constraints of human language use.

This new look at the communication process is likely to refresh theory building in general psychology. On the one hand it is a way to bring the notion of irreversible time—elaborated a century ago by Henri Bergson in philosophy, and made notable in the physical sciences in the 1970s by the work of Ilya Prigogine—to become a core axiom in psychology. All human psychological processes emerge, take form, and become extinct, in irreversible time. Secondly, the perspective of Franz Brentano on the inherent intentionality of psychological phenomena could be brought into the center of theory building. All meanings that are used in sensemaking have a direction ($\rightarrow$), so a particular meaning {A} is not merely a concept-in-itself (paraphrasing Immanuel Kant) but concept-with-direction {A$\rightarrow$...} (in contrast to its opposite direction {...$\leftarrow$A}). The specific object of that direction need not be directly evident in this concept. In fact it may acquire its object in the process of sensemaking.

Sergio Salvatore's book continues the important sequence of theoretical monographs in our series. From the very beginning we have been publishing monographic texts that innovate the discipline. Alex Gillespie's (2006) look at the Self <> Other relationship dynamics in the case of people who as tourists visit far-away countries, and Tania Zittoun's (2006) theory of ruptures were there at the beginning, and were followed by Per Linell's (2009) comprehensive theory of dialogicality, as well as Mario Carretero's

(2011) dissection of the cultural-psychological mechanisms of patriotism. Most recently, an innovative take on creativity (Tanggaard, 2014) came into existence. Cultural psychology is a colorful mosaic of perspectives, from which only at times new theoretical breakthroughs emerge. *The Psychology in Black and White* is a remarkable new step in the actively developing field of cultural psychology.

Jaan Valsiner
Aalborg, October 2014

NOTE

1. I purposefully use the otherwise negatively stigmatized notion of *arrogance* in the most positive sense. I consider breakthroughs in science possible when the thinker is capable of playful handling of serious scientific matters—including theoretical presentations. For examples of how such attitude works out at the Nobel Prize level, see Andre Geim's *Random Walk to Grapheme* (http://www.nobelprize.org/nobel_prizes/physics/laureates/2010/geim_lecture.pdf)

REFERENCES

Bühler, K. (1965). *Sprachtheorie* [Theory of language]. Jena-Stuttgart: Gustav Fischer. (Original work published 1934)

Cairns, R. B. (1986). Phenomena lost: issues in the study of development. In J. Valsiner (Ed.), *The individual subject and scientific psychology* (pp. 97–111). New York, NY: Plenum.

Carretero, M. (2011). *Constructing Patriotism: Teaching history and memories in global worlds.* Charlotte, NC: Information Age Publishing.

Gillespie, A. (2007). *Becoming other to oneself.* Greenwich, Ct: Information Age Publishing.

Linell, P. (2009). *Rethinking language, mind, and world dialogically.* Charlotte, NC: Information Age Publishing.

Rudolph, L. (Ed.). (2013). *Qualitative mathematics for the social sciences.* London, England: Routledge.

Salvatore, S., & Zittoun, T. (Eds.). (2012). *Cultural psychology and psychoanalysis: Pathways to synthesis.* Charlotte, NC: Information Age Publishing.

Tanggaard, L (2014). *Fooling around: Finding creative learning pathways.* Charlotte, NC: Information Age Publishing.

Zittoun, T. (2006). *Transitions: Symbolic resources in development.* Greenwich, CT: Information Age Publishing.

INTRODUCTION

Psychology as the Science of the Explanandum

> Life is in colour, but *black and white is more realistic*
>
> (Wenders, 1982/1983)

In *The State of Things* (Wenders, 1982/1983), the director Munro intuits that the core of human experience is not experiential and so one has to step back from the experience—to use the black and white—in order to grasp what is essential about it.

This book is grounded on such an insight.

It aims at laying the foundation of a *Psychology in Black and White*, namely a psychology that welcomes the director Munro's invitation to consider the difference between the experience of reality and the reality of experience and as a result, recognizes the need to re-think itself in terms of *theory-driven science*.

I am aware of the fact that the project of a theory-driven psychology is quite a radical proposal compared to the data-driven, evidence-based line predominant in contemporary psychology. A theory-driven psychology is a psychology that gives up concepts defined in terms of phenomenical experience, to model from within the objects and categories it takes as the target and means of its investigation. This involves pursuing an abstract form of knowledge quite remote from the concreteness of daily experience—namely, learning to see the psychological object in black and white.

Psychology in Black and White: The Project of a Theory-Driven Science, pp. xxi–xli
Copyright © 2016 by Information Age Publishing
All rights of reproduction in any form reserved.

As more developed sciences show, this distance is not the problem, but the solution: it is just what is required to enable science to go beyond what appears and grasp the core of human experience.

OVERVIEW

Psychology Suffers From Common Sense

Psychology addresses phenomena defined by common sense, that is, by the daily life way of thinking people have as members of a cultural environment.

Consider the format of psychological scientific knowledge in the terms of the following generic relation:

$$P = R(C_y) \tag{1}$$

where P stands for the phenomenon to be known (i.e., the *explanandum*, what has to be explained) and C_y for the psychological (set of) construct(s) mobilized in order to say something psychological about the phenomenon (i.e., the *explanans*, what explains); R stands for the (usually empirical) linkage built between the phenomena and the construct. Thus, (1) states that the psychological scientific knowledge consists of a relationship that is set between the phenomenon that has to be known and the psychological construct; and this is the same as saying that the phenomenon is explained as a function of the psychological construct. Needless to say, there are a variety of functions R in terms of which phenomena and construct may be linked. Causality is one of them. In this case, P is regarded as the effect of C_y, and their linkage acquires the meaning of explanation; covariation, interpretation, functional explanation, modeling are other kinds of R.

Consider some classical psychological theories. The decay of memory (P) is the effect (R) of the interference of new information (C_y). Intelligence (C_y) correlates (R) with positive scholastic outcome (P). The therapeutic alliance correlates (R) with positive psychotherapeutic outcome. The social representation (C_y) has the function (R) of making the unfamiliar (P) familiar. Outgroup aggressiveness (C_y) has the function (R) of defending in-group cohesion. And so forth.

These examples, though so different from each other, share an aspect: in all cases P is defined outside psychology, in terms of common sense—one does not need to study psychology to understand the meaning of notions like decay of memory, thinking, efficacy of the school career and so forth. Everyone learns to use these notions just by participating to daily life.

Thus, psychology seems grounded on a division of epistemic labor with common sense. It leaves the task of defining the objects of knowledge to daily language in order to concentrate its efforts on the development of the scientific constructs required to explain (*latosensu*) such objects. In this sense, psychology appears to be a *science of the explanans:* a system of knowledge aimed at producing instances of C_Y enabling us to understand instances of P that are independently defined by common sense.

This shows most emblematically psychology's tendency to consider itself a science studying commonsensical phenomena that lie in the sectoralization of the discipline in terms of domains as defined by social-cultural categories and systems of activities: organizational psychology, school psychology, sport psychology, health psychology, psychology of tourism, and so forth. The point here is not so much the differentiation in itself, but its aim, the epistemological implications of its use: sectoralization is not seen as a conventional device to be used to identify a class of professional figures that have become homogeneous due to their shared professional context; instead, the sectors are conceived as autonomous areas of psychological discourse that are characterized by their own particular objects and methods of enquiry. Now, the fact that an area of psychological discourse is defined in terms of a certain sector of the social system clearly means that the discipline finds its objects in phenomena as they appear through the eyes of the common sense, rather than in terms of constructs enrooted in the scientific theory.

Addiction is an example of this way of constructing the psychological object: addiction is not a natural phenomenon but a social construct; a model of social practice generated by the dialectic between individual ways of acting and historically determined forms of institutional control. As a result of this dialectic, rather than as result of a scientific differentiation, some patterns of action are classified as addiction (use of drugs, pornography, Internet, but also great involvement in work), while others are not (consumption of art, reading, supporting one's soccer team, a very strong romantic relationship with one's partner, and so forth). In sum, addiction is not a psychological construct, but a phenomenon of reality, defined prescientifically. Psychology is called on to explain it, not to define it.

The limitations of sectoralization have been pointed out from all quarters (*inter alia*, Carli, 2002). I myself have criticized it, with particular attention to the meaning to be given to the idea of scholastic psychology (Salvatore, 2003). Recalling this discussion may help to further clarify the issue at stake. In short, scholastic psychology cannot be interpreted as a specific, autonomous domain of psychology because school is not a systematic domain endowed with psychological specificity. What happens in schools is obviously of interest to psychology; however, the phenomena the psychologist finds in school do not acquire psychological meaning by the fact of occurring in this context. For instance, the learning processes that take place in school do not follow different forms of organization from other learning processes that may occur in other human domains.

The Weak Status of Psychological Knowledge

I maintain that the fact that psychology works as a science of the *explanans* is the fundamental source of its weakness, of its incapability of producing scientific innovation, of the *cul-de-sac* of the empty empiricism in which it is encapsulated (Toomela & Valsiner, 2010)

This criticism is the necessary corollary of the recognition of the semiotic nature of the psychological object. Psychological phenomena consist of meanings and connections among meanings. As Smedslund (1982, 1988a, 1988b, 1992, 1995) showed, this means that in the case of a psychological phenomenon the relation between *explanandum* and *explanans* it given beforehand, deposited in the common sense. Consequently, connecting the phenomenon with the construct has the epistemic value of being an operation of making pertinent/explicit an area of meaning already present in the cultural environment. In other words, *psychology ends up working as the descriptor of the implicit linkages active within common sense.*

Take a person playing roulette and winning a certain amount of money. It is evident that one may not consider winning as the effect of playing. Winning is already part of the meaning of playing roulette. It is one of the scenarios entailed in such a script. Therefore, one cannot say that playing causes winning, in the same way that one cannot say that the term "dog" causes "being the human being's best friend". Winning, like "being the human being's best friend" are definitions/pertinentizations of their respective topic (playing roulette and dog, respectively). The former derives from the latter. The same kind of semiotic linkage qualifies most (if not all) psychological phenomena, when the latter are defined by common sense. Consider the conceptualization of school drop-outs (P) in terms of students' lack of motivation (C_y). Well, actually this is not an explanation, for the very reason that the lack of motivation is not an independent agent coming from outside and producing the drop-out; rather it is part of the pragmatic definition of drop-out, and vice versa. The same consideration can be applied to the other examples of theories mentioned above. Interference of new information does not cause decay; rather, the decay of previous information is part of the meaning of interference—interference is the effect that something produces on something else with which the former enters a relation. Intelligence is entailed in the notion of positive school outcome; it is not that the student produces good scholastic outcome because of its being intelligent. Rather, being intelligent means succeeding in school (as well as in other intellectual activity). Again, once one considers that the efficacy of psychotherapy logically entails seeing it as a goal-oriented social activity, then the collaborative attitude of the participants has to be seen as part of the meaning of the concept of psychotherapy, entailed in the description (though sometimes implicit) of it as goal-oriented. Therefore, to say efficacious psychotherapy already means therapeutic alliance; where there is no therapeutic alliance, by definition there is the failure of psychotherapy; consequently, the linkage between psychotherapy and therapeutic alliance is not a matter of contingency to test empirically, but a matter of reciprocal implication in the definitions of the two terms. Similarly, the very notion of representation means changing something that before was unrepresented/unknown (unfamiliar) into something that is now part of what is known (namely, familiar). Finally, out-group aggressiveness entails logically and semantically—not factually —the reference to the in-group; this is clear if one considers that any act entails a subject acting it; therefore, to say that out-group aggressiveness causes in-group cohesion is the same as saying, for instance, that running causes the runner or observation causes the observer.

In sum, the idea that many excerpts of psychological knowledge are no more than (sometimes sophisticated) truisms has to be taken seriously into consideration. It is worth noting that this situation does not concern all the field of knowledge in a generalized way. In the case in which the (phenomenon referred by the) construct has a factual relationship with the *explanandum*, the mapping of such a relationship is not a truism. By factual relationship I mean that the *explanans* construct is independent from the *explanandum*, namely that it does not semantically entail a relationship with the *explanandum*. For instance, take the relationship between gas pressure and temperature. The definitions of both concepts do not entail any kind of reference to the relationship with the other term. Therefore, the concept of pressure is independent from the concept of temperature. A further example may help to distinguish factual and semiotic relationship between phenomenon and explicative construct. Take a person that is slapped. Due to this, the person feels pain on her cheek and is deeply annoyed with the slapper. Well, these two feelings are in different logical relationship with the slap suffered. The pain is the effect of the slap: there is no semantic relationship between the two terms—the meaning |being slapped| does not hold the meaning of |to feel pain|; thus the relationship |being slapped|–|to feel pain| is factual. In contrast, |being slapped| and |to be annoyed with the slapper| are semiotically linked: the latter is entailed in the sociopragmatic significance of the former act. To slap someone is a specific sign, different from other similar acts (kicking, punching...) and similar to other different acts (e.g., spitting), having a specific repertoire of meaning: punishment, offending, expressing one's anger, and the like. The semiotic valence of the relationship between being slapped and feeling annoyed is shown by the fact that in some countries to punch and to slap a public official are *defined as* two different crimes: respectively striking and offending a public official. And it is obvious that the law does not identify the effect of punches and smacks according to the psychology of the public official; rather it draws it from the commonsensical definition of these two pragmatic signs.

The consequence of the misrecognition of the semiotic nature of the linkage between P and C_Y has had a major negative impact on the epistemic status of psychological knowledge. It has made psychological statement pseudo-empiric (Smeslund, 1982, 1988a, 1988b, 1992, 1995) and has produced the deterioration of the scientific status of its language, step by step transformed into a replication of common sense.

Pseudo-Empiricism: Psychology Discovers the Hot Water

Psychological statements do not go beyond what is already known or however entailed implicitly within common sense. This can be expressed in the terms of a second generic relation:

$$\text{When } P = S(CS) \tag{2},$$

$$\text{Then } C_Y = S(P) \tag{3}$$

Namely, when P is a semiotic function – S – of common sense – CS –, namely it is defined in terms of naïve layman's language, the psychological construct C_Y is a semiotic function of P, namely it is implicated in P.

Now, if one substitutes (2) in (3), one obtains:

$$\text{When (2), then } C_Y = S[S(CS)] \tag{4}$$

which may be rewritten as

$$C_Y = S'(CS) \tag{5}$$

with (5) to be read that when the psychological phenomenon is defined in terms of common sense, the psychological construct is also a function of common sense.

One can seek proof of this by looking for counterintuitive ideas in psychology. I have my doubts that the research will be productive – even if it is enlarged beyond the mainstream domain. Being grounded on common sense, psychology is unable to produce ideas going beyond it. This is true particularly in domains where psychology deals with problems that are not exclusively of specialist interest, namely problems on which other social figures also express interpretations; in these cases the discipline tends to produce knowledge that systematizes and/or gives an empirical legitimization to what is already part of the more or less tacit, socially shared knowledge. This statement is admittedly a generic simplification of the vast range of psychological literature. However, if one compares sciences like physics, chemistry, and also linguistics, one cannot help being struck by the chasm separating psychology from the capacity of these sciences to produce knowledge not simply confined to deepening the furrow of what people in the street are already able to experience and conceptualise, but which builds new worlds that revolutionise the very structure of the naïve experience of the phenomena in question.

Another indication of the closeness of psychology to common sense is the ease with which psychology becomes part of the communicative contexts of everyday life and by the corresponding permeability of psychological language to everyday discourse. One could almost formulate a kind of *Murphy's law* on this: the more trivial the subject (either because it is irrelevant or because there is no interest in intervention), the more likely it is that a psychologist will be asked to comment on it. It would be far too easy to cite the proliferation of psychologists and mannered "psychologisms" in the mass media as proof of this law and more generally of the ease with which psychology tends to spill over into common sense. In the same way, one could recall the widespread idea that rather than being a skilled function based on scientific knowledge, psychology is a personal quality that everyone possesses in varying degrees.

Deterioration of the Psychological Scientific Language

This issue is even more critical than that entailed in pseudo-empiricism, because it extends the epistemic weakness of psychology to the future. The fact that the relationship between P and C_Y is regulated by commonsensical reciprocal semiotic implication is the same as saying that criteria of validity of scientific statements are, in the final analysis, defined outside scientific language.

Westen, Morrison, and Thompson-Brenner (2004) provided a thoughtful, emblematic illustration of this point. They analyzed the validity criteria grounding Evidence Based Medicine's (EBM) assumption that the experimental design of the Randomized Clinical Trial (RCT) represents the golden standard methodology in psychotherapy research. They argued convincingly that this assumption, which works as the basic normative

criterion of validation of psychotherapy research, has no scientific validation itself. And one can add: it is clearly grounded on the metaphorical assimilation of psychotherapy to pharmacotherapy (Stiles & Shapiro, 1989),
namely, on a typical way of working of the common sense, that transforms
similarities into equivalence.

Unfortunately, this is not the worse part of the affair. The very negative
consequence of this is that psychological constructs, too, are unavoidably
destined to lose their semantic boundaries and logical consistency and be
transformed into commonsensical notions. This happens as a result of two
converging tensions.

On the one hand, one has to take into account that the P works as an
attractor pushing psychologists to shape C_Y in order to enable the latter to
be assimilated by the former. This cannot be but so, because in any kind
of discourse (maybe with the exception of humor), and therefore also in
scientific discourse, it is the argument/object/*explanandum* which defines
the constraints and the terms according to which the predicate/construct/
explanans may be put in relation with it. In other words, any scientific statement has to set relationships between *explanandum* and *explanans* that are
not only empirically supported, but also plausible. And this plausibility
rests mainly on what the naïve layman already knows about the *explanandum*. (It is true that in some cases the relationship stated produces a rupture in the already acquired knowledge on the *explanandum*. Yet also in this
case the new relationship is acceptable only if it is also joined with a new
conception of the *explanandum*). During the 2010 soccer world champion-
ship, the whole world was astonished at the octopus Paul' ability to foresee
the outcome of the German team's matches. He managed to predict 8
results out 8, each time choosing the right box between the two, each of
them marked with the color of one team—Germany and its opponent.
In terms of probability, the possibility that Paul could reached this result
by chance was less than 0,04. Nevertheless, no one actually thought that
Paul was actual able to predict results. There had to be another explanation! And this is not because the level of probability is not sufficient—in
psychology a lot of statements that are trusted as the truth are based on
much higher probability threshold), but because the explanation in terms
of Paul's ability to make predictions is sharply in contrast with our representation of octopuses.

On the other hand, psychology as science concerning human affairs
cannot but adopt constructs which are sourced from the same phenomena
of life they have to model. Therefore, most psychological concepts are
originally commonsensical concepts and as such they are largely used in
parallel with their scientific appropriation. One does not need to study
psychology to be able to use notions like *emotion, aggressiveness, culture, representation, mind, thought, motivation, therapeutic alliance, unconscious*, and so

forth. Consequently, even though psychological science may be involved in elaborating very specific definitions for these terms (and actually this is not the most common case), they are constantly subjected to the attraction of the polysemic, fuzzy, contingent way they are used in the daily language game. And this is so because the scientists that use them are at the same time persons participating in such a daily language game.

These two sources of tension are inherent to any kind of science, in particular of human and social science. Yet if common sense enters the inner realm of scientific discourse, as happens if P is defined in terms of daily language, this means that the constraints contrasting the common-sensical power of attraction are greatly weakened. The result of this is that the language of contemporary psychology is full of terms whose superficial semantic self-evidence hides their theoretical opacity. Constructs like *emotion, representation, context, mind, discourse, text, culture, unconscious, act, agency, normality* are used by psychologists in a variety of significances that would be unthinkable in other sciences—imagine the credit that would be given to a physicist who stated as premise of his/her model something like: "according to my definition, an atom is...." Analogously, many constructs —*leadership, group, commitment, motivation, development, community, dialogue, meaning, addictive behavior*, and the like—are directly accepted in their na-ïve semantics, with the secondary but not at all marginal result that *what should be explained is transformed into what explains*. This is clearly evident, for instance, in the use made in transcultural psychology of the construct of culture as an independent variable—the phenomenon, instead of being modeled, is moved onto the other side of the scientific statement and transformed into the *explanans* (maintaining the commonsensical assimilation with the daily notion of people sharing a language and a country; for a discussion of this point, see Valsiner, 2007).

A corollary of the deterioration of the scientific status of psychological categories is the tendency to use them not as constructs, namely concepts that, as the name itself indicates, *construct* the objects of the discipline in modelistic terms, but to use them as pieces/states/qualities of the world. From this point of view, psychologists have been through the same process of objectification that Moscovici (1961/1976) saw as characterizing the relation between scientific knowledge and its appropriation by everyday discourse contexts. Ultimately, both psychologists and the naïve have contributed to setting scientific psychological language adrift. Nowadays, not only the construct of "the unconscious" referred to in Moscovici's study, but also many other psychological concepts, are treated as if they described pieces of reality, thought to be hidden, but endowed with ontological substance. Examples of this way of treating psychological concepts abound, across the various domains of theoretical discourse, research and professional practice.

Emblematic of the reification of a psychological construct is the way the notion of the personality trait is treated. Despite the fact that this kind of construct resulted from procedures of factorial analysis concerning the variability of the whole population by definition, and despite the cyclic methodological and theoretical warning (e.g., Lamiell, 1998), traits are diffusely used as intra-individual dimensions, both as dependent and independent variables, in clinical, differential and social psychology as well.

Survival Strategy

Smedslund (1988) proposed a radical solution to the epistemic weakness of psychological language derived from the closeness to common sense. He claimed that this closeness is not the problem, but the condition of validity and the source of the goal of psychological science. According to him, psychology has to develop as a deductive system of statements aimed at bringing order, making the commonsensical meanings about psychological affairs explicit and linking them with each other. To use an image, psychology has to "clean up" and bring order within common sense. Smedslund's reference is geometry. Geometric laws are deductive, not empirical. The assertion that the sum of the angle of a triangle is 180° is not the description of a state of fact, but a theorem derived deductively from other theorems. In this sense, geometry is an a-prior form of knowledge. Its development is a matter of deductive unpacking of what is potentially already in the mind, not of inductive discovering. The same is proposed for psychology, whose mission would be the unpacking of common sense.

Smedslund's solution is fascinating, but it makes things even worse than the problem it addresses. It is as if the therapy the doctor proposed after having diagnosed the illness, was to call the disease normal. Because of that his thoughtful, seminal criticism of inductivism in the psychological field had a smaller influence on psychology than it deserved.

On the other hand, if one goes beyond the surface, Smedslund's program of a psychology as systematization of common sense is paradoxically what is (implicitly) carried out by contemporary mainstream psychology. Psychology's blind inductivism (Salvatore & Valsiner, 2010) produces an enormous amount of studies whose global effect is the creation of a discourse on human affairs that is no more than a translation into technical language of what is already entailed in the naïve knowledge of the world.

It would be wrong to consider such a mountain of data offered by the scientific mass-production to the symbolic market as lacking in any function and value. Rather, it is a powerful source of sociopolitical legitimization enabling psychology to acquire financial, institutional and symbolic resources. The fortune of the professional psychology is grounded on this exchange. Psychological discourse reinforces common sense and thanks to this enjoys the social demand, which finds in it a powerful tool to consolidate the normative assumptions on which it is grounded (Carli, 1996; Salvatore, in press, a; in press, b; Salvatore & Valsiner, 2014). The half-century history of psychotherapy research is an exemplary instance of this collusive exchange. Psychotherapy research began to develop when Eysenck (1952) provocatively questioned its efficacy. What moved researchers was mainly the necessity to legitimize the professional system: Eysenck's article challenged the legitimacy of psychotherapy being supported by the insurance companies. If one considers this basic motivation, it is not hard to understand why the methodological and conceptual progress of psychotherapy research has been so slow and however systematically constrained within the framework of the assimilation of psychotherapy to the medical model (Wampold, 2001): psychotherapy research has had as its main concern the socioinstitutional request to demonstrate the efficacy—a request that cannot but assimilate psychotherapy to medical care—rather than the scientific commitment to developing clinical theory.

In sum, the survival strategy adopted is to sell psychology to society for the sake of psychologists' social success.

Psychology as Science of the Explanandum

This book starts from the idea that an alternative is possible. Its aim is to pave the way for this different route. The alternative strategies consist of this: *Psychology has to radically distance itself from common sense*. This requires two complementary operations to be carried out. On the one hand, psychology has to put common sense outside its language. On the other hand, it has to develop an analytic and methodological apparatus enabling to handle reflectively the inherent semiotic gravitational attraction that the common sense exerts on its language.

As stated above, the Trojan Horse of common sense is the definition of the phenomena psychology takes as its objects (i.e., the *P*). As long as this definition is made in terms of naïve language, the whole psychological language will be deteriorated by such promiscuity. Therefore, what psychology has to do is to give up the current division of epistemic work with common sense and to begin to define its objects in terms of its own scientific language. In other words, it has to pass from being a *science of the explanans* to be a *science of the explanandum*.

This shift is somehow a Copernican shift: the change from of an empirical science, as contemporary psychology self-represents itself, into a modelistic science. Nevertheless, it is a pathway already trodden. The history of science provides many indications that this shift is the precondition and the ground of development of scientific thought, which makes science an autonomous intellectual enterprise. Physics is the paradigmatic example of this kind of development. Its objects are defined from the inside its own scientific language, essentially in terms of mathematical constructions. To give an example, quantum mechanics is not only an explicative theory but a framework which constructs the objects that on the other hand are studied. Given that these objects are constructed in accordance with the inner rules of the language of physics, they are fully independent from daily conceptions, as far from common sense as Wonderland is. The consequence of this is that those who are not competent in the language of physics cannot understand not only the explanation (i.e., the *explanans*), but more deeply the phenomenon the explanation concerns (i.e., the *explanandum*). In this there is the radical distance between physics and psychology—most statements of the latter being so accessible and consistent to the naïve.

On the other hand, the development of science in modelistic terms (here I adopt this definition to denote science that defines its object of investigation theoretically) is not an exclusive prerogative of the hard sciences. Several disciplines within the realm of social sciences have assumed the status of modelistic sciences. Think of semiotics. It calls itself the science of signs and of signification (Eco, 1975). Now, signs and signification are not empirical phenomena that semiotics finds before it starts up. On the contrary, they are modelistic constructions made by semantics itself and providing the object of knowledge grounding and targeting the scientific enterprise. Linguistics is another example of this kind. Economics provides another powerful example of modelistic science. Economic objects are not empirical phenomena. They do not exist independently from economics. *Value, distribution*, as well as *market, demand, offer, choice, pay-off, inflation*, and so forth, are theoretical constructions, not categories of common sense. Or rather, they are both scientific constructs and common sense notions. But this is so for the opposite movement compared to psychology: Economics has exported its constructs toward common sense, rather than assimilating forms of daily language. Luhmann's theory of society (e.g., Luhmann & De Giorgi, 1992) is another example of the modelistic construction of the scientific object of investigation. According to Luhmann, sociology is the study of the society; yet the society studied by sociology is a theoretical object that does not have the same meaning as the naïve definition. For Luhmann, society is the recursive system of social linkages. Thus, society is not composed by persons as we naively believe, but by linkages.

Modelistic logic is not totally extraneous to psychology. The first part of the Freudian theorization is worth considering essentially modelistic. The Freudian topographical model, the rule of dream-work, the notion of primary process, the very idea of psychic determinism: all of them are examples of theoretical construction of the scientific object, rather than instances of explanations of commonsensical phenomena. Then, with the development of the psychoanalytic movement, and the preeminent role assumed by clinical professional practice within it, this original modelistic attitude was progressively marginalized.

The Self-Referentiality of Science

A science that defines the object of investigation from within its own language is by definition self-referential. And this can easily raise intensive criticisms. In particular, one can object that self-referentiality would mean cutting the linkage with the world of the facts and events, therefore losing any external criterion of validation. In so doing, at the best psychology would be led back to philosophy.

I think that there are several reasons for rejecting this criticism/concern.

Firstly, one has to consider that the commonsensical definition of psychological phenomena is however a construction. More, it is a construction that because of the social nature of the process producing it, tends to be contingent to structures of power, systems of values and interests and the like (Teo, 2005). Therefore, the version of the world that common sense provides to psychology is neither a direct channel to grasp reality nor a stable enough basis for building theory. One can find a huge amount of instances of the unreliability of common sense. Think of psychopathological theory that defines the phenomena of interest according to the evolution of social values and structures of power—for instance, two centuries ago in the Southern States of the United States the slaves that did not surrender to their condition and tried to escape were considered affected by the mental syndrome of Runaway Slave Disorder (*drapetomania*) (Grasso & Stampa, 2011). And that this is not the exception but the rule is shown by the fact that even nowadays some psychologists still persist in seeing homosexuality as a disorder.

From a complementary point of view, one has to take into consideration that giving up the common sense foundation of phenomena does not mean remaining without criteria of validation for selecting theories. Even if the vision of science as a perfect rational world not affected by the social dynamic active in the other domains of human life is a myth (e.g., Kharlamov, 2010), it is reasonable to think that the scientific normative criteria derivable from the modelization of the object are far more consistent with the aim of the scientific enterprise. In comparison with criteria derived from common sense, scientific criteria are more transparent, more visible, and therefore more negotiable and dynamic, less contingent to particularisms, more stable and less polysemic. Thus, as one defines the object of knowledge X in psychological terms, this definition produces *ipso facto* a set of constraints and regulative criteria defining the condition of validity of the theorization at stake in a more efficient and efficacious (and further developable) way than relying on the taken-for-granted normative beliefs provided by common sense. Take the case of a researcher aiming at analyzing communication. Imagine that he/she adopts the naïve definition of this object. This definition is polysemic, and therefore it does not provide systematic syntactic and semantic constrains on how the phenomenon can be addressed and what may be said about it. For instance, imagine that the researcher has to define a parameter of the participant's involvement in the communication. One possibility could be the time spent communicating; another possibility is the symbolic costs the participant agrees to pay in order to be part of the communication. Well, the common sense definition does not provide a criterion on which to decide which of the two parameters is more consistent with the phenomenon. Or rather, due to its polysemy, the common sense definition provides many criteria. It would be different in the case of the modelistic construction of communication. In this case, given that it would be made in the same language as the further operation of investigations, the definition itself would work as regulative criterion for the following conceptual and methodological operations.

In sum, refraining from referring to the commonsensical definition of phenomena does not mean giving up constraints and the possibility of selecting theories. Rather, it means overcoming a source of misleading implicit criteria in favour of more consistent and efficacious parameters of validation. On the other hand, disciplines like economics, linguistics and semiotics show that self-referentiality does not mean giving up the validation/selection of theories.

Another important aspect to underline is that modelistic science does not mean antiempirical science. A theory-driven psychology would not do without data; the empirical dimension would not disappear but it would be redefined in its role. Indeed, in modelistic science data do not build the theory but are informed and shaped by the theory. And this is just another way of claiming that modelistic science is neither deductive nor inductive, but abductive (Salvatore & Valsiner, 2010). According to abductive logic, empirical investigation is not a mere matter of data retrieval, but of production of a version of the world in terms of theory. In other words, in modelistic science empirical research performs the function of generating a local version of the theoretical object in the space-temporal setting of the investigation. The experiments conducted with the particle accelerator provide a good example of this particular linkage between theory and experience. The particle accelerator is not only a mediator between the reality and the observer. Rather, it is the generator of a specific version of the reality produced in accordance and for the sake of mirroring physics' model of the object. This is evident in the name itself: an accelerator of subatomic particles is thinkable and producible only because and on the grounds of a theory stating the subatomic composition of matter. Obviously, the accelerator produces data; yet these data are epiphenomena of a world that is instantiated by the theory; therefore, such data can be recognized, collected, understood and used only through the mediation of the theory. Thus, physics is involved in empirical investigation, but a kind of empirical investigation that is theoretically driven. Yet such a prominence of theory does not mean that physics is unable to select and develop theories. Indeed, the modelistic approach ensures that physics can develop consistently with its own criterion of validity: being realistic does not necessarily mean being in close correspondence with (the naïve representation of) the world. It can be more realistic to shape the world so as to make it a representation that is more consistent with the aim of the observer.

Opportunities

So far I have proposed arguments to defend the self-referentiality of modelistic science from criticism. In this paragraph I want to go a step ahead and show why modelistic science represents a prospect of development for psychology.

First, I have already mentioned that overcoming the commonsensical definition of psychological phenomena has the fundamental aim of defending the language of psychology from the deterioration it is exposed to by the promiscuity with common sense.

Second, not assuming phenomena as defined by common sense does not mean isolating psychology from the world. In Part I have addressed this point by discussing the issue of empirical investigation in the case of modelistic science. More in general, self-referentiality means not assuming the world directly, but however dealing with it, through the mediation of theory. Thanks to this mediation psychology could be empowered to enter epistemic and pragmatic relationship with the world. Other sciences provide examples of this. For instance, take the economic theory of price. This is a modelistic theory, part of and concerning a theoretical object (the market as an abstract concept). Nevertheless (or rather, thanks to this), it works as a powerful heuristic tool both at the level of policy formulation and at the level of the layman engaged in buying or selling something. More in general, mathematics and geometry provide clear examples of how the knowledge produced by scientific domains, not being directly in touch with the world, can be spent usefully in and for the world. There are no triangles and squares in the reality, and that is exactly why geometry is so useful because it enables us to think of some forms in terms of triangles or squares.

Third, the modelistic construction of the object is a way for empowering—rather than preventing—psychology's capacity to produce innovative statements on the world. This is because the modelistic attitude weakens the conservative power of common sense. Indeed, common sense works with the mind of researchers like ancient maps, where the limit of the known world were marked by "*hic sunt leones.*" The more common sense participates in the construction of scientific knowledge, the more cogent these constraints are. Therefore, distancing oneself from common sense is the way to produce thoughts not yet thought. For instance, if psychologists remain within the common sense assumption that what we represent as our thought is the product mirroring the inner state of our thinking, then this assumption places serious limits on the production of innovative ways of conceiving many aspects of subjectivity and relationship. An analogy with mathematics helps to highlight the latter point. Irrational numbers openly violate our naïve idea of numbers. It is hard for us to imagine them, to consider them consistent with reality. It is not by chance that they are called "irrational." Well, this kind of number is adopted in several computational procedures whose output has important concrete applications in the world. This suggests that violating the mundane norms can be the best way of pursuing mundane goals in a consistent way: again, the reality is experienced in color, but we can grasp it better in black and white.

This latter consideration leads to the last point I intend to make. Psychology, as the science of the meaning and sensemaking, pursues the epistemic task of analyzing and understanding common sense. Needless to say, insofar as it stays just within the Hercules's columns of naïve assumptions, it cannot carry out this task effectively. A psychology that is a prisoner of common sense is a psychology that acts it, rather than understanding it.

THIS VOLUME

Main Focus: Psychology as the Science of Sensemaking

The following chapters present my contribution to the development of modelistic psychology. It is grounded on the foundational idea that sensemaking is the object of psychology.

A great many works address phenomena and aspects concerning meaning and sensemaking (e.g., Guidi & Salvatore, 2014; Linell, 2009; Moscovici, 1961/1976; Sato, 2011; Valsiner, 2007, 2012, 2014; Valsiner & Rosa, 2007; Zittoun, 2006). These works focus on important characteristics of its functioning (e.g., dialogicality, hierarchical organization, semiotic mediation, embodiment, and so forth) or provide ideas as to how it works and/or analyses specific pattern of meanings and their role in psychological life. Unlike most of those works, my aim is to define a fundamental model of sensemaking, a model depicting its basic, constitutive dynamic. Accordingly, my focus concerns what I consider the core theoretical issue that any modelistic construction of sensemaking has to address and solve —*presentification*, namely the inherent capability of semiosis of making the world present for the sensemaker. Sensemaking is a matter of signs that in the final analysis consist of body modifications—yet the semiotic dynamic endows such modification with *value of life* (Salvatore, 2012), namely it enables the sensemaker to live them as the experience of the world-out-there.

The issue of presentification is not new. Gestalt theory has considered it as the constitutive process grounding the very perceptual construction of the object. People do not perceive pieces of experience that are first collected and then signified. People perceive totalities. And, given that—as the Kanizsa (1955) experiments showed—these totalities are not held in the field of experience—they have to be conceived of as the product of the mind's inherent constructive activity—indeed, of its capability of presentification. Yet, contemporary psychology has disregarded this notion, shifting the focus onto *representation*. In this terminological shift there is a major conceptual change. Cognitive psychology did not care how the value of life of the representation came about, namely the fact that representation is re-presentation. Its functionalist standpoint led to scotomize the issue of the generative process of psychological life, fully substituted by the task of describing its way of working.

My goal is to retrieve this conceptual problem, which I consider a necessary step to address in order to develop psychology as the science of sensemaking. In the final analysis, the point is to elaborate a model of the basic psychological operations that enable the mind to work semiotically, that is, to process the experience in terms of signs referring to things through the linkage with other signs. To use an image, my interest concerns something like a theory of the Big Bang of the psychological universe: the model of the very first moment of subjectivity. Needless to say, in the case of psychology the idea of a very first moment has to be considered not in a chronological sense, but in accordance to a plurality of other dimensions– namely, from a phylogenetic and ontogenetic point of view, as well as from logical and microgenetic standpoints. As a matter of fact the psychological operations generative of the mind occurred during the phylogenetic path (Corballis, 2011), and have a developmental course within the individual life. Moreover, many daily life situations show how phenomena of presentification vary in their probability and condition of occurrence (e.g., take what happens to someone watching a film: they can feel part of the story, caught up by it—or consider it just a series of fictional representations on the wall).

Dynamic, Process, and Phenomenon

In order to make the focus of my model of sensemaking clear, a distinction is worth making between dynamic, process, and phenomenon. The phenomenon is what one experiences: it is the content of our representation as it is shaped by the categories of common sense in which we are embedded. Thinking of something, feeling a given state, acting in a certain way, expressing beliefs: these are all phenomena, just like dropping out of school, delusion, memory decay, dreaming, making love, and so forth. I see the dynamic as the basic rule constituting the field, namely the constitutive dimension of sensemaking. Therefore, the dynamic is by definition a theoretical object, definable only within and in terms of a conceptual framework. From the standpoint of the dynamic, life is quite monotonous: everything that happens is a function of the same general rule. The dynamic cannot change—it is the source of change. Process is what somehow links the dynamic and the phenomena. It is the field's local way of functioning, as it is shaped in accordance with the contingent interaction of the pertinent elements. The relationship between process and dynamic is pluralistic: the same dynamic generates many local processes. In turn the same process can generate different phenomena, just as the same phenomenon can be the product of different dynamics. This is so because in the final analysis psychological processes are in a open relationship with behavior (i.e. the phenomena): the same psychological state (*latosensu*) can be associated with many behaviors, just as the same behavior can be the marker of many different psychological states (Salvatore & Valsiner, 2010; Toomela, 2008). For instance, the intense romantic commitment to another person can in some cases trigger caring behavior as well as aggressive acting out in others.

The analogy with language can help to clarify the distinction among these levels. The grammar of a given language can be considered the equivalent of a process. It is the way language works locally (i.e., in the spatial-temporal portion defining a given linguistic community). Grammars change over time and through space. Grammar, thus, is unable to define this change, by the very fact that it is the product of it. In order to study the evolution of grammars, one needs to consider such evolution as responding to some basic invariant and general tenets. If not, grammars would be incommensurable with each other. This level is what I mean by the dynamic. On the other hand, each grammar is a *post hoc* modelization of how language is used, that is, of language phenomenology. The use of language is the equivalent of what here is seen as the level of phenomenon.

> As I see it, the enterprise of language theory stands or falls with the realizability or unrealizability of the research idea of finding out something of consequence about the structure of human language in the singular, and of interpreting the known difference in the make-up of the languages as different families as possible variants of language in the singular. (Bühler, 1934/1990, p. 158)

In parallel with the distinction among process, dynamic and phenomenon, we can find corresponding levels of theory. Dynamic is the content of the *general theory*. In the final analysis, its mission is the understanding of the difference: how the unitary functioning of the whole generates variability. *Local theories* address processes. Their aim is to understand the various psychological processes that the dynamic fosters. *Pragmatic theories* concern phenomena: they reconstruct the process characterizing a certain field in the language of the phenomena. As the reader may notice, this distinction is not particularly new. It reflects on the one hand the emicetic dialectic. Moreover, it has similarities with Marr's (1982) distinction between functional, procedural and algorithmic levels of description.

One last point. My approach is radically dynamic. I consider meaning and sensemaking in terms of emergence and I focus on the definition of the constitutive dynamic generating such emergence. According to my approach, and within the specific aim of the theoretical task I address in this book, the structure is precisely what has to be understood, not what enables us to understand. I see this methodological choice as unavoidable, given that the reference to a structure in the definition recursively raises the issue of the definition of the structure, *in a regression ad infinitum*. I recognize that it is not possible within the constraint of our language to completely eliminate the reference to structures (Toomela, personal communication, May 2010): it is sufficient to use a substantive to reify a structure. Therefore, the dynamic approach has to be considered an asymptotical criterion.

The Structure of the Book

The book is divided into three parts.

The first part (Chapters 1–4) aims to present the model of the sensemaking. The second part (Chapters 5–8) is devoted to highlighting theoretical implications of the general model presented in the first part. The third part (Chapters 9–12) concerns methodology. Chapters that are included in the last section are dedicated to presenting methodological criteria and strategies as well as exemplificative cases of empirical investigation drawn from the modelistic approach outlined in the previous two parts.

The book is the (hopefully provisory...) ending point of a path of theoretical and methodological work I have been undertaking for the last decade. This is signalled by the fact that many parts of it are a more or less deep revision of papers I have published in recent years. I am aware of the fact that the usage of such already published materials somehow reduces the level of "newness" of the work. Yet it seemed to me the most appropriate way of proceeding. This is for three main reasons. First, I intended this book as the way of transforming elements having local, contingent aims and targets into components of a single Gestalt. Thus, thanks to the book the single works I have published over the last few years have become the fabric of a more general, ambitious theoretical plan that I am now able to present to readers. Second, I like the idea that most of the ideas discussed in the book have already been subject to a process of peer review. Personally, I consider the fact that such ideas have incorporated the eye of others in their very formulation—as happens any time a process of peer review is carried out—an antidote to wishful thinking. And this makes me more confident of offering readers something meaningful, even if they do not necessarily agree with me. Finally, the fact that many of the papers sourcing this volume were written in collaboration with colleagues, allows me to mention the enormous debt I have to so many friends and colleagues: through our discussions I have come to develop the idea I am proposing now.

So here I will simply express my gratitude to Evrinomy Avdi, Andrea Auletta, Angela Branco, Mario Carretero, Nandita Chaudhary, Enrico Ciavolino, Carla Cunha, Franco Di Maria, Santo Di Nuovo, Viviana Fini, Maria Francesca Freda, Guglielmo Forges Davanzati, Francesco Fronterotta, Omar Gelo, Angelo Gemignani, Alessandro Gennaro, Alex Gillespie, Miguel Gonçalves, Massimo Grasso, Marco Guidi, Pernille Hviid, Antonio Iannaccone, Marco Innamorati, Irini Kadianaki, Lewis Allen Kirshner, Hroar Klempe, Katrin, Kullasepp, Rosapia Lauro-Grotto, Franco Lancia, Claudio Longobardi, Maria Lyra, Terri Mannarini, Pina Marsico, Mariann Martsin, Anastassios Matsopoulos, Gianni Montesarchio, Piergiorgio Mossi, Yair Neuman, Rosa Maria Paniccia, Rocco Quaglia, Élias Rizkallah, Alberto Rosa, Philip Rosenbaum, Joâo Salgado, Giampaolo Salvatore (who happens to be my brother), Gordon Sammut, Michel Sanchez-Cardenas, Alfonso Santarpia, Josè Saporta, Giampaolo Sasso, Tatsuya Sato, Giuseppe Scaratti, Ahmet Suerdem, Lívia Mathias Simão, Andrea Smorti, Paul Stenner, Luca Tateo, Claudio Tebaldi, Marco Tonti, Aaro Toomela, Wolfgang Tschacher, Giuseppe Veltri, Claudia Venuleo, Brady Wagoner, Tania Zittoun, all the friends with whom I have discussed ideas this book tries to bring together.

I have many reasons to be thankful to Jaan Valsiner—the preface he wrote would be enough for that! He has been encouraging my efforts for a whole decade; many pages of this volume carry tracks of the practice of otherness that discussions with him have always been for me.

This book provides the chance to me of saying thank you to Renzo Carli and Anna di Ninni. What my eyes see today depends on what they shared with me years ago.

Good reading!
Sergio Salvatore
Lecce, August 31, 2014

ACKNOWLEDGMENTS

Section 3 of Chapter 1 is a slightly revised version of Section 1 of the paper: Salvatore, S., & Venuleo, C. (2013). Field dependency and contingency in the modelling of sensemaking. *Papers on Social Representation [Online Journal]*, *22*(2), 21.1–21.41.

Chapter 2 is a revised and extended version of the first section of the paper: Salvatore, S., & Venuleo, C. (2013). Field dependency and contingency in the modelling of sensemaking. *Papers on Social Representation [Online Journal]*, *22*(2), 21.1–21.41.

Section 2 of Chapter 4 and paragraphs 1–3 of Chapter 5 are slightly revised versions of parts of the paper: Salvatore, S. (2013). The reciprocal inherency of self and context. Notes for a semiotic model of the constitution of the experience. *Interacçoes*, *24*, 20–50.

Section 4 of Chapter 5 is based on Salvatore S., & Gennaro A. (2012). The inherent dialogicality of the clinical exchange. Introduction to the special issue. *International Journal for Dialogical Science*, *6*(1), 1–14.

Chapter 7 is based on Salvatore, S., & Zittoun, T. (2011). Outlines of a psychoanalytically informed cultural psychology. In S. Salvatore, & T. Zittoun (Eds), *Cultural Psychology and Psychoanalysis in Dialogue. Issues for Constructive Theoretical and Methodological Synergies* (pp. 3–46). Charlotte, NC: Information Age Publication.

Section 1 of Chapter 8 is a revised version of part of the work Salvatore S. (2011). Psychotherapy Research Needs Theory. Outline for an Epistemology of the Clinical Exchange. *Integrative Psychological and Behavioural Science*, *45*(3), 366–388.

Section 2 of Chapter 8 is based on the paper: Salvatore, S., & Guidi, M. (2007). Note per una rivisitazione del costrutto |Gruppo|. [Notes for rethinking the concept |Group|. *Scritti di Gruppo, 1*, retrievable at http://www.iagp.it.

Section 3 of Chapter 8 is based on the paper: Guidi, M., Fini, V., & Salvatore, S. (2012). Lo sviluppo quale fenomeno semiotico [Development as semiotic phenomenon]. In D. De Leo, & V. Fini (Eds.), *Attualità dello sviluppo. Riflessioni in pratica per costruire progetti locali di qualità* (pp. 146–157). Milano: Franco Angeli.

Section 4 of Chapter 8 is a slightly revised version of Section 2 of the paper: Forges Davanzati, G., & Salvatore S. (2012). Institutions and job flexibility. A psychological approach. *Dialettica e filosofia, 4*(1), 1–13. http://www.dialetticaefilosofia.it/public/pdf/94psicoinstitutions.

Chapter 9 is based on parts of the following papers: Salvatore, S., & Valsiner, J. (2010). Between the General and the Unique: Overcoming the nomothetic *versus* idiographic opposition, *Theory and Psychology, 20*(6), *817–833;* Salvatore, S. (2014). The mountain of cultural psychology and the mouse of empirical studies. Methodological considerations for birth control. *Culture & Psychology, 20*(4), 477–500; Salvatore, S. (forthcoming). The contingent nature of psychological intervention. From blind spot to basic resource of psychological science. In G. Sammut, G. Foster, R. Ruggieri, U. Flick, & S. Salvatore (Eds.), *Methods of psychological intervention. The Yearbook of Idiographic Science Series, Volume 7.* Charlotte NC: Information Age Publishing.

Section 1 of Chapter 10 is a revised version of the subparagraph 2.2 of the paper: Salvatore, S., & Venuleo, V. (2013). Field dependency and contingency in the modelling of sensemaking. *Papers on Social Representation, [Online Journal], 22*(2), 21.1–21.41

Section 4 of Chapter 10 is based on Salvatore, S. (in press). Lotteries, bets, Coca-cola and Octopus Paul. The extraordinary of ordinary. In G. Marsico, & L. Tateo (Eds.), *Ordinary things.* Charlotte, NC: Information Age Publishing.

Chapter 11 is based on the papers: Salvatore S., Tonti, M., & Gennaro, A. (in press). How to model sensemaking. A contribution for the development of a methodological framework for the analysis of meaning. In M. Han (Ed.), *The Subjectified and Subjectifying Mind.* Charlotte, NC: Information Age Publishing; Salvatore, S., & Venuleo, C. (2013) Field dependency and contingency in the modelling of sensemaking. *Papers on Social Representation, [Online Journal], 22*(2), 21.1–21.41; Lauro-Grotto R. P., Salvatore, S., Gennaro, A., & Gelo, O. (2009). The unbearable dynamicity of psychological processes: Highlights of the psychodynamic theories. In J. Valsiner, P. Molenaar, M. Lyra, & N. Chaudhary (Eds.), *Dynamic Process Methodology in the Social and Developmental Sciences* (pp. 1–30). New York: Springer.; Salvatore S., Lauro-Grotto, R., Gennaro, A., & Gelo, O. (2009). Attempts to grasp the dynamicity of intersubjectivity. In J. Valsiner, P. C. M. Molenaar, M. Lyra, & N. Chaudhary (Eds.), *Dynamic Process Methodology in the Social and Developmental Sciences* (pp. 171–190). New York: Springer.

Paragraphs 1–7 of Chapter 12 are based, respectively on the papers: Salvatore, S., Tebaldi, C., & Poti, S. (2009). The discursive dynamics of sensemaking. In S. Salvatore, J. Valsiner, S. Strout, & J. Clegg (Eds.), *Yearbook of Idiographic Science-Volume 1* (pp. 39–72). Rome: Firera Publishing. First published 2006, in *International Journal of Idiographic Science [OnLine Journal]*, Article 3. Retrieved June 28 2007, from http://www.valsiner.com/articles/salvatore.htm; Tonti, M., & Salvatore, S. (in press). The Homogenization of Classification Functions Measurement (HOCFUN). A method for measuring the salience of emotional arousal in thinking; Mannarini, T. M., Nitti, M., Ciavolino, E., & Salvatore, S. (2012). The role of affects in culture-based interventions: Implications for practice. *Psychology, 3*, 569–577 doi:10.4236/psych. 2012.38085; Ciavolino, E., Salvatore, S., & Calcagnì, A. (2013). A fuzzy set theory based computational model to represent the quality of inter-rater agreemen. *Quality and Quantity, 48*, 2225–2240. doi:10.1007/s11135-013-9888-3; Salvatore, S., Gennaro, A., Auletta, A., Tonti, M., & Nitti, M. (2012). Automated method of content analysis. A device for psychotherapy process research. *Psychotherapy Research, 22(3)*, 256–273; Auletta, A., Salvatore, S., Metrangolo, R., Monteforte, G., Pace, V., & Puglisi, M. (2012). The study of therapist's interpretive activity: The Grid of the Models of interpretations (GMI). A transtheoretical method. *Journal of Psychotherapy Integration, 22(2)*, 61–84; Salvatore, S., Gelo, O., Gennaro, A., Manzo, S., & Al-Radaideh, A. (2010). Looking at the psychotherapy process as an intersubjective dynamic of meaning-making. A case study with Discourse Flow Analysis. *Journal of Constructivist Psychology, 23,*195–230.

PART I

MICROPHYSICS OF SENSEMAKING

This part is devoted to presenting a semio-dynamic model of sensemaking (SDMS).

In Chapter 1, some preliminary considerations are provided in order to frame the presentation of the model presented in the following chapters. To this end, I start by sketching out the traditional way of viewing meaning, namely the idea that it is an autonomous entity existing before its expression and motivating it. Then, I provide critical arguments against such a view. Finally, based on some ideas from Wittgenstein and Peirce I outline the pragmatic and processual view of meaning that is the grounds of the SDMS. According to such a view, sensemaking can be seen as an infinite flow of signs, each of which has the bivalent function of interpreting the previous sign and triggering the following one.

Chapter 2 is devoted to presenting the basic concepts of the SDMS. In particular, two core ideas are discussed. First, the idea that meaning is not an autonomous entity existing before the process of its production and communication; rather, meaning is the emerging field property of sensemaking. Second, the idea that sensemaking works through the interplay of two components—on the one hand, a perceivable component (the *significance in praesentia*, SIP); on the other hand, the latent semiotic scenario working as the condition for interpreting the SIP (the *significance in absentia*, SIA) (the tenet of *the bivalence of sensemaking*).

Chapters 3 and 4 complete the presentation of the SDMS, sketching out the microdynamic that brings about the semiotic processes as envisaged by the model. More specifically, Chapter 3 focuses on two issues: (a) how the following sign (the interpretant) does its job of interpreting the previous flow of signs, in so doing allowing the semiotic chain to go on *(hermeneutic issue); (*b) how the sign triggers its interpretant, selecting it from the infinite set of possibilities *(issue of causality)*. Chapter 4 focuses on the third issue concerning the microdynamic of sensemaking: how a given set of unrelated sensorial occurrences acquires the status of sign *(issue of the constitution of the sign)*.

CHAPTER 1

THE MEANING OF
OUR DISCONTENT

THE DAILY-LIFE IDEA OF MEANING

Consider the following statement.

I am sitting in front of my notebook, thinking of the best way of expressing my ideas on meaning, how to put it into words. I have already written several versions of the text, but I am not satisfied with them—I do not consider these versions fully convey the idea I have in mind.

Three aspects of this are worth pointing out. First, the writer—the "I"—assumes that his/her ideas on meaning (that is, the meaning of meaning) are something existing within his/her head, before he/she expresses them. Second, the writer can have the intention of expressing his/her ideas simply because she/he believes she/he has ideas in his/her mind that can/have to be expressed. And this is the same as saying that it is the meaning held in the mind which motivates its expression: there can be a representation of the meaning (broadly speaking, a text) insofar as there is something which can be—and strives to be—represented. Third, the writer may have tried various forms of expression of his/her idea, writing and rewriting the text, only because s/he assumes that this trial and error strategy does not affect the idea contained in the mind. Rather, it is the alleged knowledge of the inner idea that works as normative criterion for defining whether—to what extent—the way it is expressed is a valid representation of it. The latter point is evident in statements like the following: "I did not mean that"; "do you really believe what you said?".

Psychology in Black and White: The Project of a Theory-Driven Science, pp. 3–17
Copyright © 2016 by Information Age Publishing
All rights of reproduction in any form reserved.

These three aspects are the elements that characterize the daily-life conception of meaning—namely, the idea of meaning as an autonomous entity existing beforehand and being essentially independent from its expression.

This idea can be found at the root of two classical conceptions (Eco, 1975). On the one hand, the view of meaning as the piece of the world the sign refers to (e.g., Frege, 1892/1980). This is the referential interpretation of meaning, known also as *extensional theory* (the extension of a concept is the set of cases it can be applied to). According to this interpretation, the meaning of a sign is the set of elements it can indicate/stand for. On the other hand, the view of meaning as the concept that the sign stands for (Saussure, 1916/1977). In this case the meaning does not reflect the segmentation of the world in (i.e., objects, events...), but the conceptual structure of the language, namely, the network of relationship among the semantic units it consists of. This is the *intensional theory* of meaning (the intension of a concept is the set of criteria defining its content). Extensional and intensional theories of meaning are profoundly different. However, they share the basic idea of meaning as separate and independent from its expression. Frege's (1892/1980) distinction between *meaning* and *sense* highlights this idea of autonomy. According to him, while meaning is the thing the sign refers to, the sense of the sign is the way of denoting it; thus there can be many senses for the same meaning—for example, the "Moon," the "white ball on the night sky", the "only satellite of the earth" are signs that have the same meaning, even if this can be affirmed through a plurality of senses. Now, if a plurality of senses corresponds to a single meaning, this implies that the meaning remains constant, regardless of the way of denoting it—that is to say that the meaning is independent from the way of expressing it. De Saussure's distinction between *langue* (i.e., the abstract system of signs) and *parole* (the concrete use of the language performed by persons) is even clearer in this direction. He explicitly regards meaning as an exclusive matter of the *langue*, which has to be understood without taking into account the level of the *parole*. And this is the same as saying that meaning is a self-contained system (*langue*) not affected by how people actually use it (*parole*).

SIX ARGUMENTS OF DISCONTENT

The view of the autonomy of meaning shapes our way of experiencing. Yet it has been subjected to a major revision in the last three decades as a result of the increasing interest in the work of authors like Wittgenstein, Peirce, Bakhtin, accompanying the linguistic and semiotic turnaround in psychology (e.g., Gergen, 1999; Gillespie, 2010; Harré & Gillet, 1994; Kirshner,

2010; Lepper, 2012; Linell, 2009; Salvatore, 2012). Without trying to be exhaustive, I list the main criticisms below, in the form of six arguments.

Argument 1: The Mind-World Hiatus

The assumption that meaning exists *a priori* transforms this construct into an entity—a piece of the world that has the capacity of producing an effect on the world (e.g., on the brain's functioning, on the actor's actions). This form of hypostatization raises fundamental problems; in particular, the issue of how meaning, being an *a priori*, is able to enter into relation with the world and therefore to affect it.

The classical way of addressing this issue is the Kantian solution, namely the (not necessarily explicit) metaphysical assumption of the transcendental capacity of the mind to be in correspondence with the world. Thanks to this assumption, the problem of the meaning-world relation is simply eliminated, rather than solved. Yet, this happens at the cost of closing meaning within the mind of the individual, as a transcendent property of the epistemic subject. This cost can be paid by those who—like Piaget and Chomsky—are interested in the invariant, formal epistemic structures of mental functioning. Yet it is too high when the interest concerns the intertwining of action, history, social and individual life, namely how meaning and the world develop through their capacity to transform each other recursively (Valsiner, 2007, 2014; Vygotsky, 1934/1986).

In the final analysis, the transcendental solution confines the understanding of meaning within the vision of an a-historical mind. In so doing, it leaves open the problem of how to link it to the world. For instance, one can find such a problem in the Fornari's psychoanalytic theory of coinems (Fornari, 1979, 1983). *Coinems* are conceived of as universal *a priori* unconscious categories, inherent properties of the transcendental mind. The theory of coinems states that the content of these universal *a priori* sustains the connotation of the experience (cfr. Chapter 7); nevertheless it does not say how the formal, invariant coinemic categories are able to connect themselves with—and therefore express themselves through—the variable, ever-changing contents and signs available within the contingent, historically situated sociocultural and interpersonal domains.

The history of the Piagetian theory is another instructive illustration of this point. Insofar as the Piagetian program of research set out to define a formal model of the development of cognitive structures, it used the principles of cognitive organization (accommodation, assimilation, equilibration) as transcendental rules whereby to depict the epigenetic process. This indeed was Piaget's interest: to understand the general universal epistemic structure through which living systems develops through the interaction with the environment. Yet, when students began to be interested in the microgenesis of the dynamic of development—an interest motivated both by theoretical and practical reasons (e.g., for the sake of dealing with educational tasks)—the focus was progressively shifted from the transcendental structure of the epistemic subject to the intersubjective and contextual communicative practices in which subjects are involved (Perret-Clermont, Pontecorvo, Resnick, Zittoun, & Burge, 2004). And alongside this evolution, meaning was seen less and less as a preestablished reality regulating the intersubjective practices from the outside, to be conceived of more and more as part and parcel of such practices and of the psychological process associated with them (Valsiner, 2001).

From a complementary point of view, the Kantian solution entails a downward model of causation—the transcendental meaning is the product emerging from the physical world (i.e., neurobiological activity) and at the same time a phenomenon acting upon that physical world. Now, the notion of downward causality is a much debated problem (Andersen, Emmeche, Finnemann, & Christiansen, 2000), given that even if it provides an appealing solution for mind-body dualism, it does so on the condition of violating the basic metaphysical tenet of the closure of the physical world (Kim, 2000; for a criticism of this kind specifically concerning meaning and psychological theory, see Fodor, 1983).

Argument 2: The Explanans-Explanandum Inversion

This argument is connected with the previous one. The entification of meaning entails an inversion between *explanans* and *explanandum*: what has to be understood (i.e., the meaning produced by and at the same time regulating sensemaking) is transformed into what allows understanding. In other words—given a psychological event E (e.g., a thought, an utterance, an act), it is explained as being motivated—for example, as the effect, the reaction, the regulated output, the defence from, and the like—by the meaning M. Therefore, M is the source of the explanation, rather than the target phenomenon to be explained; namely, $E = f(M)$, rather than $M = f(E)$—for example, "the individual has acted thus (E) because she had an inner representation of herself (M) leading her in that direction."

The *explanans-explanandum* inversion raises a number of issues. Below, I will merely indicate two main points. First, it leads to a kind of explanation that can hardly avoid the classical problem of the *homunculus*. Say that the meaning M motivated the event E; now, this raises the question of how M does so. And the answer to this question cannot but bring into the discussion an inner interpreter (the *homunculus*) of M, having the function of representing the meaning of M and transforming this representation

(*M'*) into a decision/action. Yet, in turn, this raises the question of how such an interpreter works. And the answer to this question cannot but bring into the discussion an inner interpreter of the inner interpreter, having the function of representing the meaning of the inner interpreter (*M'*) and transforming such representation (*M"*) into a decision/action according to which the inner interpreter produces its decision/action. And in turn, this entails an inner interpreter of the inner interpreter of the inner interpreter, and so forth *ad infinitum*. Second, it involves the *post hoc ergo propter hoc* fallacy: *M* is considered to be the cause of *E* just because the latter is alleged to occur beforehand. This fallacy consists of confusing a necessary condition with a sufficient condition—*M* has to come before *E* for it to be considered a cause of *E*. Yet, the fact that *M* comes before *E* is not a sufficient reason to consider *M* the cause of *E*—for instance, the fact that I am going out my house with an umbrella after hearing the weather forecast for the day, does not mean that if it rains in the next hour this depends on the fact that I have taken an umbrella. On the other hand, the very fact that meaning comes before its manifest expression is a hotly debated topic. Though controversial, Libet's (1999) classical experiments have provided evidence in favor of the fact that the action comes before the representation of the inner state that is assumed to be the agentive factor motivating the action at stake.

Thus, it seems to be less problematic to consider the notion of meaning as a *post hoc* description enabling us to order data of experience, rather than the causative source of such data. This shift is clearly expressed in relation to the role of rules (Salvatore, Forges Davanzati, Potì, & Ruggieri, 2009; see also Croom, 2012). From the classical point of view, the mind's functioning—for example, the way of using language, the way of reasoning – is the consequence of the application of rules; therefore, according to this point of view, rules have a causative role. Yet, this assumption is clearly contrasted by the experience of daily life: people first learn to act (to reason, to speak a language, to perform in accordance to given scripts) in a certain way—they acquire habits, in Peirce's terminology—and then interpret such a way as a mode of following a given rule. Thus, it is not the rule that comes before and causes the phenomenon (of thinking, of speaking, of acting…); rather, the rule is the *post-hoc* representation.

Argument 3: The Scotomization of the Genetic Standpoint

From the standpoint of the psychological theory, the entified idea of meaning as a causative agent puts a constraint upon the programmatic scientific agenda. Insofar as the meaning is already given and is independent from the semiotic process which it triggers (i.e., sensemaking), theory has no interest in addressing the microgenetics of meaning—namely, how it emerges and is reproduced through time, by means of which conditions/processes it defines the shape it assumes (Valsiner, 2007). More deeply, psychological theoreticians are prevented from asking *what* meaning *is* and what are the semiotic dynamic and properties which enable it to have psychological saliency (Salvatore, 2012).

Cognitive psychology is a clear example of this scotomization. Even when it recognizes the role played by the semantic content in regulating mental functioning (Bruner, 1990; Johnson-Laird, 1983; Neisser, 1987; Sanford, 1987; Tversky & Kahneman, 1981)—such semantic content is assumed to be a prepsychological datum whose theoretical status does not require further investigation (for a criticism of this approach in the field of economic psychology, see Salvatore et al., 2009).

In the final analysis, psychological theory ends up working as a domain specific theory. It ends up resembling disciplines such as Ballistics (Salvatore, 2011). Ballistics does not deal with the basic rules (e.g. gravitational theory) governing how bullets define their trajectories. Rather, it adopts these rules as taken for granted assumptions defined beforehand by the basic science (physics) and uses them in order to understand their effects in a circumscribed domain of application. Psychological theory does the same: the basic rules—namely, the rules informing the dynamic through which "meaning" emerges and works—are taken for granted as if they concerned other levels of knowledge (sociocultural investigation, semiotics, neuroscience), while what is relevant is how such meaning regulates/affects the trajectories of psychological bullets—thoughts, words, acts.

Argument 4. The Fallacy of the Photographic Metaphor

The assumption that meaning is autonomous from its expression leads to the constructive role played by sensemaking being underscored, even scotomized. According to such an assumption, sensemaking is like a photograph—it retrieves what is held in the sensemaker's mind. Take a subject who states: "I want a pizza". According to the classical view of the autonomy of meaning, the subject is expressing a meaning (M, the desire of having a pizza) held in his/her mind, by means of a verbal representation (VR, the statement made). The M is active in the subject's mind before he/she expresses it. Consequently, the VR is a more or less precise and valid description (photo) of M, but it does not modify what it represents.

Yet the photographic metaphor does not hold up when faced with facts. One reason is that the photographic metaphor presupposes that the mind is inspectionable—namely, that the sensemaker is capable of being a competent photographer of his/her own thoughts. Now, much empirical and theoretical work, both from dynamic and cognitive psychology, has shown that such an assumption is not justified: it has to be considered a staple of common sense, but not a valid scientific statement. In their classical review, Nisbett and De Camp Wilson (1977) convincingly reported evidence to show that there is a deep divergence between the representation that subjects have of the factors motivating their actions/reactions/feelings and the actual processes causing subjects' states of mind. For instance, while subjects were convinced that their selection of a product to buy depended on the inherent characteristics of the product, their selection proved to be a function of the position of the product in the box, with the characteristics of the product being irrelevant (for convergent considerations on the limits of self-representation and methodological implications, see Grasso & Stampa, 2011).

Argument 5: The Scotomization of the Pragmatic Dimension of Meaning

The classical conceptions entail the focalization on the semantic dimension alone, with the pragmatic dimension being scotomized. This implication is clearly expressed by de Saussure himself, when he claimed that linguistics concerns the language in itself (*langue*), not the use of it (*parole*). On the other hand, the scotomization of the pragmatic dimension of meaning is a necessary corollary of the autonomy of meaning. Pragmatic meaning is inherently contextual (Austin, 1962; Freda, 2008; Gillespie, 2010). It depends on how signs are combined in communicative practices (Linell, 2009; Salvatore, 2013; Salvatore, Gelo, Gennaro, & Manzo, 2010; Salvatore & Venuleo, 2013). Consequently, once the pragmatic dimension of meaning is recognized, it follows that meaning is contingent and contextual, namely that at least for a major aspect (the pragmatic) it is not autonomous, but contingent to how signs are used, namely to the local dynamic of sensemaking. In Wittgenstein's terminology, meaning is the sign's function of regulating the forms of life carried on by language-games. And it is evident that this regulative function is not inherent to the sign, but it depends on the virtually infinite circumstances of the social exchange serving as the setting of the speech act (Nightgale & Cromby, 1999). Accordingly, Austin (1962) distinguishes between *meaning* and *force* —namely, what people do *in* and/or *with* saying what they say.

Imagine person A saying to person B: "Are you able to tell me what time it is?" Anyone competent of the linguistic code used by A would be able to recognize the semantic content of the utterance: A wants to know if B has the capacity to tell him/her the time. But understanding such content is far from sufficient for B for the sake of realizing the pragmatic meaning (namely, the sense) of A's act of asking the question how, when and where it was asked. In order to understand the sense of the act, B needs to take into account the intersubjective circumstance within which it takes place. The sense will be very different if A is a friend of B who has arrived late, or if A is a practitioner making a neurological assessment of B, or if A has just gifted B with a watch.... That is to say, sense is local, depending on the intersubjective field, and it is an essential part of what comprises the (inter)subjective value of the communication.

Thus, the scotomization of the pragmatic dimension of meaning saves the consistency of the assumption that meaning is autonomous. Yet it does so at the price of sharply underscoring an essential aspect of the experience of daily life—namely, the quite evident fact that when people use signs they do not only express a given content, but they also (and often: especially) carry out an action and regulate intersubjective exchanges.

Argument 6: The Idealization of the Semantic Order

This argument is a complementary aspect of the scotomization of the pragmatic meaning. If the pragmatic meaning is not taken into consideration, one is unavoidably led to conceive of it as an ordered self-contained structure of semantic relationship between pieces of content clearly and sharply differentiated from each other. In so doing, the inherent fuzziness and multidimensionality of meaning is de-emphasized (Salvatore & Freda, 2011; Salvatore, Gennaro, Auletta, Grassi, Rocco, & Gelo, 2011). In the concrete circumstances of communication, signs always occur within an array of connections with many other signs; therefore, meaning depends on how the interpreter selects some of these connections as relevant, leaving others in the background. Any sign is a set of potentialities of signification (Salvatore, Tebaldi, & Potì, 2006/2009; Visetti & Cadiot, 2002).

Take the following utterance:

I hope this book offers a relevant contribution for the further development of psychological theory.

It allows several interpretations—it can be understood as concerning: (a) the content of the writers' thoughts; (b) the nature of the feeling at stake; (c) a statement on the quality of the book; (d) the role of the paper within the psychological literature; (e) a reference to psychology's capability of developing; (f) an example given for the sake of making the argument clear; (g) a way of convincing the reader, and so forth.

Now, the interpreter makes a selection within this set of potential meanings, in accordance with her point of view and scope. In so doing, one meaning is made pertinent while the other potential ones are moved into the background. In sum, meaning is not fixed in the signs, but in the constructive, hermeneutic relationship between signs and interpreters.

A DIFFERENT VIEW OF MEANING. FOUNDATIONAL ISSUE

Semiosis is Action

The arguments against the classical conceptions push us to search for an alternative approach, in order to avoid the pitfalls of the entification of meaning. To this end, it is useful to come back to Wittgenstein and Peirce, whose theories provide the conceptual tools for a dynamic and semiotic model of meaning.

Wittgenstein (1953/1958) proposed that the meaning of a word (more in general, the meaning of any sign) is how it is used. From that it follows that the meaning does not stand before its use—namely, before the action that comprises the use of the sign. Rather, meaning is the action, its effect on the listener(s).

The latter point is clearly highlighted by how Wittgenstein (1953/1958) interprets statements referring to emotions. According to Wittgenstein, the reference to an emotional state is not a description of a fact occurring within the mind of the subject; rather it is an act that produces an effect on the interlocutor and this is what makes up its meaning. For instance, take someone saying to their son "I am very angry now." This statement has a series of pragmatic consequences: it leads the person to act in a certain way (e.g., not to talk to the son), and the son to perform a certain act as the right answer to the parent's action of making the statement (e.g., to apologize; to avoid the parent, to challenge her/him). All of these pragmatic consequences are not the effect of the anger as such; rather they are produced by the language game implemented by the statement on the specific form of life underlying the parent-son relationship. In sum, Wittgenstein enables us to see how *meaning is not an entity but the pragmatic effect of the use of signs*, namely of the sensemaking. In other words, meaning is made up of action—it is action that comes after action—action that affects the following action. In sum, the meaning is part and parcel of the world of actions (Austin, 1962).

Peirce (1897/1932) provides a way for taking a further step ahead. His triadic theory of signs offers the conceptual devices for understanding the pragmatic effect of signs, and therefore reach a fully dynamic model of meaning. According to Peirce, semiosis is the ongoing, never-ending process of interpretation of signs through the following signs. Any sign

> or *representamen*, is something which stands to somebody for something in some respect or capacity. It addresses somebody, that is, creates in the mind of that person an equivalent sign, or perhaps a more developed sign. The sign stands for something, its object. It stands for that object, not in all respects, but in reference to a sort of idea which I have sometimes called the ground of the representamen. (p. 228)

Such a definition implies that the foundational condition of possibility of the semiosis comes from the inherent inability of the sign to represent its reference fully. Any sign stands for the reference "not in all respects" —it stands for it only "in some respect or capacity" (the ground), in the aspect that is relevant to somebody. For instance, the photo of a cake may stand for the cake as regards its shape and color (for somebody) or as regards the name of the person being celebrated (for somebody else); but it does not usually stand for the cake's weight or taste, although theoretically one cannot exclude that there might be at least one person for whom this ground applies. Incidentally, the probability of there being such an exceptional ground can be seen as inversely associated with the person's upholding of the cultural norm. Accordingly, one could conceive of psychopathology as a matter of distance between commonsensical ground and personal ground—for example, delusion as the constrained enrooting in a very idiosyncratic ground.

Due to its "incompleteness," the standing-for relation between a sign and the object requires the interpretative intervention of another sign— the "equivalent sign, or perhaps a more developed sign" (Peirce calls it *interpretant* too). The interpretant's interpretative task is a form of selection: it reduces the virtually infinite possibilities of standing-for—namely, the infinite "respect(s) and capacit(ies)" the previous sign could stand for—to a finite set. But the interpretant is still a sign, and therefore it is open to virtually infinite standing-for options as well. Consequently, it also needs to be interpreted by a subsequent interpretant, and so forth, *ad infinitum*, in a neverending process of backward interpretation—backward in the sense that the interpretant performs its job on the previous sign. Sensemaking is precisely such a flow of signs interpreting previous signs in their relation with previous signs, in an infinite asymptotic tension to fill the hiatus between the sign and the object. In this sense, it can be concluded that *the meaning is the sign that follows,* namely the event of enacting a sign as a consequence and for the sake of interpreting the previous sign enacted.

The infinite semiotic flow entailed in Peirce's (1897/1932) triadic theory of signs (see Figure 1.1) represents a radical change of the commonsensical view of meaning. It leads us to recognize that the sign has no content within itself. Rather, it is a relationship (i.e., the process of standing for) which, on the one hand, relates back to a previous relationship and, on the other hand, relates forward, triggering another relationship, the latter to be specified in turn. Thus, meaning is inherently pragmatic and dynamic. It is dynamic in the sense that the backward interpretative relationship between the representamen and the interpretant is a temporal one— namely, *the meaning is the sign that follows*. And it is pragmatic in the sense that the sign that follows is an event, something a certain person performs according to the capacity that is relevant for her/him. In other words, any sign does not represent/convey what is already within it (its content) but acts on the current state of the semiotic process, in the sense that it rewrites the semiotic process, selecting the relevant aspect of the previous semiotic relationship.

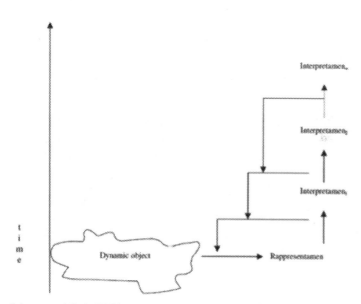

Source   Salvatore and Freda (2011).

Figure 1.1.   Peirce triadic model of sign.

Incidentally, this idea of meaning can be represented in terms of the analogy with the quantum physics notion of superposition (Neuman & Tamir, 2009). The system (i.e., the position of the particle) is contemporarily—from a probabilistic standpoint—in a multiplicity of states (superposition), taking one of them (i.e., a position) only when it is measured (observed). Likewise, the upcoming sign can be conceived as the measurement of the previous one, because it allows it to shift from the superposition (the potential multiple aspects it can stand for) towards a well-defined state, assuming a specific ground (i.e., only one given position).

In sum, thanks to Wittgenstein and Peirce, the very distinction between semantics—the stable content of the sign as defined in the system of language (*langue*, in de Saussure's terminology)—and pragmatics—the use of semantics for communicational and relational aims (*parole*)—has to be questioned. Wittgenstein and Peirce allow us to realize that the semantic is the effect of the pragmatic, rather than vice versa.

Meaning as the Domain of Pertinence of Signs

Peirce's (1897/1932) theory provides the basis for building a model of meaning on which one can ground psychological theorization and empirical investigation. From Peirce's definition of signs one can draw the idea of meaning as the *domain of pertinence* of the sign (the representamen), as established by the following sign (the interpretant).

The domain of pertinence is what Peirce (1897/1932) calls the "ground" of the representamen. Yet there is a slight difference between the two terms, which is worth underlining. As it is clear from the quotation reported above, Peirce speaks of the ground as the relation between the representamen and its object—the latter elsewhere called "dynamic object" (cf. Figure 1.1). The dynamic object is a kind of noumenal reality—the piece of the world, in itself ungraspable, motivating the sign. Thus, according to Peirce, the ground is the relation between the representamen and the noumenal thing (i.e., the dynamic object). However, the dynamic object lends itself to be conceived of as just a virtual starting point of the semiotic flow. Insofar as the new sign is created, as the first interpretant of the first representamen, then it is followed by a new interpretant, which performs its interpretative job on the relation between the previous interpretant and its target, namely the representamen. This means that the relation between the object and the representamen (i.e., the ground) is continuously reproduced by its reinterpretation through the flow of signs, each of them working as interpretant of the previous and at the same time as representamen of the following (cf. Figure 1.1).

Incidentally, this view allows a modelistic solution to be found to the problem of conjugating the referential tension of language and more generally of sensemaking (i.e., the fact that we use and experience meanings as a way of representing the object), and its autonomy, its operational closeness (i.e., the fact that any sign cannot but refer to other signs, in a web from which is not possible to escape; e.g., Lahlou & Abric, 2011).

It is worth repeating that the domain of pertinence is not an inherent property of the representamen; rather, it is one (a subset) of the "capacities" that the following sign sets among the infinite number possible. One just has to imagine how many uses there are of a photo of a cake to get a—limited—idea of the infinite potential capacities that could underlie the domain of pertinence. The interpretant does not activate the subset of capacities but selects them, creating a boundary between the ones that in so doing become pertinent and the others, left in the background.

Peirce (1897/1932) provides the following picture of such a dynamic.

> Namely, a sign is something, A, which brings something, B, its interpretant sign determined or created by it, into the same sort of correspondence with something, C, its object, as that in which itself stands to C. (pp. 20–21)

Thus, A's domain of pertinence, namely the capacity of A to stand for C– in the final analysis: the meaning of A– does not lie statically in the relation A–C. Rather, it comes from the relation between B, namely A's interpretant, and C. In other words, B's entry into the chain of signs makes the relation B-C equivalent to the relation A–C and so forth along the ongoing never-ending course (i.e., A–C = B–C = B' –C = B''–C = B'''–C = ... –C) (cf. Figure 1.2).

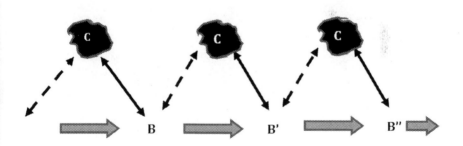

A<>C=B<>C=B'<>C=B''<>C=...<>C

Figure 1.2. The semiotic chain.

Consider the following excerpt as an example. Somebody looks at the sky (intended as the object, namely C), and exclaims (or just thinks to themselves): "How many clouds" (A)[1], "It will rain shortly" (B). Then they go on: "I'd better take my umbrella" (B'). "It's a nuisance to have to take it with me" (B")—"yet it is better to have it than to be completely soaked" (B'''). "I would not like to have to give up the week-end because of having caught a cold" (B""'). As one can see, the representamen A ("How many clouds") stands for the object (the sky) just for a certain capacity—the capacity to present many clouds. The sky is pertinent for this capacity, and not pertinent for any other potential capacity (for instance, for its capacity to appear blue). Yet, this domain of pertinence is not defined once and for all by the representamen A. Actually, if there were no further (implicit or explicit) interpretant, there would not be any domain of pertinence. In the example, the domain of pertinence emerges only when the interpretant B comes into being. Before that, one cannot grasp the sense of A, simply because it is B that defines A's ground. When this happens, the A–C semiotic relation (i.e., A's function of standing for C, namely A's meaning)—is defined in terms of B, more precisely in terms of the equivalence between B–C and A–C. Thus, one realizes that the "capacity" of the sky that the statement "How many clouds" stands for, is equivalent to the sky's "capacity" to stand for the coming of rain. One knows what this equivalence is only in the terms that it is equivalent to the recognition that it is better to take an umbrella, and so forth. This chain of equivalences between semiotic relationships defines the domain of pertinence and at the same time reproduces it through time. No sign grasps the object; yet the referential tension is maintained through the ongoing, never-ending chain of interpretation, each of which rewrites and at the same time feeds the signs' semiotic relation of "standing for."

CONCLUSION

In this chapter I have set out to lay the foundations of the dynamic and semiotic model of sensemaking that will be presented in the following chapters of Part I.

To this end, I first sketched out the commonsensical way of viewing meaning, namely the idea of it as an autonomous entity existing before its expression and motivating it. Second, I briefly discussed six critical arguments against such a view, that, on the one hand, shed light on the limits of the classical (extensional and intensional) conceptions of meaning, and, on the other hand, pave the way to a processual conception of the meaning, namely to the idea that meaning is the product of the use of signs— that is of sensemaking—rather than the entified premise of it.

Arguments highlight how the hypostatization of meaning makes it hard to understand the relation between mind and world (1), producing an inversion between *explanans* and *explanandum* in the field of the psychological knowledge (2) as well as preventing psychological theory from addressing the genetic issue, namely the understanding of how meaning emerges (3). Moreover, the entification of meaning fosters the fallible assumption of the inspectionability/accessibility of the states of mind for the sensemaker (4) as well as the scotomization of the pragmatic dimension of sensemaking (5) and the complementary absolutization of the semantic component (6).

In the third part of the chapter I have picked out some ideas from Wittgenstein and Peirce in order to outline the pragmatic and situated approach to meaning that forms the framework of the model of sensemaking that will be presented in the following chapters. Such an approach enables us to think of sensemaking in terms of an infinite flow of signs, each of which has the bivalent function of interpreting the previous one backwardly and triggering the following. Accordingly, the meaning is not inside the sign but *it is the sign that follows*, namely the force of the sign to trigger and channel the unfolding of the semiotic flow.

NOTE

1. The example above uses signs corresponding to concepts. Yet this does not mean that signs are only conceptual. For instance, affective states, sensations, gestures, icons can work as signs (for a discussion of this aspect, in the perspective of an embodied theory of semiosis, see following chapters—in particular 2, 3, and 7; see also Salvatore & Freda, 2011).

CHAPTER 2

THE SEMIO-DYNAMIC MODEL OF SENSEMAKING (SDMS)

SENSEMAKING AS TRAJECTORY OF SIGNS

In the previous chapter a view of sensemaking has been outlined. According to such a view, meaning is the way signs combine with each other in the recursive movement of interpreting the object they stand for. Accordingly, meaning is given by the capability of semiosis to keep signs in (some kind of) correspondence with the reality they refer to by means of their connection with other interpreting signs, in turn in correspondence with reality by means of yet other interpreting signs, and so on in an infinite semiotic flow. Every new interpretant rewrites the relationship of equivalence that the previous sign has with the object (cf. Figure 1.1). At the same time, in the very fact of doing so, it keeps this relationship active, opening to further potentiality of signification (one can find considerations consistent with this view in Sovran, 1992). Thus, in the final analysis, sensemaking can be seen as the chain of interpreting signs unfolding through time and meaning as the shape of the trajectory mapped by the chain.

According to such a view, and on the grounds of a consolidated tradition in linguistics (e.g., de Saussure, 1916/1997; Jakobson, 1956/1971), it is worth depicting the semiotic flow in terms of two components: the syntagmatic and paradigmatic axes. The syntagmatic axis is the time line whose points represent the sequence of signs that carry the semiotic flow forward instant by instant. The paradigmatic axis is the class of signs that can be activated in any instant of the semiotic flow, namely it

Psychology in Black and White: The Project of a Theory-Driven Science, pp. 19–40
Copyright © 2016 by Information Age Publishing

is the dimension of each point represents one of the infinite signs that could be potentially instantiated at a given point of the syntagmatic axis. Incidentally, it is worth observing that for the sake of simplicity syntagmatic and paradigmatic axes are considered here as one-dimensional. Actually, both should be conceived of as hyperdimensional. The syntagmatic axis is the reductive representation of a plurality of temporal scales that run coextensively through the semiotic flow (i.e., just to focus on the domain of language, the transition among signs can be mapped at the level of words as well as of utterances, topics, and so forth; for a model of the mind as working contemporarily on a plurality of temporal scales, see Manzotti, 2006). The paradigmatic dimension is a hyperspace, of which each dimension represents a particular form of equivalence among signs. For instance, the words "banana", "apple" and "sphere" do not have a single relationship with each other. Their relationship can be mapped in terms of many dimensions—on one of them (e.g. the one concerning the fact that they are edible), "banana" and "apple" would have the highest probability of being engaged in a relation of equivalence, compared to "banana" and "sphere" and "apple" and "sphere." On a different dimension (e.g., the one concerning their shape), "sphere" and "apple" would have the highest probability of being considered equivalent.

Phase Space, Field Contingency and Polysemy of Meaning

Figure 2.1 models sensemaking in terms of trajectory of signs moving through the syntagmatic axis in terms of the instant-by-instant selection of a point on the paradigmatic axis. The bidimensional space defined by the syntagmatic and paradigmatic axes can represent the basic *phase space of meaning*. Each point of such space maps the signs instantiated in a certain time t, as the interpretant of the sign occurring at time $(t-1)$, in turn followed by the interpretant at time $(t + 1)$. Accordingly, the meaning emerging from the semiotic flow consists of the shape of this trajectory of signs.

Figure 2.1 represents the paradigmatic axis as a continuous line. This means that the paradigmatic axis is an infinite set, namely the number of signs that can be activated on the syntagmatic axis is infinite, just as the number of points comprising a line is infinite. The infiniteness of the paradigmatic axis is the geometrical representation of the polysemy of signs—if for any sign an infinite class of interpretants can follow then any sign can assume infinite meanings, depending on which sign—among the infinite signs possible—follows it.

It is worth noting that such polysemy is something different from the fact that many signs (first of all, words) are associated with multiple semantic content. The content, even if multiple, is however something already given, associated in a static, invariant way to the sign, as if it were an inner property of it. Instead, polysemy is an inherent consequence of the *field contingency* of meaning, namely of the fact that meaning is not within the sign, but is *produced locally*, as the way the sign enters relationship with previous and following signs. In the final analysis, the polysemy consists of the property of any sign to be able to relate virtually with any other sign and therefore to participate in the emergence of an infinite set of meanings.

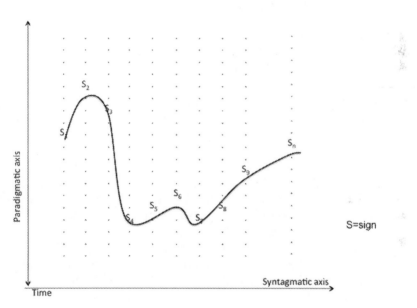

Figure 2.1.   Sensemaking as trajectory of signs.

Ideas for a Field Theory of Sensemaking

The field contingency of meaning leads us to step back from the commonsensical view of meaning as a discrete, punctual-like element. According to the commonsensical view (cf. Chapter 1), "sign *x* means *y*" is interpreted according to the assumption that "*y*" is a finite state: when we meet words, icons, gestures we treat them as associated with circumscribed contents (be they an idea, a thing, a reaction, a pragmatic effect, another signs). Physics comes to our aid in finding an useful analogical way of detecting the field nature of meaning. According to the general theory of relativity, gravity is not the effect of discrete elements. Nothing "pushes" the bodies towards each other. The idea of gravitational attraction is a description, adopted to make the *post hoc* representation of the effects of the gravity meaningful—rather than to model its functioning. The general theory of relativity models this dynamic in terms of the shape of space-time. Space-time is curved by the presence of a mass and this affects the movement of other smaller masses. One can image the first mass as a big ball on a sheet that has a certain degree of elasticity. The big ball modifies the sheet's shape, producing a dip in it. As a result of this deformation of the sheet, the small ball will be subjected to acceleration in the direction of the centre of the dip, which will appear—at a descriptive, global level—as the little ball being attracted by and pulled toward the big one. In sum, gravity is a property of the field, the effect of the space-time form of the universe. The theory of relativity means that gravity is not the effect of a discrete body on another—since this phenomenon is an inherent characteristic of the shape of the field (i.e., the curvature of space-time).

As I began to explain in the previous section, the semiotic field consists of the probability of connection among signs (Salvatore, Tebaldi, & Potì, 2006/2009; Salvatore & Zittoun, 2011a). Connection is for the theory of sensemaking what attraction is for the theory of gravity. The dictionary (or rather, the collection of all dictionaries) can be used as an image of such a semiotic field. Any dictionary can be transformed into a quadratic matrix having the same words both in rows and in columns. Row-words are the ones to define, column-words as the defining ones. Any ij-*th* cell holds the binary probability (presence or absence) of the j-*th* column-word's occurrence in the definition of the i-*th* row-word. Now, imagine taking the set of all dictionaries available for a certain language and aggregating the quadratic matrixes each of them corresponds to. In the new aggregated matrix so obtained, the ij-*th* cell holds the probability (this time from 0 to 1) of the j-*th* column-word's occurrence in the definition of the i-*th* row-word. For instance one could find the value 1 in the cell (i = dog; j = animal), while the value 0,45 in the cell (i = pen; j = ink) – which would mean that the word "animal" occurs in the definition of the word "dog" in all the dictionaries, while "ink" is associated with "pen" in 45% of the dictionaries.

On the other hand, unlike the dictionary, sensemaking concerns the use of signs in daily life rather than the mere definition of lemmas. Therefore, in the case of sensemaking, the model of the matrix can be adopted only if we introduce some further specifications. First, rows and columns of the matrix are not only words, but many kinds of symbolic resources (Zittoun, 2006)—icons, gestures, acts and so forth. Second, the probability in the ij-*th* cell concerns the way the i-*th* and j-*th* sign combine in social exchanges —rather than the presence of the latter in the definition of the former. Finally, this probability lends itself to be seen in terms of the relative frequency of the combination of the i-sign and the j-sign in the practices of sensemaking. This has two important implications. First, the matrix is an ongoing process, with the value of the cells constantly changing through time as a result of the way signs are used. Second, the changing of the values within the matrix is inherently a global dynamic. In other terms, any combination of signs occurring in the sensemaking changes all the values of the matrix. Even if one focuses on the cells showing the greatest effects, nevertheless the change concerns the whole matrix. In the final analysis, the meaning produced by sensemaking *is* this change: the moment-by-moment transformation of the state of the semiotic field.

The ongoing dynamic of the matrix can be understood through the same analogy of the elastic sheet used in the case of the general theory of relativity. In the analogy, the signs correspond to the ball. Their "mass" is their potentiality of combination with the other signs. A very specific sign, —namely, a sign that can enter into combination with only a very limited number of other signs—has a weaker mass than a very generalized sign occurring in the practice of sensemaking in association with many signs. In any given instant, the masses shape the form of the sheet-field. Thus, dips will be created—the heavier the mass-potentiality of combination, the deeper and broader the sinking it produces. In turn, the sinking will affect the space-temporal trajectories of the masses, that is the way signs combine with each other—the deeper and broader a dip, the higher number of signs will be "attracted" within it, namely, the higher number of signs will tend to combine in accordance to the sign-mass producing the sinking.[1] One is thus lead to conclude that meaning is a function of the state of the field.[2]

The field model outlined above leads us to see the interplays among signs as processes reflecting the topology of the whole semiotic field, rather than the inherent characteristics of the signs at stake. In order to move further in this direction, it is useful to take into account the view proposed above of the semiotic field as a space where the distance between any dyad of points corresponds to the probability of combination of the corresponding dyad of signs.[3] Therefore, the less the distance between two points, the more the probability that the corresponding signs are associated within the discourses.

With this premise, we are ready to interpret various sensemaking phenomena in terms of the field's topology. For instance, the basic processes of abstraction and generalization (Valsiner, 2007) can be conceived as the consequence of generalized signs (e.g., goodness, wellness, sufferance, honesty, nation, race, Muslim, and the like)—as such endowed with heavy semiotic mass, therefore producing deep and broad depressions in the field that can deviate the space-temporal trajectory of the lighter semiotic masses. The homogenizing power of the affects is another phenomenon that can also be modeled in terms of field. Feelings tend not to stop at the object they refer to. Rather, they spread out from it to everything that is contiguous, regardless of whether or not there is any semantic or functional association (Salvatore & Zittoun, 2011a; cf. Chapter 7). Thus, for instance, when we feel good, we see everything in a different light from when we feel sad. Stereotype is another paradigmatic instance of this semiotic process of affective connotation. Stereotyped thinking assumes a generalized class (e.g., Arabs as fundamentalists, chauvinists ...)—and makes the individual equivalent to the class, therefore connoting it with all and only the absolutized, affectively loaded properties associated with the class. In this way any individual is made identical to the others projected in the same stereotypical class. Such forms of affective homogenization can be depicted in topological terms too, as the phenomenical effect of curvatures of the semiotic field. More specifically, take a very deep, narrow sinking of the field. On the one hand, it will bring the signs very close to each other (i.e., it will make their connection very probable). On the other hand, a large distance will separate these signs from other signs falling into a different sinking of the field—thus, for instance, the signs "Arabs" and "progress" will not be a probable combination at all). Moreover, take the signs that serve as very basic assumptions of experience. This kind of sign is embedded within the culture of a community, and as such plays the role of what allows and orients thinking and speaking. Signs like "life," "human nature," "person," "Self," "intentionality," "agency," are more than the content of specific beliefs—they are the pillars of any belief. They are felt to be taken-for-granted truths referring to self-evident states of affairs; they are basic categories of organization of experience, like space, time, substance and movement. In this sense, those very basic meanings are even more fundamental than religious beliefs—they ground the religious beliefs rather than being grounded by them. Now, these very basic meanings can be interpreted as reflecting the global property of the semiotic field of being a non-Euclidean space. A space of this kind is withdrawn on itself, rather than endowed with homogeneous extensionality. This means that if one takes a certain set of points delimiting a surface, while the surface of the area remains the same, the distance between the points is not constant, changing in accordance to the region of the field where the area is set. As a result of this global property of the field, some points of the space are inherently closer than others. In sum, the view of the semiotic field in terms of curved space makes it possible to model how some areas of the space (i.e., the one corresponding to the basic categories discussed above) channel the movement of the sign-masses, as an inclined plane does with balls moving on it. People do not experience this orientation directly but as the alleged natural capability of their mind to reflect the unquestionable nucleus of reality.[4]

SCENARIOS AND THEIR DYNAMICS

The Sign Transition

The recognition of the inherent polysemy of signs raises the puzzling issue of how a sign is selected from the paradigmatic class so as to work as the interpretant reproducing the semiotic flow. If the paradigmatic axis were characterized by a homogeneous distribution of probability, namely all signs of the infinite class had the same probability of being selected, then no sign would be selected, because no discrimination would be possible. On the other hand, if the distribution were heterogeneous—namely, signs had different probabilities of being selected—this would make it possible to select the sign, yet no polysemy would be at stake, because any sign would be associated with a unique interpretant (or a finite set of interpretants).

This issue is overcome if one assumes that the distribution is globally homogeneous (and this guarantees the polysemy) but locally heterogeneous (and this allows for the discriminative selection). This is not paradoxical if one models the distribution of probability of the paradigmatic class as a metadistribution, namely a *distribution of distributions of probabilities,* each of them characterized by heterogeneous values of probabilities associated with signs. To use an image, the paradigmatic class should be seen as an overlapping of slices, each of them defining a specific set of asymmetrical relationships among signs.

A way of outlining this kind of metadistribution is provided by the geometrical description of a multidimensional matrix of data subjected to a *principal component analysis.* If one uses all the components extracted, and projects the single variables on the hyperdimensional phase—the space so defined—what one obtains is a cloud of points that is very similar to the description of the paradigmatic class provided above—any sign could be equivalent to an infinite number of other signs, at least one for any component extracted. As the analyst does in the case of *principal component analysis,* the same happens in the case of sensemaking (for an interpretation of the emergence of meaning in terms of component analysis, see Andersen, 2001): a subset of the components (i.e., a slice of the whole distribution) is magnified (Eco, 1975) and in so doing a specific distribution of probability is made to work.

Incidentally, various models focusing on different psychological phenomena (learning, communications, semantic comprehension) adopt the same basic idea, namely, the model of meaning as emerging from the reduction of the dimensionality of the phase space (e.g., Landauer & Dumais, 1997; Salvatore Tebaldi, & Potì, 2006/2009).

The Scenario of Experience

In sum, the sign that follows is selected from the paradigmatic axis due to the fact that a certain component—a "slice"—of the latter is involved. Any slice represents a local asymmetrical distribution of probability in accordance to which some signs are more probable than others to follow as interpretant, others are possible but not probable, others are very improbable, even impossible. Thus, any slice represents a boundary constraining the infinite polysemy—a hierarchy of probabilities on the paradigmatic axis imposing an order upon the infiniteness.

I propose to conceptualize this form of boundary in terms of *scenario of experience* (henceforth, scenario). Culturally defined markers—segmentation of activities, scripts, social roles, modalities of communication, spatial-temporal units of perception and action, and so forth—segment the flow of experience into discrete patterns of co-occurring signs, with spatial-temporal extension, namely in lived events endowed with existential value for those who experience them (Stern, 2004). By the term "scenario" I mean a pattern of this kind: a meaningful unit of subjective experience of the world sustained by a redundant (micro)domain of life characterized by a somewhat stable dynamic network of co-occurring signs, and therefore a particular distribution of the probability of their being related.

As defined here, the scenario recalls Wittgenstein's notion of language game. However, the term scenario is not limited to the linguistic dimension of semiosis—it encompasses bodies and acts too—namely, not only what Peirce calls the logical interpretant, but the emotional and the dynamic interpretant as well. In this sense, it can be associated with Bartlett's notion of schema.

I strongly dislike the term "schema." It is at once too definite and too sketchy. The word is already widely used in controversial psychological writing to refer generally to any rather vaguely outlined theory. It suggests some persistent, but fragmentary, "form of arrangement," and it does not indicate what is very essential to the whole notion, that the organised mass results of past changes of position and posture are actively doing something all the time; are, so to speak, carried along with us, complete, though developing, from moment to moment. Yet it is certainly very difficult to think of any better single descriptive word to cover the facts involved. It would probably be best to speak of "active, developing patterns"; but the word "pattern," too, being now very widely and variously employed, has its own difficulties; and it, like "schema," suggests a greater articulation of detail than is normally found. I think probably the term "organised setting" approximates most closely and clearly to the notion required. I shall, however, continue to use the term "schema" when it seems best to do so, but I will attempt to define its application more narrowly. "Schema" refers to an active organization of past reactions, or of past experiences, which must always be supposed to be operating in any well-adapted organic response. That is, whenever there is any order or regularity of behaviour, a particular response is possible only because it is related to other similar responses which have been serially organised, yet which operate, not simply as individual members coming one after another, but as a unitary mass. Determination by schemata is the most fundamental of all the ways in which we can be influenced by reactions and experiences which occurred some time in the past. All incoming impulses of a certain kind, or mode, go together to build up an active, organized setting: visual, auditory, various types of cutaneous impulses and the like, at a relatively low level; all the experiences connected by a common interest: in sport, in literature, history, art, science, philosophy and so on, on a higher level. There is not the slightest reason, however, to suppose that each set of incoming impulses, each new group of experiences persists as an isolated member of some passive patchwork. They have to be regarded as constituents of living, momentary settings belonging to the organism, or to whatever parts of the organism are concerned in making a response of a given kind, and not as a number of individual events somehow strung together and stored within the organism. Suppose I am making a stroke in a quick game, such as tennis or cricket. How I make the stroke depends on the relating of certain new experiences, most of them visual, to other immediately preceding visual experiences and to my posture, or balance of postures, at the moment. The latter, the balance of postures, is a result of a whole series of earlier movements, in which the last movement before the stroke is played has a predominant function. When I make the stroke I do not, as a matter of fact, produce something absolutely new, and I never merely repeat something old. The stroke is literally manufactured out of the living visual and postural "schemata" of the moment and their interrelations. I may say, I may think that I reproduce exactly a series of text-book movements, but demonstrably I do not; just as, under other circumstances, I may say and think that I reproduce exactly some isolated event which I want to remember, and again demonstrably I do not. (Bartlett, 1932, pp. 201–203)

The Scenario as a Fitting Function

Scenarios are the product of the subject's participation in the cultural world. On the one hand, each scenario is shaped and regulated by a canon, namely a system of generalized and more or less latent normative meanings (a form of activity, a genre, a script, a ritualized interaction). One can imagine a range of scenarios corresponding to the cultural meanings according to which the ever-changing flow of life can be segmented and semiotized. These normative meanings define and foster the regularities that the subject experiences in terms of redundancy of the patterns of co-occurring signs, therefore in terms of meaningful gestalt of experience. For instance, in the scenario of encountering a friend at the cafe by chance, co-occurrences like: (a) saying hello, (b) having a feeling of pleasure, (c) offering her a drink, are canonically expected—while a pattern like: a) not saying hello and (b) shouting at her to leave the cafe, would be a violation of the canon.

People experience the scenario in a partial fashion, since they encounter only a very limited portion of its manifestations, from a specific position. Therefore, the scenario that they assimilate does not reflect the canon in itself, but the partial experience of this canon within their biography. In sum, the organization of the scenarios depends on—and reflects—how people organize their lives and in so doing cluster signs in quite stable patterns. Needless to say, no pattern of experience is the same as the previous ones. Yet, from the very beginning of psychological life, people assimilate the new patterns to the previous one (for a clinical developmental model of this process, see Muller, 1996; see also Stern, 2004; Tronick & Beeghly, 2011). In so doing, people are able to acquire autonomy amidst the flow of experience, and to enhance a sense of stability and continuity of the relation between the self and the world that would be impossible if any experience produced ever-new scenarios.

According to the considerations made above, given that the scenario consists of a specific organization (i.e., a cluster of co-occurrences) of signs, then it can be seen in terms of the *matrix of distribution of probability of signs' transition*—the probability that signs are associated with each other. Thus, for instance, in the scenario of falling in love, after a thought like "I really love her," the probability that the lover goes on to think "so much" is decidedly higher than the probability that he goes on to think "very red." This is because in the scenario of falling in love, the feeling involved is canonically seen as measurable, rather than depictable in chromatic terms (as for example Kandinsky's chromatic theory of feeling would claim). Thus, one can come to consider the scenario as a specific *fitting function*, which, on the basis of the matrix of probability and given the current state of the field of experience, identifies the fittest following sign, namely the one that—given current conditions—expresses the highest value of appropriateness to the canon (whatever the parameter of appropriateness at stake might be).

Scenario as Domain of Sense

These considerations allow the twofold role scenarios play in the dynamic of sensemaking to be highlighted. On the one hand, scenarios are the product of the previous chain of signs. In other words, the way previous signs have been combined in the semiotic flow defines which (set of) scenario(s) is involved. On the other hand, the scenario at stake works as the attractor shaping the trajectory of the chain of signs. This means that the following sign is selected from the subset of signs making up the scenario in question—it is the fittest sign (i.e., the most probable) given that particular scenario. This means that the set of scenarios in question works as a constraint on the paradigmatic axis and in so doing it leads to the selection of the following sign, which in turn participates to reshape the scenario. For instance, imagine that in a certain circumstance of communication the utterance "she is a girl" comes about when the ongoing flow of signs has made pertinent a scenario magnifying the valorizing of age. This scenario will work as a mode of selection on the possible following sign: it will make it more probable that the following sign is selected among those that will keep the youth-age opposition in play, rather than, say, the subset of signs concerning the beautiful-ugly or male-female opposition and so on. Thus, the following sign could be something like: "yes, she is still young" or "but she is so mature for her age" and the like. And according to which following sign occurs, the boundaries of the scenario are reproduced or change to a varying degree.

From a phenomenological standpoint, any set of scenarios corresponds with a specific *domain of sense*. Insofar as the boundary is set, the trajectory of a sign is loaded with a certain domain of sense. The domain of sense is the subjective equivalent of the dynamics of scenarios—it is to the boundaries of the scenario what the experience of heat is to the dynamic of molecules. Thus, any trajectory of signs activates and reproduces through time a certain dynamic of scenarios and in so doing it is experienced by sense-makers as the (domain of) sense implemented by the signs.

One can arrive at a topological interpretation of the interplay between trajectory and scenario. The trajectory, in the way it unfolds, shapes the topology of the phase space, determining curvatures in it that work as attractors towards the ongoing trajectory. As outlined above, this dynamic process can be imagined in terms of the movement of a heavy ball on an elastic sheet. The movement of the ball on the sheet changes the shape of the sheet, creating a specific panorama of dips that determines the further trajectory of the ball.

The latter analogy leads us to conclude that the trajectory of signs making up meaning is not only a dynamic phenomenon; it is also *nonstationary* in the sense that the way the trajectory works—its shape—changes through time as a result of its way of working—the trajectory modifies the topology of the distribution of probability of interconnection among signs (i.e., the set of scenarios). The distribution works, in turn, as an attractor for the trajectory, in a recursive global dynamic where input and output, cause and effect can be distinguished only in conventional terms.

Fuzziness and Other Characteristics of Scenarios

Scenarios are in a fuzzy relation with each other. They overlap each other, in a multiplicity of ways and levels (see Tronick, 2010). Figure 2.2 shows the fuzziness of the organization of scenarios. It depicts how the same pattern of signs can be part of several scenarios at different levels of generalization/abstraction and having different kinds of relationship amongst them. For instance, in the current moment, part of my experience is sustained by a scenario consisting of a cluster of co-occurring signs —the sensation of my fingers on the keyboard, the light of my laptop, the words on the screen, the sense of being unable to grasp what I have in my head, and so forth; most, if not all, of these co-occurring signs are part of other microscenarios too: the sensation of typing is shared with scenarios like the ones involved when I write e-mails to friends; or when I surf the net; in the same way, the sense of an ungraspable idea is perhaps the same as what I felt when I was not able to find the words to specify a certain vague and at the same time persistent negative sensation to my doctor. Thus, scenarios overlap, sharing a more or less broad number of co-occurring signs. Moreover, scenarios can be nested within each other.

From a complementary point of view, signs and their co-occurrences have different levels of *representativeness* of the various scenarios they are part of—namely, a different level of probability of being associated with the scenario. For instance, the white color of my home computer is a sign that is sometimes part of the scenario I-WHEN-USING-THE-COMPUTER, but not always (my home computer is white, but my notebook is black). Thus, being less systematically associated with the scenario, the white color is not as representative of the scenario I-WHEN-USING-THE-COMPUTER as the sounds and tactile sensations associated with fingers typing the keyboard.

The boundaries of scenarios depend both on the cultural organization of life and on the personal biography of which such organization is part. For instance, take two different scenarios: I-WHEN-USING-THE-COMPUTER and I-WHEN-USING-MY-NOTEBOOK. This distinction would be allowed by the differentiation in the technology market, and it would reflect my personal biography as well—not only the fact that I have both a home computer and a notebook, but that I use them in different circumstances—associated with different operations, feelings—differentiated stably enough to serve at least as different domains endowed with subjective meanings, namely: scenarios.

Finally, it is worth noting that scenarios have different extents of *generalization*—namely, the number of circumstances of life they are associated with—and *abstraction*—namely the amount of co-occurrences of signs qualifying them (Bühler, 1934/1990). The scenario GOING-TO-A-RESTAURANT is less generalized than the scenario HAVING DINNER, since the former is associable with a lower number of life circumstances than the latter. The scenario SPEAKING is more abstract than the scenario CHATTING, because the former is identified by a narrower set of co-occurring signs than the latter (e.g., to identify CHATTING, the reference to a specific social scenario involving acquaintances is required; for SPEAKING it is not). As I discuss below (in Chapter 7) emotions lend themselves to be interpreted in terms of hype-generalized and hyperabstracted scenarios.

Figure 2.2. The fuzziness of scenarios.

SIGNIFICANCE IN *PRAESENTIA* (SIP) AND SIGNIFICANCE IN *ABSENTIA* (SIA)

The discussion above depicts sensemaking as a flow of signs unfolding through signs emerging because of the scenario of experience at stake. This view leads to conceiving of meaning as inherently *bivalent,* namely, made up of two components (for similar views, see Abbey & Valsiner, 2005; Carli, 2007; Valsiner, 2007). On the one hand, meaning has an observable, perceivable side: the portion of the world (or rather, of the transformations of the world; cf. Chapter 3; see also Eco, 1975) used as sign—for example, a sound, a gesture, an image as well as an event or a body state. On the other hand, it consists of the *set of scenarios involved in working as the condition for selecting the following sign*. The latter is the second component of meaning. It defines a border, namely the pertinent subset of the paradigmatic infinite set of signs that are virtually available. Pertinent following signs are the ones that *may* follow the representamen as a valid —"senseful"—interpretant of the relation of equivalence at stake. For instance, faced with a photo of a cake, people can react in a great many ways, but for each of them one can imagine a great many other ways that are not usually acted out. For instance, one does not usually say: "please put the rest of the photo in the refrigerator after cutting your slice."

I have proposed calling the former component *significance in praesentia* (SIP), reserving the label *significance in absentia* (SIA) for the latter (Salvatore, 2013).

From a complementary standpoint, SIA can be conceived of as entailed in the very distinction between *sameness* and *equivalence*. Equivalence between two signs—more in general between two elements—is always with respect to a particular standpoint—what Peirce calls the ground of the representamen (cf. Chapter 1); two elements are in a relation of equivalence as concerns a property, a criterion, a certain state of the art. The equivalence may be broad or less broad, but it never fully saturates the infinite dimensions upon which two elements can be placed in relation. If it were so, the equivalence would be *sameness* (Sovran, 1992). Therefore, equivalence always entails *pertinence*—namely, the subset of dimensions the relation consists of. In the final analysis, to establish an equivalence between two or more elements means setting a boundary distinguishing between a region of the relationship seen to be pertinent and all the other infinite dimensions pushed into the background, as not pertinent.

It is worth underlining that, as conceptualized here, the SIA is not a SIP that does not occur or which is implicit or hidden. Rather, it is an inherent component of meaning, namely the pertinent gestalt of linkages among signs (i.e., the scenarios) in terms of which the following interpreting signs are selected. In other words, the SIA is not content, but *the condition of interpretability of signs*. And this means that the SIA is not represented, it is *enacted*, namely, it is instantiated and reproduced through time by means of the action of producing the interpreting signs (see Chapter 3).

The Dynamic Bivalence of the Meaning

The dynamic bivalence of meaning (Abbey & Valsiner, 2005; Carli, 2007; Ribeiro, Gonçalves, & Santos, 2012; Valsiner, 2007) lies in the fact that meaning does not consist of the SIP alone; the phenomenical component of meaning—the SIP—is not enough to produce semiotic values. The meaning *is the effect of the cooperative tension between SIP and SIA through time*—namely, the product of the dynamic positioning of signs within the field of possibilities defined by the pertinent scenario (i.e., the SIA).

Take the lottery: the prize associated with a given number—and therefore the meaning of the selected number—depends neither on its content (whether it is 1 or 1,000 is irrelevant), nor on the very fact of having been selected in itself. Rather, what defines the prize is the relationship between the number and all the others that may be selected. The number would have a different value if extracted from a set of 100 numbers or from a set of 10,000 numbers. In the same way, meaning is *a matter of positioning within a field of possibilities*. Thus, one can see meaning as the transformation of the potentialities of the SIA into the instantaneous actuality of the SIP.

Actually, the example of the lottery is valid only as an initial approximation. In the case of the lottery, indeed, numbers all have the same probability of being selected; consequently, all the cases have the same value, the same meaning. And this condition does not vary through time. It is not so in the case of the transition between signs. The distribution of probability (i.e., the probability of transition to the following sign) which comprises the SIA, is not homogeneous and invariant. Rather, the SIA's boundaries are contingent to local circumstances of sensemaking. Boundaries change through time, as a result of the semiotic flow that they trigger: which dimensions allow a given semiotic relationship of pertinence to be foregrounded depends on the state of communicational field. Take the previous example of the photo of a cake. Actually, we can imagine a situation in which the utterance "please put the rest of the cake in the refrigerator after cutting your slice" is uttered in a senseful way—for instance, in the context of a game between a child and her parent. The chips used in the casino are in a relation of equivalence with money in the casino where they are distributed; in that scenario, and only in that scenario, they stand for money and can be used in place of money.

Moreover, as has been said above, the SIA is an aggregation of a set of local distributions—those concerning the scenarios involved. Thus, the fact that a certain following sign *s* is produced means that a certain set of scenarios has to be involved, namely a certain geography of distributions of probabilities whose global effect is that *s* proves to be the fittest following sign.

My thesis is that, in the final analysis, the *meaning is this geography of scenarios*, namely it is the distribution of probability (the SIA) due to which a certain SIP acquires the status of following sign (S_2).

Consider a person saying to an interlocutor: "I am quite hungry" (S_1). One can imagine very many utterances and actions as SIP, namely as the sign (S_2) following S_1—for example, "Do you want to go to a restaurant before going home?"; "And what about your sleep?", "Shall we have a break?" Each of these SIPs is the fittest following sign in terms of a pertinent

SIA, consisting of a given set of scenarios. Therefore, to understand (to interpret) the SIP means defining the SIA in which the S_1–S_2 transition makes sense. Thus, for example, if the following SIP were "Do you want to go to a restaurant before going home?", then the interpreter should imagine a scenario of two people negotiating where to have dinner, in order to make sense of the transition; instead, if the following SIP were "and what about your sleep?", the scenario involved could be something like a medical visit, with a doctor collecting data on the patient; if the following SIP were "Shall we have a break?", one could imagine something like two colleagues that have to decide together when to stop working. Needless to say, one can imagine many other scenarios as well. However, whatever scenario is involved, S_2 acquires *"sensefulness"*—namely, it enters the semiotic flow as a sign allowing/demanding to be interpreted—only because of and in terms of a certain SIA.

The scenarios activated vary depending on their level of abstraction and generalization. These levels depend on the nature of the relationship between S_1 and S_2 in the context of the circumstances of the communication. In some cases, the scenarios could be quite specific—that is, with a low level of abstraction and/or generalization. In other cases, the pertinentization is confined to shaping more abstract and extended affective scenarios (I will come back to this point in the next chapter).

In sum, meaning is dynamic and bivalent. It is bivalent because it emerges through the relationship between SIA and SIP; it is dynamic because such a dialectical relationship defines its state instant by instant. To express this with a formula:

$$M = f(SIP, SIA, t)$$

where M stands for meaning, and t for time.

Sensemaking Works Through a Mutual Part-Whole Tension

The bivalent model of meaning requires a view of the part-whole relation that can be considered a version of the hermeneutic circle (Ricoeur, 1981). This is so because the SIA may not be conceived of as coming before the SIP, as if it were a super-order meaning framing the selection of the following sign. Such a view would sneak in through the back door the reification of the meaning that has been ushered out through the front door (cf. Chapter 1). Thus, in order to avoid the conceptual problems raised by the reified vision of meaning, and consistently with the dynamic standpoint adopted here—that is, the idea that it is the movements of signs that produce meaning, not the meaning that moves signs—one is led to conceive the selection of the SIP and the instantiation of the SIA as two outputs of the same iterative mechanism of optimization of the form of experience. The new sign is selected as the fittest solution within the constraints of the SIA which, in their turn, are shaped so to allow the optimization of the solution. In sum, parts produce the whole that guides the activation of the parts.

Free schema crosswords provide an image of this interactive mutual constitutive tension between *parts* and *whole*. Free schema crosswords cannot be solved by separating two such components—that is, finding the right word and the setting of constraints defining the compositional order of words. It is not possible to address them as two sequential tasks, to solve one and then to move on to the other, using the solution of the former as the basis for pursuing the latter. This is so because both tasks require that the other task is addressed in order to be addressed—one has to search for single words in order to establish the constraints; at the same time, establishing the constraints is necessary in order to identify the words.

The iterative mutual constitutive tension between parts and whole proposed above could seem counterintuitive. Yet, this is so only if one assumes the commonsensical conception of the nonextensionality of points of time, namely that time is made of elementary units (i.e., instants) devoid of duration. As thoughtfully discussed by Stern (2004), psychological time does not work in this way. *The psychological instant has duration.* The enduring psychological instant of time is the temporal room hosting the iterative tension between the bottom-up process of inference (i.e., the process of selecting the SIP) and top-down constraints (i.e., the enactment of the SIA).

It is worth noting that during the psychological instant the enactment of the SIA is more precisely the enactment of a variation of the SIA. Indeed, the iterative process does not start any instant from 0; instead, it moves from what is already involved, introducing progressive variation in the search for the optimal solution. Accordingly, one can integrate what is stated above—that is, the idea of meaning as the geography of scenarios— with saying that the meaning emerging from sensemaking consists of the instant by instant variation of such geography, namely of the variation of the domain of sense such geography instantiates.

Humorous stories often provide clear examples of the latter statement. Take the following joke. A patient goes to the doctor and says: "Doc, every time I have a coffee, I feel a pain in my right eye." The doctor answers: "Have you tried taking the spoon out of the cup?" What is funny about this story? According to the model provided above, it is the shift of domain of sense generated by the sudden variation of the boundary of the SIA. As the story starts, the linguistic cues (doctor, patient, pain) contribute to the instantiation of a SIA corresponding to a domain of sense about health problems, illness, medical semiotics, and so forth—namely, as if it were a scenario of CARING FOR SUFFERANCE. The interlocutor's reply provides a sudden shift, instantiating the image of a person able to damage him/herself by the very simple act of drinking a cup of coffee—a scenario of, say, STUPIDITY TO BE HANDLED.

SENSEMAKING IS INHERENTLY ABDUCTIVE

The view of sensemaking in terms of mutual part-whole tension is consistent with a systemic notion of causality, which holds that the dynamic of a process is a matter of transformation of the field as a whole, rather than a cause-effect sequence of discrete events (for a discussion of this model in the domain of sensemaking, see Cabell & Valsiner, 2011).

One can refer to several daily life experiences to find instances of this tenet. For example, consider two persons talking with each other. It would be hard to consider the language they are using as the cause of the words they use. Rather, the language they use is the *condition of production and interpretability* of the words they use. The same applies now, as I write. The utterances I have just written are not caused by the English language I am using. Rather, the English language defines the field conditions that make the trajectory of meaning as defined by the previous signs (the preceding utterances) develop in terms of the utterances that follow—namely, the conditions for the latter to be considered part of the semiotic flow in question.

To take another example, consider a performative utterance—for example, "I baptize you," "I curse you" (Austin, 1962). Well, in cases like these, the meaning of the utterance is what it performs. Thus, we see a shift: it is not the meaning that performs something, but the performance that produces meaning (i.e., the transformation of reality brought about by the performance). In the same way, it is not the SIA that causes the SIP (i.e., the S_2), but it is S_2 that creates the conditions for the instantiation of the pertinentized SIA.

Every time a person produces an interpretant, she is instantiating a SIA, namely the field conditions of possibility allowing the interpretant (i.e., the following sign) to work as an equivalent sign to the previous one. This instantiation reflects the basic abductive way of functioning of sensemaking (Eco, 1975; Peirce, 1897/1932; Salvatore & Valsiner, 2010), namely, the tendency of people to experience the discrete elements as a single whole. On this point it is interesting to refer to Stern's (2004) notion of *present moment*, namely the current experience of nowness to be intended as a gestalt with its own temporal extension (a few seconds), whose elements are experienced in terms of a whole. As Peirce (1897/1932) highlights, that is

precisely what abduction is—in his terms: the "reunification of the predicates" (see also Pizarroso & Valsiner, 2009), namely, the presentification of
a totality encompassing—and in so doing interpreting—the plurality of
the elements experienced.

The game of rebus (Figure 2.3[5]) provides an image of this mechanism.
The player's starting point is that the letters are meaningful parts of the
semiotic organization of the game—namely, they have the status of SIPs.
Grounded on this assumption, the interpreter shapes the SIA sourced by
the images in the background (that provide infinite potentialities of connection), in order to select the scenarios that allow the gestalt to be closed
and thus the SIPs to acquire the status of meaningful signs within it and
based on it. On the other hand, till such a gestalt is closed, the letters do
not gain the status of SIPs (or rather, they acquire the status of sign in reason of a different scenario—the scenario of PUZZLING-PROBLEM).

Rebus: (2, 8)

Source: http://www.linkiesta.it/blogs/neverland/--sogni--giochi--realta/rebus--english

Figure 2.3.   A rebus.

The Kanizsa triangle (Figure 2.4, cf. Kanizsa, 1955) provides a further
example, at the level of perception, of the abductive process of presentification of the gestalt totality. The triangle is not comprised in the stimulus; rather the perceiver adds the sides that close the figure as a good
form. An equivalence can therefore be established: the three uncompleted
black circles and the black lines correspond to the pattern of co-occurring
SIPs—what is seen; the sides of the triangle in the foreground correspond
to the SIA, which the perceiver adds in order to connect the SIPs in a
meaningful totality. The triangle emerges in the tension between these
two components.

One last example of the backward production of SIA: miming. The mime produces some movements that work as a sign (SIP). The spectator sees these movements as a "senseful" action, a sign having the meaning M. For the spectator, the SIP stands for M. Yet it would be misleading to consider M the content conveyed by the SIP. M is not contained in the SIP; rather it is the spectator that presentifies M as the interpretation of the SIP. Moreover, the spectator performs this interpretative activity by adding a set of further data of imagination (i.e., scenarios sourced from memory) that work as the SIA of the SIP; in so doing s/he defines the gestalt totality providing the *condition of interpretability* of the SIP. The mime moves his arms and hands in a certain way; yet the interpretation of these movements—say "pulling a rope"—requires the spectator to complete the gestalt with a scenario concerning a long thin object being grasped, connected at the opposite end with something that resists his efforts. In sum, the meaning of the mime consists of the cooperative tension between what is seen and what is added to make what is seen interpretable. It is only on this condition that the mime's movements can be interpreted as "pulling a rope." The interpretation starts, is constrained by and has the SIP as its target; yet, strictly speaking *it does not concern it.* Rather, the SIP is the catalytic trigger for the interpreter's hermeneutic activity of shaping a SIA which has to be added to the field of experience in order to make the latter a meaningful gestalt. *The interpretation of a sign does not specify something that is "within" the interpretant—it adds something further to it.* In sum, when the spectators give meaning to the mime's movement, their interpretative work is not limited to the representation of what they perceive. Rather, they provide something else, complementing the gestalt. It is the pertinentization of the SIA which allows the closure of the gestalt that makes interpretation possible. Abduction is not one of the possible modalities of sensemaking—it is the inherent logic of its functioning.

CONCLUSION

In this chapter I have started to present the semio-dynamic model of sensemaking (SDMS) that is the central focus of the first session of the volume. The SDMS can be summarized in terms of three basic tenets.

First, the claim of the *primacy of sensemaking over meaning*. The meaning is not an autonomous entity existing before the process of its production and communication (i.e., before the sensemaking). Rather, it is the emerging field property of sensemaking, so meaning is not within the signs, as their inner content; instead, it consists of the way signs iteratively combine with each other in the local circumstances of communication. I have summarized such a view in the statement that *sensemaking is the chain of interpreting signs unfolding through time and meaning the shape of the trajectory drawn by the chain.*

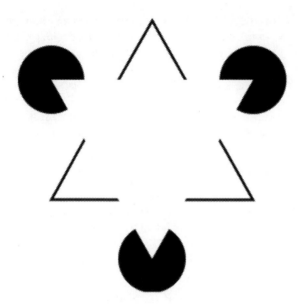

Figure 2.4.   Kanizsa's triangle.

Second, *the dynamic bivalence of sensemaking*. Sensemaking is not completed in its observable side. Any new sign is selected from the infinite set of possible sign in accordance to and thanks to the fact that the semiotic flow is always characterized by a *scenario of experience* defining the condition of interpretability of signs. As defined in this chapter, a scenario is a meaningful unit of subjective experience of the world characterized by a somehow stable dynamic network of co-occurring signs. Thus, sensemaking works through the interplay of two components—on the one hand, the perceivable component (the *significance in praesentia*, SIP), namely the piece of world—for example, a sound, a gesture … —used as sign; on the other hand, the set of scenarios working as the condition for selecting/ interpreting the following sign (the *significance in absentia*, SIA). Meaning emerges from the instant-by-instant cooperative tension between these two components, namely, as the projection of the SIP upon the SIA and the complementary transformation of the SIA.

Third, *sensemaking works through a mutual part-whole tension*. The relation between SIA and SIP has to be conceived of in terms of iterative mutually constitutive tension between SIP and SIA. The selection of the SIP is performed through the optimization of the SIA and at the same time the enactment of the SIP is performed in terms of the optimization of the SIP. More specifically, the SIP defines the constraints that trigger/force the interpreter to shape the boundaries of SIA in a certain way, so that the transition to such a SIP is made possible. In sum, *meaning is the border of the potentially infinite SIA under the condition of the SIP, and sensemaking is the process of making such bordering-pertinentization*. And this means that sensemaking is inherently abductive—it works as an ongoing process of "reunification of the predicates" that allows parts and whole to be constituted through the other.

In the next chapters I will go on to present the SDMS, sketching out the microdynamic that brings about the processes described above.

NOTES

1. A similar analogy can be drawn with the movement of animals in a wood. Each animal's trajectories depend on the shape of the wood. Given a certain point in the wood, the less dense the vegetation, the more probable it is that the animal will pass through that point. At the same time, the movement thus regulated transforms the wood, and in so doing affects the animal's future trajectory.

2. One can add that such a state lends itself to be detected by means of many different scales of observation, each of them focusing a certain space-temporal dimensionality corresponding to the pertinentization of certain local effects of sensemaking rather than others. Thus, as the choice of the scale of observation leads Newtonian, relativistic or quantum phenomena to meet, so the choice of a given dimensionality of sensemaking leads us to see semantic or pragmatic levels of meaning, as well as cultural process we usually regard as concerning individuals, interpersonal and group relationships or society—either occurring in the present moment or spread over other time scales. This view provides a shift in how to consider the phenomenical levels —micro-meso-macro. Accordingly, such levels do not mirror ontological substances but represent epistemological choice—namely, they are the product of the chosen scale of observation. Fronterotta and Salvatore (in press) have proposed a re-reading the mind-body problem based on this view.

3. The more the signs, the more dimensions in the space. For the sake of simplicity, here I will simply consider a bidimensional space given by the combination for adjacency between two signs. Nevertheless, the reasoning can be extended so as to encompass hyperdimensional spaces, given by the combination among many signs.

4. Fractal geometry seems to be able to provide suggestive opportunities for the modeling of sensemaking in terms of topology. Such an approach could provide an interesting pointer to address sensemaking's tendency to produce semiotic forms that are redundant in spite of the different spatial and temporal scale of observation of the practices of sensemaking producing them—think, for instance of the fact that some semiotic forms tend to be present in different domains (art, politics, science), as well as levels (institutional, group, interpersonal) of discourse.

5. Solution: T, O, B eatrice—To Beatrice

CHAPTER 3

MICRODYNAMIC OF SENSEMAKING

THE FUNCTION OF THE SIGN

In this chapter and in the next I intend to make a step ahead towards defining a model of the microdynamic of sensemaking, namely, of the S_1–S_2 transition. More specifically, my aim is to shed light on how the cooperative tension between SIP and SIA works and which basic mechanisms carry it out.

My starting point is the triadic nature of the sign. As a result of this characteristic, the S_1–S_2 transition is a two-sided process. Any time a sign enters the semiotic flow, it works as the representamen motivating the following interpreter sign; at the same time it works as the interpretant of the previous sign.

The model proposed below treats these two functions separately. On the one hand, it addresses the issue of *causality*: how the representamen motivates its interpretant – namely, which processes make it happen that the position S_2 of the S_1–S_2 transition comes to be occupied by the occurrence x, rather than y, or w, or z or the like. On the other hand, it addresses the *hermeneutic* issue: how the interpretant sign defines-develops the meaning of the previous sign (see Peirce's definition of the interpretant as a "more developed idea").

A further point has to be highlighted. As stated above, a sign is supposedly a discrete entity existing independently from the semiotic flow and ready to enter it. This assumption is consistent with common sense as well

Psychology in Black and White: The Project of a Theory-Driven Science, pp. 41–63
Copyright © 2016 by Information Age Publishing

as with the basic implicit metaphysical grounds of the mainstream psychological theories, according to which the world is made of discrete stable
units, as such suitable to be perceived and understood (for a criticism of
this assumption, see Manzotti, 2010). Actually, one has to distinguish the
dynamic of sensemaking as seen from the inside of that process and the
way this dynamic works. From the inside, the interpreter experiences an
ongoing chain of signs. Yet this does not mean that signs are the basic
units of functioning of sensemaking; rather, they are to be considered intermediate output. Peirce considers such output in terms of *Thirdness* (see
below).

Individuals are immersed in the world and the basic, elementary, immediate experience of it comes in a cascade of patterns of sensorial occurrences lacking any inherent order, any reciprocal relation. According to
Peirce's typology of the conditions of experience, such patterns are experienced in terms of *Firstness*. They lack a relation because infinite possibilities of relation are possible. For something to be used as a sign, it has to
be assumed as *something* before, namely, as a *persistence* producing an effect
on the perceiver and the world; in Peirce's terminology, it has to develop
itself as *Secondness*. Yet, the passage from the undifferentiated totality of
the unrelated *Firstness* to the *Secondness* of the discrete "something" is not
obvious; rather it is the product of how the field of experience is "cut" and
ordered in stable enough clusters of co-occurrence. Objects we perceive
and address are the result of this process of discretization, pertinentization and presentification leading to the construction of a world of entities:
objects, facts and qualities in the foreground and all the rest as noise in
the background (Bickhard, 2009). In this instant (actually, an instant ago,
before I moved my attention to the margin of my field of experience for
the sake of producing this example), the noise of the air conditioner in
my office is in the background, merged with many other occurrences, like
the quality of the light, sensations of muscular tension, the reflex of the
computer screen on my glasses and so forth. That basic capacity of making
some occurrences pertinent compared to all the others left in the background enables me to extract a meaningful connection within the flow of
experience, and therefore to perceive objects. And this capacity entails a
task that is inherently semiotic—it represents the grounds of the semiotic,
the *dark side of sensemaking*: the part of sensemaking which is not its content, but instead its basic constituent.

In sum, a more fundamental model of sensemaking is needed, a model
whose starting point is the *Firstness* of the whole field of experience (Rosa,
2007), namely, the unrelated clusters of co-occurring states of the body-
environment physical interaction, sustaining the subject's instantaneous
consciousness of being alive (which is broader than awareness; see Stern,
2004; Tronick, 2010). Such a model must not only conceptualize how signs

work and produce meaning, but also how sensemaking produces the signs through which its dynamic unfolds. This is the third issue that the model outlined below has to address—the fundamental issue of the *constitution* of the sign.

In the final analysis, the three issues that the model is designed to address follow the trajectory entailed in Peirce's triad model: from the *Firstness* of undifferentiated experience (the constitution issue) to the *Secondness* of the object in relation with other objects (the causality issue) to the *Thirdness* of the semiotic mediation (the hermeneutic issue). However, for the sake of the discussion, I have inverted the order of exposition. In this chapter I deal with the hermeneutical issue and the causality issue. Chapter 4 is devoted to the constitution issue.

THE HERMENEUTIC ISSUE: THE INTERPRETANT'S JOB

The Semiotic Value of the Sign: The Bootstrapping Mechanism

As far as this issue is concerned, the central point to address is the *backward process* entailed in the abductive process of pertinentization of the SIA. This dynamic does not lend itself to being conceived of in terms of ready-to-use meanings selectively triggered by the SIP. This view is problematic. Indeed, the idea of SIAs as a collection of ready-to-use meanings entails the reified view of meaning, which is inconsistent with the dynamic nature of meaning discussed in the previous chapters.

As an alternative view, I propose to consider the abductive process of pertinentization of the SIA in terms of what I define the *bootstrapping mechanism* (Salvatore, Tebaldi, Potì, 2006/2009; see also Tronick & Beeghly, 2011). This mechanism works through two stages—a stage of *propagation* and a stage of *reduction*. Below I provide some details on such a two-stage bootstrapping mechanism (Figure 3.1).

Take the S_1–S_2 transition. According to my argument, S_2 triggers the propagation stage—namely. *all connections between signs are activated*. This process of propagation can be understood in the light of Matte Blanco's (1975, cf. Chapter 7) bi-logic theory. Accordingly, the propagation works in terms of the principle of symmetry: *any relation of contiguity among signs is transformed into identity; consequently, a homogeneous totality of connection is activated, tending to encompass the infinite set of signs the sensemaker has stored in memory*. One can consider this global state of activation as a potential absolute SIA.

The propagation is antagonized by the opposite movement, which characterizes the second stage: the *fading off of the nonpertinent connections*.

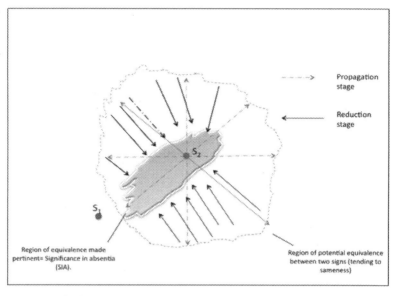

Figure 3.1. The bootstrapping mechanism of semiosis.

This movement of reduction consists of a process of competitive differentiation of the absolute SIA. It does not work randomly; rather, it is channelled by the fuzzy boundaries of the scenarios. Thus, any connection tends to fade off, unless it is consistent with scenarios containing the S_1–S_2 co-occurrence. For instance, say S_1 is "apple" and S_2 is "orange"; then the connection "orange-sugar" could remain active, because it is found in scenarios like GOING SHOPPING and HAVING BREAKFAST that also contain the triggering "apple" – "orange" transition; conversely, the connections "orange-logistic regression" would probably be ruled out because it would hardly share scenarios with the "apple" – "orange" transition. Thus, the many connections sharing few or no scenarios with the S_1–S_2 transition fall into the background, while the survived co-occurrences stay in the foreground. In so doing, they emerge as the SIA, namely, the domain of equivalence between S_2 and S_1.

This can be shown by referring to the example of the photo of the cake already given. The domain of equivalence of the photo compared to the cake made of chocolate, milk and eggs consists of all the scenarios in which the co-occurrence is active (e.g. scenarios concerning circumstances like: seeing the photo album of a past birthday, choosing the cake for a wedding party, and the like); in those scenarios the photo can work as interpretant of the cake. Whatever they are, such scenarios define the ways the photo can be used as an equivalent sign of the cake. This is what has to be considered the *semiotic value of the sign*—its meaning.

It is worth noting that, given the fuzziness of the SIA, the S_1-S_2 co-occurrence is part of scenarios that might be very different from each other. Two scenarios are differentiated when they share few connections. Therefore, it must be assumed that a certain level of constraints is at work for the SIA to remain at least partially consistent. This means that there should be a competition among divergent scenarios, so that a subset of candidate scenarios survives while the others fade off. For example, the sensations of liquid slipping down my throat, that I feel when I drink, is a pattern of co-occurrences that is part of a scenario of pleasure—yet it is also part of a quite divergent scenario, related with the unpleasant scenario of me as child, forced to take a very bitter cough mixture. These scenarios share the sensations associated with the swallowing of a liquid—but very few other occurrences. And when I drink my favorite ice drink on the beach, only one of the two scenarios stays in foreground (usually not the latter).

If one were to ask which parameters regulate the competitive selection of scenarios, a plausible hypothesis is to conceive of it in terms of an *optimization-seeking criterion of good form*. One could depict such a parameter in terms of the following rule, entailing two partially contrasting dimensions: in order to get the most efficient closure of the gestalt, the fading off has to optimize the generalization of the SIA and the representativeness of the transition signs (i.e., S_1 and S_2).

In sum, one can conceive of the reduction stage as a bootstrapping process where many selections are compared in terms of their capacity to produce a good form. The optimal one is that which survives as the gestalt comprising the SIA. It is this gestalt that works as the most efficient grounds for the S_1-S_2 transition.

The way scenarios have been conceptualized above makes it clear that they cannot be considered structures already defined. Rather, they have to be seen as potentialities of connection among signs working as parallel—partially convergent and partially divergent—attractors involved in the competitive selection of the reduction stage. In this sense, scenarios look more like sprinters than golfers. All the racers start from the same line, with the same possibility of winning. The competitive capacity of the sprinters is potential and is actualized only after the race, in terms of its outcome. In the case of golf, instead, the capacities of the competitors are registered before the competition, in terms of the handicap each golfer has to start from.

Moreover, as we have said above, scenarios are neither categories contained in the individual's transcendental mind nor semantic content stored somewhere in any Platonic world. Rather, they reflect the individual participation in the redundant patterns of the social world. Therefore, the more two individuals share experiences and spheres of life, the more their scenarios tend to converge and to be compatible, yet never emerging as the same. Consequently, the two-stage mechanism is implemented in ways that are highly idiosyncratic and at the same time express the participation in a shared cultural system (providing the basic form of redundancy that makes up the scenarios).

The Freudian energetic model (Freud, 1895/1950) works as a useful analogy of the two-stage bootstrapping mechanism: in the propagation stage, operating under the domain of the primary process, the libidinal charges are free to fluctuate and spread themselves over the whole memory, namely, over the network of signs it stores. Thus, the network is activated in a global and homogeneous way, with each zone having an equivalent, low rate of charge. Then, as the secondary process comes into play, a progressive asymmetrization emerges in the distribution of the charges. Thus, some regions of the network prove to be competitively activated—and therefore come to the foreground—compared to others that prove to be unactivated—that is, pushed into the background.

From a further standpoint, the two-stage model proposed above depicts the SIA as the output of a process of sculpture, rather than of painting, as distinguished by the classical student of art, Giorgio Vasari. Painting is a way of representing by adding on the emptiness (i.e., putting chromatic pigments on the white canvas), while sculpture is a way of making the figure emerge by taking off from the whole (i.e., eliminating something from the block, so to extract a form).

The same "sculptural" logic of the mechanism placed at the functional core of the bootstrapping model proposed above can be found in several theories addressing different kinds of phenomena from a variety of standpoints. In the psychoanalytic field, Bucci's (1997) multiple code theory claims that representational contents emerge from a process of progressive extraction from the continuous embodied field of experience. Kintsch (1988) has conceptualized the process of comprehension of written texts in terms of a two-stage model having a somewhat similar logic to the one proposed here. According to this author, when read, the word triggers a process of global activation of the semantic network, so that all potential meanings associated with the word are activated, and this activation is propagated to the further meanings associated with the former. The irradiation of the activation is then antagonized by a second stage of reduction of the active linkages within the network, performed on the basis of the cues provided by further incoming words. Moreover, the basic idea of meaning as emerging from a process of constraining—the sculpture-like function of taking off—is entailed in the Landauer and Dumais's (1997) model, which sees the understanding of lexical meaning in terms of a mechanism of multidimensional mapping of the relations among the words implementing an optimizing procedure of space reduction.

Change by and Change of Sensemaking

The two-stage mechanism proposed in the previous section entails the basic argument that the sensemaking is a dynamic that seeks inherently to maintain its own continuity, namely, to connect the incoming sign of the semiotic flow backwards. According to this view, any transition between signs produces a perturbation and thus a response from the system aimed at restoring steadiness (i.e., at finding the most efficient way for restoring the gestalt closure). What such a response produces is what we experience as meaning—namely, the "stuff" making up the semiotic value of the transition between signs.

This last consideration leads us to make a fundamental distinction between change as concerning the dynamic of sensemaking and change as concerning its content. Insofar as one assumes that sensemaking is a dynamic inherently oriented to restoring steadiness, one is led to conclude that, in the final analysis, according to a certain standpoint, *sensemaking does not change*—rather, it uses the change (the difference) as the perturbative mechanism of its reproduction. In other words, sensemaking is a self-organized dynamic that uses perturbations to constantly self-regulate itself. Thus, the perturbations are at the core of the functional identity of sensemaking. Imagine the sign *x* followed by the sign *y*. Now, the interpreter is allowed rightly to consider that a change has happened in the transition from *x* to *y* – *y* is different from *x*. This is true, obviously. Nevertheless, *y* is a sign produced from within the same semiotic flow, as a further interpretant sign of the ongoing flow, not something coming from outside the sensemaking. And as such, it creates a linkage with the previous semiotic instant (*x*), in so doing reproducing the continuity of the semiotic flow. And this is so always, whatever the distance between *x* and *y* may be.

This might seem paradoxical. Nevertheless, at a more careful glance, it is consistent with the experience of daily life. Here is an example of this.

xzslfqw

How has the reader approached the string above? Regardless of what she/he has thought of it (an example, an error, a world in a different language…), what she/he cannot but to carry out has been to create a bridge between the semiotic flow represented by the previous text and the string. One can consider the string as the input sign of the transition (i.e., S_1); the way of understanding it represents the output sign of the transition (i.e., S_2). A new sign (S_2) is however performed, for the sake of retaining the continuity of the semiotic flow, namely, to define in what way S_1 can be treated as a sign, that is, as something standing for something else. Also to think that the string has no meaning, that it is just an error, *would however be a way for grounding its connection with the semiotic flow*, namely, to treat the string as a sign—standing for the fact of being an error.

Now, it is worth highlighting that the striving to ground the transition and keep up the continuity of the semiotic flow is a ubiquitous dynamic; it does not concern only the situation of rupture, as in the case of the previous example. Rather, any transition introduces a (variable) quantum of perturbation and therefore a need to restore the continuity of the flow.

Thus, when considering semiotic processes, it is worth distinguishing between a *descriptive* and a *structural* level of change—the former concerns the content that is the output of the sensemaking, the latter the organization of its dynamic. I propose to refer to the former in terms of change *by* sensemaking and the latter as change *of* sensemaking. This distinction is required because the change *by* does not necessarily entail and reflect the change *of*. Indeed, the previous example of the meaningless string provides a case in which the *change by* could be considered relevant—the string produces a rupture in the inner consistency of the text—but that does not mean it must represent a significant transformation of the dynamic of sensemaking.

Mossi and Salvatore (2011) provide an example of the by/of difference. They mapped the systems of meaning of students engaged with the transition between two scholastic systems (junior school and high school), finding that while at the level of content major changes occurred, the structural organization of the sensemaking remained constant—no change happened at the level of the basic way of interpreting the experience of being a student.

Conversely, one can imagine situations in which the change *of* sensemaking has no correspondence with the descriptive level. I tend to consider (at least a certain kind of) humor a case of this kind, when limited changes at the level of content produce a sudden reorganization of the trajectory of sensemaking. Some time ago, David Letterman, after having been made a target of Fatwa, introduced himself in the following episode of the *Letterman Show* explaining that he was late because he had just needed to check whether his life insurance covered Fatwa. The few words he said were taken as a very brilliant piece of humor—people saw them as an example of Letterman's ability as a stand-up. Something obviously happened at the level of the dynamic of sensemaking for him to be able to produce such an effect on the public. Nevertheless, whatever happened, it is hard to see it as a mere matter of content—what he said was not so descriptively divergent (strange, hyperbolic, incomprehensible …) from a mere apology for arriving late.

To make things even more complicated, in many circumstances the change of the content—namely, the change by—is used as a sign in the following semiotic dynamic, and thus works as a factor of stability of sensemaking. This is particularly evident in the clinical domain, where, on the one hand, significant perturbations of the dynamic are nuanced by slight movements at the level of content (Salvatore & Tschacher, 2012) and, on the other hand, in some cases impressive changes at the level of the patient's discourse and action reflect the need to defend the *status quo*—on this, see the Freudian notion of escape into health (for a general discussion of this issue in the field of psychotherapy research see Salvatore, 2011).

In the final analysis, the fact that change *by* and change *of* are not necessarily related depends on the fact that the former, unlike the latter, is a function of the contingencies and social norms defining the quality and the content of what it is said and enacted. Therefore, it is contingent to circumstances, actors' purposes, and so forth. And the recognition of this cannot but make us recognize that a criterion is needed to enable the mapping of the change of sensemaking regardless of the normative value of its content. In other words, we need a theory according to which the change can be seen and appraised in terms of the dynamic of sensemaking involved (Salvatore, Lauro-Grotto, Gennaro, & Gelo, 2009), rather than in terms of normative descriptive criteria—*we need a theory of semiotic identity —namely, a theory of the self-organization of sensemaking—as the grounds for a dynamic theory of change.*

A Typology of Change of Sensemaking

The arguments put forward in the previous section pave the way for outlining a model of the change of sensemaking. On the basis of the idea of the bivalence of meaning and on the two-stage bootstrapping mechanism, the change of sensemaking could be conceived of in terms of the self-regulative dynamic of the SIA that sensemaking performs in order to keep its own continuity. Such transformations could be appreciated in terms of the *ongoing modification of the geography of scenarios sustaining the SIA.*

More in particular, the transformations of the geography of scenarios could be depicted in terms of the two basic parameters we have already mentioned: abstraction and generalization (cf. Chapter 2). On the one hand, scenarios have different degrees of *abstraction*, namely, they encompass a set of co-occurring signs. This set may vary in size—the smaller the amount of co-occurring signs, the more the abstraction of the scenario. In other words, the abstraction concerns the number of signs that are part of the constitution of the scenario. Thus, for example, the scenario HAVING BREAKFAST WITH THE FAMILY is less abstract than the scenario HAVING A BUSINESS BREAKFAST (even if one has experienced the latter more often than the former), because allegedly HAVING BREAKFAST WITH THE FAMILY entails more redundant co-occurring signs—in the final analysis when one has break-fast with the family, one always encounters more or less the same people, in the same place, eating more or less the same food, and so forth. Instead, when one has a business breakfast a lot of aspects that are stable in the former circumstance are variable, therefore not part of what sustains the scenario. On the other hand, as already observed, the scenarios can be more or less generalized, namely, associable with various circumstances in life. The more the circumstances, the more generalized the scenario. HAVING BREAKFAST WITH THE FAMILY is less generalized than HAVING A BUSINESS BREAKFAST because it is activated in association with a narrower set of circumstances compared to the latter.

The dynamic of the SIA can be viewed in terms of the two parameters of abstraction and generalization. Thus, one can distinguish between different kinds of changes of sensemaking. According to a first type (say, *type 0*) the SIA keeps both parameters more or less constant. This is what one might expect to happen when, for instance, the sensemaking keeps going on in a specific circumstance, according to the pragmatic and semantic norms of that circumstance, or when a change of context of activity occurs between two social settings characterized by the same level of social regulation and therefore of abstraction and generalization. I call the change characterized by the decreasing abstraction of the SIA, *type A–* change. This is what happens when a less abstract scenario comes to be pertinentized as the way of interpreting the new sign. Conversely, one can talk about *type A+* when sensemaking produces an increase in the abstraction of the SIA—like when a more conventionalized scenario is activated, as such qualified by a narrower number of co-occurring signs. With *type G+*, I mean the change associated with the increase in generalization – what happens when a more generalized scenario comes to be activated. And also in this case one can refer to the opposite trend—*type G–*, characterized by a reduction of the generalization.

A typology of dynamics of changes can be obtained as combination of the types presented above (see Table 3.1).

- *Concretization by pleromatization* (for a more detailed discussion of the role of pleromatization in sensemaking, see Valsiner, 2006) is the dynamic characterized by the combination A–/G–. It consists of the decreasing abstraction of the scenario, producing an enrichment of its particular character, of its individualized concreteness. An example of this dynamic is provided by the circumstances in which a social exchange shifts from a more conventionalized and ritualized script to a more contingent, individualized and idiosyncratic canon. Imagine husband and wife talking with some acquaintances during a dinner—the conversation is following the canonical rules of politeness (i.e., highly conventionalized scenario). At one point, the wife throws a discrete glance at her husband as a tacit, private commentary on what is going on. Such a glance entails a private, idiosyncratic scenario of the couple; it is in accordance to such a scenario that the glance acquires the value of a sign—a sign charged with meaning only for the two people exchanging it. This is an example of concretization by pleromatization because the scenario constituted by the idiosyncratic history of the couple is on the one hand a form of decreasing generalization of the scenario—that is, a shift from the extended conventionalized scenario TALKING WITH ACQUAINTANCES to the scenario of, let's say, OUR PRIVATE UNDERSTANDING; on the other hand, the latter scenario, since it is restricted to the couple alone, will supposedly be a very rich pattern of signs, which the idiosyncratic rituality of the couple's life has led to cohere into a dense whole, encompassing fragments of experience from a vast range of circumstances and contexts.

• *Individuation by schematization* is the label I use here to indicate the dynamic marked by the combination of increasing abstraction and decreasing generalization $(A+G-)$. Schematization is the semiotic process of reducing the complexity of the sign (Valsiner, 2006). Such a reduction, in this case, is functional to the complementary reduction of the extension of the scenario. Thus, in this kind of dynamic the "lightening" of the scenario is performed for the sake of constraining the scenario to a more specific set of circumstances. A photographic portrait could be considered a prototype of this kind of dynamic—it is a schematization, in the sense that it is the output of the selection of only some aspects of the face represented (abstraction); yet, its semiotic effect is to provide a sense of presence of the person that has been photographed. Thus, when one speaks to or kisses the photo of a significant person, this shows that a process of reduction of the complexity of the representation can be performed with the result of making it a concrete exemplar, rather than a general category—that is, my son John, her cousin Eleanor, rather than son-ness or cousin-ness. Another example of individuation by schematization is provided by what happens when two people from the same country meet abroad. They will seek a more individualized and closer linkage with each other by reducing the connotation concerning their identity. Generally speaking this tends to be proportional to the distance from home; thus, a man coming from New York and a man from Los Angeles would probably consider themselves as being both from the United States, if they meet in Shanghai. In sum, they would seek to make their connection more individualized through a process of schematization, in this case performed in terms of the reduction of elements qualifying their scenarios. Incidentally, I tend to think that a stereotype concerns this kind of dynamic: it is a simplified version of the other, performed for the sake of creating a form of concrete representation of it.

- *Schematic abstraction* concerns the opposite output of individuation by schematization. In this case the increasing abstraction of the scenario serves the process of increasing generalization $(A+G+)$. This is typical of a dynamic of sensemaking that follows the path of conventionalization—namely, the shift in the direction of a scenario regulated by norms that are generic enough to be applied in a general way. For an example of this, take what happens when a group of classmates shifts from the informal, idiosyncratic way of acting to the formal, rule-based way, as a result of the teacher entering the room. Their informal way of acting is typical of their microculture, while the formal, institutional mode reflects rules that have a broader application—how to act in the formal school time is not so different from the way of acting in other public and work contexts. At the same time, the formal scenario is generalized precisely because it is composed of a pattern of signs that, however broad they may be, will be less highly charged than the idiosyncratic, informal scenario the students experience.

- Finally, I use *affective generalization* to refer to the dynamic marked by decreasing abstraction and increasing generalization $(A–G+)$. At first glance this would seem hard to conceive of—one might expect that density tends to be inversely associated with generalization. Actually, the combination of density and generalization makes sense if one considers this kind of dynamic in terms of affective semiosis (Salvatore & Freda, 2011; Salvatore & Zittoun, 2011a; see also Chapter 7). Thus, according to my proposal, this dynamic is associated with feelings and generalized values (honesty, freedom, goodness, trust...). This is so because feelings and values have an affective (symmetrical, in Matte Blanco terms, cf. Chapter 7) ground. Owing to this, on the one hand they constitute scenarios sustaining an infinite number of signs cohering in homogeneous wholes. On the other hand, meanings like happiness, freedom, anger will not be constrained – they tend to spread and assimilate with every domain of experience (Salvatore & Freda, 2011). As Tolstoy wrote, happy families are all alike—in the bright light of affects and values everything is white. In sum, affects are both dense (not highly abstract) and generalized.

Table 3.1. A Typology of Changes of Sensemaking

		Generalization	
		+	−
Abstraction	+	schematic abstraction	individuation by schematization
	−	affective generalization	concretization by pleromatization

THE CAUSALITY ISSUE: THE REPRESENTAMEN'S JOB

How is the New Sign Motivated?

In this section the causality issue is addressed, namely, the question of how the following sign is brought about—how it is selected among the alternatives so that the S_1–S_2 transition is made.

My basic thesis is that this process is a function of the SIA.

One can pick up a clue of this aspect by comparing what follows after the same sign in two different scenarios. Take a person arriving late at the office and being asked what time it is by her boss (Scenario A) and the same person asked the same question, yet this time by an unknown person met by chance on the street (Scenario B). One can expect that in Scenario A, the person reacts in terms of justification (or challenge, avoidance, shame and so forth, depending on the circumstances and previous history of the persons involved and their relationship), while the person in Scenario B tells the asker the time.

The example highlights how the following sign (S_2) is selected in accordance with the SIA involved, the latter performing a *causative function* in the activation of the incoming sign—the SIA works as the punctuator in the selection of S_2. Incidentally, it is worth noticing that the two functions of the SIA—the hermeneutic one discussed in the previous sections and the causative function addressed here—do not correspond to different mechanisms—they are two outputs of the same process. Take the set of cases from which the lottery winner number is extracted—the extension of such a set is *both* the parameter defining the probability that a given case is extracted *and* the parameter according to which it defines its value. It is the latter because it is the former.

A way of understanding the causative function of the SIA is to conceive of it as a *fitting function* (cf. Chapter 2). This view introduces an articulation of the definition provided above, where the SIA has been defined in a dichotomic way—as the set of signs that may potentially follow. What I add now is that such potentiality is continuous, ranging from almost 0 to almost 1 (I speak of "almost 0," rather than 0, because any sign has a possibility, albeit very low, of following any other sign; consequently, no transition can reach probability 1). Thus, in general terms, given the current state of the field of experience, the SIA identifies the following sign that has the highest capacity of fitting the field.

The idea of the SIA as a fitting function needs to be further specified. Indeed, the SIA does not lend itself to being interpreted in a traditional way, as a super-ordered semantic frame guiding and regulating the selection of the signs. As already pointed out, this reified view of meanings is untenable in the case of the SIA. Below, I list some of the reasons for this. First, SIAs are fuzzy sets of scenarios of experience. As such, they are unsuitable as hierarchical criterion of ordering and selection. The fuzziness of the SIA makes it hard to think of it as part of a top-down mechanism. Secondly, unlike the basic metaphysical representationist assumption that the world is made of discrete stable units (Manzotti, 2010), experience is a processual gestalt—it is not composed of autonomous discrete objects, but sustained by an infinite amount of interacting co-occurrences enslaved to the field dynamic; consequently, experience does not provide elements that are stable and differentiated enough to enable the hierarchical rule to operate—the rule states: if x then y; but experience does not contain "x's" (for a similar argument, see Bickhard, 2009). Third, a sharply ordered system of categories framing sensemaking would rule out the possibility of understanding a series of phenomena of sensemaking related to its inherent ambiguity—for example, the fact that meaning is not a discrete but a continuous dynamic as well as the fact that meaning is multidimensional (Salvatore, Tonti, & Gennaro, in press). Finally, the idea of specific categories existing prior to the sign is hardly consistent with evidence—for instance that provided by the neuroscientific domain (Damasio, 1999) showing how even the computational processes grounding rational choice and economic reasoning are rooted in gestalt, embodied states of the mind (see also Ziemke, Zlatev, & Frank, 2007). In the final analysis, the view of a stable-enough patterns of experience working as a frame regulating sensemaking in a top-down way, has to be rejected as a reification that slips the traditional vision of meaning "in through the back door" while the pragmatic standpoint tries to go beyond it.

Thus, the way of conceptualizing scenarios and SIAs proposed in this work does not entail a top-down logic. Rather, scenarios have been modeled in terms of sculpture, instead of painting, namely, as the result—not the premise—of the semiotic dynamic (see the two-stage mechanism discussed in the previous section).

As it seems to me, such a view provides a synthesis between the top-down and bottom-up approaches—it avoids the untenable reification of the top-down logic, while recognizing that the bottom-up dynamic develops alongside asymmetrical field potentialities. Such potentialities, however, cannot be regarded as preexisting entities exercising a guiding power on the dynamic; rather, they are instantiated in the same instant in which the development of the dynamic is revealed as their effect. In sum, the synthesis of bottom-up and top-down logic requires a new (old) vision of the entangled relation between cause and effect.

The Semiotic Hyperspace

A geometrical interpretation of the SIA can be a helpful tool for the sake of a better understanding of the mechanism grounding the causality function. Signs can be regarded as points on a space—which I call *semiotic hyperspace* (SH). Thus, the position of the points-signs on the SH in a given instant provides the whole map of the linkages among signs, as they appear at that instant through their use in the world so far. The distance between point x and point y of the SH indicates the probability of the sign y to follow the sign x in the transition $S_1 \rightarrow S_2$—the less the distance, the higher the probability of the transition (for an operative method based on this rationale and applied to textual analysis, see Salvatore, Gennaro, Auletta, Tonti, & Nitti, 2012; see also Chapters 11 and 12).

Each dimension of the SH corresponds to a component of the meaning, namely, a pattern of co-occurrences among signs resulting from a specific way they have been used through time. Examples of dimensions—as one could name them—could be |purposefulness|, |movement|, |pleasantness|, |color|, |shape|, |density|, |mother-ness—each of them associated with a certain organization of the behavior of signs—that is, a certain distribution of probability of connection between them (Salvatore, Tonti, Gennaro, in press). Note that the SH has to be considered hyperdimensional because of the infinite number of components of meaning active in the semiosphere, that is, of the infinite possibilities of combination that signs have with each other.

One can identify many SHs, according to the kind of combination among signs one intends to focus on (e.g., the probability of co-occurrence within a more or less narrow temporal span; the probability of immediate contiguity). Below, for the sake of discussion I take a simplified SH, the one mapping the probability of transition between two signs alongside the temporal line—from time 1 to time 2 (i.e., $S_1 \rightarrow S_2$).

Moreover, one can identify many kinds of SH in terms of the kind of portion of the world taken as the universe of analysis. Thus, one can take a given local circumstance of sensemaking as the universe—for example, a given scholastic community, the exchange between patient and therapist of a specific psychotherapy. Again, one can consider only verbal signs or also other kinds of signs. From a complementary standpoint, one can focus on the universe constituted by a single person's sensemaking (i.e., how he/she experiences a sign or uses the experience of a sign in the concrete domain of his/her life) or consider the entire semiosphere—that is, the global behavior of signs within the world (in a certain temporal space). In the latter case the SH acquires the conceptual meaning of a geometrical model of the cultural system as a whole.

On the other hand, these different focuses are not in contrast with each other. In the final analysis, in fact, if one conceives of the SH as the global map of the semiosphere, one can treat any more specific focus as a *region* of the whole SH—that is, the portion of the SH concerning that specific spatial-temporal unit of sensemaking. Incidentally, according to this approach, the individual memory can be interpreted as a region of the global semiosphere.

At any instant the position of the signs within the SH is given by the history of how the signs have been used so far—if sign b has followed sign a more times than c has, then b will be nearer to a on the SH than c will. This means that any time a sign (say b)—enters as S_2 in a transition triggered by a certain sign (say a), sign b comes closer to sign a—thus changing the position of all other signs too. Anytime an $S_1 \rightarrow S_2$ transition occurs, it produces (micro)movements of nearing and distancing among signs.

However, such movements concern only the dimensions of meaning (i.e., the region defined by such dimensions) involved in the transition, not all the dimensions of the whole hyperdimensional SH. For instance, imagine that the transition from "star" to "fame" occurs in the context of a conversation concerning the fantasy of being involved in the Hollywood system; then, the sign "fame" will come nearer to the sign "star", but only alongside the dimensions of meanings that are active in the context of the conversation in question (say, |envy|, |desire|, |pleasantness|, |movement|, and so forth), not on all dimensions of SH (say, not on dimensions like |color|, |shape| |density| |mother-ness|). Therefore, after the transition the sign "fame" will be nearer to the sign "star", but only in terms of the dimensions: |envy|, |desire|, |pleasantness|, |movement|. If one saw the positions of the two signs from the standpoint of an inactive dimensions—such as |color—the two signs would be found unchanged in their reciprocal positions.

This shows that SH is a dynamic space, changing instant by instant. Moreover, such change concerns two different aspects. On the one hand, as just noted, the position of the signs; on the other hand, the very shape of the space, namely, the dimensions that are pertinent. Indeed, in any circumstance of sensemaking only a subset of components of meaning is active, compared to the infinite possible dimensions available in the cultural system. Therefore, in any instant a certain region of SH shaped by the active components of meaning is pertinentized, and the movements of the signs will be carried out only on that subspace.

Generally speaking, the movements of signs on the SH are quite slow. This is so because a single transition cannot but have a limited impact on the accumulated transitions that have already occurred. For instance, if the transition between a and b has occurred 1,000 times, a new transition will increase the linkage between a and b by a probability of 0,001. Yet the speed and depth of the changes in positions vary in accordance to the subspace of SH involved: if the a–b transition occurs in a region where in the past it has only occurred very few times, the nearing of b to a—in that subspace—will be dramatic. For instance, imagine that in the region a the $a \rightarrow b$ transition has already happened just once. The new occurrences of $a \rightarrow b$ will double the probability, which will reflect in a considerable nearing of b to a, but this only in the subspace a. Incidentally, this provides a way of understanding how innovation in meaning can happen through new linkages among signs in marginal domains of sense that create strong local connections that then spread progressively as long as such marginal domains combine with more central domains.

It is important to underline that the geometric model of SH proposed here is grounded on an antisemantic and antiagentive view. Indeed, it is assumed that the current conditional probability of a given transition is the sufficient condition for the possibility that such a transition will occur in the future. This assumption allows us to avoid the reifying recourse to any *ad hoc* explanatory mechanism being responsible for the transition. According to the argument proposed above (i.e., the transition as resulting from a fitting function), the following sign is neither the object of a more or less purposeful choice of an agent, nor the mere reaction to the inner value of the triggering sign. Rather, it is the output of a transcendental mechanism, based not on the content, but on a dynamic rule—something like:

> //compute the conditional probability of all the transitions in which S_1 is involved in the context of the kinds of circumstance like the one involved here, and choose as S_2 the sign the co-occurrence with which has the highest value//

In the final analysis, this antisemantic and antiagentive view allows the SH to be considered a map of both the history of sensemaking that has already occurred—indeed the positions of signs represent how signs have been combined thus far—and a way of depicting the immediate future trajectory—indeed, the sign that will follow in the next instant is the nearest to S_1 (in the pertinent SH region).

Now, it is worth insisting on the fact that the nearness of two signs depends on the space's dimensionality, namely, on how many and which dimensions define the region of SH on which the points are projected and their distance measured. This can be made clearer through the following example. If the space were of dimension $= 1$, then there would be only one criterion of nearness. But if the dimension were $= 2$, the possible measures of nearness would become 2, and so forth. Therefore, in a hyperdimensional space, the number of relationships of nearness tends to the infinite. This means that given a sign, there are infinite transitions as the most probable, one for each dimension or combination of dimensions of the hyperspace. On the other hand, just one sign is selected to carry on the semiotic trajectory. This means that any time a transition between two signs is established, this happens because a specific region of the SH has been activated—has been pertinentized—so to make it possible to fix a local position of the points-signs and therefore to allow the transition to be made (a similar idea, recalling the quantistic notion of superposition, is provided by Neuman & Tamir, 2009). Figure 3.2 shows the process of pertinentization of the SH's region in terms of reduction of dimensionality.

The view of the establishment of sign-connections as the precipitate of the reduction of dimensionality allows us to state that sensemaking is not at all a repetitive phenomenon. On the contrary, the mechanism hypothesized is a way of addressing the extreme variability and fuzziness of sensemaking, at the same time modeling it in terms of an invariant general dynamic. Indeed, the probability of transition is contingent to the region of the SH being pertinent at that instant (in turn resulting from the previous trajectory of signs). This is the same as saying that the geometric model proposed here is consistent with and helps to understand the fact that transitions are contingent to the local circumstances of sensemaking—sign a will probably be followed by b in circumstance W, but by c in circumstance Z.

In the final analysis, the geometrical model allows for a connection between the search for an invariant rule and the striving to grasp the uniqueness of the phenomena (Salvatore & Valsiner, 2009, 2010; Valsiner, Salvatore, Gennaro, & Travers, 2010)—it views the dynamic as a fixed, transcendental property of the mind, while the concrete processes of sensemaking resulting from this dynamic as variable, fuzzy, contingent to the context (on the dynamic-process distinction (cf. Introduction; see also Salvatore, 2011).

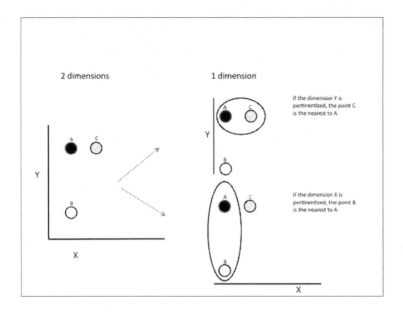

Figure 3.2. The closeness among signs as resulting from the reduction of dimensionality of SH.

The geometrical model proposed above has more than one point of contact with Matte Blanco's geometrical conceptualization of the unconscious as a hyperdimensional space (Matte Blanco, 1975; see Chapter 7). Moreover, it is consistent with the logic of the French school of *analyze des données* (Benzecri, 1980). Several authors have more or less explicitly considered this computational logic to be isomorphic to the way the mind works (Andersen, 2001; Carli & Paniccia, 2002; Landauer & Dumais, 1997). Andersen (2001) has proposed an antiextensional model of how people understand word meaning, based on the idea that the mind interprets the significance of words through an iterative process of mapping of co-occurrences—a process that resembles factorial analysis. Carli and colleagues (Carli & Paniccia, 1999, 2003; Carli & Giovagnoli, 2011) have developed a method for interpreting the affective meaning of text based on the multidimensional analysis of co-occurrence of signs.

Semiotic Hyperspace and Sensemaking

As conceived above, the SH provides the ground for interpreting in geometrical terms the bivalence of meaning and its role in sensemaking. The main points involved are summarized below.

The absolute potential SIA of S_1 is the set of all distances linking S_1 to all other points-signs. And this is equivalent to saying that the absolute potential SIA of a sign is the position of that sign on the SH, in relation to the concurrent positions of other signs.

The scenario can be conceived of as a subset of dimensions of SH. As a result of the projection of signs on the region defined by such subset, the position of the points acquires a specific local geography. And this is the geometrical equivalent of the definition of scenario as fitting function, reflecting a specific cluster of co-occurring signs characterized by a particular matrix of probability of transitions between them.

Since the SIA corresponds to a set of scenarios that are active and placed in the foreground, it can be conceived of as the subspace generated by the reduction of the dimensionality of SH. The SIA always has fewer dimensions than SH (for any n, it is always given that $n > N$, where n means the dimensionality of SIA and N the dimensionality of SH). This is so because it is not possible that a scenario holds all the infinite possible connections of a sign. In Vygotsky's terms sense is always a potentiality broader than its actualization in terms of meaning—sense is the "totality of the psychological events aroused in our consciousness by the word" (Vygotsky, 1934/1986; p. 305, as translated by Valsiner, 2001, p. 89).

Every sign has a local position on the region of SH defined by the SIA, namely, every sign entertains probabilistic linkages with the other signs that are specific for every SIA. In accordance to the distribution of such probabilistic linkages, a given sign becomes the most probable candidate for the position of following sign, namely, for the position of SIP. And this means that the SIA is the *fitting metafunction* consisting of the convergence of the fitting functions, each of them corresponding to one of the scenarios composing the SIA in question.

Thus, one can conclude that the reduction of dimensionality $N \rightarrow n$ is the way the $S_1 \rightarrow S_2$ transition is brought about.

Note that n varies in magnitude. The lower the n – that is, the stronger the $N \rightarrow n$ reduction – the more the constraints on the SIA, namely, the specificity of the criterion of nearness (as defined above); in contrast, the higher the n, the more undifferentiated the relations are between the signs as mapped on the SIA, namely, the more the signs that hold the same level of nearness with the previous sign (S_1), therefore that are equivalent to each other as possible candidates to assume the position S_2 in the transition.

According to this last point, one can map the dynamic of sensemaking in terms of the ongoing dimensionality of the SIA (Salvatore, Tebaldi, & Potì, 2006/2009). A low dimensional SIA lends itself to being considered the marker of a process of sensemaking working in a highly differentiated and articulated fashion, namely, characterized by a use of signs subjected to many articulations and constraints. On the contrary, a high dimensional

SIA would mark a process of sensemaking characterized by less constraints and differentiation in the transition between signs. The former kinds of process are expected to be found more typical of conventionalized circumstances of activity, while the latter can be associated with a greater role played by affective meanings, usage of metaphoric communication, and reference to generalized values.

The conceptualization of sensemaking in terms of dimensionality sheds a new light on some important characteristics of affective sensemaking. Here I will just briefly mention one of them—the fact that the affective contexts are contagious, namely, they are easily shareable—people do not need to negotiate to share feelings and emotional states (what Carli calls *collusion*, see Carli & Giovagnoli, 2011). This characteristic can be understood in terms of the geometrical model in the following way. The fewer dimensions the SIA has, the more specific it is and therefore the higher the number of elements required to trigger it. On the contrary, the more dimensions the SIA has (as in the case of affective scenarios), the more homogeneous and generalized it is, therefore the smaller the number of elements required to trigger it. Thus, the higher the degree of homogeneity and generalization of the scenarios associated with segments of social praxis, the higher the probability that people share them as SIA.

Two last remarks before concluding.

First, the above model does not underrate time and the temporal perspective. At a first glance, indeed, the transition would seem to be just the dyadic S_1–S_2 linkage, as if what had happened before S_1 were irrelevant. Yet that is not so. The current state of the semiotic flow is responsible for the new transition, but in turn, the current state is the cumulative product of the infinite sequence of past states (always having occurred as current states) as well. Thus, according to the dynamic point of view adopted here, the past is not an entity acting on the transition between the present and the future—the present has no memory. Rather, it is the shape of the potentiality of the transition, as modeled by what happened beforehand. This can be said from the viewpoint of the geometrical model too. According to such a standpoint, the impact of the past can be depicted in two complementary ways. As concerns the brief-to-middle temporal scale, one has to consider that the positions of S_1 and S_2 are defined not in absolute terms, but always in terms of the region of the space that is active in the given instant. And the shape of that region—that is, the dimensions defining it—depends on the trajectory of the previous chain of transitions. Therefore, the past is active in the present in terms of the form of the conditions leading S_2 to acquire the nearest position to S_1. In sum, *the past is the shape of the current SIA*. As concerns the long-term scale, as pointed out above, the positions of signs change, and with them the global form of the SH. In the final analysis, the geometrical model allows us to integrate in a single view the two main units of analysis of the dynamic of sensemaking —microanalysis focused on the local communicational exchanges and activities, characterized by the ongoing reshaping of their situated contexts, and macroanalysis focused on the ecological systems of meaning working in a normative fashion on how individuals think and feel (Ratner, 2008).

Second, while the mechanism of reduction of dimensionality is universal and common among people, which dimensions are made pertinent is the result of the dynamic interaction between the structure of the social order and the idiosyncratic biography of the individual experience—namely, how any person has mapped the configurations of combinations of signs they have met through their own life. Thus, a cultural system can be seen as the system of boundaries defining the distance between the similarities and differences of people's fields of experience.

CONCLUSION

In this chapter I have started to outline a model of the microdynamic of sensemaking, aimed at deepening the understanding of the semiopoietic capacity of sensemaking, namely, of the capacity of sensemaking of producing meaning as the emerging output from its dynamic. To this end, I have focused on two fundamental issues entailed in the backward-forward process of sign transition, that is the transition between the representamen and its interpretant, with the latter being motivated and at the same time interpreting backwards from the former.

First, I have focused on the *hermeneutic issue*, namely, how does it happens that a given interpretant comes to assume its *semiotic value*, and in so doing to move the semiotic flow further ahead. I proposed to model this issue in terms of a two-stage bootstrapping mechanism—the interpretant triggers the activation of all possible connections between signs (propagation stage); this process is antagonized by the opposite movement of fading off of the nonpertinent connections (reduction stage), working according to an optimization-seeking criterion of good form. As a result of this dynamic, the optimized set of scenarios (the SIA) comes into being.

Second, I have addressed the *issue of causality*—namely, how the representamen triggers its interpretant, selecting it from the infinite set of possibilities comprising the paradigmatic axis. I conceptualized this issue using a geometrical model—the semiotic hyperspace (SH). Each point of the SH represents a sign; the nearer two points-signs on the SH, the more the probability of transition between them. The SH has infinite dimensions, corresponding to the number of components of meaning active in the semiosphere. Therefore, the reciprocal position between two signs, and thus the probability of the transition from the one to the other, requires a reduction of dimensionality of the SH, thus the pertinentization of a subset of dimensions constituting a region of the SH (i.e., a SIA). The new sign is the nearest one in the region made pertinent.

The next chapter is devoted to the third issue—the issue of constitution, namely, how patterns of experience emerge from the flow of sensorial occurrences, as the precondition for their taking on a semiotic function (i.e., the function of being signs).

CHAPTER 4

THE SEMIOTIC BIG BANG

THE CONSTITUTION ISSUE

This chapter addresses the third issue, that of the constitution of the sign —how a given set of unrelated sensorial occurrences acquires the status of sign. In what follows I propose the thesis that signs emerge from the same field of experience that they shape in terms of meanings. It would be beyond my scope and my competence to present a complete model of the dynamic of the constitution of signs. My intention is more limited—the considerations offered below are designed to highlight how relevant this aspect is for the development of the semiotic standpoint in psychological theory. In the final analysis, the issue at stake is the elaboration of a comprehensive model of sensemaking that does not see signs as a taken-for-granted reality. Rather, the challenge is to be able to model sensemaking so that also its input (i.e., signs) can be understood in the light of its dynamic.

This purpose may seem megalomaniac if interpreted according to the current status of psychological science, fragmented in subdisciplines legitimized by their anchoring to "scientific objects" that actually are the reified consequence of the division of the intellectual labor that they should justify (Salvatore, 2011). Nevertheless, the perspective of a comprehensive theory of sensemaking is consistent with a more general vision of psychology as a single science—a vision that has strong roots in the history of the discipline—just to mention one instance, the gestalt theoreticians adopted the same basic logic and concepts to deal with perception and thinking.

Psychology in Black and White: The Project of a Theory-Driven Science, pp. 65–83
Copyright © 2016 by Information Age Publishing

The "Effected" Body

The way with which I propose to approach the process of the constitution of signs is based on the dynamic and embodied interpretation of the basic concepts of the gestalt theory, inspired by the innovative work of authors like Bickhard (2009) and Manzotti (2006, 2009, 2010, 2011).

Instead of considering subjects as immersed in the environment—which would entail the idea of the environment as something existing before and independently of subjects—I adopt a radical interactionist standpoint (Christopher & Bickhard, 2007). According to this standpoint, the subject (or rather, the subject's body) acts on and is acted on by external processes, namely chains of spatial-temporal contingencies of energy-matter, brought about by causative sources lying outside the body.[1] (Henceforth, I will adopt the term "world" to indicate the whole set of external processes).

Spatial-temporal contingencies have no inherent order. It must simply be assumed that they are somehow endowed with a dynamic, namely that what happens in the world varies through time and space and that such variations are subject to constraints—not everything can happen (e.g., according to quantum physics, particles cannot occupy every position). The fact that external processes have no inner order (if by "order" we mean a specific form) means that they are not to be considered as phenomena; rather, they can be seen as potentialities of phenomena. And they come into existence as phenomena in terms of the pertinentization of one of the infinite structures of order (i.e., spatial-temporal patterns of relationships) that could be extracted from them as potentiality. In sum, processes provide the *constraining conditions* required for phenomena to be able to come into being.

If we take in a radically consistent way the assumption that processes are not phenomena, then we have to conclude that the presentification of the world is a mechanism that does not lend itself to being seen in terms of the combination and selection of pieces of experience. Indeed, the pieces of experience are already an output of a deeper microgenetic stage. In the beginning, there is *Firstness*—the unrelated totality of the field of experience. Thus, we have to take a step ahead and consider occurrences not as something already lying in the world and as such picked up, combined, selected and coded by the interpreter. Rather, occurrences, as well as the relationships between them, are the effect of processes on the body (Manzotti, 2006, 2011; Maturana & Varela, 1980; Ziemke, Zlatev, & Frank, 2007). In this sense, the view proposed here is radically interactionist and microgenetic—the phenomena do not exist in the body or in the world as separate entities (and given that no phenomena would exist if body and world were considered separate, separation itself being meaningless); they exist because they are the output of such interaction, namely as the effect of the world on the body. In sum, the *body is the effect thanks to which its cause comes into existence, in the form of this effect* (for a systematic discussion of this processual ontology, see Manzotti, 2009).

The effect of the world is constrained by the characteristics of the causative processes, but the phenomenical form it takes depends on the configuration of the body—namely, on how the body is organized to be "effected" by the world. Indeed, the body lends itself to be effected by a limited and peculiar set of components of the external processes. Thus, the process of being effected is the process of the construction of a specific portion of the world as the significant one for the interpreter (its own *Umwelt*; von Uexküll, 1920/1926). For instance, the human body is not made to be effected by sounds having a wavelength higher than a certain threshold. Thus, strictly speaking, ultrasounds do not exist as phenomena for the human being, while they are part of the world of a dog.

Incidentally, it must be noticed that the very distinction between cause and effect has to be considered in a different light. As matter of fact, the body itself is part of the world and therefore the effect of the rest of the world on it has to be interpreted *sensustricto* as part of the whole causative chain making up the process. Only the conceptual distinction between body and world makes the punctuation of this whole chain of cause and effect meaningful.

Although limited compared to the potentiality of the world, the effects on the body are extremely vast and multiform. Every point of the body's boundary is configured to enter one or more causative chains with the world. Thus, the basic form of experience is a collection of a huge number of ever-changing, local, sensorial-motor modifications (e.g., tactile, acoustic, visual, kinaesthetic patterns of activation), which come to be in parallel, as an unrelated totality. Phenomena—the consciousness of the experience—emerge once relations are imposed on this condition of *Firstness*. Incidentally, I speak of imposition because the sensorial-motor modifications have no inherent, necessary linkage among themselves—their being aggregated in the unrelated totality is just a matter of their convergent spatial-temporal contingency (i.e., when I type on the computer keyboard, an aggregate of tactile, acoustic, visual and kinaesthetic modifications come into being as an undifferentiated whole, which is a whole because I act according to a social, historical contingent format of activity).

Mechanisms of Organization of the Field of Experience

In general terms, the imposition of relations can be conceived of as the organization of the field of experience in terms of gestalt principles of order. What follows is a possible way of modeling the microgenetic mechanisms enacting those principles.

First, I adopt the general idea that the mind scans the body states (Damasio, 1999). Such an action of scanning is done following a huge number of different maps. Every map could be defined by two basic parameters: (a) *a set of markers*, to make the map sensitive just to one class of states; (b) a *system of thresholds* associated with each marker, to make the map sensitive to a certain range of intensity of changes. In sum, the body states are detected by means of a set of independent markers.

Second, I propose to compute these markers so as to cluster them efficiently—where the criterion of efficiency could be viewed as the balance of two parameters: the *stability* of the partition and the *minimization* of the differentiation. The former parameter concerns the maintenance through time of the pattern of organization imposed on the input. This criterion means that the clusters are shaped so as to keep the within-cluster variability (i.e., the variations of the relations among markers belonging to the same partition through two contiguous states) below a certain threshold. On the other hand, the search for stability could be performed in terms of an infinite mechanism of iterative differentiation, performed on the field of experience. This is so because, given a certain way of segmenting the field of experience, the computational system could always seek stability by increasing the gradient of its differentiation. Therefore, given the bounded nature of computation (Gigerenzer & Todd, 1999; Simon, 1957) one is led to assume that a further parameter, constraining the differentiation of the field of experience, is involved. This is what I mean by the second parameter: the minimization of differentiation. According to this parameter, a further gradient of differentiation is introduced only if and when the required level of stability cannot be satisfied by the previous way of segmenting the field.

The clusters of markers are the *Secondness* that emerges as the output of the microgenetic mechanism. They start to work as phenomenical objects. In sum, *phenomenical objects are the solution for optimizing the tension between stability and differentiation of the field of experience.* Thus, for example, I see the markers corresponding to a photo as a single cluster (i.e., the image of the photo) because this solution is the most efficient, given that it groups the markers in a way that maximizes information and keeps itself substantially stable through time. It would not be efficient to see the photo as a collection of independent objects (e.g., as the frame, the paper, the colors; or the man on the right, the tower on the ground, and so forth). In sum, to use an image, imposing a criterion of organizational efficiency to the unrelated totality of the basic experience is akin to constructing a mosaic—the constructor has very many tiles available and has to cluster them in meaningful patterns.

Incidentally, what has been said above means that already at this basic level sensemaking is dynamic—time is an inherent part of the construction of experience; this is so because it is not the map of the markers in itself that is addressed, but the difference between two temporally contiguous states. It is as if the mind calculated the derivative of bodily states. Incidentally, this is consistent with Stern's (2004) observation that states of consciousness are always associated with or triggered by a some kind of violation, variation or rupture. To come back to the image of the mosaic, in the case of the sensemaker the tiles are not material pieces, but derivatives of bodily states—the information lies in the difference (Bateson, 1972).

The Plurality of Units of Experience and Their Organization

Two further aspects have to be added to make the picture more precise. First, if we think about it carefully, we easily recognize that our own experience is not portioned at a single level, according to just one spatial-temporal unit/scale. Our state of consciousness collects "pieces" of experience that have a different spatial-temporal extension (Manzotti, 2006, 2011; Tronick, 2010). Such states cohabit, even when they exist in the same region of experience of the world. An indication of this cohabitation is provided by the very fact that the sensorial registers have a different temporal extension—therefore, already at this very basic level the duration of the body states is not a single parameter. However, according to the view proposed here, it is plausible to think that the utmost variability in the space-time extension of the units of experience depends on the fact that the *mind adopts many different temporal lags at the same time for the sake of comparing the body states*. And given that the amount of body movement is a function of time, any temporal lag corresponds to a spatial-temporal extension. Thus, for example, my experience is the experience of just an instant—for example, the instant marked by the appearance of the letter on the screen associated with the tactile sensation of my finger on the keyboard and the sound produced by the pressed key—and *at the same time* a more extended space-time—for example, the experience of writing in my office with the sun out the window. And it is worth underlining that these experiences unfold in parallel, even if the focus of my attention is just on one of them—in other words, the more extended experience is not a secondary product of the summation of the narrower ones. In the final analysis, we experience a plurality of realities in parallel, each of them produced by a spatial-temporal scale. This conclusion is consistent with the inherent nonlinearity of psychological time (Rudolph, 2006a, 2006b). Thus, for example, in relation to the previous example, a picture can be a discrete phenomenical object—namely, a stable pattern of experience (i.e. a cluster of markers)—and at the same time a nonautonomous element of a broader gestalt—for example, a banknote.

Second, there are many ways in which a gestalt can be imposed on the field of experience. This is a consequence of the previous point. Insofar as there is a cohabiting plurality of realities, there must be many ways of composing them in stable phenomenical objects. Indeed, one has to consider that the interaction between interpreters and the world is bidirectional. Persons move and act and their perceiving—more in general their sensemaking—is embedded in their moving (Gibson, 1979). Therefore, as the spatial-temporal scale decreases, the articulation of the field of experience tends to increase, and vice versa—namely, the derivative between two contiguous states increases. In other words, the narrower the unit, the more analytic the experience is. This is akin to what happens with a video: the faster the coding, the smaller the temporal unit of a single map of the field, the greater the amount of details and density of the information. Thus, a very narrow spatial-temporal frame is like examining something through a microscope: one sees very detailed aspects, which change to a large extent as a result of even a very slight perturbation.

All this leads us to conclude that as the spatial-temporal scale changes, the search for a stable pattern of experience varies in its complexity and in the way it is performed. Indeed, the narrower the units of experience, the more the markers are brought together, and therefore the more the competing ways of performing the clustering. To use an image, if a cook and an art designer look at a table, the former sees forks and spoons, the latter forms endowed with aesthetic value.

The Contingent Ground of the Organization of Experience

The variability of the way the field of experience can be organized into a stable object of experience leads us to go beyond a transcendental vision of this process. If the search for stability were performed only in terms of invariant gestalt tenets of organization (i.e., in terms of *a priori* universal categories), it would be hard to understand the plurality of objects of experience we are able to shape in the contingency of sensemaking.

A way usually adopted to make the transcendental view consistent with the variability of the phenomenal experience is to consider *a priori* categories as being entailed in the basic process of construction of experience, and the variability as resulting from higher psychological functions. Yet such a solution has a cost that is not worth paying—the separation between the basic psychological process and sensemaking (see below; in his discussion of the aesthetic belief, Croom (2012) argues cogently against such separation).

On the other hand, there is evidence that leads us to think that we do not organize experience, even at the basic level, in invariant, encapsulated ways (for a diametrically opposed position, see Fodor, 1983), but in accordance to contingent criteria of ordering. For instance, it is well-known that the capacity to discriminate between objects increases with specific training—a sommelier is able to recognize the bouquet of wines in a far more subtle way than the naïve drinker. One could argue that such capacities are however universal and fixed and that the training just makes them more available, increasing the capacity to access them. But in the final analysis this means that a cultural, contingent circumstance, the training, defines the hierarchical organization of the criteria based on which persons shape experience into phenomenical objects. Thus, the point is not the presence of transcendental principles of organization—in some circumstances (e.g., the Ames room) they prove to play a role in perception. Rather, the point is that the transcendental principles of organization are not autonomous, but are enslaved to the dynamic of sensemaking that is regulated by culturally acquired, contingent ways of imposing form on experience.

My thesis is that such culturally acquired, contingent ways of ordering experience are simply the way scenarios of experience work at the microgenetic level. Conceiving the principles of order in terms of scenarios allows the latter concept to be defined better, and levels of sensemaking to be linked in terms of a single, basic general dynamic of functioning. According to this perspective, a scenario is a redundant pattern of experience, lived many times in the course of time and for this reason working—and experienced—as a steady point in the shaping of the totality of the field of experience. Scenarios work in this way because they are associated with quite redundant culturally shaped patterns of activity (cf. Chapter 2). Thus, any scenario represents a solution to the task of ordering experience—a solution that fits because and insofar as it has been applied to similar, redundant circumstances. For instance, take an infant at the mother's breast. Own field of experience is constituted of a plurality of markers, relative to the different stimulations composing the instant by instant body states, which are in turn caused by/associated with what happens in the world—for example, the movement of the mother, her smell, the level and temporal profile (Stern, 2004) of the lights and sounds and so on (for a discussion on the ontogenetic process through which phenomenical objects emerge, see Salvatore & Zittoun, 2011a). Now, the circumstance of breast-feeding is socially regulated—for instance, mothers tend to feed their infants in calm conditions, avoiding abrupt noises, strong fragrances, and so forth. Thus, the infant encounters a redundant field of experience, largely composed of quite similar relations among markers.

Consequently, the organization of such fields of experience—insofar as it is able to bring the redundant markers into the foreground and leave the more contingent ones in the background (i.e., those that change through the circumstances)—will tend to be generalized as a fitting solution for all those similar circumstances.

In sum, the previous discussion leads us to two complementary conclusions. On the one hand, it gives us a better understanding of the ontogenesis of the scenarios: they are solutions to the organization of the experience that have proved to work—that is, to shape experience efficiently—in a class of redundant circumstances, because of the fact that they reflect the social organization of activities. On the other hand, it provides a suitable hypothesis of which role they play in the construction of the phenomenical objects—they are attractors that are active in the clustering of the markers, in so doing orienting the shaping of the phenomenal objects (on the interpretation of the perceptual solution in terms of attractor, see Rumelhart & McClelland, 1986).

The Abductive Valence of Experience

Let us see in more detail how scenarios can be said to work as attractors.

First, it is worth noting that the mechanism is oriented to the detection of difference. This is entailed in the thesis that the mind calculates the derivative between body states sustaining contiguous spatial-temporal units. On the other hand, this is consistent with daily experience—we do not perceive invariant stimuli (for instance the basic smell of our skin); we perceive variations.

Second, as we have said, the organization of experience can be conceived of as the most efficient solution, namely the clustering of the markers that presents the higher level of stability of the two contiguous units. Thus, in general terms one could say that the mechanism at stake is a dialectical tension between searching for difference and assimilating them in terms of restoring constancy. Now, the central point is how such constancy is reached. Indeed, because of the fact that human beings and more in general living beings have moving bodies, most markers change through time, even in the case of very contiguous spatial-temporal units. Now, on the one hand the mind tries to encompass as many markers as possible in a whole gestalt (according to the criterion of efficiency); on the other hand, however it has to "give up" some—the ones that it would not be efficient to include in the gestalt—and put them into the background, as noise.

Incidentally, notice that these movements (i.e., selection and combination) are not two different processes; rather they are sides of the same mechanism of competition among parallel solutions—namely, the solution that provides the best point of equilibrium between the two criteria wins. And this solution is the pertinentization of some markers against the others that are backgrounded—and at the same the way of combining them. Let us return to the example of the mosaic. As presented here, the way of constructing the phenomenal object resembles a constructor of mosaics that has not an already defined motif to create and intends to use the highest number of tiles. Thus, she will explore several solutions each of them entailing a certain selection of tiles and a certain combination of them—selection and combination are a function of each other.

This leads to a final, important remark. The process of selection-combination of markers is not limited to the current field of experience, namely to organize the marker active in the current instant. Rather, it goes beyond the current field, adding further elements in order to close the gestalt so as to optimize efficacy and stability. This process of constructive closure is performed through the projection of the current markers onto the fittest scenario, namely, the scenario that assures the best solution for the closure of the figure. In such a perspective, the current collection of markers, the ones in terms of which the experience is mapped in a given moment, is subjected to the competitive attraction of many scenarios, each of them providing a certain organization of the field of experience. The scenario that allows the organization of the field endowed with the highest level of efficacy and stability is the one onto which the current collection of markers is projected. Needless to say, such a process of competition among alternative scenarios does not entail computing all the possible virtual alternatives—indeed, the state of sensemaking in the current instant somehow constrains scenarios potentially involved.

It is worth noting that as above conceived, the relation between the markers and the scenario is different than how it is traditionally seen in the notion of frame. A central aspect of the scenario makes it something different from a frame: the scenario does not normatively regulate the organization of the field from the outside; rather it is part of the construction of the object, providing the element required for closing the figure. And it is in this sense that the semiotic construction of the object, already in the passage from *Firstness* to *Secondness* is inherently abductive—it is not a matter of representation, but of *presentification*: the "unification of the predicate" that is possible insofar as one introduces "something more" enabling the closure of the form. According to this perspective, one can conclude that the object is the ongoing presentification of the scenario, triggered by the catalytic function of the current markers of the experience (for a discussion of the notion of catalysis in the realm of psychology, see Cabell, 2010, 2011). In sum, the phenomenal construction of the object is akin to watching a film—some photograms correspond to the collection of markers in a given instant; the flow of photograms represents the differences detected instant by instant; yet what the watcher sees is not the flow of photograms, but the gestalt closure of the form triggered by this flow and in the final analysis obtained through the something more added by the watchers themselves, as the best solution for providing order and continuity to the flow of images.

The idea of the presentification of experience as carried out through what is experienced in the current instant, but not consisting of it, might sound counterintuitive. Yet it is consistent with several daily perceptual phenomena. Kanizsa's triangle (cf. Figure 2.4, Chapter 2) is a clear example of this class of phenomena—the triangle is added as the best solution for closing the figure in accordance to the basic constraint defined by the figure's need to have a ground. Stroboscopic movement provides another example of the process. This phenomenon also helps to highlight the criterion of efficiency entailed in the way the gestalt is closed. The spectator sees the (apparent) movement of the light, instead of the sequence of single episodes of switching on/off because, given a certain length of the line of light bulbs and a certain length of the interval of the switching on/ off, the apparent movement provides the fittest solution, the one unifying the highest number of predicates: a single object (the movement of the light) versus a sequence of many dichotomic events (the switching on/off of light bulbs). Finally, it is interesting to refer to the study of Schenellenberg (1996; cit. in Stern, 2004) which shows that people, not only professional musicians, are able to anticipate correctly the conclusion of the musical phrases being listened to. And this happened also when they were unfamiliar with the type of music (e.g., Westerners listening to Chinese music). This result is interesting for the sake of the current discussion because it bears witness to four important issues: (a) people presentify a continuity through the segments of experience—they link the segments in a whole; (b) the difference can be detected only because there is the whole through time—if there were no continuity, the remaining part of the musical phrase would be a new independent phrase; (c) people are inherently led to close the gestalt by adding something more to the current field of experience—indeed, the piece of the phrase they foresee is not in the inherent field of experience in the moment in which they add it; (d) they do this in an efficient way, namely in a way that corresponds to a valid closure of the perceptual gestalt.

On the other hand, the hypothesis that the presentification of the object is brought about in terms of an abductive process of addition is prompted by a functional consideration. Indeed, it is hard to think that the presentification process would be possible if it were based only on a bottom-up mechanism, namely if the organization of experience were limited to the manipulation of the markers currently being experienced. This is so because the processes of the world corresponding to the object are an infinite potentiality of producing experiential phenomenical forms. Consequently, no already experienced versions of such processes can exhaust the ways the object can be presentified. Rather, any set of markers in any local circumstance of experience provides the "stuff" for what is, however, an only partial detection of the object. And this means that, even in the immediate following spatial-temporal unit, the proportion of markers liable to change are the majority, compared to the ones remaining constant. And this is just a different way of saying that it would not be possible to construct stable objects of experience. To clarify this point, consider a very large set of elements (say $N = 1.000.000$), each of them representing a possible marker of the object, namely a marker that at least once has been involved in the construction of the object. According to what is said above, in a certain transition between two contiguous spatial-temporal units, the markers detected are a limited subset of the set of potential markers (say $n_1 = 100$). Because of the inherent dynamicity of body states, in the following unit most of such 100 markers will be changed with more or less the same number of markers. Consequently no stability would be kept. To give a concrete example, take a person intending to follow the movement of an object in her visual field—say a car while she is crossing the road. As discussed above, the object is actually a process of the world that comes to be an object insofar as and in terms of the effects such processes produce on the body states. And these effects are mapped through a set of pertinent markers, whose differential trajectory is monitored in terms of a certain spatial-temporal unit. Now, the experience of the car is just a very limited subset of markers compared to the infinite ones that could potentially "saturate" such an experience (in function of the distances from it, or the position, the intention toward it, and so on). Moreover, due to both her movements and the car's, most of the few current markers change instant by instant. Therefore, it would be hard to guarantee stability to this pattern of markers so as to ground the presentification of the object on them. Rather, individuals would experience discrete single, instantaneous patterns of experience, as objects having a very rapid time of decay.

The picture changes considerably if one assumes that the person completes the set of current markers by adding further markers to it provided by the optimizing scenario. Accordingly, also in this case the current marker would change, but they would be just a limited proportion of the whole set of markers used for closing the figure. And given that the markers added through the assimilation of the scenario are shared with the contiguous temporal unit, they feed the stability of the closure, therefore grounding the presentification of the object.

A final remark concerns the scenario. The idea of the cohabitation of a plurality of spatial-temporal units of experience allows us to provide a material ground to this notion. I have proposed to conceive of the scenario as a redundant pattern of experience, having a specific spatial-temporal unit. The broader the unit, the more generalized and abstract the scenario. Thus, affective scenarios are conceivable as scenarios based on very broad spatial-temporal units (and this would be consistent with feelings as an experience being outside time), while the presentification of a concrete object can be seen as entailing scenarios based on a very narrow spatial-temporal unit, as such analytically focused on basic microcomponents of the experience—for example, the distribution of the light; the orientation of the figure, and so forth; the embodied metaphors illustrated by Lakoff and Johnson (1980) could represent a way of describing microcomponents of this kind.

It is worth observing that the definition of the scenario in terms of the mechanisms supposedly involved in the basic process of presentification of the object of experience allows us to connect the level of sensemaking (*Firstness, Secondness, Thirdness*) in a single theory. According to this perspective, the notion of scenario concerns a unique quality of the dynamic of sensemaking—that is, the multidimensionality of sensemaking as its inherent dynamic principle of order—that acquires different meanings and definitions (e.g., fitting function, attractor, collection of markers…), due to the descriptive level used in expressing the understanding of the process of sensemaking. I recognize that this increases the complexity of the discussion. Yet, this is a cost that I think it is worth paying in order to avoid a multiplication of the concepts and the consequent ontological reification of the epistemological levels of the scientific description.

THE MICRODYNAMIC OF SENSEMAKING

For the sake of simplicity, the three issues discussed in this and the previous chapter have been addressed separately; yet they are interwoven components of a unique, unitary dynamic. In what follows I provide a global look at it, so as to integrate the various elements discussed above into the whole they comprise. The model focuses on a narrow temporal window, corresponding to the semiotic flow of few transitions between signs. In general terms, it conceives of the microdynamic of sensemaking as having an oscillatory trend. It is a trajectory of signs moving through time; at the same time, any step ahead, namely any new sign, leads to a backward movement of interpretative rewriting of the previous transitions between signs (cf. Figure 4.1a, b, c).

The Emergence of Firstness

Consider the instant of time (t_0). Say that at t_0 an action (more in general, a certain form of environmental event: E_0) triggers, at the following

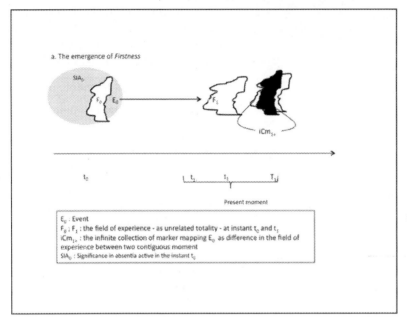

Figure 4.1a. The microdynamics of sensemaking.

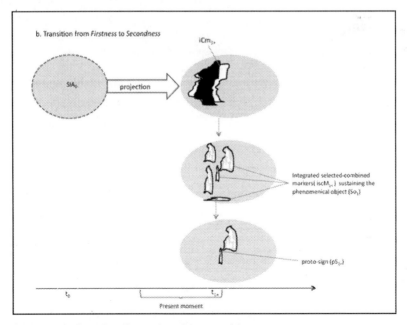

Figure 4.1b. The microdynamics of sensemaking.

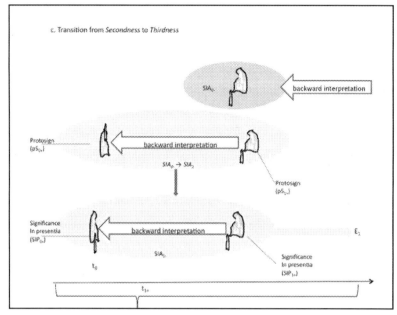

Figure 4.1c.   The microdynamics of sensemaking.

instant t_1, an array of physical processes whose first output is an unrelated totality of the effects (F_1) on the sensemaker's body (for simplicity just one sensemaker is considered). For instance, take the person A that is exposed to person B. A moves her hand and says to B: "hello, my dear." Such an event (E_0) produces a very high number of effects on B's body, namely a lot of microtransformations of its previous states—for example, changes of the surface of the retina, of the acoustic receptors, of the physiological state, and so forth.

It is worth noting that such micromodifications are not caused just by A's action. Indeed, at this very basic level of organization of the experience, A's action is not yet distinguished from the whole field of experience that goes with it. Therefore, for instance, the set of effects (F_1) on B are triggered by A's act as well as by an infinite number of other occurrences that are contingent components of the same field—for example, the level of temperature, the quality of the light, the colors of the walls in the background, the shape of objects that are present in the visual field and so forth. All these components that comprise the E_0 trigger physical processes that produce a series of independent effects on B's body. The set of such effects is what is called F_1 here.

At time t_{1+} the difference of F_1 compared to the previous state F_0 is mapped in terms of an *infinite collection of markers* (iCm_{1+}). This is the first shift in the dynamic—*Firstness has come into being* (Figure 4.1a). Note that the notations "$_{1+}$" and "$_{1-}$" used here and below, mean that the collection at stake has been activated immediately before or after t_1, however in the temporal surrounds subjectively belonging to t_1 (for a discussion of the present time as having duration, therefore making it possible to consider present as having a past as well as a future side, see Stern, 2004).

According to this view, in the final analysis the basic form of perception consists of the map of the body's microtransformations caused by the on-going flow of energy-matter which makes up the environment. As one can see, such a view is indebted to the phenomenological idea of the embodiment of mind (Maturana & Varela, 1980; Ziemke, Zlatev, & Frank, 2007). On the other hand, it has to be highlighted that perception is not the mere registration of such embodiment; rather, from the very beginning it is a *form of interpretation through selection*: the body recognizes only the micro-transformations it is equipped to map, namely, the microtransformations it has the markers to detect. For instance, person B of our previous example will be able to map the effect on her produced by A's tone, as well as the change in the light caused by A's movements, while she has no markers for mapping the minimal change of temperature produced by the presence of A's body. Therefore, such a component of F_1 simply does not enter the field of experience. In sum, according to such a view, the body is the *measure* and the *content* of the basic form of perception that makes up *Firstness*. The paradox of the body lies in this: it causes experience through being "effected" by the world, and in so doing shapes it.

From Firstness to Secondness

Now, assume that a SIA is already active at t_1, as the precipitate of the previous dynamic of the semiotic flow (for this reason, defined as SIA_{0-} in Figure 4.1a). I adopt the notation "$_{0-}$" to indicate that this SIA is the precipitate of the backward interaction between E_0 and what has happened just before it. The projection of iCm_{1+} on SIA_{0-} brings about the gestalt organization of the field of experience (Figure 4.1b), namely, the selection/ combination of markers, integrated with the elements of SIA_{0-} ($iscM_{1+}$, *integrated-selected-combined markers*), so as to get an efficient and stable enough closure of the form—namely, the presentification of a set of phenomenical objects So_1. Daily life provides many cues of this twofold process of blending and abductive abstraction. For instance, take a person with a very intense aesthetic sense: she perceives occurrences as being blended in a unique gestalt, where other people perceive objects that have no relation to each other.

In turn, So_is are subjected to pertinentization in terms of SIA_{0-}—some So_is are foregrounded, others moved into the background; this process of abductive abstraction (Bühler, 1934/1990) leads to the discrimination of the discretized field of experience on a constrained focus of attention (i.e. a sentence, a gesture, a sound, a network of a few elements compared to the many potentially involved)—I call this constrained portion of discretized field of experience the *protosign* (pS_{1+}). This is the second shift in the dynamic—*the transition from Firstness to Secondness*.

From Secondness to Thirdness

The pS_{1+} is on the edge of the semiotic world—on the one hand, it is not yet a sign, because it is still unconnected with the previous semiotic flow. On the other hand, however, it is the effect of the previous semiotic flow, being motivated by the interaction between E_0 and SIA—namely, it is what Peirce refers to as the reaction motivated in the mind of the interpreter. Here the third shift comes into being (Figure 4.1c). The pS_{1+} is quite a stable content of consciousness (though not necessarily, even rather rarely, endowed with awareness; on the fluctuating dynamic of consciousness, see Allen & Williams, 2011); as such it is able to trigger the backward interpretation of the previous sign. As a result of the action of this backward interpretation, the reproducing/reshaping of the SIA_{0-} comes about —SIA_{0-} is transformed into SIA_{-1} (the notation "$_{1-}$" indicates that it is the SIA active at the instant t_1, concerned with the backward linkage of continuity between the current state of the semiotic flow and that of the previous instant, namely, pS_{0+}). The $SIA_{0-} \rightarrow SIA_{1-}$ transformation is the way of defining the ground of pS_{1+}, therefore, of building its condition of interpretability, so as to have it loaded with semiotic value. At the same time, the backward connection between pS_{1+} and the previous protosign pS_{0+} leads to the constitution of the latter in terms of SIP_{1+}. *Thirdness is achieved.*

Note that what said above means that *the semiotic value of SIP_{1+} is its capacity to interpret pS_{0+} in terms of and under the condition of SIA_{1-}*. Moreover, it is worth noting that pS_{0+} fulfills its own status of sign only when it is interpreted by pS_{1+}—indeed a sign is such insofar as it is interpreted by the following sign. Needless to say, SIP_{1+} shares the same destiny as pS_{0+}—it has to wait for the following sign to gain semiotic status.

In sum, this view entails that the protosign reaches the status of sign in terms of its capacity to interpret the previous protosign, namely, to make it a sign. Yet, at the same moment, it triggers a further protosign that will backwardly reinterpret it—which means that it loses its quality of sign coming to be a protosign. This dynamic of ongoing, never ending backward reinterpretation is evident in (though is not exclusive to) any situation in which the SIA is subjected to a sudden shift. In cases of this kind, any previous sign (at a gradient decreasing in proportion to the distance) is rewritten according to the shift.

This process is the basis of many jokes. Take the following story. A lifeguard on the beach is eating a very tasty bowl of spaghetti. A boy arrives and stands in front of him. The boy is very tiny, seems unhealthy, and looks at the spaghetti longingly. He seems very hungry, as if he has been starving for long time. The lifeguard goes on eating, seeming not to notice him. The boy keeps his gaze on the spaghetti. After a while the lifeguard seems to realize the presence of the boy, raises his eyes from the dish, turns to the boy and kindly asks: "You haven't eaten for a long time, have you?"

The boy, very happy and at the same time shyly nods and says "No, I haven't," his eyes like saucers and moving closer to the table. The lifeguard immediately answers: "Ok, so you can go for a swim."

It is worth insisting on the fact that SIP_{1+} and SIA_{1-} are shaped through a reciprocal process of optimization, aimed at creating the best continuity with the current semiotic flow. Thus, from a phenomenological standpoint (i.e., from the point of view of the sensemaker experiencing the semiotic flow), SIP_{1+} instantiates SIA_{1-}, which in turn is the way of linking SIP_{1+} to the previous chain of signs. Therefore the former makes the latter interpretable and enables it to reinterpret the whole chain in reverse, backwardly.

Finally, the SIP_{1+} takes the semiotic chain further, working as the next event (E_1) waiting to be semiotized (i.e., interpreted) by the effect it produces—an effect that in turn will be semiotized in terms of its capacity to interpret its cause.

In sum, the model of microdynamic of sensemaking proposed here follows a forward-backward, recursive movement: SIA_{0-} allows SIP_{1+} to emerge from the undifferentiated field of experience (constitutive function). In turn, SIP_{1+} instantiates SIA_{1-} (namely, reshapes SIA_{0-}).SIA_{1-}, on the one hand, allows SIP_{1+} to emerge (causal function), and, on the other, grounds the linkage between SIP_{1+} and E_0 (hermeneutic function), so that the infinite circle of the semiosis can go on.

CONCLUSION

In the first section of this book I have outlined a model of sensemaking based on a semiotic, pragmatic, contextual, dynamic, view of meaning and mind. I based my arguments on a preliminary critical analysis of the reasons that lead one to be unsatisfied with the classical way of considering meaning and sensemaking—namely, the view of meaning as an entity contained in the sign that conveys it, independent from the process of sensemaking. This is consistent with the commonsensical view. I therefore considered it necessary to highlight the issues that motivate to challenge it.

On this basis, I have presented an alternative view, whose core point is the inversion of the relation between meaning and sensemaking—namely, the idea that meaning is the effect of how signs are used in the circumstances of communication, namely, the effect of semiosis, rather than its premise. Needless to say, this idea is not new; it is rooted—*inter alia*—in Wittgenstein and Peirce's theories of sign and meaning. On the grounds of these theories, I have addressed the issue of how such an effect comes to be—through which processes meaning emerges, and which mechanisms instantiate such processes. To do this has required encompassing three lines of argumentation.

First, a structural standpoint, focused on modeling meaning in terms of its basic components and relations among them. At this level, I underlined the bivalence of meaning—distinguishing between what I propose to call: *significance in praesentia* (SIP) and *significance in absentia* (SIA). Moreover, I deepened the structure of the SIA, proposing to consider it a fuzzy set of *scenarios of experience*, each of them sustaining of a distribution of probability of co-occurrence among signs. Accordingly, I have conceptualized meaning as the cooperative tension between these two basic dimensions.

Second, I have provided a general view of how such cooperative tension works, based on the idea that the interpretation of signs is an *abductive backward process of presentification*. According to this thesis, meaning is what the interpreted adds to the SIP in order to make it *senseful*, namely, to link it to the semiotic flow.

Third, I have outlined a possible way of modeling the microdynamic of such backward process, in terms of a two-stage bootstrapping mechanism. Regardless of their specific content, the thesis I have proposed on this point entails a more general epistemological and methodological standpoint, that can be summarized in the following two statements: (*i*) the development of a general model of sensemaking requires that the issue of understanding the specific mechanisms through which semiosis works have to be addressed. In this sense, the semiotic view of the mind can be grounded on Peirce but has to go beyond Peirce, insofar as he provided the descriptive and interpretative tools for viewing the psychological processes in terms of dynamic of signs, but did not give us a model of how this dynamic takes place; (*ii*) a general model of sensemaking has to deal with the challenging issue of the constitution of signs, namely, the process though which a brute state of the world experienced in itself (*Firstness*) acquires the semiotic status of something standing for something else (*Thirdness*). I devoted the previous and this chapter to outline a general model of such a kind.

In the final analysis, ideas proposed in this first part of the book bear witness to the effort to loosen the constraints of conceptual separations that affect the development of contemporary psychological science. Distinctions like the ones between first and third persons, computational and functional models, basic and higher processes do not picture separate worlds, but polarities of a whole dialectics, commitment to which is the magisterial path of science. Next chapters are devoted to deal with such polarities.

NOTE

1. In order to avoid reifying the spatial metaphor of the environment, it would be preferable to use a formulation like "other-than-body," rather than "outside the body." However, having said that, I will continue to use, for the sake of simplicity, terms like "outside" and "external."

PART II

THEORETICAL EXPLORATIONS

The chapters in this second part (5–8) are devoted to developing the theoretical implications of the SDMS outlined in first part.

The aim of this part is to develop the heuristic richness of the SDMS in terms of its capacity to foster an innovative approach to psychological theory. A rather radical view, that is not confined to proposing a different explanation of psychological phenomena, but is committed to providing new definitions of basic psychological categories, transforming the eyes through which psychology sees human affairs. In this sense, the following chapters are an exercise of the shift to the explanandum envisaged in the Introduction as a different possible perspective for psychology.

Chapter 5 is devoted to discussing how the SDMS entails a view of the mind and psychological processes that, focusing on the constitution of the experience, goes beyond the distinction between subject and object, thus providing the way of modeling it. Chapter 6 addresses the same issue, with a rereading of the notion of context, designed to overcome a reified interpretation of it as something affecting the mind from the outside, in favour of a view of the context as an inherent component of the mind. Chapter 7 provides a semiotic interpretation of the notion of *affect*, highlighting its role in the basic semiotic dynamic of the constitution of experience. Finally, Chapter 8 proposes a conceptual analysis of other notions that are quite popular in different areas of psychological science such as psychotherapy, group, social development, and economic choice. In so doing, it is intended to provide a further test of the heuristic fertility of the SDMS, together with the chance of showing the theoretical and practical opportunities revealed by the approach this book proposes.

CHAPTER 5

THE CONTEXTUALITY OF MIND

CONTEXT AS THE VERSION OF MIND

The model of sensemaking outlined in the first part of the book entails the view that the mind is not just held within the skull, but is produced in relation with the context.

Such a view finds very many supporters. Problems start when one tries to define more clearly what is actually meant by the term "context" and how this relation works specifically. Psychology and more in general the social sciences have proposed many theories of the context, each of them providing a specific interpretation of the way mind and world are related. Environment, activity, culture, intersubjectivity, social representations, collective unconscious, Dasein, otherness, language games, frame, voices: these, and others, are terms denoting ways of interpreting the entanglement between mind and context and the role the latter plays in psychological phenomena.

Needless to say, such an array of theories is so articulated that any generalization is condemned to be a simplification. Nevertheless, one can reliably recognize a basic conceptual attitude that crosses many theories: the view that the context and the mind are two different entities that, as such, can be studied in their reciprocal engagement. I define that view as the *separateness* of the context. Thanks to this, the context lends itself to be treated as an *explanans*, namely, something that, when referred to, enables

Psychology in Black and White: The Project of a Theory-Driven Science, pp. 87–102
Copyright © 2016 by Information Age Publishing

something else to be understood more clearly (in this case, psychological phenomena).

The separateness of the context manifests itself under many semblances. One can track it, as it were, indirectly, in the critical reactions it raises in different theoretical areas. Several theoreticians interested in the development of the dialogical view of mind have pointed out that the specificity of such a view lies in the role played by otherness in the very constitution of the self (Grossen, 2009; Linell, 2009; Salgado & Clegg, 2011; Salvatore & Gennaro, 2012). The constitutive role of otherness is what distinguishes dialogical theories from other relational theories, which, even if they attribute a major role to otherness, conceive of it as something that is secondary, namely, as a dimension which the self—assumed as a self-contained entity—engages with. A basic criticism that cultural psychology addresses to cross-cultural psychology is that the latter considers culture as being outside the mind, a context-container individuals belong to and therefore are characterized by. In opposition to this view, cultural psychology underlines that culture is a constitutive dimension of the mind, a process sustaining it rather than acting on it externally (Valsiner, 2007). Recently, Cousin (2012) has addressed this kind of criticism to cognitivism. Even if one may disagree with the solution he proposes, the point he raises is central—cognitivism treats the representation as the basic unit of analysis of mental processes, as if the fact that they are endowed with psychological value (i.e., with meaning) were something obvious, rather than the basic problem psychology should address. In the final analysis, what Cousin underlines is the oddness of a view of cultural meanings as a taken-for-granted, preexisting, separate reality acting from the outside on the psychological process of construction of experience. Similarly, both from within and outside the field of social representations theory many voices have been raised against a representationist interpretation of such a notion (Sammutt, Daanen, & Sartawi, 2010; Valsiner, 2009a; Verheggen & Baerveldt, 2007). Also in this case, in the final analysis such criticisms share the basic dissatisfaction with platonism entailed in the vision of knowledge as an entity placed somewhere outside the mind, and from there interacting with—grounding, guiding, constraining (e.g., Doise, 1986)—individual minds. Juxtaposed to this view, is the idea of knowledge as the embodied participation in a system of practices—"Knowledge is being" (Verheggen & Baerveldt, 2012, p. 283). Accordingly, shared knowledge is not a matter of negotiated representations, but the shape of the world of actions one is immersed in. Context and psychological life cannot be separated. As Verhegge and Baerveldt (2012) highlight, this view is indebted to Heidegger's idea of being as constituted by its inherent membership of the world.

Dialogism, cultural psychology (in particular the cultural psychology embracing a semiotic perspective, see Valsiner, 2014), enactivism, phenomenology, are streams of thought—partially intertwined, partially running in parallel—that have elaborated thoughtful models of the inherent reciprocal constitutiveness of mind and context, of their being part of a dynamic totality. The semio-dynamic model of sensemaking (SDMS) outlined in the previous chapters shares the same view of the reciprocal inherency between mind and context, providing a view of the microdynamic comprising their constitutive linkage—namely, the microgenetic mechanisms through which mind and context are reciprocally brought about. Thus, as I argue in this chapter, the SDMS helps to avoid the commonsensical reification of the notion of context—namely, the view of the context as an entity standing outside the mind and interacting with it - providing a way of considering such a notion that is more consistent with the theoretical mission of the psychological science.

CONTEXT AS THE VERSION OF MIND

The SDMS entails a specific view of the self and context, and their relationship. Self and context are not two separate entities, but two forms of experience emerging as complementary output from the same semiotic dynamic. More in particular, the context is what in another work I defined as the *version of mind* grounding the interpretation of the experience (Salvatore & Freda, 2011). A version of the mind is the set of scenarios that are salient in a given instant in time . As has been said, each scenario identifies a specific pattern of co-occurring signs (see Chapter 2). Therefore, the salience of a scenario—of a set of scenarios—constitutes a specific way of defining the condition of interpretability of the signs—namely, the peculiar distribution of probability in accordance to which the following sign emerges.

What the latter statement implies is that the distribution of the co-occurrence among signs is not a homogeneous pattern. Rather, it is a set of distributions, each of them reflecting a specific form of life (cf. Chapter 2). For instance, take the statement "I don't like it". The association of this sign with the following sign "I do not care what you like" will be rather weak in the case of the scenario of, say, AFFECTIVE CLOSENESS (here and henceforth the small caps denote the scenario) and rather high in the case of the scenario of, say, CONFLICT. In other words, the answer "I do not care what you like" is more likely to be triggered as the following sign in the latter scenario than in the former. Thus, the probability of association between the two signs varies over scenarios and therefore the global probability is a combination of very many local distributions, each of them corresponding to a given scenario.

It is this characteristic that leads to a scenario being interpreted in terms of *version of mind*. A collection of scenarios defines a peculiar dynamic pattern of probability of association among signs and therefore a peculiar condition of the semiotic field governing the way the interpretative trajectory unfolds. And this in the final analysis means that the mind works in different ways, defined locally and contingently, due to the set of scenarios that are salient in that circumstance of space and time. We are not always the same. Rather, depending on circumstances, we think and feel in different ways, each of them corresponding to one of the infinite versions of mind we are—CONFLICT, CLOSENESS, ACTIVENESS, FULFILLING, EMPTINESS and so forth (and their combination).

Needless to say, scenarios are not clear-cut, sharply defined states of mind. Rather, they have different levels of generalization and fuzzy boundaries, resulting from their bottom-up nature—namely, from the fact that they emerge as patterns of co-occurring signs experienced with a certain stability. Thus, for instance, FRIENDSHIP is more general than CLOSENESS, yet the latter is not only contained in the former, being connected with other scenarios too.

According to this perspective, the mind can be conceived of as a hyperdimensional space populated by an infinite set of scenarios (cf. Chapter 3). Similarly to what happens when the researcher selects a subset of dimensions among the ones emerging from a multidimensional analysis (i.e. a factorial analysis, multidimensional correspondence analysis), the subset of dimensions of the mental space that is salient at a given moment defines the patterns of scenarios in the foreground. This pattern is the version of mind involved at that given moment (Salvatore & Freda, 2011).

A good indication of the salience of versions of mind is provided by the way the mechanism of pertinentization works. A simple mental experiment can illustrate this. Imagine showing the photo in Figure 5.1 to several people, and asking them "please tell me just what you see, without spending too much time thinking about it."

Probably many will answer "the Eiffel tower," but other might answer: "Paris," "a very nice photo," and the like. In brief, the following sign they select is constrained by the previous, but not determined by it—it will be the one that will emerge in accordance to the version of mind working as attractor.

The above mental experiment provides the chance to come back to two important points discussed in the previous chapters. First, the reality provides a lot of opportunities—the version of mind is the semiotic attractor thanks to which a choice is made among them. In the final analysis, the version of mind consists of a form of *foregrounding*—a modality of reducing the hyperdimensional space of mind so that a specific form can emerge. Second, the mind does not work in an invariant way even at the level of the

Figure 5.1. What do you see?

constitution of experience, namely, when the perception is charged with meaning. Incidentally, this is the reason projective tests work—what one sees in a Rorschach test is an indication of one's version of mind at work. On the other hand, unlike the way of interpreting answers to projective tests, the idea of version of mind means that the following signs associated to the stimuli do not mark stable characteristics of the person, but one of their specific components that is salient at that specific moment, namely, a contingent version of mind.

The view of the mind in terms of an ongoing dynamic of versions of mind is consistent with several models that conceive of psychological processes in a dialogical and relational way. Notions like object relationships (Klein, 1967), inner working model (Bowlby, 1969), voices (Hermans & Hermans-Konopka, 2010), positioning (Harrè & Gillett, 1994), personal culture (Valsiner, 2007)—just to cite a few—entail the general idea that mind works in terms of its engagement in what is other-than-it. The SDMS shares this basic, general idea, at the same time providing a way of modeling the mechanism thanks to which such engagement is carried out. Moreover, in doing so, it allows a very central quality of such engagement to be recognized—it neither depends on what is inside the mind, nor does it depends on external conditions somehow introjected by the mind. Rather, it comes before the distinction between mind and world, grounding it (see Chapter 6 too). In fact, the interpretation of the context in terms of scenario models the constitution of experience and more in general psychological processes as a unique semiotic dynamic from which mind, self and therefore their complement: the world—emerges. Paraphrasing the Bible, *in the beginning, there is dia-logos* (namely, semiosis).

Further Remarks

Such a view of context could appear reductive, in the sense that it interprets the context as a local, contingent state, void of ontological substance; rather than being a phenomenon emerging from the semiotic dynamic. Thus, one could also criticize such a view as intrapsychological because it negates the historical and material embeddedness of mind. In sum, it could seem that the striving to highlight the intimacy of the relation between context and mind ends paradoxically in the cancellation of the first term. Actually, this cancellation is only apparent. This is so for two basic reasons.

First, because the idea of psychological processes as a semiotic field dynamic entails that the local, contingent condition of the field is the precipitate of its whole history. The geography of scenarios defining the conditions of interpretability of signs as well as their shape and boundaries, are historical products—the sedimentation in a given instant of all previous mundane facts as they have come to be due to the semiotic dynamic they have shaped (cf. Chapter 6 too). Thus, the definition of the context in terms of contingency does not reduce the salience of the relationship between mind and world. Rather it provides a microgenetic model for interpreting it, so as to avoid the pitfall of conceiving the context in a reified way, as something that is there and, because of that, acts on the mind.

Second, the idea of scenarios as the distribution of probability of connections among signs somehow "incorporates" the context within the semiotic dynamic. Yet this does not mean that the model is intrapsychological. On the contrary, it is radically externalist. This is so because it provides a modality of conceptualizing psychological processes because of their engagement with reality—as a matter of fact the field conditions of semiotic dynamic are the precipitate of the forms of life—yet without violating its operational closeness (Maturana & Varela, 1980). The mind is a semiotic dynamic and as such by definition it works only in semiotic terms, as transformation/connections of signs with other signs, being in itself totally blind to "facts" and "events" supposedly populating the mundane reality. This is not the place to go into the philosophical and epistemological implications of this form of weakness of many contextual theories, as they more or less implicitly assume that the world can act directly on the mind. Intrapsychological theory finds an easy target in such weakness—see for example the criticism of extensionalism that Fodor (1983) addresses to notions like frame, context, and mental model as proposed by psychologists such as Bruner (e.g., Bruner, 1990). Thus, the semio-dynamic model proposed above is worth considering as a radical contextual model precisely because it shows how, at the basic level of the constitution of experience, the world plays a role in psychological process even if (or rather, for the very reason that) such psychological process works in terms of operational closeness.

From a complementary point of view, one could add that the microgenetic model concerns a dimension of psychological processes where the very distinction between subject and world is not yet given. In the final analysis, the constitution of experience is just that: the emergence of the sense of subjectivity as engaging with something that is out-of-it (this point is deepened in Chapter 6). Accordingly, the model proposed is intrapsychological in the sense that it is aimed at understanding the way the psychological subject is continuously constructed through the flow of experience. Yet it is radically contextual as well, because it assumes the construction of experience as the output of a semiotic dynamic embedded in and fed by the world.

FROM ENTITIES TO EMERGENT PROCESSES

As a premise, it is worth noting that the very fact that the SDMS concerns the microgenesis of experience means that it considers the basic categories of psychological theory and experience—mind, context, self, meaning—as something that needs to be conceptualized in its making, rather than foundational conceptual building blocks. It is in this sense that I have proposed the SDMS as a theory of the "psychological big bang," namely, a theory aimed at modeling how the psychological universe comes about (cf. Chapter 4). Unlike physics, however, it is assumed that the psychological big bang of the constitution of experience has not occurred once, as the starting point (or cyclically, as some cosmological models assume), but it is coextensive to the psychological experience it brings out, in an ongoing, never-ending recursive backward-forward dynamic.

Thus, according to the SDMS, the basic psychological terms are not natural entities having the causal power of generating/modeling experience, but basic forms/contents—categories, indeed—of experience. In other words, there is not a self with a mind that generates experience through one's interaction with a context in terms of meaning; rather, *experience is shaped in terms of* a self that has a mind interacting with a world. In the final analysis, notions like "mind," "self," "context," are not primitive but, as the discussion in the previous chapter should have shown, they lend themselves to be conceived of as the product of more fundamental psychological processes.

This view is counterintuitive. Yet it is part of a perspective that is already present in psychological theory. For instance, Feldman Barrett (2006) has put forward a similar view as concerns emotions. She has argued convincingly that emotions are not natural entities, as generally assumed by contemporary psychology and common sense, but forms of interpretation of basic affective experience.

> In the history of psychological science, there are several notable examples where psychologists have progressed from thinking about psychological phenomena as unitary faculties of the mind—entities, if you will—to thinking about them as emergent phenomena that vary with the immediate context. (p. 21)

It can be seen that this perspective uses its own particular definitions of the basic psychological categories. Specifically, for our interests here, self and context lend themselves to be conceived as hypergeneralized meaning —more precisely: SIA (significance in absentia; cf. Chapter 2)—emerging from the semiotic dynamic and at the same time grounding its unfolding.

Invariance and Variation in the Shaping of Experience

The latter statement requires a premise to be clear. The semiotic dynamic can be seen as an ongoing process that has to establish invariance continuously and recursively upon the ever-changing flow of the field of experience. If it were not so, we would be immersed in a perennial present time, where any instant would be incommensurable with the previous and the following one. Actually, the very notion of previous and following, and therefore of time, would be not-given. Invariance is thus the fundamental epistemic structure of experience, the "stuff" of its constitutive valence: *duration*. Needless to say, we experience variability—the fact that things happen, that they change: first they are not, then they are and then are not again. Yet such happenings can be experienced only because they have duration, namely, they persist as invariant over instants of time. From a complementary point of view, they can be experienced as happenings, or *events*—something that has a beginning and an end—only in relation to a ground, that is, in relation to something else having a more extended invariance.

Experience follows the same mode as the perception of movement. Like the latter, it requires the exercise of a mechanism of mutual constitution between variance and invariance. Movement is not absolute. It is given compared to a ground, a point of observation that has a condition of stillness compared to it. The task of the ground is to provide the basic persistence in terms of which the variations over time—the variations of position in the case of movement, the body transformations in the more general case of a semiotic dynamic—can be related to each other. On the other hand, such a relation—the sign by means of which it is carried out —is nothing but a new form of invariance extracted from the variation (or rather, an abstractive transformation of the variation into a new form of invariance), the one in which the sense of the persistence of the objects over time (more in general of the continuity of the experience) is maintained.

In sum, the sense of the continuity of experience is provided by the transformation of the infinite set of occurrences in a single dynamic gestalt. One can see the same X simply because it is not the identical X. To see the same X means transforming a variation (x1 – x2) into a more abstract invariance (X). And this is performed in terms of the identification of a relation between x1 and x2. Variation, therefore, is at the service of invariance—purely because invariance is the ongoing transformation of variation. The classical example of this view is provided by a river: we never see the same water, since the molecules are always different. Precisely for this reason—not despite it—we see the same thing—the river—persisting over time. The river emerges as the transformation of the ongoing variability of the molecules in a single, dynamic gestalt. Parmenide and Heraclitus need each other and collaborate with each other.

In brief, one is led to conceive of experience as emerging from a recursive process of mutual constitution of variation and invariance. Invariance is the ground thanks to which it is possible to experience variation. In turn, the experience of variation leads to the definition of a dynamic gestalt that persists over time. In the final analysis, the experience of a variation is its transformation into an invariance.

Self as a Metastable Set of Scenarios

What I have said above paves the way to seeing the mutual constitution of self and context. Self and context have to be considered as very generalized SIAs working as metastable grounds enabling the unification of experience (Salvatore, Gennaro, & Valsiner, 2014). They are not entities, but embodied meanings, the projection of the flow of experience which allows the variation to be transformed into invariance. More specifically, we consider self and context as *grounds of grounds*, namely, very generalized conditions of interpretability that become salient insofar as there is the need to handle ruptures in the steadiness of the semiotic dynamic. An example can help to make the latter claim clear.

Imagine a person engaged in a certain routine activity—for example, she is reading the newspaper in front of a cup of black coffee in her kitchen, just after waking up. The radio is broadcasting the breaking news in the background. Such a flow of experience unfolds in terms of quite a stable regularity. However, it is worth noticing that such regularity is not invariance, but a hyperdimensional flow of instant by instant variations that can however be transformed into invariance through its projection onto a partially stable set of scenarios (cf. Chapter 4). Therefore, the regularity is the phenomenological precipitate of the steadiness of the set of scenarios working as SIA and as such allowing the abductive construction of the sense of continuity of experience (Salvatore, 2012). Now, imagine that something totally unexpected suddenly happens. For instance, a sharp, piercing noise breaks the routine. As such it does not fit with the set of scenarios at stake. The dynamic steadiness is disrupted. How is it retrieved, so as to maintain the feeling of continuity? In circumstances like that, the person can experience the rupture just because they project it onto a more generalized ground: the self, in fact. Accordingly, they experience the divergent occurrence in terms of perturbation of their state, as something breaking the sense of continuity that comprises the self. By means of such projection, the variation of scenarios brought about by the disrupting event is assimilated—that is, becomes part of a more generalized totality serving as a synthetic ground. In this way, the rupture, and what happens before and after, as well as around it, can be unified in a certain form of experience of continuity. In the final analysis, to experience a discontinuity is the basic form of constructing the continuity of experience—this is so because of the simple fact that the feeling of discontinuity entails an invariance which enables the discontinuity to be defined (Martsin, 2014; Tarsi & Salvatore, 2013).

In sum, the self is not a natural thing as such having its own properties by which one can explain the unitary nature of experience and other psychological phenomena. Rather, it is a very basic, embodied hypergeneralized meaning working as the fundamental condition of interpretability of experience. And the same thesis can be extended to what are conceived of as transcendental qualities of subjectivity—intentionality and agency. Unlike ontological claims, I am proposing to consider them from the inside of the semiotic dynamic, as its basic products that at the same time play a grounding function for it. *The semiotic dynamic produces the self and uses it, and so reproduces itself as well as the latter over time* (Salvatore, Gennaro, & Valsiner, 2014).

DIMENSIONS OF THE CONTEXTUALITY OF MIND

The above considerations lead us to distinguish different concepts within the generic notion of context.

In particular, three aspects have to be considered. Each of them high-lights the inherent mutual linkage between context and mind, constituting the psychological process and the phenomenological experience of them.

First, the context has to be considered as the source of the constitution of the self. As we have observed, the self emerges as the required ground to encompass the variations in a dynamic gestalt. Thus, the context enters into play as the mundane source of such variation. I use the term *environment* to depict this component of the semiotic dynamic. It is worth observ-ing that even as environment, the context does not exist in itself, instead being the ongoing product of the coupling with the semiotic dynamic. As a matter of fact, it enters into play only through the mediation and in terms of the body modifications mapping it—namely, as *Umwelt* (von Uexküll, 1920/1926). In this sense, consistently with the lesson of phenomenol-ogy, the environment is not the mere source of the bodily modifications, but the whole causal process of energy-matter transformation that causes bodily modifications and that therefore allows the latter to be considered as the map of the former (Manzotti, 2006). In other words in contrast to the traditional view of a self-contained external reality made of discrete mundane entities that act on a separate body, I am endorsing the idea of a single process where the capacity of the body to be effected is the way pat-terns of environment are extracted/constructed, and in the final analysis, brought into existence. Thus, the inherent mutuality of environment and body (here intended in the broad sense, as the basic source of psychologi-cal processes) lies in this: *the body causes the environment by means of being "effected" by it* (cf. Chapter 4). Incidentally, such a view entails a kind of pro-cessual ontology. One has to assume the existence of the world out there, sourcing the energy-matter contingency. Yet this assumption is made not as a metaphysical statement, but as an instrumental, epistemological de-vice enabling the abductive understanding of the phenomenon at stake, in order to be able to model the constitution of the experience.

Second, the SDMS entails the view of the context as scenario. As mod-eled above, the scenario is a certain distribution of probability of link-ages among signs defining the boundary enabling the following sign to emerge. Also here, one can observe how context does not lend itself to be conceived of as a reality affecting/regulating the mind from the outside. This can be seen from two different standpoints. On the one hand, the sce-nario does not define or "push" the selection of the sign following. Rather, it works as a constraint limiting the potential infinite set of possible follow-ing signs. This means that the following sign emerges however from within the semiotic dynamic, as a product of its contingent state interpreting the constraint. This can also be expressed in the following way, which recalls what has already been said of the environment: the mind uses the reality's constraints to perform its job. From a complementary point of view, one can see, as I have made clear above, that the scenario is before the distinction between mind and world—it is at the same time mind and world. It is world because the probability of distribution comprising it is the form of the world in which the person has participated, the way she has experienced it. There is a certain distribution among signs because practices are structured culturally in terms of scripts, routines, codes, enacted assumptions and so forth that shape life in terms of certain regularities. At the same time, the scenario is a constitutive, inherent component of the semiotic dynamic, what allows the flow of experience to come into being as experience (I will come back to this point in Chapter 6).

Third, in the previous paragraph I have proposed a radically semiotic view of the self, as a hypergeneralized embodied meaning working as metastable ground of the interpretability of the flow of experience. From this thesis one can draw a further component/interpretation of the context that is worth considering: the context as *constitutive otherness* (Salvatore & Gennaro, 2012). This definition becomes clear if one considers that the boundary of the hypergeneralized SIA of which the self consists, is *ipso facto* the definition of what-is-not-self. This is a logical, relevant consequence of the interpretation of the self in semiotic terms. Insofar as the self is conceived of as an entity, it would be possible to see it as a discrete self-contained phenomenon. In contrast, as highlighted above (Chapter 2), meanings are constituted by oppositional linkages; this is so because any boundary defining a scenario is performed in terms of foreground/ background differentiation. This means that the self emerges as a figure in the contrast with the otherness serving as the background the self is projected upon. In brief, the emergence of the self is also the constitution of the context as what is other-than-self.

One can find traces of this basic mechanism of reciprocal constitution of self and otherness in the experience of the situation where an increase in variation (in terms of intensity, dynamicity, and so forth) occurs. In cases like that, when an affective reaction arises—for instance, one feels happy, surprised, anxious—the latter is experienced as content, namely, as something that one has/that is happening to oneself, rather than the very form of one's own self: one has an emotion, *feels* it, rather than *being* it. This means that the "I" which feels and the feeling being felt (the *me*, in James' terminology) make up each other. The person lives itself as the experience of being further and other than the content of its own experience, namely, as I-as-not-coincident-with-what-I-experience. In other words, the *experience of otherness* (i.e., the presence of the object for the subject) *feeds the otherness of the experience* (the recognition of the subject as something more and else compared to the experience and as such the source as well as the target of the experience) *that feeds it*, in a never-ending circle.

THE DIALOGICALITY OF THE SDMS

The discussion above allows to specify in what sense the SDMS is dialogical as well.

Indeed, among the relational approaches it is worth distinguishing between dialogical and interactional models, according to the role otherness plays for the subject (Grossen, 2009). In brief, while interactional models conceive of otherness—implicitly or explicitly—as an external device having a *function* in the subject's organization/development, the dialogical models treat it as a *constitutive* dimension of subjectivity.

The Other as a Function

A set of relational interpretations of otherness shares the basic idea of the original autonomy of the subject. According to this idea, the other is a necessary condition and a device for the subject's development and more in general for its life, but not a constitutive element of it.

Henceforth I refer to two versions of this interpretation. First, the idea of otherness as entailed in all those theories that regard the encounter with difference as triggering psychological functioning. Piaget's theory of cognitive decentering is emblematic of this line of thought. The subject finds in what is outside itself the constraints of its own way of functioning and thus is compelled to decenter and reorganize itself at a more developed level. The neo-Piagetian authors have further underlined the social nature of this process, highlighting how otherness is in any case an experience concerning the interpersonal world (Perret Clermont, 1993). The other, in this perspective, is the *perturbing limit* of the self. Another instance of this interpretation is the Vygotskyian notion of zone of proximal development (ZPD), which sees the role of otherness as the device triggering the subject's competence. In this case the other is not a dialectic counterpart of the subject, but a supportive scaffold of its functioning. And yet it remains an external resource that the subject encounters and with which it interacts simply because both exist prior to and independently of their encounter, as two separate and autonomous entities. In sum, the subject is made *by* the encounter with the other, but it is not made *of* this encounter —otherness is like the weights for the body-builder: a necessary device for the sake of the subject's functioning and development, but not by that a constitutive part of it.

A further version of this approach is provided by those authors that use it as a way of interpreting the meaning-making process in terms of coconstruction and negotiation of significance (Angus & McLeod, 2004; Hoffman, 1998). The logic of this interpretation is no different from the previous one: the other is seen as the source of a semiotic conflict allowing the subject to move from a given position (as expressed by speeches, narrative forms, forms of discourse or of action) to another, so as to reconstruct the desired (or however required) equilibrium of the interaction. In sum, also in this case the coconstruction, the negotiation of meaning and positions, is a dynamic grounded on the subject's agency, rather than a process constituting such agency (even though, obviously, the product of that dynamic affects the form and quality of the agency).

The Constitutiveness of the Other

Conceiving otherness as an inherent constitutive dimension of subjectivity means that even the basic aspects of psychological life are sustained by and through the presence of the other. Which means that there is no subject prior to and independent of its relationship with the other—the subject is made up of such a relation.

One can find different—more or less radical—versions of this conception. One interpretation is provided by those theories that assume the subject's psychological states are inherently intentional, namely, always and in any case concerning the experience of something. From this perspective, the other plays its constitutive role as the *reference* of the subject's experience: subjectivity is (the experience of) *what* the person relates to and *how*. The dialogical self theory's idea of the mind as a society of selves (Hermans & Dimaggio, 2004; Hermans & Hermans-Konopka, 2010) provides a version of this interpretation: any position that articulates the multiplicity of the self reflects a model of relationship with a specific form of otherness. Klein's (1967) object relation theory is another example of this vision. According to that theory, the individual mind is the precipitate of the representations of the early experience of relationship (i.e., inner objects); the subject experiences the present reality by assimilating it to the movements of this archaic internalized relationship. Broadly speaking, one could say that according to this interpretation the subject is inherently relational because it is constituted of the desire *for* the other: the subject lives on and in terms of the other that is experienced.

An extension of this interpretation is provided by the Bakhtinian vision of language and more in general of meaning-making as acts that are always shaped by their inherent addressivity (Linell, 2009). The subject feels, thinks and speaks *of* the experience of the other person and *in terms* of such experience, but also addresses such acts to the other—its psychological activity is directed at and shaped by *the engagement with the other person*. This means that the other enters into defining the very way the subject addresses it—how and what the subject thinks, feels and speaks reflects how it anticipates the response of the other person to whom it is addressed (Rommetveit, 1992). In sum, this interpretation adds to the previous one the idea of the other person (the anticipation of its answer) as the feed-forward regulative device in the constitution of the subject.

A further interpretation of constitutiveness lies in the idea that psychological life is shaped by forms (categories, signs, tools, symbolic resources) that persons find in the social space. The theory of symbolic mediation (Valsiner, 2007; Vygotsky, 1934/1986) is an instance of this way of looking at the constitutiveness of the other person. One can also refers to Lacan's notions of Symbolic order as the place of the other's signifier, inhabited by the subject (Muller, 1996). What these notions propose is the vision of the social world as shaping the subjectivity in its constitutive elements – the way of thinking and feeling, the very structure of the subjectivity and its dynamic is sustained, regulated and nourished by the discourse of the other (culture, symbolic resources). From the standpoint of this interpretation, the subject constitutes itself *through* the (signs of the) other. This can be seen as a more radical interpretation of constitutiveness, because otherness is regarded not only as the reference and the measure of the subject, but as its very substance, that which provides the stuff of which the subject is made.

Finally, one can distinguish a further, pragmatic variant of the latter interpretation, considering those semiotic theories that focus on how the other contributes actively to building the subject's experience. According to this view, any subject's condition is not a self-contained state, but it is the precipitate of the combination of the subject's act and the other's response. In this sense, subjectivity is constituted by the other's *answer*. This vision is expressed by Peirce's triadic semiotic model. According to this author, meaning is not contained in the sign but is the interpretant (another sign) in terms of which somebody interprets the sign. Thus, the meaning is not in what the subject says, acts and feels, but in how all this *is interpreted by somebody* – the meaning has a backward dynamic—it is what follows in the gaze of the other (Salvatore, 2012). An interpretation of this kind leads definitively to decoupling subject and individual—the subject is extended and concerns not the individual, but the constitutive work of otherness on it. The subject is inherently an *intersubject*.

CONCLUSION

In this chapter I have looked more deeply into the implications of the SDMS as regards the contextual view of the mind it implies. Such a view is different from the current idea of context as something that affects experience—and more in general psychological processes—from the "outside." This reified idea is a good metaphor, but no more. As a conceptual model it is quite weak and therefore it limits the development of a convincing, comprehensive model of the mind. In particular, it does not allow clarification of what is specifically meant by the notion of "context," nor does it enable a clear conceptual boundary to be set between the mind and what is not mind and thus to model their reciprocal engagement.

The SDMS provides a different theory of the context. It is the grounds of a general view of the context as inherently linked to the mind. Accordingly, mind and context cannot be conceived as separate entities interacting with each other. Rather, they are the forms of description on different spatial-temporal scales of the same basic dynamic of semiotization. The self and context are the same thing—two sides of the same coin.

The view of context as immanently linked to psychological process has consequences in the way of seeing the role it plays. As I have argued above, it entails the idea that persons shape experience through and in terms of the context—rather than being affected/framed by the context. When a person feels or thinks, the field of experience in this instant state of mind emerges as the interpretative transformation of the state of the previous instant and the condition for the emergence of the following one. According to the SDMS model, it is thanks to the context that the state of mind of any instant is able to source the following state of mind as well as to make sense of the previous one. On the other hand, such an ongoing, never-ending chain of interpretative transformations is what sustains the person's sense of being a self that is experiencing the world. This leads us to conclude that, in the final analysis, the context is the grounds of the sense of continuity and fullness of the self and the experience of the world—namely, the *value-of-life of signs* (Salvatore, 2012). A rather radical change of perspective is involved here: it is not the ontological quality of the world that grounds the sense of continuity of the experience. Rather, it is the sense of continuity of the experience that feeds our embodied feeling of the ontological subsistence of the world.

The next chapter is devoted to discussing further implications of this reversed perspective.

CHAPTER 6

BEYOND SUBJECT
AND OBJECT

PRESUBJECTIVITY AND
INTERSUBJECTIVITY OF SENSEMEANING

As argued in the previous chapter, the SDMS entails a view of sensemaking as inherently dialogical. The dialogicality of the meaning, however, has to be interpreted in two complementary ways.

As a starting point, it is worth considering that meaning emerges from and through the backward and forward linkages among patterns of experience, the latter acquiring the status of sign thanks to such linkages (i.e., the function of standing for something else; see part I). Yet, semiotic dynamics are possible *only because they are grounded on a system of redundancies* —in SDMS terms: on the basic components of the SIA. The very possibility of selecting a sign (a SIP) from the paradigmatic axis is grounded on the fact that a SIA is instantiated. Moreover, the experiential content of the meaning—what is called the *domain of sense* (Chapter 2)—consists of the variation of the SIA's boundaries over time.

As conceptualized above, the system of redundancies is the historical precipitate of social life. This is the same as saying that sensemaking emerges from and it is embedded in a network of linkages, in a form of life that transcends the local circumstances of the sensemaking, working as the landscape of it. Language is the perfect example of the salience of such a landscape. Any newborn learns language because her/his experience

Psychology in Black and White: The Project of a Theory-Driven Science, pp. 103–113

occurs within and through an environment that has a linguistic shape, which transcends her/him and within which she/he is embedded.

Thus, one is led to a first conclusion: the *dynamic of sensemaking is inherently presubjective*, namely, it is the enactment of a form of life that comes before—and motivates—the very distinction between self and other. In other words, the fact that the interpreting sign is provided by the same "somebody" that has provided the previous sign or by another "somebody" makes no difference as to the dynamic fostering the semiotic chain (while, needless to say, it makes a difference in the specific trajectory of the chain). Phenomenology as well as psychoanalysis has highlighted how subjectivity and meaning emerge from the dynamics of the linkage (Bion, 1962; Lacan, 1978; Mitchel, 1988; Sasso, 2011; Salvatore & Zittoun, 2011b). As Winnicot (1960, p. 587, f. 4) stated: "There is no such thing as an infant," namely, there does not exist a mother and an infant as two separate entities. Incidentally, the presemiotic constitution of sensemaking leads us to recognize that the constitution of experience is the core theoretical problem of any psychological theory of meaning. In other words, psychology has to explain not only how meaning is elaborated, negotiated, communicated, shared and changed, but also how it comes into being as a basic psychological experience, as the precipitate of the semiotization of presemiotic being in the world-namely as precipitate of sensemaking as the enactment of the embeddedness in the lived world.

On the other hand, having recognized the presubjective valence of sensemaking, it is now necessary to recognize that this is not the whole story. What has to be considered is that sensemaking produces meaning and such meaning is a constitutive part of sensemaking, shaping its following trajectory. To be precise, one should not even separate meaning and sensemaking: meaning is the evolution of sensemaking as experienced in a given portion of time—namely, the state of sensemaking that determines the further evolution of its dynamics (see below). The very self and the other—together with an array of connected signs such as mind, will, intention, and so forth—rather than primitive entities, represent the basic semiotic output of sensemaking, namely, stable enough meanings to make experience steady, and therefore to work as building blocks of our sense of reality (Salvatore, 2012; Salvatore, Gennaro, & Valsiner, 2014; cf. also Chapter 5). The self-other semiotic distinction brings about the social space, namely the mapping of experience in terms of relationship between subject, object and the former's project for the latter, to be performed through the mediation (the support, the constraints) of otherness.[1] In other words, the self/other distinction provides the semiotic devices shaping the experience in terms of a landscape made up of one's feelings, desires, plans, objects to which they are addressed, and other persons and objects (e.g., institutions) that play a meditational role in such addressing.

Within and through such a landscape, meaning acquires its status of *inter-subjectivity*: it lends itself to be represented as object/target of negotiation and communication, then to be distributed, stored, used, even changed thanks to and for the sake of human relations.

To summarize, the social space (i.e., the distinction self/other) is a generalized meaning working as an attractor of trajectories of signs within the phase space: a SIA grounding the condition of interpretability of other meanings. It is what allows meanings to be represented and handled both at the individual and collective level. The self/other distinction makes it possible to interpret signs as signs of/to/from the other and therefore to consider them a matter of negotiation, as well as properties of someone (one's own and/or other's). Accordingly, the claim of the intersubjectivity of sensemaking is not merely descriptive, but as claimed by developmental (e.g., Stern, 1985) and psychoanalytic theories (Hoffman, 1998; Mitchell & Aron, 1999; Odgen, 2004) sensemaking is genetically intersubjective. It is grounded on the self/other distinction.

The discussion proposed above leads to the conclusion that sensemaking is both presubjective and intersubjective (Salvatore & Gennaro, 2012; cf. Chapter 5). This raises the issue of the relation between these two conditions. To address this issue, it must be taken into account that, as argued above, presubjectivity generates intersubjectivity, and intersubjectivity also produces presubjectivity. As a matter of fact, if one has to assume an embodied, presubjective state of coordination among bodies[2] at the very grounds of sensemaking, at the same time one has to recognize that such coordination is in turn based on and made it possible by a cultural environment made up of artefacts and social practices built and reproduced through the mediation of signs (rules, norms, system of knowledge, and so forth). This means that sensemaking enables the coordination of action through the meaning that it itself produces. In the final analysis, *the building and reproduction through time of that lived world which is the crucible of sensemaking is at the same time the product of sensemaking*.

NORMATIVITY AND VARIABILITY OF SENSEMAKING

The SDMS is able to take into account two seemingly contrasting properties of sensemaking, namely, the fact that it is constantly open to variability while at the same time it works somehow in a normative way, namely, by showing a redundancy which allows individuals to coordinate with each other and to have the experience of being part of a shared world.

Take what happens in the case of language. Two trajectories of linguistic signs hardly ever follow the same path, even when it is the same person enacting them. Nevertheless, this does not hamper a certain level of predictability on the further development of the trajectory. Usually, we cannot forecast the specific word that will follow, but we expect that this word will be selected from a certain set—and this is made evident by the reaction of surprise when incoming words do not match the expectation. Broadly speaking, common sense considers such variability as depending on the intervention of the subject's will, or as a result of malfunctioning (i.e. madness), or of further situational factors—for example, the person has answered Z (instead of the expected X) because she wanted to pursue W/ because she has the problem P/ because F led her to move from X to Z. Yet explanations like W, P, and F are, at best, post hoc descriptions, linguistic transformations of the event to be explained (Smedslund, 1988), that do not solve the issue of modeling Z in terms of the specific dynamics of sensemaking producing it. Moreover, solutions of this kind are inevitably exposed to the homunculus fallacy—namely, the fact that the explanation just moves the problem of providing a model of the mechanism involved a step ahead instead of solving it. In other words, it leaves open the issue of how W, P or S work and are able to provide Z as their effect. In the final analysis this leads us to conclude that the trajectory of signs has to be considered subject to deterministic rules and that the explanation of Z requires such rules to be modeled. Moreover, these deterministic rules have to be able to model not only Z, but also the fact that Z is selected when X is a potential alternative. In other words, the model of sensemaking has to address the variability $X <> Z$.

The SDMS offers a solution to this puzzling issue. The interplay between variability and normativity of meaning lends itself to be understood as the precipitate of the historicity of sensemaking, namely of the fact that the mind is shaped by the whole history of the co-occurring signs it has been exposed to. A possible way of depicting the way the historicity of sensemaking plays a role is briefly outlined below.

Once we take a long enough time span, some patterns of sign co-occurrence prove to happen with a frequency higher than 1. Now, even if this frequency is quite low, it will be relatively much higher if compared to the frequency of the infinite patterns of co-occurrence distributed within the time span. This is due to the fact that in a long enough time span the number of patterns is extremely high—almost infinite—their probability tends to 0. Therefore, the very fact that one pattern appears a second time makes the difference.

Now, if one assumes the multidimensionality of the distribution of probability making up a certain scenario, it can be concluded that some of these components map the patterns of signs that have high relative frequency. In other words, these components map what is invariant across the intra- and interindividual experience—they are the precipitate of the exposure of persons to the same cultural redundancy across space-temporal circumstances. So any scenario has to be conceived of as having a homogenizing ground working as the "semiotic gravitational force" fostering the normativity of sensemaking. As a result of this semiotic gravitational force, even if no sign trajectory is identical to any other, the instantiation of a new sign is constrained so as to allow sensemaking to reproduce the condition of redundancy, which, in the final analysis, makes up the domain of sense. Incidentally, this means, according to the computational standpoint adopted here, that the culture can be conceptualized as the redundancy of the symbolic environment.

On the other hand, any person has his own idiosyncratic map of the scenario, representing the precipitate of the trajectory of signs experienced in their own life. As we have said, some components of this distribution map the redundancy of the symbolic environment and its constancy through space-time circumstances. Yet other components are the precipitate of the experience peculiar to the single person. To use an analogy, a scenario is like a wave that can be decomposed in a cumulative array of waves with different frequency and length. In the case of the scenario we will have a basic wave that is constant across people, and a lot of other waves of greater or lesser importance, representing the idiosyncratic individual components of the experience.

These considerations provide the basis for understanding the variability of sensemaking, both at the intra- and interindividual level. While the gravitational force expressed by the redundant components constrains the paradigmatic variability within a certain area, the idiosyncratic components of the scenario guarantee that in any circumstance of sensemaking the trajectory of signs is also a function of the uniqueness of the participants involved in it. And this means that sensemaking is determined by the collective history of its unfolding but that this does not mean it locks out the local variability (even innovation) as produced by means of the situated interplay of the idiosyncratic components of sensemakers' biographies.

One could say, paraphrasing the basic tenet of chaos theory, that sensemaking is *a deterministic system sensitive to local conditions*.

THE ONTOLOGICAL UNIQUENESS OF MEANING

The last statement has two important interconnected consequences. First, it leads us to see the presubjective embodied linkage not as a self-contained reality that exercises its influence on sensemaking from the outside, but as a product of semiosis itself. Incidentally, it is worth highlighting that this view is consistent with the hermeneutic recognition of how the presymbolic linkage constitutive of the being-in-the-world is dialectizated by the effort to semiotize it: preunderstanding grounds understanding and in so doing determines the conditions for going beyond it, for the partial and never fully defined autonomy of the thought from the linkage (Ricoeur, 1981).

Second, it follows that the self/other semiotic distinction has to be recognized as having an ontological status as well, albeit peculiar. This is so because the ontological status has to be attributed to that which produces effects (Manzotti, 2009). Thus, according to a psychological theory of sensemaking like SDMS, the semiotic self\other distinction is a piece of reality in itself, regardless of the quality of its referential linkage with the world (Salvatore, 2012).

Here Meinong's distinction between *subsistence* and *existence* is relevant (Albertazzi, Jacquette, & Poli, 2001; Valsiner, 2009b). Existence is an accidental property of entities, namely a given object can be predicated to have or not have it. Consequently, one has to admit that entities have to be part of the world at a higher order level (they *subsist*, in fact) in order to be predicated in terms of absence of existence (Valsiner & Salvatore, 2012). As Eco (2009) shows, this idea comes from Avicenna, who claimed that existence is an accidental property of the object (i.e., it does not precede and ground the object; rather, it may or may not be a value of it). It is logically required by the recognition of the fact that to state that something has no being, this something must already subsist. Thus, according to this stream of thought, the psychological object has a content of being that is independent of its ontological status; some objects (mathematical entities, objects like a gold mountain, square circle, or the current king of France), even if they do not exist in the world, namely even if they are lacking any extensional property, *subsist*. Now, if one accepts that the subsistence of the object is independent from and fundamental to its very existence, one has to conclude that the psychological presentation of the object is not based on, and does not mirror, its value of empirical existence; rather, it grounds it.[3]

Meaning and Action

It is worth highlighting that the recognition of the ontological status to intersubjectivity does not necessarily entail an ontological pluralism. This conceptual pitfall can be avoided if one considers the sensemaking an autopoietic dynamic (Maturana & Varela, 1980), namely, a system working in a condition of operational closeness, for this reason able to recursively self-produce the condition of its unfolding.

This last claim is a more generalized way of stating the homogeneity of meaning and action. Accordingly, action and meaning lend themselves to be view as sensemaking—as the unique reality that manifests itself differently at different levels of observation. Where such levels of observation can be modeled as different spatial-temporal frames of analysis (for a similar perspective, see Leiman, 2000; Matusov, 1996). Take the relation between the waves and the coast. The wave occurs in the here and now, presenting an ever-changing shape that requires a local frame of observation to be represented. Such a frame of observation assumes as given, as a fact, the form of the coast, considering it (one of) the parameter(s) which the shape of the wave, as well as its dynamic over time, depends on. At the same time, however, the shape of the coast is the sedimentation of the dynamic of the waves—a dynamic that requires a broader frame of observation through which the ever-changing shape of the wave is described in terms of a more generalized model and its effects recognized. According to the analogy, intersubjective phenomenology is what the observer sees of the sensemaking when a local frame of observation is adopted—namely, the contingency of the situated interaction; while presubjective phenomenology emerges as a fact insofar as a broader frame of observation is adopted—namely, a standpoint broad enough to enable us to see sensemaking's capacity to create redundancy through time. An example of this recursion that requires a hierarchy of frames of observation to be modeled is provided by language. Individuals talk and in the ongoing process of communication they do that as a way of performing their projects and desires, in accordance to the intersubjective landscape at stake. At the same time, in a different, broader spatial-temporal frame, such performances can be conceived of as the precipitate of long-standing semiotics regularities (e.g., language structure, ideologies, social representations, and so forth) that unfold through the local performances of language.

THE EXPERIENCE OF MEANING AND THE MEANING OF EXPERIENCE

The considerations put forward in the previous sections of this chapter have interesting implications as regards the relation between experience and meaning, an issue that crosses several domains of inquiry. The core of this issue concerns the autonomy of experience from meaning. It can be summarized in the following question: does the meaning interpret the experience (*the meaning of the experience*) or is the experience in itself a product of meaning (*the experience of meaning*)?

The dialectics between hermeneutics and phenomenology is an example of the point at stake. Even though he does not negate the phenomenological view of a level of prereflexive meaning constitutive of the human experience, Ricoeur (1981) claimed the possibility of experience to free itself from that constitutive linkage, once such experience is objectivized in texts that have their own life distanced from the author. In cultural psychology this question is prompted by the debate on the differences among cultures. Cultural psychologists (e.g., Cole, 1996; Valsiner, 2007) criticize cross-cultural studies for the implicit view of culture that informs such studies— namely, the fact that they assume a view of meaning working from the outside on how and what people act, feel and think. This assumption, in the terms of the discussion here, entails the idea that experience (how and what people feel, act and think) is a separate phenomenon acted upon by the system of meaning (the culture). On the grounds of this assumption, the cross-cultural variability in the forms of experience can be explained in terms of variability of meaning seen as independent variable. In the domain of social representations theory (SRT) a debate has been developing in the last few years over the interpretation of the term "social" qualifying representation. Very briefly, two different positions are involved. On the one hand, it is argued that the specification "social" attributed to the representation of any object is pleonastic (Verheggen & Baerveldt, 2007) because objects cannot but be social, since the representation of them is a social meaning constituting the very experience of them. On the other hand, there are those who instead consider the experience of the object an enough autonomous phenomenon, which as such enters the consensual universe of communication, thus acquiring the value of a form of social knowledge (Chryssides, Dashtipour, Keshet, Righi, Sammut, & Sartawi, 2009). Incidentally, in what is only a seemingly paradoxical way, the former position is criticized as individualistic, because in fact it assumes that the "social-ness" of the representation is an inherent quality of the experience, which as such one could be modeled in terms of processes placed at the level of the individual mind (see Chryssides et al., 2009). In contrast, the second position is targeted at the criticism of hypostatizing what has to be explained, namely the fact that the social valence of the representation— and its normative functions—are treated as an explicative criterion rather than what has to be explained (Verheggen & Baerveldt, 2007). Consider the Bauer and Gaskell (1999) toblerone model, which conceptualizes the representation in the interplay of subject, object and project. The authors make it clear that the three terms cannot be considered separately, because they constitute each other. Nevertheless, in the final analysis such terms are considered self-contained entities interacting with each other. Thus, the difference is subtle but theoretically substantial—according to the idea that meaning is inherent to experience, subject, object, project (and to be precise, also time, because it is not a natural fact but an experience) cannot be the dimensions of the conceptual space through which the social representations are modeled. And this is so because such notions are themselves forms of meaning, therefore, in the final analysis, social representations.

The recursive character of sensemaking in the SDMS provides the bridge for integrating the two standpoints. On the one hand, as we have said, the SDMS considers sensemaking as presubjective. In so, the model is consistent with the phenomenological view of prereflexive meaning as constitutive of experience. Individuals are part of the world and this being part is the lived semantics comprising experience. As already underlined, action and meaning are ontologically nondistinguishable. The SIA is how SDMS conceptualizes such lived semantics—the concept of SIA depicts at the computational level the inherently presubjective being part of the world, lived in terms of the redundancy of patterns of experience (following Wagner [2011] one could say—the rhythm of signs), working as the generalized embodied meaning feeding the sensemaking. On the other hand, the SDMS underlines the recursion of the semiotic flow, namely that any SIP is projected both backwards, to interpret what went before, and forwards, to trigger its own interpretant. As a result of that, sensemaking is able to develop the quality of the SIP through its very unfolding. In Peirce's terms the interpretant is "perhaps a more developed idea."[4] The prereflexive meaning triggers its interpretation in terms/by means of "more developed" signs, namely in terms/by means of signs being part of a symbolic system. This corresponds to saying that the prereflexive, embodied meaning is projected onto the domain of symbolic semiosis and through this projection it can be interpreted and reinterpreted through the course of social communication. This is so because the projection of the embodied meaning onto the domain of language does not entail its transformation. Projection does not eliminate the embodied meaning; rather the latter is linked to "more developed" signs. Thus, the embodied meaning, so to speak, keeps its semiotic force, working as the vital ground and experiential substance of the symbolic signs. Thanks to the projection, then, on the one hand the embodied meaning becomes autonomous from the local condition of its *presentification*—namely, the instant by instant bodily transformations mapping the ongoing coupling with the world—and therefore able to be *represented* for the sake of communication (Valsiner, 2013); on the other hand, the symbolic sign is enrooted in the world, acquires existential and affective value for the sensemaker (Lakatoff & Johnson, 1980), charged with what I proposed to name *value of life* (Salvatore, 2012; Salvatore & Freda, 2011; cf. Chapter 7).

In sum, the SDMS considers the experience of meaning and the meaning of experience as two states of functioning of sensemaking, expressing its nonstationary dynamic. According to some authors (Sasso, 2011; Valsiner, 2007) the relation between these states follows a sinusoidal rather than linear trend—a kind of accordion movement: states of embodied activation are elaborated in symbolic terms and this triggers further forms of embodied activation (for a computational model of such movement, see

Chapters 3–5). Immediacy and mediation are not two alternative models, but two components of the same dynamics (Valsiner, 2009a)

CONCLUSION

In this chapter some implications of the SDMS model have been outlined.

First, *meaning's sensitivity to the local condition.* The redundancy of the symbolic environment produced by the historical sedimentation of the practices of communication (i.e., the way signs have been combined with each other through time, so as to expose each person to certain distributions of frequency of co-occurring signs) works as a basic attractor modeling the shape of any current trajectory of signs. In this there is the normative valence of sensemaking. At the same time, however, idiosyncratic components of the personal biography of exposure to the symbolic environment work locally, in the situated circumstances of communication, as sources of intra/inter individual variability of sensemaking.

Second, *the hermeneutic circularity of sensemaking.* Sensemaking is a pre-semiotic, presubjective embodied dynamics embedded within the lived world. At the same time, it semiotizes such conditions and in so doing transforms it in a symbolic intersubjective reality. Thus, basic distinctions like self-other can be attributes of ontological status, yet not because they mirror self-contained states of the world, but because they are part of the recursive dynamic of sensemaking that uses their semiotic products as their constitutive elements.

Ontological homogeneity of meaning and action. Meaning and action cannot be distinguished ontologically from each other—meaning is a form of action and action is the way sensemaking unfolds. Needless to say, this does not mean that meaning and action cannot be separated (just by calling them differently one does so). Rather, it means that a distinction of this kind is an epistemic operation whose validity depends on the heuristic project pursued (the frame of observation associated with it), rather than the mirror of a state of affairs.

NOTES

1. This definition is similar to the *toblerone model* (Bauer & Gaskell, 1999). What differentiates it is the theoretical interpretation of the terms. In the case of SDMS, subject, object, otherness (although the latter term is not present in the toblerone model) are generalized meanings and as such they acquire the status of reality (Salvatore, 2012).
2. I regard them as bodies because at this conceptual level they are not yet indi-viduals—the individualization of bodies comes as the precipitate of the self/

other distinction. In other words, action produces its own actor. Individuals are the output of the semiotization of bodies.

3. Contemporary psychology has pushed aside the notion of presentation, moving the focus onto representation. In this terminological shift, there is a major conceptual change. Cognitive psychology is not interested in how the psychological value of the representation comes about—namely, the fact that it is a re-presentation. Its functionalist standpoint led to the scotomization of the issue of the generative process of psychological life, fully substituted by the task of describing its way of working.

4. The recursion of sensemaking is entailed in several models, in particular the ones interested to link affective experience to language (Bucci, 1997; Valsiner, 2007; Salvatore & Zittoun, 2011b).

CHAPTER 7

AFFECT AND DESIRE AS SEMIOTIC PROCESS

The SDMS outlined is deeply indebted to the psychoanalytic theory. For the sake of simplicity, I refrained from addressing this aspect in the previous chapters, just making some marginal reference to it, in particular to Matte Blanco's theory (Chapter 3). Yet the recognition of such a linkage with psychoanalytic theory is quite relevant, because it allows us to pursue a twofold theoretical purpose. On the one hand, it empowers the grounds of the SDMS, through the enrooting of semiotic dynamics within the affective level of the mind's functioning. On the other hand, it brings with it a re-reading of central psychodynamic constructs, in so doing contributing to the development of a semiotic approach to psychoanalytic theory (Neuman, 2009; Salvatore & Zittoun, 2011b). This chapter is devoted to taking some steps toward such a twofold theoretical goal.

PSYCHOANALYSIS AND SEMIOSIS

Psychoanalysis is not a homogeneous theoretical domain. Wallerstein (2000; see also Pine, 1988) claimed that there is not one psychoanalysis, but many. In what follows the focus is on the psychoanalytic approach and concepts that more than others lend themselves to be interpreted according to a semiotic standpoint, namely, the psychoanalytic view that sees the mind as a process of unconscious/affective signification of experience. This vision is typical of (a segment of) contemporary psychoanalysis. Yet

Psychology in Black and White: The Project of a Theory-Driven Science, pp. 115–142

it can be found throughout the whole history of the movement, starting from some of Freud's seminal elaborations. In particular, two aspects of the Freudian theorization are relevant for a semiotic reading of psychological processes: the notion of primary process and the theory of anxiety.

Freud's Very Discovery

One of the basic constituents of the classic psychoanalytic architecture is the intrapsychic and quasi-biological notion of drive (*inter alia:* Brenner, 2002; Ellenberger, 1970; Modell, 1984; Rapaport, 1960). Freud (1915/1957) conceptualized drive as an element standing on the boundary between the somatic and the psychic: a source of stimulation coming from the body and working on, or through, the mind. In brief, a somatic demand of work addressed to the mind.

The modeling of the psychic processes in terms of drives entails an energetic conception of the mind. Such a conception founds its grounds on the concept of *cathexis* (*Besetzung*), which constituted a constant through the various formulations and revisions of Freud's (1915/1957) thought. Freud depicted drives as distributions of libidic (or aggressive, after having introduced the death drive) charges modifying the body's state of equilibrium. This modification is perceived by the psychic system in terms of excitement. The activity of the psychic system is moved by the need to restore the condition of equilibrium in the distribution of the charges, by means of motor and/or mental operations aimed at their discharge. This is what is stated by the Freudian principle of constants: the psychic system tends to keep the stimulation as close as possible to the zero point; satisfaction consists in the reduction, rather than the increase, of the stimulation.

Yet, in parallel with the notions of drive and cathexis, Freud also developed a semiotic conception of the mind. In *The Interpretation of Dreams* (Freud, 1900/1953), he conceptualized the unconscious as a *mode of expression*: a language having its own syntax (characterized by the rules of condensation, displacement, plastic representation, symbolic transformation, absence of negation and absence of time) and creating a specific form of meaning. As one can see, this formulation implies a model of the unconscious which differs from Freud's topographical model (namely, the model according to which the unconscious is a place-container of repressed thoughts) and structural model (according to which the unconscious-Id is an entity of the mind). In Freud's theorization of the dream work, the unconscious is conceived of in a semiotic way: as a *mode of combining signs, generative of images and texts*.

The concept of the unconscious was already present in the scientific knowledge of Freud's time. As Freud (1933/1964) himself recognizes the main contribution of him is not the discovery of the unconscious as such (Ellenberger, 1970), but rather, the depiction of the modes whereby the unconscious works, namely, of the notions of *primary* and *secondary process*. The notion of secondary process describes the logic of diurnal mode of linking ideas, admitting succession, causality, no double contradiction. The notion of primary process designates the privileged mode of working of the unconscious. This mode is not the mere weakening of the secondary process, a reduction of the constraints of rationality. Rather, it is a specific, autonomous and radically different way of functioning of the mind (Freud 1900/1953; cf. also Bucci, 1997; Brakel, Shevrin, & Villa, 2002; Matte Blanco, 1975; see below). Primary process is the magic and hallucinatory way the mind works, typical—yet not exclusive—of dreams. It is grounded on the possibility of freely combining (condensing, moving) representations, insensitive to the constraints imposed by the reality test and by the distinction between inner and outer world.

The notion of primary process has allowed psychoanalysis to read the idiosyncratic expressions of human beings not as the by-product of the lack of rationality, but as the emergence from a specific modality of the mind, different from rationality, yet endowed with its own inner systematic logic. This can be considered the main contribution of psychoanalysis to psychology—the acknowledgement of the unconscious way of working of mind, as the grounds of the understanding of psychic expressions otherwise destined to be considered as void of value and meaning.

The Semiotic Theory of Anxiety

The shift in the theory of anxiety is the other point in Freudian works where a semiotic standpoint is evident. Initially, Freud (1895/1950) proposed the so-called "toxic" model of anxiety. According to this model, anxiety is the effect of the accumulation of instinctual energy that the mental apparatus has been unable to discharge. Yet, 30 years later (Freud, 1926/1959) he radically changed his views, proposing that anxiety should be considered as a signal produced by the *ego* in order to warn that an unconscious source of undesirable conflict is going to arise, thereby making the ego itself ready to cope with it. This is quite a significant theoretical change. It has been made possible and motivated by the elaboration of the triadic structural model (e.g., ego-super-ego and id) and the consequent centrality gained by the notion of ego within Freudian thought.

Such a change has had highly relevant implications for the further development of psychoanalytic theory—and more specifically for the psychoanalytical theory of the affect. According to the toxic model, anxiety is a subjective reflex of the energy flow—the psychological precipitate of a somatic state. In contrast, the idea of anxiety as a signal entails a semiotic conception of this kind of affect: a given state of the body (i.e., the anxiety) is not treated as an effect explained in terms of its somatic cause, but as a signal understood in terms of its function of *standing for something else* (the emergence of an undesirable conflict).

As concerns the focus of the current discussion, two aspects of the signal theory are worth underlining. First, this theory opened the way to theoretical elaborations that have led the notion of affect to gain a central place within contemporary psychoanalysis. With the signal theory the idea of the affect as an epiphenomenal correlate of the dynamic of drives is abandoned and replaced with a vision of it as the fundamental source of semiotic regulation of the psychic apparatus. Thus, the signal theory has allowed the affect to be charged with an important, specific role within the psychoanalytic architecture of the mind. According to it, the affect performs the function of connoting the state of the intersystemic relationship (i.e., something like the following warning: "the relationship between the ego and the id is going to enter a critical condition") and consequently of triggering the ego's response in coherence with this connotation (i.e., in terms of activation of defense mechanism for coping with the danger coming from the id). Second, the theory of anxiety as a signal provides a semiotic perspective encompassing biological and psychological domains, making them strictly intertwined. The theory asserts that a state of the body (anxiety) works as the interpretant sign of the psychological condition (the undesirable conflict to be coped with), that is, its representamen. In sum, with the signal theory Freud allows affect to enter within the semiotic domain, where relations are defined in terms of interpreting linkages.

The Affect in the Klein Object Relations Theory

Melanie Klein and her followers have developed the seminal Freudian idea of the semiotic nature of the affect. According to Klein (1967), from the very beginning of their life, persons are engaged with an activity of affective connotation of the world leading them to feel every experience in terms of a relation with a positive (loved) or negative (hated) object (i.e., inner representation of relational experiences).[1]

Klein (1967) conceives the affect as the process of attributing basic meanings to experiences—love and hate, which she sees as the psychological precipitates of the drive of life and drive of death. Thus, M. Klein keeps the Freudian concept of drive, but uses it in original way, making it part of a semiotic dynamics. Accordingly, the drive assumes the theoretical status of a basic, enrooted bodily meaning according to which the state of the self-object relationship is shaped. This is very clearly expressed in the way Klein models the relationship between mother and infant. From the beginning of its life, the infant has to deal with the alternation of presence and absence of the mother, she/he experiences this in terms of global and intense bodily states—for example, presence as a condition of satisfaction and warmth, associated with the mother's care; absence as a state of suffering, associated with the sense of hunger. The infant does not have the cognitive competences to modulate these bodily states, therefore she/he experiences them as very intense, extreme affective condition—of total pleasure or of total catastrophic displeasure. As M. Klein maintains, these two affective conditions are not associated with the representation of the same external object—the actual mother—as she is alternately present with or absent from the child. Rather, the two affective conditions are felt to be due to two different objects, according to the instinctual duality (life and death drives): the good object providing love and warmth, and the bad object attacking and seeking to destroy the infant.

Thus, in the object relation theory, the affect does not merely connote the experience—for example in terms of positive, joyful or unpleasant reactions; rather, the affect psychologically *generates* the object (Stein, 1991). In other words, the affect being active in a certain circumstance (e.g., the pleasure associated with seeing a nice landscape, or of talking with a beloved friend) is *ipso facto* (at the unconscious level) the object associated with/triggering that affect. For instance, the state of pleasure that a person may be filled with is—at the unconscious level—the presence of the loved, pleasant object.[2]

Unconscious Process as Symbolization

The semiotic perspective has been developed after Klein (Klein, Heimann, & Money-Kyrle, 1955). The leading Italian psychoanalyst Franco Fornari (1979, 1981, 1983; for a presentation of Fornari's Fornari in English: Giannakoulas, 1984) proposed a model of the unconscious as a process of symbolization. Fornari (1981) described the unconscious as a semiotic device fostering the subject's striving to signify itself and the world in terms of very basic affective categories—"coinems" in the terminology of the author.

> Psychoanalytic philosophy radically changes, if exploring the unconscious, we assume a subject wanting to signify her/himself, marked by a primal facultas signatrix, or we assume a subject that always has to hide behind the modes in which it manifests. (Fornari, 1981, p. 13, italics in the text, our translation from Italian original)

Fornari (1981) takes coinems as Kantian-like, a-priori, preconceptual categories, attached to/sustained by fundamental vital dimensions (life, death, parental relationship, parts of the body). According to him, individuals reveal two coextensive ways of signifying: one working under the socially shared rules of formal thinking—that is, the secondary process, what Fornari refers to in terms of the "diurnal" side of operative categorization—and one working according to the primary process— the "onirical" side of the affective symbolization, which works in terms of the mobilization of coinems. Accordingly, the affective symbolization is the process of projecting every object of experience onto coinems. In so doing, the individual charges every element of the experience with affective meaning. For instance, the student projects the teacher onto the affective category (i.e., the coinem) of "mother," consequently feeling and interacting with him/her as if he/she were the student's mother, that is someone having a function of holding, feeding and taking care of him/her. Coinems are just a few—Fornari speaks of the coinems as "the few things oniric symbolism deal with" (p. 73, our translation from the Italian original); they thus work as generalized classes, homogenizing the experience: patterns of experience that have no semantic linkage can be made identical by being projected onto the same coinemic category.[3]

Fornari's (1981) model is relevant to the current discussion for three reasons. First, it offers a processual notion of the unconscious that leads to it being seen no longer as an entity but as a *mental activity of semiosis*, characterized by a specific modality. Second, it puts the notion of affect at the centre of the understanding of the unconscious. According to the theory of coinems, and thanks to it, a semiotic standpoint in psychoanalytic theory equates to a theory of the affect—better, a theory of *affective semiosis*. In so doing Fornari goes beyond the Kleinian semiotic use of the notion of drive, radically freeing the psychoanalytic theory of this notion (substituted by a reference to linguistics and semiotics).[4] Third, Fornari's way of modeling affective semiosis preserves the nature of the primary process. This is evident for example in the way Fornari (1983) reconceptualizes the method of free association. The author highlights how, according to the traditional mode of using free association, what the patient says after having recounted a dream, in answer to the therapist's request to freely saying what is passing through her/his mind, is conceived of as a content of the unconscious connected to the images of the dream. On this basis, the content of the free association is very often used as the signified of the dream, the latter considered as the signifier. For example, if the patient says he has dreamt of a policeman getting angry with him, and afterwards, when asked by the therapist to freely associate, says that the day before he had been shouted at by his father, then the therapist would interpret that the policeman is the signifier of the father. Fornari highlights how this way of using the free association contradicts the primary process principle, because it assumes a structural difference between the patient's account of the dream—treated as a signifier—and the following statement produced in regime of free association—treated as signified. If one does not make such a distinction, in so doing keeping the "primariness" of the dreaming activity, then one cannot but take everything said by the patient as signifiers, whose combination has to be interpreted.

Despite these three major merits, coinems theory has a fundamental limit, in particular from a dialogical standpoint: it shares with the Kleinian theory a Kantian vision of the mind. In both approaches, the basic meanings sustaining the affective semiosis of experience—drives and *coinems*, respectively—are conceived as universal *a priori*, inherent properties of the transcendental individual mind. Although the content of these universal *a priori* clearly connote and therefore regulate relational contexts, nevertheless they do not depend on the intersubjective experience provided by such a context.

Interpersonal Psychoanalysis

A different path of development of the psychoanalytic theory gives a more radical alternative to the transcendental Kleinian model of mind and affect. A primarily American, post-World War II tradition has proposed a rereading of psychoanalysis with a strong focus on interpersonal relations (Gill, 1994; Greenberg & Mitchell, 1983; Hoffman, 1998; Mitchell & Aron, 1999; Modell, 1984; Stolorow, Atwood, & Brandchaft, 1994). Proponents emphasized the dialogical nature of the mind and the role of relational experiences in the organization of the psyche (Sullivan, 1953), coming to radically criticize the original Freudian theory of drives. One of the most representative authors of this approach, Mitchell (1988), stated that mind does not preexist relationships, but emerges within and by means of the intersubjective communication. Consistently with this idea, interpersonal psychoanalysis underlines that affective meanings and the relational field are recursively linked, each being the source and the product of the other. Being part of an intersubjective field elicits patterns of experiences of self and the other made of sensations, fantasies, ideas, feelings, acts and so forth. These patterns acquire subjective meaning according to the constellation of generalized emotional and relational experiences associated with positive or negative affective valences (e.g., pleasant, unpleasant; dreadful, disgusting and the like). Thus, previous experience provides a context for giving sense to the present moment (Stern, 2004) in terms of an affective meaning onto which the here and now is projected. In brief, the affective meaning works as the basic interpretant of the ongoing intersubjective field.

In place of Freud's topographical and structural theories of mind we envision an organized totality of lived personal experience, more or less conscious and more or less contoured according to those emotional and relational experiences. Instead of a container we picture an experiential system of expectations, interpretative patterns and meanings.... Within such a system or world, one can feel and know certain things often repetitively and with unshakable certainty. (Stolorow, Organge, & Atwood, 2001/2006, p. 675)

The Loss of the Primary Process

As outlined above, contemporary psychoanalysis has developed a semiotic approach to the mind, giving room to the notion of affective semiosis and at the same time overcoming the hypostatization of the affective meaning entailed in the implicit reference to a transcendental subject. Nevertheless, mainly in Northern American streams of psychoanalysis, this has not been achieved without a cost, namely, the abandonment of the psychoanalytic-specific reading of the unconscious in terms of primary process. This abandonment is the common ground of theoretical approaches that are quite different in other respects.

On the one hand, the quote from Storolow and his colleagues reported above highlights how interpersonal psychoanalysis tends to overlap notions of *unconscious* and *not-conscious*, and to conceive of affective semiosis as a form of sensemaking that works according to the rules of rational thought (secondary process, in psychoanalytic terms). Accordingly, affective semiosis is drawn as a form of mental activity which stays in touch with reality, though in a somewhat fuzzier and less constrained way than rational thinking does. In such terms, interpersonal psychoanalysis misses out on the specificity of affective semiosis. What remains is a form of subjective reaction to the environment, and emotions commonly called happiness, sadness, loneliness, and so forth. The "experiential system of expectations, interpretative patterns and meanings" to which Storolow and his colleagues (2001/2006, p. 675) refer is a constellation entailing an idea of the psychological reality as strongly shaped and regulated by idiosyncratic passions, desires and relational memories. Nevertheless, this kind of constellation has nothing to do with primary process, that is, the specificity of unconscious processes as described by Freud (1933/1964). In the final analysis, contemporary interpersonal psychoanalysis seems to have given up the specificity provided by the nuclear and foundational notion of primary process (Eagle, 1987).

On the other hand, a line of psychoanalysis striving to anchor Freudian theory to psychology has performed such a task by assuming a descriptive, non dynamic idea of the unconscious, defined in negative terms—namely, as *not-conscious*. Indications of this trend can be found in the work of authors revising psychoanalytic theory in the light of cognitive science (Epstein, 1998; Erderlyi, 1985; Singer, 1998). In a similar vein, the loss of specificity of the notion of the unconscious is provided by those models which propose a functional interpretation of it. According to this kind of interpretation, the unconscious is endowed with plans and goals, even though not under the control of conscious thought. A well-known example of this approach is provided by Weiss, Sampson and the Mount Zion Psychotherapy Research Group (1986) with their clinical theory centered on the idea of "unconscious plans"—the patient engages with the therapist with the unconscious aim of being confirmed in his/her own pathogenic beliefs concerning her/himself and others. For example, a patient asks the therapist to be held and understood; yet at the same time he behaves toward the therapist in a provocative way, so as to trigger negative feelings in the clinician. According to this approach, the patient is guided by the unconscious plan of finding confirmation of his unconscious pathogenic belief that nobody can welcome and understand him. Clearly, concepts like plans, aims, beliefs, goal-oriented action entail the idea that the unconscious has, or is the reflex of, a computational competence, namely, that it works in terms of secondary process.[5]

In conclusion, one has to ask if the renounce of the specificity of the psychoanalytic unconscious is a convenient cost to be paid. The argument put forward in the following pages is that psychoanalysis can contribute to a semiotic and dynamic model of sensemaking insofar as it takes into account both the horizontal dimension of intersubjectivity, and the vertical dimension of the intrapsychological processes sustaining both unconscious and conscious forms of functioning (Green, 2002/2005).

AFFECT

The discussion in the previous paragraph has hopefully provided indications of the complex role played by the affect in psychoanalysis. A psychology that wants to capture the dynamics of sensemaking has to account for this essential component of human experience. Unfortunately, the notion of affect is one of the most ambiguous and polysemic within the psychoanalytic tradition, and more generally, the psychological realm, where it is subject to a wide number of definitions and uses. It is therefore necessary to clarify how it is used in the current discussion.

A Notion Seeking a Definition

Freud did not use the term "affect" in one single way. In various parts of its writings, he implied a quantitative and somatic conception of such a notion, considering it as derivative of the drive—more specifically, as the amount of charge associated with the drive (i.e., as "sum of excitation") or as the somatic process of discharging the drive energy (i.e., as *cathexis*). In other part of his works, especially in those concerning clinical topics, the affect is conceived in terms of feelings working as *regulators*. This is already evident in *Studies on Hysteria* (Breuer & Freud, 1893/1955) as well as, even more clearly, in Freud's later work on signal theory (Freud, 1926/1959), which models anxiety as the affective state associated with bodily sensations fostering a feeling of displeasure that pushes the subject to react.

The *reference* of the affect is another source of variability in Freud's (1926/1959) theory. As concerns this aspect, two general ideas can be found. On the one hand, the affect is seen as representation and inner reproduction of experiences of the external world. Typically, in Freud's theory of trauma the affect is a quasi-hypnotic state of the mind resulting from traumatic experiences. It works to keep such experiences continuously active—somehow maintaining the mind outside of time, in the suspended present of the traumatic event. When the affect cannot be metabolized and remains, as it were, "undigested," then the traumatic experience preserves its power of colonizing the mind, and therefore of sustaining the person's psychic realty. On the other hand, Freud provided an idea of the affect as inner perceptions, that is, as representations of the body's state of activation.

> In 1915 and in 1923, in the first and second topographical theories, affects were placed in a system and were seen not only as springing from the drives but as being activated by the ego as well, being regarded as inner perceptions.... They were seen as unmediated inner perceptions, more primordial and influential than external perceptions and more commensurate in intensity and quality to inner bodily processes. (Stein, 1991, pp. 32–33)

Contemporary Views

Contemporary psychoanalysis has updated the original Freudian thesis on the affect, yet the conceptual articulation found in Freud's writings has been kept. Thus, the initial physiological modeling of the affect in terms of drive derivative has been updated as a result of the re-elaboration of the concept of drive in accordance with advances in biology, ethology and neuroscience. A trace of such updating is provided by the role the concept of arousal has gained in the contemporary psychological theory of affect. According to the classical theory of emotions of Schachter and Singer (1962), arousal is the state of generalized and undifferentiated neurovegetative activation elicited by the environment. This state is then subjected to interpretation (*appraisal*), and in so doing it is differentiated in terms of a given emotion, consistent with the contextual circumstances (for a similar, recent theory, see Barrett, 2006). What is interesting to notice here is that, in the final analysis, the concept of arousal is germane to the notion of drive, a sort of translation of the latter into psychological language (Stein, 1991).

On the other hand, the notion of appraisal paves the way to the recognition of the connections between affect and meaning. A way of highlighting this connection has been the recognition of the close, recursive linkage between emotion and cognition. According to this view, emotions are conceptualized as innate schematic values connoting the environmental objects and events in an unreflexive and unmediated way (Lazarus, 1991). Appraisal is thus inherent to the emotions: the individual enters into contact with the world primarily and very quickly in terms of generalized judgments (pleasant, unpleasant, dangerous, awful, and so forth) selecting and orienting the further analysis of the experience. This kind of approach is consistent with neuroscientific modeling of emotions. LeDoux (1996) distinguishes two circuits through which the brain processes the information concerning a dreadful stimulus. One path (that gets to the amygdala via the thalamus) is very fast, entailing only a rough computation of the sensorial information. The other path involves the cortical structure, and a more sophisticated, slower analysis of the stimulus. Moreover, the idea of the emotion as attribution of subjective value is close to the psychoanalytic theorizations that have tried to conceptualize the notion of affect in psychological terms, that is, in terms of feelings. For instance, consistently with the Kleinian view, Sandler and Sandler (1978) pointed out that the affect is the way of representing and connoting the state of the objectual bond, thereby performing a fundamental function of regulation of the self (and the relationship with the object).

Unconscious and Feeling

The conceptualization of the affect in terms of subjective value has constituted a major advance within psychoanalytic theory as well as a bridge between psychoanalysis and psychology for two main reasons. First, this idea has allowed the recognition of the motivational and communicational valence of emotions, evident for psychologists (Ekman & Rosenberg, 2005; Tomkins, 1970) and clinicians (G. S. Klein, 1976; Lichtemberg, 1989), as well as for the layperson. Emotions are subjectively felt as an impulse to act and are associated with reactions that work as very immediate signals for others, thereby serving as powerful regulators of both the subject and the other. Insofar as the affect is conceived as the attribution of subjective value to experiences and objects, then it is easy to conclude that the affect is a way of mapping the world in terms of how to engage with it. In the final analysis, the notion of value leads us to recognize that affect and action are strictly intertwined: emotionally feeling an object means to be ready and inclined to move towards (against, far from, on, and so forth) it, and at the same time, to express such an inclination to the object. Second, the interpretation of the affect in terms of value allows us to address a basic paradox that accompanies the psychoanalytic theory: the issue of their unconscious nature. Briefly, the point at stake is the following. As far as one conceives the affect in terms of somatic activation, its unconscious nature is preserved. Or rather, the somatic conceptualization of the affect entails the notion of a dynamic (not repressed) unconscious, namely, an unconscious that is so not because it is the container of ideational content kept out of consciousness, but because its way of functioning (i.e., the way of working defined by primary process) makes it inherently ungraspable for the consciousness. Hence the somatic conception of the affect allows affect to be considered in psychodynamic terms, consistently with the "true psychic reality" (in Freudian terms) of primary process. On the other hand, the idea of the affect in terms of feelings, that is, as subjective representation of the value of object, entails a secondarization of the unconscious, and this means giving up the dynamic nature of the affect and conceiving it in terms of representational contents that can be computed by the subject, in a way that is not so different from how the subject computes other contents of consciousness.

Alongside the path paved by Freud with his definition of the affect in terms of inner perception, several psychoanalysts have tried to address this issue, proposing the idea that affective feelings could be unconscious. Nevertheless, this solution raises more problems than it solves, because it leads to the paradox of a category of feelings that are unfelt. A way of avoiding such a paradox is to give up the view of the affect in terms of feeling—reserving such a term to the conscious representational domain (i.e., the linguistic self-description of emotional experience)—and focus on emotions, intended as embodied meanings. Accordingly, emotions are forms of somatic interpretation, namely, of assimilating the object to basic hedonic values. In this way, the meaning interpreting the object can be conceived of as presemantic, namely, as void of a discrete representational content; rather consisting of a specific disposition to act (which is the same as saying that it consists of a dynamic state of the body). Accordingly, the affect can be conceptualized as part of the psychological realm, as a subjective process of interpretation, and at the same time in dynamic terms, as unconscious process working according to primary process.

It is worth underlining how the idea of the emotions as embodied, unmediated and unreflexive connotation of experience forms a bridge between the psychoanalytic theory and the phenomenological vision of the situated and embodied nature of experience (De Leo, 2009; Ziemke, Zlatev, & Frank, 2007). According to this standpoint, emotions can be interpreted as the basic forms of shaping experience, or more, of knowing the world that the individual unfolds through and in the terms of her/his body, namely, in terms of basic hedonic values (positive vs. negative, exciting vs. relaxing) experienced prereflexively. Being in the world is inherent to the body and is lived in/through the body. Emotion is the first way the subject experiences the world in terms of the "lived" body. Therefore, feeling/acting the body is ipso facto the experience of the world. On this point, the French psychoanalyst Green's (1972) definition of the affect as the glaze on the moved body (p. 221) is illuminating.

To Summarize

The psychoanalytic discourse on the affect, intertwined with the psychological and neuroscientific theorization, leads to this notion being conceived in accordance with the following basic processes:

- *Somatic activation as embodied appraisal*. The affect is a dynamic of generalized bodily activation, that is, the basic way of prereflexively experiencing the world in terms of embodied meanings (emotions), consisting of basic hedonic values (positive vs. negative, exciting vs. relaxing) qualifying and construing the experience;
- *Self-other regulation*. The immediate appraisal of the experience has an inherent motivational and communicational valence, thereby making the affect a powerful, situated, preconventional semiotic regulator of the social bond;
- *Symbolization as subjectivization*. The patterns of sense-motor activation sustaining arousal are subjected to a continuous and recursive process of symbolization (also sometimes called mentalization). One can conceive of this process of symbolization as a process of incorporating the embodied meanings within an associative chain of signs (Green, 1973), thereby transforming raw experience (Bion, 1962) into representations, that is, the subsymbolic into the symbolic (Bucci, 1997; Damasio, 1999; Barrett, 2006).
- *Feelings* are the self-reflective output of this process, resulting from the introduction of the body into the realm of the secondary process, mainly through language. These feelings can then in turn activate the whole dynamic again, for instance as triggers for further affective activation.

AFFECTIVE SEMIOSIS

In the previous paragraph the general coordinates of a psychodynamic oriented theory of the affect have been outlined. On this grounds, a specific model of the affect—or rather, of affective semiosis—and the role it plays in sensemaking is provided below. Such a model rests on the idea that affective semiosis works mainly according to primary process. The presentation is divided into three steps. First, a model of the unconscious in terms of affective semiosis is presented. To this end, I focus on the seminal contribution of the Chilean psychoanalyst Matte Blanco (1975) who conceptualized primary process in logical terms. Second, some characteristics of the functioning and the phenomenology of the affective semiosis are described. Finally, in the following paragraph the contribution of the affective semiosis to sensemaking is discussed.

Matte Blanco's Bi-logic Theory of the Unconscious

Matte Blanco (1975; see also Carvalho, Ginzburg, Lombardi, & Sanchez-Cardenas, 2009; Rayner, 1995; Sanchez-Cardenas, 2011) proposed a theory of the unconscious to which one can refer, if one wants a semiotic understanding of the dynamic of primary process and its interaction with secondary process. As far as I know, no other model addresses this central issue in such a systematic way, a circumstance that makes Matte Blanco's "bi-logic" theory a cornerstone for those interested in modeling affective semiosis.

Following the Freud (1900/1953) of the *Interpretation of Dreams*, Matte Blanco's (1975) bi-logic theory assumes the unconscious as a specific modality of the mind's functioning. His formal analysis, based on the principles of the unconscious that Freud had recognized as the basis of dreams (condensation, displacement, plastic representation, symbolic transformation, absence of negation and time), shows that the unconscious logic is different from the rational mode grounded in the principle of noncontradiction, but none the less systematic.

Matte Blanco (1975) described the logic and semantic relations sustaining rational thought as *asymmetrical*. Such relations are asymmetrical in the sense that the positions of the terms of any proposition are not changeable—they may not be inverted without affecting the proposition's value of truth. For instance, if the proposition "A > B" is true, then "B > A" cannot be true at the same time; similarly, if it is given that "Marco is the father of Bruno", then "Bruno is the father of Marco" cannot be true.

In contrast, unconscious process is free of these constraints. Matte Blanco (1975) called the *symmetry principle* what he saw as its fundamental rule of working: The unconscious *does not set limits to the exchangeability between the terms of the relation*; this means that the unconscious treats all propositions generated by all possible permutations of their terms as the same.

Thus, for instance, for the unconscious dimension of mental functioning, Marco is the father of Bruno, and Bruno is the father of Marco as well.

According to Matte Blanco (1975), the exchangeability between the terms of the relation—as defined by the principle of symmetry—is the specificity of the logic of the unconscious. Such a logic openly and radically violates the noncontradiction principle of Aristotelian logic grounding asymmetrical thinking; its full application cancels any differences and produces homogeneity among signs that are part of any relation—insofar as Marco and Bruno are at the same time father and son of each other, they are not distinguishable from one another. In the final analysis, this means *that the logic of the unconscious transforms any relation of contiguity between two signs—namely, any association between these—into a relation of identity*.

Matte Blanco (1975) does not consider the two logics—asymmetrical and symmetrical logic—as juxtaposed, but as complementary. The asymmetrical way of thinking works in terms of setting categorical distinctions-relations within the homogenizing (symmetrical) way of functioning of the mind. Accordingly, symmetrical and asymmetrical logics are two *coextensive* ways of mental functioning that are antagonistic and complementary: every psychological process is the output emerging from their interaction, and therefore, a concrete act of thinking is always a mixture of both. One can differentiate various forms of thinking according to the proportion of symmetrical and asymmetrical logic characterizing the mixture. In the case of formal thought asymmetric logic is strongly prevalent. However, even this mode of thinking retains a degree of symmetry, in terms of unreflexive assumptions, analogical thinking, metaphoric linkages, unconstrained pertinentization, and so forth (Matte Bon, 1999). Conversely, even the delusional thinking of a schizophrenic is never the instantiation of the pure symmetric principle. This is so because working in terms of pure symmetry would mean a condition where no relation, therefore no mind process, would be possible. One can imagine the pure unconscious as an absolutely undifferentiated, presymbolic field of activation, produced by the encounter between the mind and the world, where no distinction has yet been made (for similar views, see Bucci, 1997; Valsiner, 2007; cf. Chapter 3). In sum, the unconscious process is the mental activity characterized by the strong predominance of the symmetrical logic associated with a quantum of asymmetrical logic, which is however present. The asymmetrical logic introduces elements of differentiation within the symmetrical totality (namely, the virtual condition of the absolutely undifferentiated field of activation), in so doing allowing the production of first basic relations, that is: the first protocategories—in the final analysis, the first forms of experience.

Emotions as Infinite Sets

Matte Blanco (1975) depicted this function of differentiation performed according to asymmetrical logic as the creation of "bags" of symmetry within the symmetrical totality's indistinctness.

> The fact that classes are differentiated from one another means that there
> are asymmetrical relations which differentiate them. Viewed in this light, a
> class, if and when the principle of symmetry rules, can be considered a por-
> tion of "symmetrical being" surrounded by a layer or skin of asymmetry. As
> the mind and the unconscious deal with various classes, we can say that there
> are as many "bags" of symmetry surrounded by films of symmetry as there
> are classes in our unconscious. (p. 104)

Bags are separate (therefore asymmetrical) from each other (one bag is
different from another), as the result of the basic activity of differentiation
carried out by the hedonic values, but each of them conserves symmetrical homogeneity inside itself. The very basic differentiation of the unconscious totality is the one producing the opposition between two global
scenarios—the class of GOODNESS as opposed to the class of BADNESS (Klein,
1967; see also Carli & Giovagnoli, 2011; Carli & Paniccia, 2003). In this
way a basic distinction is made in the undifferentiated field of activation,
and at the same time, foundations are laid for—on the one hand—a hypergeneralized assimilation of experience (i.e., the experience-as-a-whole
understood as GOODNESS—or BADNESS) and—on the other hand—the recursive process of further differentiation of the field of experience.

Inspired by mathematics, Matte Blanco (1975) interprets bags of symmetry in terms of "infinite sets", in order to show that they have homogeneous, hypergeneralized valence yet while being constrained, namely,
distinguished from what does not belong to them (this allows them to be
considered classes). For instance, the set of odd numbers is an infinite set
—its extension is infinitely generalizable—namely, it is always possible to
add a further element to it—yet not every element (any even number) can
be added to it.

The idea of meanings as infinite sets, resulting from the antagonistic
encounter between symmetrical and asymmetrical principles provides a
powerful tool for modeling emotions as the first semiotic output of the
dynamic of emergence of meaning in the mind. Indeed, emotions can
be conceptualized as the first hypergeneralized, homogenized classes of
meaning resulting from the rupture of the undifferentiated presymbolic
symmetrical totality.

Psychology and psychoanalysis tend to conceive of the emotions in terms
of a bodily state of activation endowed with basic hedonic values (positive
vs. negative, exciting vs. relaxing) nourishing and shaping the subjective

experience of the world as well as regulating the relational engagement with it (cf. Affect section, current chapter). Matte Blanco's (1975) theory does not contradict this general vision. Rather, it can be seen as a mode of interpreting it in a way that allows us a better understanding of the genetic function of the affect for sensemaking. In accordance with Matte Blanco, *one can see the hedonic value sustaining the affect as the basic form of asymmetriza-tion—that is of creation of hypergeneralized, homogenizing (symmetrical) classes of meaning (i.e., emotions).* In other words, the hedonic values can be conceived as the first "antagonist" of the unconscious, introducing a quantum of differentiation within the symmetrical totality.

Before concluding this part of the discussion, it is worth spending some words for a terminological specification. Terms like affect, emotion, feeling (and their plurals) are often used in an interchangeable way, and they have a rather polysemic aura. Therefore, it is useful to specify how I use them in the current discussion. I reserve the term "affect" for the basic psychological dynamic of reciprocal antagonization between the primary and secondary process, namely, the fundamental asymmetricization of the undifferentiated symmetrical totality—in the Matte Blanco (1975) terminology: the creation of bags of symmetry. Once so defined, the SDMS two-stage bootstrapping mechanism of sensemaking (cf. Chapter 3) lends itself to be considered a model of affective semiosis—with the propagation and fade-off steps being the way of interpreting in terms of sign network linkages the antagonistic movements of primary and secondary process respectively. In sum, as used here, the affect is a dynamic—rather than a discrete state—and this is the reason I have avoided the use of the term in the plural (affects), preferring the use of the expression: *affective semiosis* in order to highlight its dynamic valence. In a complementary way, as is evident in the discussion in this subsection, by the term "emotion" I mean the hypergeneralized class of embodied meaning resulting from affective semiosis—namely, as the bag of symmetry, or, in the SDMS terms, as the pertinent subregion of SIA emerging from the reduction of the dimensionality of the semiotic hyperspace (cf. Chapter 3).

Thus, if one wants, the affect is to the activity of thinking as emotions are to thoughts, that is, to the product of such activity. Such an analogy allows us to highlight how the two elements are part of the same dynamic gestalt, therefore distinguishable only for the sake of discussion. As the SDMS shows, like the case of thoughts for thinking, emotions are not the external output of the affective semiosis, but the latter's instantaneous organization. To use an image, emotions are the clusters of molecules of water with their reciprocal positions that one can observe if one pictures the vortex, stopping it in an instantaneous spatial-temporal slice. Such a web of reciprocal position can be seen as the structure of the vortex, yet it is not a separate entity from which the process unfolds—rather, it is the instantaneous state of the process, as such resulting from the dynamic and organizing its following instantiation.

Rereading Matte Blanco From a Dialogical and Semiotic Standpoint

Only recently semiotic models have begun to consider the affect as a constitutive part of sensemaking (Valsiner, 2007). Matte Blanco's (1975) theory provides the conceptual tools for moving ahead in this direction. This is so because the Chilean psychoanalyst's theory considers the mind in terms of classes of meaning and operations on meanings; at the same time, unlike other contemporary psychoanalytic theories (e.g., Stolorow, Orange, & Atwood, 2001), the bi-logic theory keeps the basic distinction between primary and secondary process, which is the distinction defining the specificity of psychoanalysis (Freud, 1933[1932]/1964).

On the other hand, as should be clear by comparing the SDMS with Matte Blanco's theory, a re-interpretation of the bi-logic theory is required in order to use it for the sake of developing a model of sensemaking that is able to take into account the unconscious dimension of the mind. Such reinterpretation concerns the vision of meaning grounding the theory. As a matter of fact, bi-logical theory shares the same traditional vision of meaning with other psychoanalytic and psychological theories. This makes Matte Blanco's proposal essentially a structuralist model—namely, a model considering the mind in terms of relationships between invariant parts (i.e. in terms of layers; cf. Matte Blanco, 1988), as defined by transcendental modes of functioning (i.e., symmetry and asymmetry principles). Those parts of mind vary in their specific phenomenological content and output; yet they are invariant in their way of functioning and in their properties.

Consider the following example given by Matte Blanco (1975) of the symmetry principle in action. He reports the case of a schizophrenic, who was bitten by a dog and for this reason went to a dentist. The Chilean psychoanalyst interprets the case in the following way. The dog bites P (the patient). According to the symmetry principle this means that P bites the dog too. Now, biting can be seen as a bad act. Therefore, the dog and P are doing something bad. Yet, as a result of the symmetric *pars-toto* identity, those who act badly are bad. Again, according to the symmetric *pars-toto* identity, the dog and P's teeth are bad as well. According to the symmetrical point of view, being bad, being damaged, being decayed is the same (all of these attributes are part of the generalized class of badness). Therefore, P goes to the dentist for his bad/decayed teeth.

One might admire the thoughtfulness of Matte Blanco's analysis, his capability of providing an innovative clinical interpretation. Yet, at the same time one cannot but recognize that this interpretation entails a vision of the patient's story that is: (a) focused on the semantic content; (b) intended as something held in the mind of the patient; (c) elaborated exclusively in terms of transcendental functions of the mind. The pragmatic aspect of the story—the fact that the patient has told it to someone, and in so doing has performed an action, with a communicative value—which in the final analysis concerns the dimension of desire—is left in the background.

Imagine two different interpersonal contexts in which the story could have been told. One context is the patient who has gone to the dentist instead of going to psychotherapy. The other context is the patient going to the dentist that he knows is the same as the therapist's. Well, according to the point of view of the content of the story and the transcendental function in terms of which it can be analyzed, such difference of contexts is irrelevant. But it is evident that it is not so at the level of telling the story, namely, at the level of the intersubjective meaning is performed by the act of telling just that story—that sequence of signs—in a specific way, to a particular addressee in a contingent interpersonal circumstance.

The thesis proposed by this book is that Matte Blanco's theory is not incompatible with taking into account this dialogical and dynamic level of communication. Yet, to move in such a perspective, one has to reframe the bi-logic theory from the traditional structural notion of meaning as categorical organization of the semantic system—a notion that in the final analysis Matte Blanco retrieved from de Saussure (1916/1977)—to the dynamic and semiotic notion of meaning discussed in the first part of this work (in particular, in Chapters 1 and 2), that conceives of it as the way signs are used in the social circumstances of language games. Such a reframing produces three major complementary shifts, which I have already addressed. First, the idea of the meanings as local models of relations among signs—rather than as semantic categories produced by a transcendental rule (*dynamic tenet*). Second, the idea that the meaning is not the content of the individual mind, but it is inherently intersubjective, since it is the product of how signs are used in the social circumstances (*dialogical tenet*). Third, the idea that such a use does not only have a semantic function, but what one thinks, feels, says and does is performed for the sake of generating objects of experience (*semiotic tenet*).

PHENOMENOLOGY OF EMOTIONS

The reading of affective semiosis and emotions in terms of symmetrical sets enables us to recognize and understand better some aspects of the way they work.

Generalization and Homogenizing Through Absolutization

Emotions signify each thing in terms of generalized classes: they do not recognize a mother as an individual, but *tout court* as the whole class of all that is associable (therefore made identical) with being a mother—that is, in the final analysis, as *mother-ness* (Rayner, 1995; Salvatore & Freda, 2011). Examples of generalization are numerous: consider the awe one can feel in front of one's superior or another figure with some authority over her/him (a teacher, a policemen, an elderly relative...). Such a feeling cannot be related to the actual attitude and power of the figure; rather, it reflects a meaning that the person attributes to the generalized class of the authoritative and powerful figures the interlocutor is identified with.

The fact that affective semiosis treats every element as identical to the class also means that all the qualities and characteristics of the class are attributed to the element, and that it will have them to the maximum degree (the unconscious does not modulate). As a result of this absolutization, every element is made identical—homogenized—to every other element that is part of the same generalized set of meaning. Stereotypic thought shows hints of this affective mechanism. All the objects that are projected in the stereotypical class are confused with each other regardless of their individual specificity, and treated according to all the properties associated with the class. Thus, to give an example, stereotypic thought tends to connote all Muslims as Arabs and all Arabs as extremist male chauvinists and terrorists—giving all of them the maximum extent of the qualities of enemy-ness, dangerousness, wickedness that are associated with the stereotype. The experience of falling in love is another manifestation of the process of absolutization. When someone is in this state, they view their beloved in an idealized way—that is, as having, to the highest extent, the totality of the qualities associated with goodness and beauty. Obviously someone falling in love understands that reality is different, but they do so by means of a further operation of asymmetrization, placing constraints on the absolutized meaning.

It is worth highlighting that it follows that the reference of affective semiosis is never the discrete object (i.e., a person, an event, a thing). This is because, given the symmetrical valence of affective semiosis, the discrete object is in any case assimilated within the hypergeneralized and homogenizing infinite class. In other words, every discrete object is experienced as the whole field provided by all the elements with which the discrete object is connected and therefore "symmetrized" (i.e., made identical). Hence, the affective semiosis is the reifying transformation of the encounter with the world—namely, the ongoing flow of stimuli—as the unitary experience of a total object. One can pick up a hint of this level of experience when a new situation is encountered. In those circumstances sometimes one may be aware of how, though very briefly, we emotionally[6] experience the situation as something of global value (threatening, warm, distancing...), before differentiating the experience through a specific attentive focus.

Reification

Conscious thought makes and keeps a distinction between the signifier and the signified, with the former standing for the latter. Thus, the signifier represents the signified, but does not substitute it. In other words, the picture of a serving of spaghetti can be used to denote the dish, but if one decided to eat it, one would not be fed.

On the level of affective semiosis things go differently. According to the symmetry principle, signifier and signifier are linked through an identity linkage. The signifier does not stand for the signified: *it is what it represents*. The process of wish-fulfilment described by Freud concerns this characteristic: unconscious representations (oneiric images as well as phantasies) are not mere figurations of the wished-for goal, but their hallucinatory satisfaction. In the same way, the infant who sucks her/his thumb is doing more than self-stimulating: she/he is experiencing her/himself being nourished. The thumb is not something standing for the breast: it *is* the breast. The same mechanism is evident in many circumstances where the affective semiosis is salient. Take the example of a flag, which in many cases, is felt and used as something more than the conventional sign of the nation: it renders the value of the country present and alive (Salvatore, 2012).

Recognizing the reifying valence of the symmetrical principle leads to conceiving affective semiosis as a device of *mental hypostatization*.[7] Affective semiosis does not attribute meaning to objects of experience that preexist to it. Rather, consistently with the Kleinian idea of the affect creating the objects subjected to emotional connoting (see above, §1), *affective semiosis generates objects within the mind, through the act of connoting them* (Salvatore & Venuleo, 2010).

It is worth recalling here the observation made by Bowlby (1961) concerning the elaboration of mourning. In this kind of circumstance, a feeling of anger against the absent object often takes the place of the first reaction of grief. The model of affective semiosis proposed here allows for an understanding of this mechanism. Anger can be interpreted as the way affective semiosis makes (hallucinates) the absent object present-for-the-mind through the act of connoting it, albeit in negative terms: because it is gone it is bad, but it is present as being bad. To use the terminology of linguistics, affective semiosis performs an inversion of the relationship between subject and predicate. It is not the argument that logically precedes the predicate (as happens on the asymmetrical level, where the predicate follows the argument, adding something not-yet-given to the latter). Rather, it is the predicate that precedes and produces the argument.

The semiotic principle of reification is well known by those who work in the field of advertising. In many circumstances the message on the product does not serve the function of informing about the object. Rather it is aimed at affectively construing (generating) it by making it present in the public's mental landscape (N. Klein, 1999). This circumstance is particularly clear in the case of paradoxical and negative advertising (i.e., "do not buy this product"; "it is a bad object").

The reifying valence of affective semiosis can be highlighted from a complementary standpoint, underlining that it has no intensionality, that is, no possibility of referring to hypothetical representations. This is an evident implication of reification. As a matter of fact, asserting that affective semiosis generates the object that it connotes is equivalent to saying that *affective semiosis always and only predicates presences*. This comes back to Freud's (1900/1953) seminal observation about the absence of negation in dream work as well as to Klein's (1999) model of the infant's affective transformation of the experience of the mother's absence into the presence of the persecutory object (see Psychoanalysis and Semiosis section, current Chapter).

Anthropomorphization

The objects generated by affective semiosis as mentally salient are not discrete pieces of the reality ("objects" in the ordinary sense). Rather, they are *embodied experiences of relationships*. In other words, objects are animated by a communicational and relational dynamism oriented toward the symbolizing subject. Affective semiosis is a kind of picturing the world shaping it as engaging with the subject. We do not feel an object as bad, rather as *bad-with-me/us*. Such an addressivity is already entailed in the Kleinian model of affective semiosis of the absent mother, who is not symbolized as a recognition of a fact, but as an object endowed with a destructive agency against the person who is symbolizing (as a persecutory object).

One can find a sign of this aspect of affective semiosis in the child's way of hitting the table it has just run into, and saying "bad" to the table. On the other hand, everyone who loves knows that this circumstance is not limited to infancy. One who loves does not feel the lack of commitment (interest, attention…) from the beloved as just a fact. She/he feels this lack as something that the beloved performs against her/him—the beloved is accused of lack of commitment and is guilty of not loving. This is evident in episodes of unfaithfulness, which are generally experienced as a form of betrayal, that is, as a presence occurring against the partner, rather than an absence in the conjugal relationship produced as a result of the presence of another relationship.

A relevant corollary of the anthropomorphization is the inherent dialogicality of the affective semiosis: This is so in accordance to three complementary points of view. First, affective semiosis is an emergent product of the dialogical dynamic. Indeed, given the fact that unconscious logic does not recognize differences between self and other, one has to conclude that affective semiosis encompasses all the contributions to the dialogue, before and regardless of any distinction of their source.[8] In this sense, affective semiosis is by definition the systemic effect of an intersubjective process. Second, as we have seen, affective semiosis concerns the whole field of experience, before and regardless of the self-world distinction. Thus, as the Kleinian theory has clearly highlighted, affective semiosis is the way of emotionally connoting the relationship in itself. Third, as the discussion on anthropomorphization should have shown, the intersubjectivity is the content of affective semiosis—this is what was meant by the previous claim that affective semiosis shapes the field of experience in terms of relational engagement. In sum, one can say that the relationship is the subject, the reference and the object of affective semiosis.

To summarize, in this section some characteristics of affective semiosis have been highlighted. In so doing affective semiosis has been pictured in its being a semiotic and inherently intersubjective process, whose product is the transformation of the flow of ever-changing contact with the world into a global, generalized, and homogenized object of experience, endowed with an inherently subjective, anthropomorphic addressivity. Connecting this statement to the ones provided in the previous paragraphs, one can add that such addressivity is signified and shaped through and in the terms of embodied meanings, that is, of hedonic values that can be considered the first form of meaningfulness, therefore of subjective mental life.

THE ROLE OF EMOTIONS IN SENSEMAKING

The discussion above should have clarified the view of affective semiosis as the basic dynamic grounding sensemaking and making it emerge from/working through the body. Like the image of sensemaking as the sculpturing entailed in the two stage bootstrapping mechanism (cf. Chapters 2 and 3) shows, the way SDMS models the emergence of meaning is based on the idea of the salience of an embodied, basic level of hypergeneralizing signification of the ongoing encounter with the world—what I have conceptualized in terms of the psychoanalytic notion of affective semiosis (after having reinterpreted it in a semiotic way).

According to the SDMS, emotions lend themselves to be rethought in terms of very highly generalized and abstracted scenarios, namely, affective scenarios made up by embodied protodifferentiations of the field of experience (Salvatore & Freda, 2011).

As has been said (cf. Chapter 2), by the term "scenario" I mean a meaningful unit of subjective experience of the world sustained by a redundant (micro)domain of life. Consistently, affective scenarios are classes of embodied meanings:

- highly *abstracted*, in the sense that they are defined and differentiated from each other in term of polarized hedonic values (e.g., pleasant *vs* unpleasant);
- highly *internally homogeneous*, because all the contents of experience within the class are defined in terms of the shared hedonic value defining the class—which means that intraclass contents are made identical with each other. To use Matte Blanco terms, relations are possible among the bags, while within any bag only symmetry works (everything is the same of everything else).
- highly *generalized*, because they cover any content of experience, assimilating it to the polarized hedonic value.

Human experience takes its basic and primary shape in terms of this kind of scenario (Salvatore & Venuleo, 2008). Thus, the affective scenario designates the basic, emotional SIA grounding the immediate experience of the world, namely, allowing and channelling the extraction of a meaningful pattern (i.e., objects) from the ongoing flow of stimulation. Thus, *the affective scenario* is the first psychological moment of subjective construction of the environment. The affective scenario is the unitary global mental state associated with the continuity of the experience the subject is embedded in, before and regardless of the articulations between past and present; here and elsewhere; me, thou, it, us, you. It is a hypergeneralized, embodied construction sustaining the mind and allowing it to have content—that is, conferring the lived sense of being in relation with an animate object.

Finally, it is worth highlighting one last point. Affective semiosis is not a separate moment from other levels of sensemaking: individuals represent the discrete elements of the reality according to an affective scenario, and their representations constitute an experience of such reality as a whole.[9] Thus, for instance, at this very moment I am typing on the keyboard striving to elaborate and express some ideas on sensemaking. At the same time, I am "immersed" in the affective scenario of my actions. It emerged this morning, when I sat down at the computer, as the local stabilization of the infinite flow of interacting signs (my feeling on my activity, my ideas, how I slept, the sensation associated with the chair I am sitting in, etc.). I can grasp this affective scenario only partially and vaguely, as it escapes language. I would depict it as a state of pleasant tension. Yet, according to the model proposed in this chapter, this scenario is not the feeling as I have tried to describe it above (i.e., the feeling of pleasant tension); rather, it is a hypergeneralized, homogenizing meaning that is active in my body —better: it is the *hic et nunc* shape of my body—and sustains the sense of myself in the present moment. Insofar as this affective meaning is an infinite set of potentiality of linkage among signs, one can only have (and give) an impression of it, by resorting to metaphoric terms. In this case, the image I find useful is the following: |being in relation with a likeable and active object, activating me and enabling my enjoyment.| The state this image evokes encompasses a very large class of experiences through one's lifetime, unified by the fact that they share the same hedonic value. This basic affective tone can be said to have its origin in the experience of the infant playing within an interaction with its mother, thus producing a pleasant movement of increasing-decreasing tension—this tension being the content of a transmodal, presymbolic experience of the intersubjective field (for an analysis of this kind of process, see Stern, 1985). The point at stake is the following: while I am typing and working on ideas that I am trying to make meaningful, obviously I am in a functional relationship with the concepts and the mediating devices—I am engaged with a discrete activity, dealing with a specific object. Yet, at the same time I am living the experience of mother-infant playing-ness.[10]

In conclusion, the affective scenario is embedded in the course of sensemaking, conveyed and reproduced moment by moment by ongoing acts of meaning. Obviously, people are usually somehow able to differentiate, to place constraints on generalization. In so doing, they generally succeed to a certain extent in focusing their attitudes and evaluation on specific objects. Nevertheless, this does not mean that the affective meaning disappears. Rather, the differentiation adds a further level to sensemaking, but it does not cancel the salience of emotions.

CONCLUSION

This chapter has been devoted to modeling affect from the semiotic perspective provided by the SDMS. The way this issue has been addressed is indebted to psychoanalytic theory, in particular to Matte Blanco's (1975) formal rereading of the psychodynamic notion of primary process. This theory enables us to get a better understanding of the basic role played by affect in sensemaking: the constitution of experience in terms of meaningful gestalts (scenarios, according to the terms adopted above) is grounded on the generalizing and homogenizing valences of the affect. Such affective gestalts can be seen as the basic, global mental states embedded within the encounter with the world, triggered and fostered by the encounter. This means that any specific engagement with a discrete element of the reality (an object, an event, a practice, a person, etc.) occurs within the global semiotic field provided by the affective scenario (the SIA, according to the SDMS). And this leads us to say that any engagement with a discrete element of the world keeps the affective valence of the scenario of its instantiation. Hence, when someone experiences the piece of reality g in terms of the sign a, they are experiencing the scenario A-$ness$—that is, they are experiencing the infinite set of signs a_n which comprises the affective meaning. In other words, the affect works as the hypergeneralized, basic and prereflexive SIA grounding the way persons interpret experience.

In sum, the recognition of the affect as a basic component of the dynamic of sensemaking enables a comprehensive conceptualization of meaning to be developed, as such consistently able to take into account the phenomenological, subjective dimension of sensemaking as well as its microdynamic.

NOTES

1. In psychoanalytic terminology the term "object" is used as a generic term to mean the piece of the world the subject relates with. Therefore, the object can be a person as well as any other content of experience taken as the target of desire.
2. The generative capability of the affect is consistent with the fact that Melanie Klein conceives it as a very basic dimension of mind, working according to the primary process. And the primary process is unable to make distinctions between the self and the object (see below). Consequently, every state of the self is experienced as a state of the undifferentiated self-world totality.
3. Incidentally, emotional response categorization theory (ERCT) (Niedenthal, Halberstadt, & Innes-Ker, 1999). provides a view of emotions based on such a homogenizing a-semantic function. According to the ERCT, persons tend to create categories of objects on the basis of the object's emotional quality— namely, things that evoke or have evoked the same emotion are categorized in the same homogeneous category.
4. Actually, this change of reference cannot be considered an absolute necessity. As a matter of fact, the concept of drive has not been totally surpassed, and its validity is not as dubious as it is often pictured. Various psychoanalysts have proposed a revision of it, in order to make it more consistent with the contemporary knowledge produced in biology and neuroscience. For instance, Kernberg, 1990—cf. Stein, 1991) has defined drive as a hierarchical system of affects, thus reversing the traditional Freudian idea of the affect

as a derivative of the drive. Other authors have set out to reconceptualize the drive in terms of motive (Lichtenberg, 1989). In these approaches, the reference to the concept of drive generally entails a functionalist vision of the mind (i.e., the mind as a mechanism to be explained in terms of causes and/or goals). Thus, despite the path of integration between drive and meaning proposed by Klein, contemporary psychoanalytical approaches referring to the concept of drive (*inter alia*, Brenner, 1973, 2002; Busch, 1993) are quite far from a semiotic vision of the psychological process.

5. Stolorow and colleagues (2001/2006) define the unconscious as the affective dynamic that the subject subtracts from intersubjective communication, because she/he feels incompatible with the regulation of the relationship. Typically such a definition condenses the two previous criticisms: it is merely descriptive and negative (unconscious as what-is-kept-not-expressed); it entails the reference to a function of directionality—the unconscious does something in order to avoid/overcoming a state of incompatibility. Note that this definition of the unconscious is germane to the conceptualization of the psychoanalytic notion of repression proposed by Billig (1999, 2003) within the frame of discursive psychology.

6. The feeling—what we can make correspond to the naïve term "emotion"—is not affective semiosis, which according to the argument put forward here follows the rule of primary process, for which it cannot be exhaustively represented by conscious thought. Nevertheless, feeling is one of the domains of human life—together with dream and delusion—where the clues of the symmetric quality of affective semiosis are more evident. For this reason here and later emotional experience is used as a source of examples.

7. Also Peirce highlighted the process of hypostatization that he described as the process of conversion of a quality into an object (i.e., the man is honest is converted into "the man possesses honesty). Neuman (2010) provides a thoughtful discussion of such a concept supported by a linguistic computational analysis. Though it is presented in a slightly different way from how it is discussed here, the hypostatic abstraction is a phenomenon of reification that can be consistently interpreted as a sign of the reifying power of the affect, therefore an indication of the constitutive role the affect plays in language and thinking.

8. This consideration means that the affective semiosis keeps its inherent dialogicality also when instead of an external dialogue performed by two or more people engaged in a communicative exchange, there is one person producing her/his idiosyncratic chain of signs sustaining an inner dialogue. This is consistent with the dialogical theory stating the intersubjectivity of thinking as well as of perception (Linell, 2009).

9. It is worth noticing that conceiving the affective scenario as ubiquitous means that it cannot be thought of as a kind of structural obstacle/limit of sensemaking, as the commonsensical view of emotions as enemies of thinking suggests. Rather, according to my thesis, the affective scenario has an essential, constitutive, systematic role in sensemaking. No act of sensemaking would be possible without the grounding of the affective semiosis.

10. According to the symmetric principle, it is meaningless to decide whether I am living it as the infant or as the mother. The context is the sense of the intersubjective field as a whole.

CHAPTER 8

EXERCISES OF
SEMIOTIC REFRAMING

The SDMS aims at being a general, foundational model providing an abstract, generalized definition of the psychological object. As such, its value does not depend only on its inner consistency, but also on its capacity to ground the psychological modeling of specific phenomena.

That is what this chapter is devoted to. Four constructs of interest for Psychology are examined: *psychotherapy*, *group*, *social development*, and *economic choice*. The choice reflects my interests: many other constructs could have been selected. However, the ones addressed are representative of a broad enough variety of psychological domains, from clinical to social psychology. For each of them, first, I provide a criticism of the commonsensical definition usually adopted; then, I propose a different conceptualization, based on the SDMS, namely, on the view of the psychological phenomena in terms of the dynamic of sensemaking. In so doing, I intend to show how the SDMS, and more in general the semiotic approach it reflects, enables an innovative, heuristically fertile approach, freeing Psychology from constraints imposed by the adherence to common sense.

THE "PSYCHOTHERAPY" OBJECT

The Ontological Assumption

In their search for the determinants and constants in the functioning of the clinical exchange, students of psychotherapy start from the founding

Psychology in Black and White: The Project of a Theory-Driven Science, pp. 143–172
Copyright © 2016 by Information Age Publishing

assumption that psychotherapy is a specific object, endowed with its own peculiar way of functioning, distinct from those associated with other kinds of human relations, and therefore to be understood in terms of a particular model of functioning.

This is quite understandable—any scientific object is such because it is characterized by a specific model of functioning differentiating it from any other object: the boundary of the object of scientific knowledge O is defined by its model of functioning M_O. Thus, for instance, the falling of stones is not an autonomous object of scientific knowledge, because such a phenomenon does not have its own way of working, compared, say, to the falling of shoes. Needless to say, the falling of stones can be an interesting target of investigation, but this is not the same as saying that being a target constitutes *ipso facto* being the *object* of scientific knowledge.

In the case of psychotherapy, the foundational assumption is evident in one aspect: if one reviews the journals that publish studies on psychotherapy, one finds articles that focus on facets and components of psychotherapy both as the object of investigation and as source of data as well. The possibility of understanding psychotherapy through the study of other forms of human relation is not considered. This choice is consistent and understandable insofar as one considers psychotherapy a specific entity—namely, insofar as one considers psychotherapy as having its own peculiar mechanism of functioning, that makes it different from other instances of human relations (e.g., the relation between teacher and pupils).

A clear expression of this ontological assumption is provided by the so-called "drug metaphor" (Russell, 1994). According to this image, psychotherapy is conceived of as a set of active factors, namely, elements endowed with the capacity to produce a curative effect on the target, exactly like a drug that is the vector of chemical factors with a curative function.

It is hard to think that such an assumption can be grounded on empirical evidence. The definition of the object comes first, as a foundational basis of the interpretation of data, rather than depending on the latter. Thus, the grounds of this assumption are theoretical—it is an ontological assumption defined at the theoretical, albeit implicit, level. According to this ontological premise of psychotherapy research, a given piece of human communication (psychotherapy, in our case) is seen as having a specificity of functioning, due to the phenomenical characteristics it expresses (e.g., modality of engagement, time, space, duration, linguistic markers, and so forth). In turn, such characteristics derive from the specificity of the psychotherapy's aim (i.e., broadly speaking, clinical change, recovering and the like) compared to other forms of human communication.

Thus, in the final analysis, the particular *function* that psychotherapy pursues is seen—generally implicitly—as constituting a particular *way of functioning*. In sum, the *function* (i.e., the psychotherapy as a particular aim of human communication) is reified, transformed into an *entity*, a piece of the world (psychotherapy as a thing peculiar to itself, having its own inherent mechanism of functioning).

The Paradox of Reification

The reification of the function is not a productive act for psychotherapy research. An analogy can be useful to highlight how theoretically untenable it is. Take two people, each of them playing roulette in two casinos —one very big and crowded, the other small and reserved for selected clients. One is a professional player, who lives on what he is able to win by playing; the other is a clinical researcher who decided to go to the casino to refresh herself from quite a boring conference on psychotherapy research. Thus, the two players have very different aims and their playing happens in two contexts differentiated in many respects (the number of players, the constraints on the bets, the size of chips adopted, the spatial-temporal contingencies of the game, and so forth). These differences will deeply affect the strategies of the two players—the type and the amount of bets, levels of attention, time spent at the green table, and so forth. But, does this mean that the mechanism at the basis of the game varies as well? Obviously not! A mathematician would not consider the personal reasons to play that the players have, relevant for the understanding the way the game functions. This is so because the mathematician would conceive of the contingent phenomenologies of the game as instantiations[1] of the same basic dynamic concerning the same fundamental object, rather than expressions of two different models of functioning reflecting two different objects—the game of roulette played by professionals versus the game of roulette played by clinical researchers. Indeed, our mathematician will consider the game of roulette itself as an instantiation of a more general abstract object (the dynamic of probabilities)—as such belonging to the same class as other instantiations like poker, blackjack, betting on sports events, and so forth.

In sum, the purposes of the actors performing a dynamic of human relationship as well as its contextual conditions are parameters that affect the way such a dynamic is expressed (i.e., the way it is instantiated); yet the model of the dynamic (its basic rule of functioning) is not dependent on such a parameter—it is always equal to itself. Someone may enter psychotherapy to solve a personal problem or to find an attentive listener for their need to pretend they have such a problem, yet the process of psychotherapy functions in accordance to the same dynamic.

The reification of the function leads to a paradoxical conclusion. If one accepts that the purpose motivating and guiding any form of human relations defines the model of functioning of such a form, then one should accept that as many objects as purposes exist and are conceivable at the level of social action. In the final analysis, one should elaborate a theory—and a corresponding theoretical field—for any cultural articulation of social action—for instance, one should elaborate the psychology of going to the museum, the psychology of eating a pizza, the psychology of business meetings, the psychology of watching soccer matches, and so forth. The futility of such an expansion of discrete context-dependent psychologies can be seen. Yet, in actual fact it is what happens. Currently, psychology includes a great many niches devoted to specific objects defined exactly in terms of the cultural articulation of the social action—for example, not only psychotherapy, but also psychology of tourism, psychology of sport, work psychology, psychology of the consumer, and so forth. What distinguished these articulations of social action that have had the honour of being chosen as the object of psychological discourse from others is precisely a cultural aspect—the social relevance of the action involved, and of the purposes implied. Thus, sooner or later one can expect that a psychological theory of the iPad user will be elaborated, as has already happened with the psychology of diving (Venza, 2006).

Psychotherapy as Procedure and as Semiotic Format

The discussion above highlights the need not to take the object "psychotherapy" for granted, and to examine its conceptual analysis in greater depth. To this end, it is worth starting by recognizing the double-sided phenomenical aspect of psychotherapy.

On the one hand, psychotherapy is a method, grounded on scientific and functional criteria guiding and constraining the clinician's action. Accordingly, it has to be recognized as a *scientifically-guided procedure*, namely, a set of rules defined by the clinical theories (psychoanalysis, cognitive therapy, and the like). Moreover, any clinical theory states that the implementation of the rules leads to a specific output, defined from within the clinical theory as well. For instance, the psychoanalytic theory states that a certain kind of therapist action—for example, interpretation—produces a specific impact on the patient—for example, insight; cognitive therapy states that the normative intervention of the therapist leads the patient to abandon the misbeliefs that are at the basis of his/her problems, and so forth.

On the other hand, psychotherapy is a *semiotic format*, namely, a form of cultural action mediated, constrained and oriented by meanings (aims, desires, scripts) that clinicians and clients negotiate through the mediation of the cultural environment they are part of. From such standpoint, psychotherapy is the result of the assimilation of the procedure to other social practices and roles (medical therapy, talking with a friend or a parent, confession). More specifically, at least in the Western cultural context, the format in which psychotherapy has developed is that deriving from the merging of the scripts of medical intervention and professional service (Carli & Giovagnoli, 2011; Wampold, 2001). As a social practice, psychotherapy is an instance of the social world: it is a form of culturally informed practice that has gathered legitimacy through being inscribed in the cultural frame of the scientific-professional activity, in so doing being symbolically construed as an activity mobilizing normative social expectations, as well as private and public resources. Thus, psychotherapy works according to the cultural environment—or rather, it exists as a product of such cultural environment—and pursues aims that are normatively defined by the social demand, as reflected in the expectation of the clients and institutions mediating the relationship of service between clinicians and clients.

Thus, the conceptual issue is how to model the relation between the two such phenomenical dimensions—scientific-guided procedure and social practice. One way of solving such an issue is to eliminate it at its root, foregrounding one dimension and backgrounding the other. As argued above, the current mainstream psychotherapy research, with its ontological assumption lends itself to be seen as a way of absolutizing the methodological-rule based dimension of psychotherapy. In contrast, but analogously, postmodern criticism of psychotherapy tends to use the recognition of psychotherapy's worldly role to negate its scientific value to the point of claiming that psychotherapy is nothing more than one of the many rituals and procedures through which people define their way of being in the world. In some cases this criticism goes so far as to consider psychotherapy a device for promoting social conformism (e.g., House, 2003). Yet, such radical criticism runs the risk of throwing out the baby with the bath water. Treating psychotherapy merely as a social practice, a ritual, does not help to understand it better and to make it a better device for addressing clinical problems. Moreover, it greatly underestimates the aspect of expertise and the specific utility that clinical practices are able to express. In the final analysis, the recognition of what psychotherapy shares with other forms of social interaction does not mean that psychotherapy is merely a form of social interaction. It is like claiming that writing a scientific paper is just a matter of conversation, because it uses the same linguistic tool as other forms of conversation.

Is it possible to avoid such diametrically opposed and complementary extremisms of negating or absolutizing the scientific content of the psychotherapy? Is there a different solution to the bivalence of psychotherapy than negating one dimension for the sake of recognizing the other one?

Freud (1904[1903]/1953) proved to be aware of this issue. His solution was to conceive of the linkage between the two dimensions in a functional way. At the beginning of the psychoanalytic movement, addressing the issue of the aim of the analysis, he recognized the difference between psychoanalysis as *method*—as such following its own inner logic, blind to the reason for its use—and psychoanalysis as *cure*—as such oriented to a goal, which is defined in the negotiation between the theory and the social expectation. Psychoanalysis as a method follows rules defined from within psychoanalytic theory—in Freud's terms: the interpretations of the unconscious for the sake of making the unconscious conscious. In contrast, psychoanalysis as cure pursues a goal that cannot but be defined in terms of, and according to, the normative system of values and the associated canonical idea of normality that is valid in the cultural environment— according to one of Freud's formulation as: "the restoration of his [the patient's] ability to lead an active life and of his capacity of enjoyment" (p. 253).

Now, what ensures that performing a blind-to-goal methodological rule of analysis makes it pursue a socially defined aim concerning the way of being in the world—for example, the "capacity to have an active life?" Freud provided quite an axiomatic answer to this question, which seems more a way of avoiding it rather than addressing it. According to him, psychoanalysis can put the two aspects into a functional relationship—to stay in conjunction with each other.

> In psychoanalysis there has existed from the very first an inseparable bond between cure and research. Knowledge brought therapeutic success.... Our analytic procedure is the only one in which this conjunction is assured. (Freud, 1926[1925]/1959, p. 256)

Anyway, Dreher and Sandler (1996) show that despite such a claim, Freud did not feel the issue was solved, and this is so in the current debate within psychoanalysis too.

> there is evidence that the two aims were not in fact evenly balanced in his [Freud's] mind, and this is a source of conflict for analysts which remains to this day. Psychoanalytic research was the gaining of knowledge *through analysing*, and the problem of the "aim of cure" as opposed to the aim to conduct research (that is, the aim to analyse), was, as we shall see, the run like a thread through subsequent discussion of analytic aims, during Freud's lifetime and afterwards. (pp. 11–12)

On the other hand, that there is conflict between the two dimensions is quite understandable. This is evident at the level of the aims. Let's assume that psychotherapy as method is able to produce a certain psychological effect (PE) in the client, as defined from within the clinical theory of reference—for example, the making the unconscious conscious. Now, by definition, PE has no value per se. What produces value for the client is the improvement of the (broadly speaking) capability of adjustment (AD) associated with PE—for example, the capacity for enjoyment. Thus, Freud's tenet of conjunction can be expressed in the following way: AD = f(PE)—the social aim pursued by the cure (the adjustment) is a function of the level of the psychological effect obtained by the method. Yet, such a formulation is insufficient for two complementary reasons. First, AD is not definable in terms of a universal condition. What has to be considered an improvement in the adjustment is a matter of historical-cultural construction. Canonical criteria of normality and desirability vary from time to time and place to place (Grasso & Stampa, 2011)—as this is quite evident in the case of homosexuality; up to not many years ago, one can find many statements in the psychoanalytic literature entailing the idea that a good analysis with homosexual patients should conclude with the change in the client's sexual preference (cf. Friedman & Downey, 1998). Today the ideal of quality of life is different and therapists are oriented to consider the capacity of living and recognizing one's own need and desire as a goal of adjustment. And thus, the normative purpose of psychotherapy has changed as well—for example, in terms of enabling/empowering the subjects' capacity to pursue their own projects and desires. Second, even if the direction of the adjustment were quite stable, the relation between PE and AD, however, is variable. A PE favors ways of feeling and behaving whose functional value depends on the forms of social life. Thus, a given PE can be a resource in a certain social context, but have no relevance in another, and even be a constraint in still another. For instance, to be suspicious, avoiding social engagement, having weak contacts with one's own feelings, can be seen as a problem in many social contexts, but could be a lever of development in other contexts as well.

More in general, it has to be recognized that the two dimensions—the rule-based procedure and the semiotic format—are independent of each other and therefore can hardly be connected functionally in a systematic, invariant way. This is evident if one thinks that the clinical procedure could be implemented through cultural formats that are different from the one represented by the psychotherapy-as-professional service. This can be seen in the transformation of psychotherapy in the passage from private practice to the public institutions of welfare (community health centres, psychiatric services). With this passage, some of the peculiar characteristics of the traditional clinical format were lost or changed (e.g., payment, number of sessions per week, the therapist's neutrality). And one could image how the format could have been different if it had been implemented in a different cultural and economic system. Moreover, procedure and format are inherently in conflict with each other. On the one hand, the procedure limits the possibilities of negotiating the format, while the latter exposes the former to a systematic pressure to adapt it to the social desire. One could write a history of psychotherapy in terms of such a dialectics, analyzing how the extra-scientific requirements and demands have progressively been able to partially transform the method, and how the method has been able to partially shape the clients' expectation.

In sum, the functional way of considering the nexus between psychotherapy as practice and psychotherapy as scientifically grounded method has the merit of avoiding the scotomization of one of the dimensions; yet, it has to be considered a way of presenting the problem, rather than a solution. In the following section, I propose a different way of conceptualizing the relation between the two dimensions, based on the view of sensemaking as a field dynamic.

Dynamic, Field Parameters, and Processes

According to my argument, one has to consider psychotherapy as a local instantiation of a general object—communicational exchange (Salvatore, 2006; Salvatore, Gelo, Gennaro, Manzo, & Al-Radaideh, 2010). This definition entails the distinction between the *dynamic* and the *process* instantiating it (cf. Introduction). The dynamic is the object's fundamental form of functioning- that which defines the object as such. The dynamic follows basic, a-temporal and invariant ways of functioning. It always repeats itself in the same way. Consequently, it lends itself to be depicted in terms of universal and abstract rules. Such rules define the logical boundary of the object—they define what can be considered a local manifestation of the general object compared to what cannot.

The dynamic is always instantiated within and through local field conditions. In the case of communicational exchange, it is carried out through the mediation of specific sociocultural contexts of opportunities and constraints, shaping the purposes and the condition of success of the exchange. Such contingent parameters do not modify the dynamic, but define the way the latter instantiates itself in a contingent phenomenical manifestation, namely, in a *process*. Thus, the same dynamics can be instantiated in terms of many processes, due to the variety of field conditions mediating its unfolding.

Consider physics. It deals with generalized objects, abstracted from their contingent empirical content—falling bodies, not falling stones, shoes, dishes and the like. Using the terminology adopted above, the dynamic of an object of this kind is modeled in terms of universal and invariant rules—for example, the theory of gravitational acceleration. Even if the dynamic is invariant, it brings about processes very different from each other, due to the variety of field conditions (e.g., the contingent parameters) involved. The trajectory of a bullet, the flight of a bird, the falling of a stone, the orbit of a planet and so forth, are phenomena that are covered by the same fundamental dynamic and at the same time are characterized as different processes, due to the field parameters associated with their functioning. Processes have to be studied *locally*, namely, in accordance and in terms of their contingent empirical content. This is what disciplines like ballistics, astronomy, and hydraulics do, as domains of knowledge addressing specific phenomenical fields. Yet, the shape/way of functioning of such phenomenical fields (in the terminology adopted here: the process) always reflects the basic dynamic concerning the general object of which such fields are the instantiation. Thus, for example, the trajectory of a bullet does not follow specific rules, different from the ones followed, say, by the trajectory of a planet or a stone or a tennis ball. What makes such processes phenomenically different are the field parameters mediating the instantiation of their common dynamic. Consequently, to understand the trajectory of the bullet one cannot disregard the model of the dynamic, namely, one cannot avoid considering the bullet as the generalized object "body endowed with mass." And this is the same as saying that the modelization of the dynamic is the conceptual ground of the field analysis of local processes.

Psychotherapy as Human Communication

According to the analogy with physics, psychotherapy is one of the very many processes of human communicational exchange. The specific form of communication comprising psychotherapy is created by the mediation of field parameters depending on the cultural and institutional system of social action. Thus, the characteristics of the semiotic format of psychotherapy—its being an institutionalized practice shaped by the cultural frame of the professional service—works as the set of field parameters of the communicational dynamic sustaining the clinical exchange. These parameters include: the professional format for the therapeutic encounter, the socially defined values of the aims pursued by the interlocutors, the organizational forms in terms of which the psychotherapy is performed (e.g., the folk models that frame the clinical procedures as "healing"). Such features make psychotherapy a specific, particular form of the communicational exchange, compared with infinite number of other field versions of the same general object, such as romantic engagement, writing scientific papers, watching a soccer match, participating in a job meeting, giving a present, selling a car, and so on.

In sum, psychotherapy works in a certain way not because of its being an ontologically autonomous object endowed with its own particular dynamic, but because of the fact that it operates through the general semiotic dynamic of human communication. Yet its specificities are set up in terms of specific field conditions that lead the general semiotic dynamic to be instantiated in terms of a unique, stable enough process—the modeling of which is the specific target of psychotherapy process research and whose stability grounds the epistemological suitability of conceiving the clinical method a scientifically-based system of criteria.

Some Methodological Implications

This view of psychotherapy has important theoretical and methodological implications. Below the three relevant ones are discussed.

Going Beyond Psychotherapy in Order to Understand It

I conclude that the basic mechanisms that shape psychotherapy—making it more or less consistent with its clinical aims—are the same that work in other forms of human communication. And this is the same as saying that there is no point in focusing only on psychotherapy if one wants to find an answer to the question of why psychotherapy works and how it works—and why certain conditions (e.g., the duration of the intervention, the kind of therapist intervention) affect it in a certain way. One can—and should—study psychotherapy also by analyzing work meetings or everyday conversation within families or at school and the like. This is so not only because in so doing one could have more data and cases at disposition or for the sake of making comparisons. More radically, approaching psychotherapy as an instance of a more general dynamic leads to a change in the scientific agenda on psychotherapy.

However, the field of psychotherapy research has moved in a different direction. Currently, psychotherapy research pursues two basic purposes (Hill & Lambert, 2004). On the one hand, it deals with the basic question of the efficacy of intervention (outcome research). According to this standpoint, the issue at stake is to what extent psychotherapy is able to carry out the clinical aims it intends to pursue (e.g., improving the psychological conditions of patients) and what are the characteristics and conditions that mediate or moderate such effects (characteristics of the patient, the therapist, the treatment). Thus a typical format of the findings of this kind of investigation is the following: the psychotherapy T (e.g., cognitive therapy, psychoanalysis) is able to produce an outcome O (e.g., reduction of the symptoms), where the relation between C and O is moderated by the factor Mo (e.g., the patient's personality structure), or depends on the presence of the mediator Me (e.g., the patient's capacity to elaborate his/ her own emotional state). On the other hand, the research is aimed at understanding the clinical process, namely, what happens within the session between client and patient and how this process produces an effect on the patient's conditions (process and process-outcome research). According to this standpoint, the issue at stake is the description of the different elements sustaining the clinical exchange—for example, the therapeutic alliance, the modalities of the relationship between patient and client, the content and the structure of the communication, and so forth—their evolution through the course of the treatment and their influence on the outcome. Thus, in this case the typical finding of this kind of research is the following: the process works in accordance with the model P (e.g., a certain trajectory of the therapeutic alliance through the sessions; the distribution of certain narrative innovations within the patient's speech), and P favors/triggers/is associated with the outcome O.

Now, this level of knowledge is relevant and helpful, but it is hard to consider it conclusive. The phenomenical connections like T(Mo, Me)O and P(Mo, Me)O—as well as their possible combinations—are just an initial, descriptive step concerning the regularity observed at the level of phenomenon. Therefore, these phenomenical connections rise, rather than solve, the issue of what dynamics bring them about as its particular effect. In sum, the actual findings of psychotherapy research are not the result of an explanation, but are what has to be explained. And the explanation that is required concerns with the basic dynamic characterizing psychotherapy as an instantiation of a more general, abstract object (Rocco, Gennaro, Salvatore, Stoycheva, & Bucci, in press). In the final analysis, the current status of psychotherapy research is similar, from a logical point of view, to that of a naïve observer who has realized, after systematic observations, that every time one opens one's hand the stone held in it falls out. Our naïve observer has produced knowledge and has acquired a capacity of foreseeing thanks to it. Nevertheless, such knowledge is an initial, descriptive step, which raises the very question: why does this regularity occur? And to address such a question the observer has to treat the phenomenical field hand-stone as a case of a more general object—the falling body. In so doing the observer becomes capable of understanding the phenomenical regularity in terms of a basic dynamic (the gravitational attraction). In the same way, seeing psychotherapy as an instantiation of human communication is required in order to deepen the understanding of mechanisms according to which psychotherapy shows certain regularities under certain conditions.

Incidentally, it is worth noting that within psychology and social science this kind of abstract and generalized approach has a strong tradition—for example, Piaget studied the child for the sake of developing a general theory of intelligence; ethnomethology studies daily communicational events as equivalent forms of distributed social competence. Nevertheless, this tradition seems to come to a halt when faced with the applied domains—and so nowadays we have work psychology modeling human behavior at work, psychology of sport modeling the human behavior in sports contexts, and so forth, through to psychotherapy that models human behavior in the circumstances defined by clinical aims and associated social expectations (health, wellbeing, care).

A further consideration is prompted by what was stated above. The negation of the ontological autonomy of psychotherapy leads not only to extending the focus beyond psychotherapy, but also to seeing other domains of psychosocial investigation as a fruitful source of innovative concepts and methodologies. Semiotics and linguistics are examples of domains that can represent very rich sources for psychological theory and methodology resources (Gennaro, 2011; Salvatore, Gelo et al., 2010; Zittoun, 2011), as well as the dynamic system theory (Lauro-Grotto, Salvatore, Gennaro, & Gelo, 2009, Salvatore, Lauro-Grotto, Gennaro, & Gelo, 2009; Salvatore & Tschacher, 2012).

The Call for a Unified Semiotic Clinical Theory of Psychotherapy

According to the discussion above, one has to distinguish between three levels/functions of analysis. One level has to be aimed at developing a general *theory of the process*, namely, to answer the basic question of how the clinical exchange works, due to what basic dynamic and how the field parameters mediate the relation (see previous section). Faccio, Centomo, and Mininni (2011) provide an example of this kind of analysis, when they propose to consider psychotherapy in terms of the analysis of constrains produced by the reified valence of the language, that trap people within their metaphors.

The other level concerns the analysis of the regulation of psychotherapy as social practice. This level can be further articulated. On the one hand, it is aimed at understanding how method-guided operations and the regulation of the social interaction that is performed through such operations, interact with each other. In general terms, this issue is raised by the inherent conflict between these two polarities—the method-guided operations do not assure the regulation of social interaction and its reproduction. This is clearly evident at the level of the inherent divergence between the aim of the client in accordance to which she/he decides to ask for therapy (e.g., "I want to be happy," "I want my wife comes back") and the methodological objective performed by the therapist (the performing of the analysis without memory and desire, to use Bion's [1967a] statement). The aim of this level of analysis is to model how this kind of dialectic works and can be functionally regulated within the clinical exchange. One could define this the level of the *organizational theory* of the clinical exchange —the analysis aimed at modeling how psychotherapy as social practice unfolds, despite—or thanks to—the inherently conflictual positions of client and patient.

On the other hand, psychotherapy research has to address the basic issue of analyzing the relationship between the output of the process—as defined in terms of the clinical theory—and the outcome of the social practice, as negotiated by therapist and client through the mediation of the cultural environment (Salvatore & Valsiner, 2014). In sum, this is where to address the issue of the dialectic relationship (Hoffman, 1998) between the application of the method and the aim of the client, who asks (and pays) for this application. One could call this the level of the *strategic theory* of the clinical exchange. As we have said above, it is motivated by the fact that psychotherapy research cannot take for granted the conjunction between method and cure (to use Freudian terminology) and is therefore required to study what, how, through what sociocultural process, and in what conditions, the output of the method (PE) is able to generate value for the client (AD).

Now, the view of psychotherapy in terms of the dynamic-field parameter-process division lays the foundation for considering these levels of analysis (processual, organizational, and strategic) as part of a unified model of psychotherapy. On the one hand, the organizational and strategic level of analysis provides the way of modeling the field parameters instantiating the psychotherapy; the theory of process allows us to understand how such field parameters shape the clinical exchange in a way that enables psychotherapy to have a strategic valence, namely, to generate value for clients.

Re-reading the Specific-Versus-Nonspecific Debate

The vision of psychotherapy as an instantiation of a general dynamic has an effect on the way of interpreting the empirical findings provided by the studies. This can be shown in relation with the historical debate concerning the specificity of the effects (Wampold, 2001). Starting from the mid-1970s, various studies and reviewers (Luborsky, Singer, & Luborsky, 1975; Sloane, Staples, Cristol, Yorkston, & Whipple, 1975; Smith, Glass, & Miller, 1980; Strupp & Hadley, 1979) have accredited the conclusion that the main forms of psychotherapy have a similar level of efficacy. As Luborsky and colleagues (1975) entitled their famous review, quoting the Dodo bird's verdict in *Alice in Wonderland*: "Everyone has won and all must have a prize." Now, each form of psychotherapy assumes that its efficacy depends on its own specific factor—for example, psychodynamic therapy considers interpretation and insight its specific factor, cognitive therapy the change in misconceptions, behavioral therapy the modification of learnt associations, and so forth. Consequently, if more or less all of these forms of psychotherapy were shown to be efficacious, then—the supposedly obvious conclusion—they were so because of their nonspecific factors—namely, the factors that all forms of psychotherapy share (e.g., the expectation of improvement, the experience of being involved and held in a warm, welcoming relationship). This was quite a paradoxical conclusion —the greatest capacity of demonstrating efficacy led to a reduction of the value of the proof! Psychotherapy is efficacious, but due to what it shares with any form of caring and holding.

Now, one can observe that the interpretation of the Dodo bird's verdict as a marker of nonspecificity of the effect is based on the assumption that the forms of psychotherapy are self-contained objects. Based on this taken-for-granted assumption, the similar efficacy of the forms of psychotherapy can be interpreted only in two ways: either as depending on the shared nonspecific ingredients, or as a collection of alternative types of efficacy, each of them depending on the specific ingredient of each form of psychotherapy. This can be explained in the following way—consider any form of psychotherapy as a set of ingredients (a, b, ...); moreover, for the sake of simplicity, consider that each set holds two ingredients: one that belongs only to the set and another that is common to all sets. The former is the specific ingredient (s_x), the latter the nonspecific (ns). Still, consider N forms of psychotherapy, each of them defined by a set (s_x, ns) – say 3 forms of psychotherapy: A (s_A, ns), B (s_B, ns), C(s_C, ns). Now, given that as regards their efficacy A = B = C, one has to conclude that such efficacy can depend on: sn (thesis of the nonspecific effect) or by s_A, s_B, and s_C (thesis of parallel specificities). And it is clear that the higher the number of forms of psychotherapy proving to have equivalent efficacy, the less appealing the thesis of parallel specificities becomes, entailing a multiplication of *ad hoc* hypotheses.

The thesis of the nonontological autonomy of psychotherapy allows a reinterpretation of the Dodo bird's verdict. If one considers psychotherapy as an instantiation of a generalized object, then the many specific ingredients can be conceived of as many contingent, local field versions of the same pattern of the basic dynamic. And this leads to overcoming the objection of the multiplication of *ad hoc* hypotheses, making it plausible to think of any specific ingredient being effective because of its being the local expression of the same generalized property/dynamic. In sum, the idea of psychotherapy as a nonautonomous object allows the Dodo's verdict to be reinterpreted in terms of abstraction, rather than of nonspecificity. According to this standpoint, the equivalence of efficacy could reflect the fact that the specific ingredients work as factors of efficacy, but not because of their contingent peculiar content; rather, their influence could be due to the fact that they reflect the same singular generalized dynamic property in different field conditions (i.e., the different forms of psychotherapy).

This can be expressed with an analogy with an imagined situation. Consider a researcher coming from a far-away planet of another galaxy —a "generalized Martian"—who is sent to Earth to study how human beings relate to each other when they go shopping. So, the Martian student chooses a store and starts to observe. And what it sees is something like the following. A first human takes some boxes from the shelves and goes to a counter labeled "pay here," where there is another human sitting behind the counter. There, the former extracts a piece of colored paper and gives it to the latter. A second human performs the same operation; once at the counter, however, it extracts a small card and inserts it in a machine, then retrieves it. Finally, a third human, after taking the same boxes from shelves, and having reached the counter, writes something on a piece of paper and hands it to the human sitting behind the counter. In all three cases the conclusion seems the same: the three humans exit from the store with the things taken from the shelves, and this seems to confirm their expectations.

Now, let us assume that on the Martian researcher's home planet there is no notion of money. How will it interpret the observation made? Indeed, from its standpoint, the acts performed by the three humans cannot be traced back to a common ground. Thus, the actions have some aspects that the Martian conceives of as nonspecific—for instance, taking boxes from shelves and going to a counter labeled "Pay here"—and some aspects conceived of as specific, being different from one human to the others –for instance, the operation performed at the counter. Thus, given that the three transactions have an equivalent positive outcome (all the three clients leave the store supposedly satisfied), the Martian will be led to conclude that this positive outcome is due to the nonspecific factors found in all the transactions. Once she returns to her distant planet she will publish an article on a very high impact journal announcing the discovery that the essential ingredient for efficacy in a trade transaction in stores on earth is the fact that whoever takes things from the shelves then goes to a counter labeled "Pay here."

Actually, given that we have the notion of money and are aware of how it works, we know that the operations performed by the three clients are three contingent versions of the same basic dynamic: transfer of values. The empirical content of such operation varies, in accordance to field conditions, but this difference concerns the way the same dynamic is performed—paying cash, paying by credit card, paying by check. Thus, what is seen as specific and differentiating factors by the Martian researcher, from a more abstracted standpoint can be conceived of as local versions of the same pattern of basic dynamic. Needless to say, this logical hierarchical shift can be carried out insofar as one has a theory of the generalized object thanks to which the contingent element can be interpreted as a local form of the same abstracted property—your Martian researcher is unable to consider the three forms of payment as local versions of the same function insofar as it does not have a theory of money and its use. And this leads us to the conclusion: abstraction enlarges our capacity for interpreting data, but requires theory if it is to be performed.

GROUP

The Ontologization of the Construct

It happens quite frequently to come across articles in which the construct |group|[3] is reified, that is, treated in naturalistic terms, so to speak, a state of reality that is gathered by the observation. Thus, the group is hypostatized—it is considered endowed with of a particular essence, as such identifiable as a peculiar phenomenon, having its identity of functioning distinguishing it from what is other than it. This trend to hypostatization can be traced in main interpreters of this area of psychological thought, as the following quotations show.

> [I...] find myself sitting in a room with eight or nine other people—sometimes more, sometimes less—sometimes patients, sometimes not. When the members of the group were not patients, I often found myself in a peculiar quandary. I will describe what happens. At the appointed time members of the group begin to arrive; individuals engage each other in conversation for a short time, and then, when a certain number has collected, a silence falls on the group. After a while desultory conversation breaks out again, and then another silence falls. It becomes clear to me that I am, in some sense, the focus of attention in the group. Furthermore, I am aware of feeling uneasily that I am expected to do something. At this point I confide my anxieties to the group, remarking that, however mistaken my attitude might be, I feel just this. (Bion, 1961, pp. 29–30)

> Seven, eight, nine patients, suitable for a common approach, meet regularly once a week for an hour and a half with the Therapist. They are comfortably seated, in a suitable room with adequate seating arranged in such a way that they face each other and the Conductor. The atmosphere is informal. The purpose of their meeting is to discuss their problems. The period over which these sessions are to continue is to be determined by their own condition. Flexibility and spontaneity are the key notes. (Foulkes, 1948/1983, p. 69)

> A therapeutic group is an ad hoc environment we create artificially ... on the basis of meetings according to certain rules, in which various people (6 to

8) interact, communicate and share the rules with each other. The meetings take place once or several times a week for a period not predetermined, although limited, terminable. (Puget, Bernard, Games Chaves, & Romano, 1982, p. 91, my translation from original in Spanish)

The group ordinarily consists of 17–35 people, men and women of average age, reunited in a room that allows to form a single circle, so that each is visible to everyone else. The conductor sits between them, supported by one or two colleagues. The group includes, usually, some observers too; these usually do not speak, even if, at some point of the course of the group, it may happen that one of them could begin to speak.... The group is open, that is continuous over the years, and is therefore susceptible to withdraws and new admissions. The use of the "thou" is a prescription. (Ancona, 2002, pp. 235–236, my translation from original in Italian)

Two aspects of the quotations above are worth highlighting. First, in all the excerpts the group is defined—or at least implicitly assumed, as in the case of the quotations from Bion and Foulkes—on the basis and in terms of a set of concrete elements: the group is made up of people, meeting in a certain space-time point, with a certain number of components. One may wonder: according to what standpoint is this kind of definition different from that provided by ordinary language, as one can find in a dictionary and used in everyday conversation? It seems to me, that there is no differ-ence—a politician, a mother, a postman, a teacher, a doctor, a greengrocer, and so forth, use the term "group" exactly according to the same meaning as used by the eminent authors mentioned above.

Intended as a limited set of coexisting interacting people (and/or what-ever else further characteristic is used), the group is not a psychological construct, but *the description of a state of the world*. The process of objectifi-cation that Moscovici (1961/1976) used to characterize the relationship between scientific knowledge and its use in daily life discursive contexts, is reversed here. Indeed, in this case it is psychology that encroaches on common language and derives its own object from it. In sum: the quota-tions reported above show what was mentioned in the Introduction: the group is not a construct generated in a modelistic way; rather, it is a con-tent of everyday life which psychology borrows as its own object.

Second, in the passages cited, functional rules are considered defi-nitional and/or characterizing the group and its use (particularly in the clinical setting): the frequency of appointments, prescription of "thou," arrangement in a circle, the fact that sick as well as not-sick members may participate, and so forth. It is not difficult to trace the implicit assump-tion that grounds these rules: the idea that the group has its own specific nature—its inner modality of functioning—and the way of handling and using it has to comply with that nature. Take in this sense, the case of the prescription of the "thou" as well as of the circular arrangement. It is obvious that these parameters make sense insofar as one interprets them as ways of making the practice of the group consistent with its nature, its essence. It is as if one said: given that the group is—that is, its essence consists of—a condition of interpersonal closeness, then it requires people to adopt forms of communication that are consistent with such a condition (hence the "thou"); in the same vein, given that the group is a context of multifaceted and distributed exchanges, then it is necessary for the spatial arrangement to go along with this feature (hence the circular setting).

The Group From Entity to Regulative Sign

In the Introduction I have already proposed a number of critical issues concerning psychology's tendency to ground uncritically the definition of the explanandum on commonsensical categories. Here I confine myself to adding an additional argument concerned more specifically with the topic under discussion: reference to the group as an entity contradicts the contextual nature of the psycho-social phenomena. Consequently, the idea of describing psychological objects (the group, but also personality, communication, learning, and so forth) in terms of entities endowed with an invariant way of functioning is a simplification which may be useful as a form of approximation or for reasons of communication but it does not lend itself to grounding scientific knowledge of psychological phenomena. In fact, if one accepts the tenet that psychological processes are situated, contingent to the context of their unfolding, then one should recognize that any arrangement of interhuman affairs can assume, if not infinite, at least a very large number of forms and dynamics of functioning. The shape of these forms and dynamics of functioning is defined due to the position played by the human affairs involved in the system of activity motivating it. Consequently, modeling such forms in terms of invariance means representing the psychological process involving an oversimplification.

An example may be useful. Consider the classroom. One might consider it a group engaged with a certain task. Accordingly, the classroom's functioning would reflect the functional and structural characteristics of the group. Actually, this is the way many psychologists and teachers look at the classroom, approaching it as if it were a group—as to this point, one can refer to the many strategies of intervention based on the idea that school activity improves as a result of increasing the quality of group bonds in the class. In the final analysis, such strategies (e.g., interventions aimed at developing group cohesion as a way of preventing drop-out) are based on the idea that the quality of the classroom functioning depends on the degree the group approximates how the group should be and operate.

Actually, according to the point of view proposed here, there is not a group as something other than the classroom; there is not a further entity grounding, making up and fostering the classroom functioning. The piece of human interaction represented as the classroom is so because of its being a classroom, not a group, namely, because of its being an institutional and organizational device—namely, a system of activity—that mediates and shapes the ongoing, reciprocal engagement among the participants to the activity (teachers, students, principal, stakeholders). It is worth adding that the ontologizing view of the class as consisting of a group is an epistemological fallacy that has heuristic and practical consequences. Indeed, as we have said above, it leads us to invert cause and effect: the contingent process of semiotic self-regulation of the system of activity is not recognized, while its effect (that is, the representation of the class in terms of group) is treated as its causative entity. Thus, the instance of human exchange is split and separate from its contextual embeddedness, that is, from its being always and just an activity—a relationship-to-do-something, therefore shaped by the situated task to be carried out. At the same time, an idealized image of relatedness (the group) is hypostatized, endowed with its own autonomous life and therefore with the capacity to foster the activity. Elsewhere I highlight the very critical consequences for psychological analysis and intervention in the school context of this double movement of splitting and reification (Salvatore & Scotto di Carlo, 2005).

Insofar as one gives up considering the group as an entity with its own intrinsic mode of operation, such a concept loses its explicative valence. However, it does not necessarily follow from this that the use of the category is also given up. Indeed, such a notion is useful, insofar as one consider it as a regulative sign, namely, a meaning in terms of which the participants to the activity self-represent their engagement (Salvatore, 2012)—for example, "we are a group." Let's get back to the example of the classroom. Students may represent their interaction as a "group." But in so doing, it is not its essence that is described, but a classroom that uses the sign "group" to talk about itself through and under the terms of the reification of an idealized relational dimension (the "group"). Thus, one is led to conclude that it is the classroom that produces the group as a symbolic device used for the sake of semiotic regulation of its functioning—rather than vice versa.

SOCIAL DEVELOPMENT
The Need of a Psychological Interpretation

The way of considering the social development is subject to several interpretations, each of them framed within a more general paradigmatic view of social phenomena. For instance, according to the economic standpoint, social development is somehow equated to growth (e.g., Acemoglu, 2009). A criticism of the equation between social development and economic growth has been carried on by those who have criticized the idea of gross domestic product as the central indicator of progress, in favor of the quality of life as the core task of societies (e.g., Hartmann, 2014; Martirani, 1985). Psychology seems absent from such debate. Needless to say, aspects concerned with subjectivity are taken into account as inherently associated with the quality of life. Thus, from this standpoint one could say that the view of development takes into account psychological aspects. Yet, this is different from providing a *psychological definition* of social development.

Actually, there are several cases where psychology has provided its interpretation of concepts coming from different scientific domains. Consider, for example, the notion of culture, originally defined by anthropology, which has been reframed in terms of sensemaking in accordance to the semiotic view of psychological phenomena (Valsiner, 2014). The same can be said for the economic notion of *demand*, which Carli (1987; Carli & Paniccia, 2003) has modeled in a psychological key—that is, the demand as the intersubjective unconscious symbolization of the user-consultant relationship grounding the exchange between consultant and user.

As to the notion of social development, it may be appropriate to reframe it in psychological key. This claim reflects the following reasoning. The notion of development that feeds the various theories and practices of social development involves the issue of resources (economic resources and/or social resources—e.g., civism); thus, social development is made contingent to the availability of resources. Yet, one has to take into account the structural, systemic crisis of (financial as well as institutional and symbolic) resources as a distinctive trait of contemporary societies. Consequently, a notion of development being depending on the availability of resource is destined to create a short-circuit: to assume as condition what has to be carried out. From that it descends the utility of rethinking such concept in order to free its definition from the dependency on resources and thus to enable it to ground innovative models of social planning and action (Fini, Guidi, & Salvatore, 2012).

The Semiotic View of Social Development

The psychological definition of social development I propose is based on the SDMS view of social dynamics as sensemaking. The semiotic approach offers a reinterpretation of the concept of development which frees this concept from the dependency on the availability of resources. According to the SDMS, the development can be conceived of as the *increase of the variability of the sensemaking dynamic*.

Sensemaking with limited variability is a social dynamic where signs come in a rigid relationship with each other. In such a system the sensemaking follows redundant, preestablished, trajectories. A system of this kind reproduces the structures of meanings given over time, assimilating the variability of the environmental states to them. The reproduction of the existing will be the rule of such a semiotic context, namely, the assimilation of the unknown to the known: the familiar as the measure of things. It is worth noting that this vision of a system with reduced semiotic variability—therefore, a low development regime—can be associated with phenomena that another language may qualify in terms of cultural deprivation and/or backwardness. Phenomena such as racism, amoral familism, privatistic use of public resources, free-rider behaviors, to name a few, lend themselves to being interpreted as epiphenomena of symbolic assimilative models that ground and foster self-referential logics of action, devoted to the reproduction of the acquired assets, unable to find a constraint in the recognition of the externalities they produce (Carli & Salvatore, 2001). The actor that absolutizes his/her own particularistic interest treats the (broadly speaking) environment as a resource of its own reproduction; in other words, interprets the world as a function of the representation of his/her own particular interest. To the extent that this form of assimilation is proposed as all-encompassing, it does not retain the ability to perceive the costs it generates in other regions of social space—which, incidentally, explains why, by definition, familism is *amoral*: it does not chose to be so; it just does not "see" beyond the membership bonds.

In contrast, a highly variable sensemaking is a social dynamic comprising a plurality of trajectories of meaning, as the result of the systematic ability to reorganize its organization, accommodating it in accordance with environmental constraints and variations. Such a system, therefore, enters into a relationship with the variability of the environment in the sense that it tends constantly to innovate itself in order to compete with the environmental variability—that is to say, to extend the capacity to map it. It is worth noting that the dynamic of accommodation (the flexibility of the structures of meaning in relation to the exploration of the not-known) that characterizes the system cannot be absolute. A system operating exclusively in terms of accommodation would be a system void of memory, immersed in an eternal present—paradoxically, not much different from a radically assimilative system. The development, then, is a matter of balance between the maintenance of systemic boundaries and the ability to make them permeable to another reality that qualifies its environment.

Development as Strangeness

The conceptualization of the notion of social development in a semiotic key provides a chance to reason about forms of social action pursuing development. From the considerations made above, a general methodological principle can be derived: *the pursuit of social development is an exercise of limits*, namely, a practice of the suspension of the assimilative self-referentiality sustaining—to a different extent—any dynamic of sensemaking.

In psychology such a suspension has been conceptualized in terms of *strangeness* (Paniccia, 2003). The figure of the *stranger* marks the intermediate space between the friend and the enemy. Both of these polarities are a reflection of assimilative self-referentiality. The friend is known—it is the one with whom one shares membership; the enemy is known as well, assimilated—even though in negative terms—so as to make it predictable and thus preserve the relation of reciprocity. The intermediate space between these two semiotic attractors is the space of openness to otherness, assumed as a potential resource because of—rather than in spite of—its condition of irreducible distance. In sum, strangeness is the ability to hold one's gaze on the otherness of the Other.

The argument I put forward is that promoting development can be thought of in terms of activating *practices of strangeness*. Quality and processes such as the use of resources, the ability to make medium-term plans, the willingness to participate in the construction of public assets and the recognition of the universality of areas of social life—in a word, what we usually call *civism, social capital*—are ultimately conceivable as forms of relationship with the strangeness, namely, the interpretation of otherness as the source of increasing the opportunity of sense.

ECONOMIC CHOICE

What follows is a view of economic choice grounded on the SDMS, and aimed at conceptualizing it in terms of the psychological mechanisms entailed in the way agents in the market labor makes their choice.

The mainstream economic model of the economic choice is largely based on the idea that individuals do behave according to the instrumental rationality axiom. Yet, as we know, several areas of economic theory have subjected this paradigm to major criticisms. As one of the exponents of the institutional theory highlighted, people pursue a plurality of aims of maximization (e.g., knowledge, reputation, visibility), each of them entailing particular payoffs (Veblen, 1899/1975). This is quite close to the everyday experience—the same person adopts different logics and criteria of computation, so that in some cases he/she seems to work according to instrumental rationality, while in others as if other kinds of rules were at stake.

This leads to a major change of focus. The issue is not whether the decision is rational or not, but to understand the conditions in which the choice is made rationally (and which other conditions apply, when other forms of decision prevail).

The psychological model of economic decision outlined below intends to address this issue. It considers the decision to be a process working in a hierarchical way. Psychological assumptions work as super-ordered (inter)subjective meanings selecting the model of payoff and the logic of its computation.

Such assumptions define it in terms of three basic dimensions:

- Model of value (MoV)
- Perception of relevance (Pr)
- Salience (S)

Model of Value

Individuals do not have monolithic selves. Rather, they are made up of a plurality of components of identity, each of them working as a subset of the system of self (Gergen, 1991; Hermans & Dimaggio, 2004; Salgado & Cunha, 2012; Salvatore & Zittoun, 2011a). Each component of identity reflects the person's experience of a sociocultural and intersubjective scenario (cf. Chapter 2 and more in general Part I): country, family, friendship, neighbor relationships, community, virtual networks, professional group and so forth. The lived experience of being part of a society is made up of participation in scenarios.

Each scenario tends to be characterized by its own system of rules, meanings and forms of subjectivity. Consequently, being positioned within a scenario makes up a peculiar *model of value*—namely, a specific pattern of feelings, intentions, desires, axiomatic tenets, ways of thinking and methods of engagement with others and the world.

It is worth noting that scenarios share some aspects and at the same time can be very different from each other (e.g., the scenario of being involved with one's children and the scenario of playing the stock market are quite different, while the latter shares some aspects with the scenario of playing poker with friends). Moreover, one has to consider that scenarios are psychological realities: *socioculturally guided and intersubjectively negotiated forms of interpretation of the world*. Positioning within a scenario is a psychological process—one need not actually be on the job to feel and act like a worker, just as one can be at work but experience it in terms of a different mental scenario (e.g., as a family).

In any circumstance of life, the components of identity somehow engage in a competition with each other. One component (or a homogeneous pattern of them) takes the foreground, with the others going into the background. I propose the term "version of identity" for the component of identity that foregrounds the self in a certain spatial-temporal circumstance. In sum, the person's version of identity is the form of subjectivity governing how the person interprets (i.e., feels, thinks, chooses, performs) the experience in a given moment.

Any version of identity is the grounds of a certain model of value. Two aspects of such a definition are worth underlining. First, as the use of the term "version" suggests, each person holds a plurality of aspects of identity—and therefore of models of value. Second, any actualization is local, that is, it is performed at a given moment, due to the circumstances that lead the person to bring a certain mental scenario to the foreground. So, the person can function in one circumstance as a father, while in another as an in-group member, and still in another as a cold thinker. In sum, the version of identity is a field dynamic process, depending on time and local circumstances.

I maintain that the model of value channels and constrains decision-making. Making decisions according to ethical rules, in terms of rationality, adherence, opposing, computing, saving, avoiding, pursuing loyalty, friendship, reciprocity, curiosity, pleasure: all of those are forms/logics of decision making grounded in a specific model of value (or a combination of some of them), in its turn enrooted in an equally specific version of identity.

More specifically, the model of value plays a central role in decision-making, because *it shapes the content of the decision*. This is so because the content of any decision is not fixed. Rather, it depends on which aspect(s) of the experience is(are) made pertinent. As the theory of frame highlights, the same logical structure of a decision can be interpreted in different ways, due to how it is experienced (Kahneman, 2003).

In the final analysis, what is exogenous and what is endogenous in the choice is not invariant, but is a function of the model of value. Take a worker: he/she can regard many aspects as relevant, therefore as the value (and combination of values) on which her/his choice is focused: security, wage, relationship with colleagues and/or clients, gratification associated with achievement, power, and so forth. Thus, any choice entails a previous process of making some aspects of the experience pertinent and of placing the rest into the background. For instance, being fired can be interpreted by some workers as an instrumental issue, while for others it could be seen as a loss of identity, something with quite a destructive impact on the self, on one's reputation, on the feeling of being a member of the community.

The idea that the model of value produces a hierarchy of the aspects of experience that potentially enter the decision-making process is consistent with the fast and frugal way of functioning of such processes (Gigerenzer, 2008; Gigerenzer & Todd, 1999). Above all, it provides a way to address the puzzling issue of the incommensurability of the components involved in any major decisional context. Take the increased risk of being fired associated with the increasing flexibility of the labor market. This risk entails a plurality of implications—for example, dramatic reduction of income, increase in free time, leaving the work group, and so forth. Now, each of these aspects is experienced in a peculiar, incommensurable way—there is no general psychological metric governing how such aspects are integrated in a single mental computation. For instance, how does the person compare the loss of income and the enhancing of free time? The answer to this question provided by the concept of model of value lies in the idea that people do not make comparisons between the components involved in the decision; rather, they create a hierarchy, placing something in the foreground and the rest in the background. In the final analysis a model of value is a specific model of hierarchization of decisional parameters.

Salience

As a premise, it has to be taken into account that the identification with a version of identity is not an all-or-nothing process. Rather, it must be considered a continuous dimension: one can identify with a certain version of identity to different extents, ranging from the lack of identification to a total level of identification. With the term identification here I mean the *existential force*—the value of life (Salvatore, 2012; Salvatore & Freda, 2011; cf. Chapter 6)—the person attributes to a given version of identity (when it is experienced as the foreground)—therefore to the experience and representations he/she makes through the mediation of such a version of identity. To identify deeply with a certain version of identity means feeling the representation/experience produced within this version as absolutely true-for-the-person, therefore having a very strong existential force —in other words not as one among other possible representations of the world, but the only true possible world.[4]

In sum, the salience of the version of identity determines how seriously the person takes the experience mediated by this version of identity, namely, to what extent he/she gives it existential force. This makes the role that salience plays in decision making clear—the greater the salience, the more the actor will be forced/constrained to adopt his own version of identity as the grounds of the choice. Conversely, the less the salience, the more the actor is able to adopt forms/logics of decision making that are peripheral to himself.

It is worth noting three aspects associated with the construct discussed here. First, salience does not concern the content of the representation, but the existential truthfulness of the representation itself, its value of life.

A representation can be felt to be highly salient even if its content consists of something considered to lack relevance. The rational paradigm of choice provides a clear example of this: a representation that, according to everyday experience is void of relevance, but that works as hegemonic paradigmatic scientific framework. The opposite situation can also be considered—a content with high relevance but void of salience. Examples of that can be found in the situations where the correct recognition of the risk does not produce a consistent decision. Paradigmatically, take a smoker who is fully aware of the risk associated with such conduct. Nevertheless, they do not stop smoking. The common sense interpretation of this contradictory decision says that this happens because the smoker underestimates the risk. But this is just a post hoc description of what happens, rather than an explanation of it. The notion of salience enables such inconsistency to be understood—the representation of the risk is correct, but the salience of this representation is lacking or is quite weak. Consequently, the representation is unable to lead to a decision—it is correct but has no existential force.

Second, salience has to be considered as the by-product of affect. From an evolutionary standpoint, affect is just that—the attribution of relevance to the stimulus preparing the subject to react to it (Panksepp, 1998). Also from the phenomenological standpoint, to be affectively activated means feeling vividly the experience, as something that has immediate and relevant value for the subject (Salvatore & Zittoun, 2011a). Finally, from the neurobiological standpoint, it has been highlighted that the damage of the neural circuits involved in the computation of affective information does not inflate the capability of reasoning; rather it leads the subject to consider the content of own thought as just conjectural, namely, void of value of life, therefore unable to motivate the individual to choose and act (Damasio, 1999).

Third, salience is a field dynamic characteristic, even if its effects concern single individuals. As a matter of fact, the absolutization of a version of identity depends on the extent to which the sociocultural and intersubjective scenario is socially shared. Take the context of decision C_1; in that context, persons share just one scenario, therefore the same version of identity. Consider now context C_2, where there is a plurality of versions of identity involved. The salience will be higher in C_1 than in C_2. To give a more concrete example, consider a firm. If in this firm the greatest proportion of workers share the version of identity "I as overworked by the ownership," then the representation derived from such a version of identity (feelings, evaluation, thoughts, decisions, acts) will have strong salience. On the contrary, if in the firm's sociocultural environment, a plurality of versions of identity circulate, then the level of salience of each of them is lower—the other workers' versions of identity operate as a constraint (as a source of strangeness; cf. previous paragraph) on the salience of one's own version of identity.

Perception of Relevance

The relevance of the object of choice plays a crucial role in affecting individual behavior. One can distinguish between relevant and irrelevant situations (or—more reasonably—between situations of variable degrees of relevance). In other words, it seems quite reasonable to assume that not all situations have the same importance for individuals (the choice between two job opportunities is certainly more important than the choice between a cup of coffee or a cup of tea) and that the loss caused by of the erroneous choice in the case of an important situation is higher.

Two aspects have to be considered further. First, it is argued that relevance derives from how the actor *perceives* the value of the object. In other words relevance is not an immediate mirror of the objective value of the object; rather it consists of how the person interprets such a value. And it is reasonable to think that this interpretation is affected by contextual and individual factors like household income, status, group affiliation, plans, history of previous experiences (e.g., desensitization to experience).

Second, in close connection with the previous point, it can be observed that the attribution of relevance is made not in absolute terms, but in accordance with a normative criterion of canonicity. No value has an inherent meaning—its meaning is construed by comparing it with what is considered normal. This means, for instance, that workers perceive the extent of insecurity not in terms of a continuous, fixed proportion scale—that is, as the yardstick used for measuring a physical distance—but in normative terms, namely, in terms of comparison with what it is canonically expected to be—therefore, in terms of "right," "excessive."

It is worth noting that the recognition of the role played by the perception of relevance in decision-making contrasts twofold with the tenet of instrumental rationality. In fact, on the one hand, it means that decision making—rather than being based on an encapsulated, computational mechanism—is a process mediated by the persons' sensemaking, affected by contextual factors (Salvatore, Forges Davanzati, Potì, & Ruggieri, 2009); on the other hand, it means that decision making—rather than working in terms of optimization—is performed in terms of maintenance/retrieval of (cultural) canons.

I claim that the greater the perceived relevance, the more the agent tends to conform his/her decision making to the decisional criterion defined by the version of identity involved. For instance, if the version of identity at stake prescribes instrumental rationality as decisional criterion, individuals tend to behave in a rational way (at least in the sense that they tend to calculate, even under uncertainty) when the choice pertains to significant events, while, by contrast, they tend to be more open to other decisional criteria in the event of less important outcomes. In the same way, if the version of identity is, for instance, family ties, and therefore the decisional criteria associated with such a version of identity is protection, affiliation, caring, then the more the perceived relevance, the more individuals tend to behave according to such criteria.

Summary

The psychological model of the economic decision outlined above considers three dimensions. One dimension concerns the shape of the decision maker's self (version of identity/model of value); one the force of this version (salience), which is variable through time, space, and persons; and the third concerns the perceived relevance of the object, which is an evaluation grounded on cultural canons. These dimensions work in a complementary way: the perceived relevance defines the value of the object in accordance to the criteria of value made pertinent by the first dimension. The salience defines the existential force of this representation of value. Working jointly, they define the logic of decision-making enacted by the economic agent. Thus, one can model the logic of decision in terms of the position on the 3-dimensional phase space—each coordinate being the value on the corresponding dimension.

CONCLUSION

In this chapter I have provided a conceptual analysis of four notions, grounded on the semiotic standpoint provided by the SDMS. In so doing, it seems to me that the tendency in psychological science to hypostatize concepts—namely, to consider them as substantive entities—has been highlighted. Whether it be psychotherapy, group, social development or economic choice—or one of many other terms (emotion, motivation, unconscious, person, and personality, identity...), psychological science seems prone to consider them as explanatory essences, namely, pieces of the world which, once seen as the causative source of the phenomenon, enable us to understand it.

Thus, what I have proposed in this chapter is an exercise in (re)turning to the *explanandum* envisaged in the introduction of this book. Moreover, I have tried to show that the SDMS can be used as the semantic ground allowing such a (re)turn. In the final analysis, the SDMS has the ambition of providing the grounds for unifying psychological science, that is, for modeling psychological phenomena thanks to, rather than in spite of, the enormously broad variety of human affairs.

NOTES

1. Here and henceforth I use the term "instantiation" to refer to the nexus between the phenomenon and the basic dynamic making it up. Saying that X is an instantiation of Y, I want to mean that X is an instance, an example, a specific object of the general class Y. My use of the term is consistent with philosophical language—the "principle of instantiation" states that any property exists only if it is instantiated in a specific object (needless to say the consistent use of the term does not mean to agree with such a philosophical thesis). I adopt the term "instantiation" for the sake of avoiding a dualistic view of the nexus between dynamic and phenomenon, entailed in the use of terms like "cause" and "effect"—namely, the dynamic as something that causes the phenomenon as its own effect. Thus, the use of the term "instantiation" is motivated by the assumption that there is just one world that one can see in accordance to different epistemic frames and levels of abstraction (Fronterotta & Salvatore, in press)—at a very abstract level one sees it as a dynamic, while at a less abstract, more local level one sees it as a specific phenomenical experience. Consider the nexus between the English language and this text. The latter is not the effect of the former. Rather, it is its instantiation, namely, an exemplar, a concrete phenomenical occurrence that inherently holds the properties of the English language. The text and the English are not two different things—rather, the latter is the form of the former just as the former is the "place" where the latter comes into existence.
2. Migone (2011) provides a brilliant discussion of the sociocultural factors grounding the technical psychoanalytic issue of the payment of a missed session. What is worthwhile in this discussion is that the author adopts a bivalent approach to the issue, considering it as both a cultural process and a matter of scientifically-grounded technical procedure.
3. Here and henceforth the notation: |group| is used to denote the modelistic interpretation of the construct, so as to differentiate it from its commonsensical meaning. Thus, "group" can be used with different meanings, one of them being |group|.
4. The following examples illustrate this issue. Take somebody watching a film—they can be caught up in the story, feeling part of it—afraid, happy, surprised, and the like, identifying with the characters. They do not feel they are a spectator of something happening outside them—rather they are within the story just as the story is part of them (in that current moment). In other cases—usually when the film is of lower quality—this does not happen and the screen images are experienced as something distant. The spectator gets bored, starting to think to other things. Now, the content of the experience does not change—what changes is the salience of such content,

namely, the existential value it conveys: to what extent the subject lives the experience as something-being-part-of-her. Another example can be found in playing. The quality of the experience of playing does not only depend on the content of the game, but mainly on the capacity of feeling the game is real, something that in that current moment is the player's whole life—in the terms of our model: as a very salient version of identity. Reference to the context of playing is useful to highlight the role of salience in choice. Consider a person playing Monopoly. It is evident that the output of her decision will not depend only on the terms/structure of the decision (payoff, resources). Her decision will also depend on the extent to which she feels the experiential scenario of Monopoly is salient—namely, to what extent the version of identity in the foreground at that moment (I as the character acted in the game) dominates the person's self. The more salient the experience of playing is (at the moment of its actuation), the more the person will follow the rules of the game.

PART III

A NEW METHODOLOGICAL APPROACH

The theoretical discussion conducted in the previous two parts lends it-self to framing a new methodology for the modeling of sensemaking and meaning—a fresh look at *what* and *how* to know the semiotic dynamics making up psychological phenomena.

As used here, methodology is something different from method—namely, from the set of procedures and tools of empirical inquiry. Method-ology is the *discourse on method:* the theoretical domain designed to define the model of knowledge bridging the general theory to the practices of investigation, so as to allow the interaction between thought and action required for the construction of scientific knowledge.

The third part of the book is devoted to outlining this new methodological framework. Chapter 9 provides a discussion about the logic of knowledge construction that is consistent with the field nature of sensemaking. Abduction—and the abstractive generalization grounded on it—is proposed as an alternative methodological framework for the psychological empirical investigation of sensemaking. Chapter 10 discusses two further core implications of the field nature of sensemaking: the need to re-think the subject of the analysis in a dynamic and situated way, going beyond the reified notion of the individual. Chapter 11 proposes some strategies of analysis grounded on the methodological framework outlined in the previous chapter. Finally, Chapter 12 presents some instances of empirical investigations that instantiate the methodological tenets presented in the previous chapters.

CHAPTER 9

FIELD DEPENDENCY
AND ABDUCTION

As discussed in previous chapters (in particular, Chapters 2–4), sensemaking can be conceived of as a field dependency dynamic. In general terms, to conceive of a dynamic in terms of field means assuming that elements are interconnected and their behavior is "enslaved" to the whole. In the final analysis, the recognition of the field nature of a dynamic leads to seeing it as contingent to the whole it belongs to. The SDMS sees sensemaking exactly in this way: no sign has an autonomous content; rather, the content is a function of the relation between the sign and the whole trajectory of signs it is part of, therefore of the position of the sign within the scenario working as the semiotic landscape grounding the interpretability of the sign. In the SDMS terminology, the value of the SIP is contingent to the SIA.

This chapter outlines a basic methodological implication of such a view of sensemaking. It concerns the logic of knowledge building that is consistent with the field nature of sensemaking. Such a view can be summarized in two tenets. First, the idea that the field dynamic requires abductive logic to be modeled: field dynamics are a matter of relation, having a contingent linkage with their empirical content. This means that the same pattern of relation (e.g., a certain SIA) can be associated and implemented by different empirical contents (e.g., a certain set of co-occurring words) and, conversely, the same empirical content can indicate different patterns of relation, according to the situated circumstances (Salvatore & Valsiner, 2010). Consequently, the inductive aggregation of data is unable to provide

Psychology in Black and White: The Project of a Theory-Driven Science, pp. 175–199
Copyright © 2016 by Information Age Publishing
175

a map of the semiotic landscape, because this strategy is based on the assumption that data holds informative content, since they are in quite a stable relation with the phenomenon to be mapped (i.e., the state a' of the marker corresponds quite stably to the state a of the phenomenon). This leads to acceptance of the argument that the analysis of sensemaking is a matter of abductive reconstruction. This kind of knowledge building consists of the inference of the phenomenon through the empirical clues available. It is aimed at defining the minimal phenomenon whose (past or current) presence makes the clues meaningful. The phenomenon is reconstructed since it serves as the ground of the plausibility of their co-occurrences. Second, as proposed here, abductive logic provides the way of integrating idiographic and nomothetic knowledge, namely, of pursuing generalized knowledge through the analysis of what is contingency. In so doing, the ideological polarization between the idiographic and the nomothetic, as if they were two alternative approaches and even two alternative points of view on human affairs, can be recomposed in a more realistic, useful, and historically correct view of them as complementary components of the single effort of knowledge building.

THE INDEXICALITY OF PSYCHOLOGICAL PHENOMENA

As we have said, this is what field dependency consists of: the meaning of signs—and more in general the psychological value of a given occurrence (a behavior, a feeling, a thought, a text)—changes according to the semiotic dynamic they are part of. Take for instance the student dropping out of school. This act occurs in a given field—a certain class, within a certain school, placed in certain sociosymbolic surroundings. Now let us say that the field at stake is affected by one of the following psychological semiotic dynamics—field A: a semiotic landscape consisting of a hypergeneralized meaning (i.e., a SIA) of anomy, enacted by persecutory connotation of otherness, and fragmented, conflicting relationship between subgroups of students and these subgroups and teachers; field B: a semiotic landscape consisting of the intensive idealization of the bond among students and teachers, leading to perceive and feel any deviation/exclusion from it as a catastrophic event. Now, one can interpret the act of dropping out in different, even opposing ways, according to the field where it occurs. If field A is involved, dropping out can be interpreted as an act of escaping from a frustrating, persecutory experience; according to field B, as a self-sacrificial act, enacting both the goodness of the bond and the student's own inability to be part of it (i.e., "I am not worthy of being part of such a wonderful world"). Needless to say, other interpretations are possible; what is relevant here is simply the fact that once the field dependency of the psychological phenomena is recognized, it must also be recognized that the psychological meaning of occurrences (acts, feelings, speeches) is contingent to the field. This is the tenet of the indexicality of psychological occurrences descending from the field dependency of sensemaking.

According to the tenet of the indexicality, the empirical content of any occurrence does not have a fixed meaning, since it depends on the synchronic and diachronic network of linkages of which it is part. This can be shown by means of the following picture. Consider field F made up of the infinite set of sequential occurrences $(o_1, o_2, o_3, ... o_\infty)$. Moreover, assume that the meaning $|m|$ of any of them is provided by the rule R: "the meaning of any occurrence from the set consists of the rank in the sequence". Consider the occurrence (o_{11}): according to the rule, the meaning of this occurrence is $|11|$, namely, its rank in the set of sequential occurrences comprising F. Now imagine another field, similar to the former but not identical—say F', comprising the set: $o_9, o_{10}, o_{11}, ... o_\infty$. In this case, according to the same rule, the meaning of the occurrence (o_{11}) is $|3|$, even if its phenomenical content has not changed. Finally, imagine another field F'', comprising the set of occurrences: $s_1, s_2, s_3, ... s_\infty$-- very different from the previous one as to its empirical content—yet functioning according to the same rule R. In this case the occurrence (s_{11}) will have the same meaning as (o_{11}) regardless of its phenomenical diversity.

In brief, the assumption of the field dependency of the psychological object leads to the claim that psychological science can consider the empirical content of the occurrences neither a necessary nor a sufficient condition to attributing meaning to them. Rather, one has to conclude that—according to the global state of the field—the same occurrence can have, even highly different meanings just as different occurrences can be associated with the same psychological meaning[1] (Toomela, 2007, 2008).

INDEXICALITY MAKES
INDUCTIVE GENERALIZATION UNSUITABLE

The recognition of the indexicality of the sensemaking—and thus of the psychological phenomena—cannot but lead to put in discussion the induction as the way of knowledge building on which current mainstream psychological science is grounded.

Inductive generalization addresses occurrences in order to detect their redundancy, interpreted as the index of the regularity conceived of as typical of the phenomenon under investigation. This is well highlighted by Peirce (1897/1932), who defined induction as "the formation of a habit." As this definition shows, within the frame of induction, occurrences are interpreted and aggregated according to their empirical, factual content.

The Population as Methodological Device

The absolute relevance of induction in psychological science is evident in the massive reference to the population as the methodological device for generating data. Populations are class defined in terms of collection of specimens collected according to a criterion of descriptive similarity. Every time one defines a characteristic, one is implicitly construing a collection of the objects that can be clustered in terms of that characteristic. It is presumed that such a characteristic *as a quality* is present in each and every member ascribed to the given population—in contrast to other populations. In terms of the *presumed quantity* of the characteristic, the individual members of the class (i.e., of the population) are allowed to vary as long as the quality is set as permanent. Moving on to consider this collection a population is easy—sometimes as a result of negotiation, often as the hypostatized gift of the researcher's preferences or society's prescribed ideology. And thus psychology is populated by an infinite set of possible populations—students, tourists, soccer supporters—as well males, females, homosexuals, extroverts, field dependent people, managers, and the like.

In sum, for the sake of producing data the reference to the concept of population makes the affair enormously easy: a property/criterion X is selected and considered an essential quality; accordingly, each subject that shows that quality is qualified in terms of such essence and therefore attributed with the status of being a specimen of the corresponding class —namely, the status of being a member of the population; finally, due to their common membership specimens are assumed to be equivalent to each other, as if they were all instantiations of the same essential transcendental quality.

Thanks to this conceptual machine psychologists have bypassed the very difficult and never completely and definitively solved methodological issue of modeling and interpreting intra-individual (temporal) variability —which entails the relation between the individual and its context.[2] This methodological challenge has been reduced to the less critical technical task of elaborating procedures of sampling and data analysis enabling the researcher to put the context aside, namely, to consider it in terms of error of measurement and as such to be separable—through the opportune psychometric techniques—from the measurement of the essential quality. In so doing, the redundancy detected at the level of population may be interpreted as if it were "purged" of the marginal, contextual noise, obtained from and indicative of the single, transcendental subject defined by the essential quality.

The Castle of Induction and Its Foundations in The Sand

The inductive construction of the transcendental subject—that is, the elimination of the contextual noise through its interpretation in terms of measurement error annullable through the aggregation of equivalent cases (i.e., through the displacement of the analysis from the individual case to the population of cases)—is an impressive conceptual castle. Yet, in the case of psychology—and more in general of social sciences—the castle is built on foundations in the sand. Indeed, induction aggregates and considers cases as equivalent according to the similarity of their phenomenical, empirical content (i.e., two cases are equivalent members of the population of males because both show the empirical indicator of masculinity). This means that induction assumes the empirical content of the cases is invariant, and can therefore indicate whether or not the case possesses the membership quality.

The recognition of the field dependency of psychological phenomena leads precisely to the invalidation of this assumption: the empirical content of any occurrence never has an invariant, therefore self-contained meaning; as discussed above, its psychological meaning depends on— consists of—the relation of the occurrence with the field dynamic of which it is part. Consequently, occurrences cannot be aggregated according to their empirical content. In sum, the tenet of the indexicality of the psychological phenomena cannot but lead to the recognition that *psychological occurrences may not be used for producing redundancy because of their phenomenological similarities* (Lamiell, 1998).

For example, consider a researcher who is interested in studying how people elaborate their sense of identity in the context of a new community. Well, imagine that the researcher has found two or more individuals that share many features (nationality, gender, age, place of living, some psychological traits, attitudes, and so forth). Despite the characteristics the two individuals share, they cannot be considered equivalent, because of the fact that their shared characteristics will be however a finite and limited subset of the whole set of occurrences sustaining the field comprising the dynamic of the phenomenon. Consequently, the researcher cannot aggregate the two individuals and treat them as equivalent because of their being members of the same population.

Classes encompassing similar phenomenical occurrences have only a descriptive value—the specimens they include may have very different psychological meaning, namely, they may signal very different psychological processes. Coming back to the example proposed above, the class "drop out" is a commonsensical, descriptive set, encompassing phenomena that may be very different according to a psychological standpoint. On the other hand, psychology should define classes shaped according to psychological processes; this means that insofar as a certain class should be defined as the set covering the occurrences of a certain psychological process, such a class would encompass phenomena that could be very different from a commonsensical, descriptive standpoint. For instance, consider the class of the self-sacrificial forms of bond idealization. This class would cover phenomena like some forms of dropping out (the one associated to field B, see above, previous paragraph), some forms of voluntary community service, some forms of terrorism, a certain parental attitude, and so forth. I know that what I have just proposed is paradoxical and lends itself to be read as a mere provocation. Actually it is paradoxical, but from the commonsensical standpoint. The development of science is to become independent from common sense (Salvatore, 2006); not to negate it, but to interact with it. Physics has developed models entailing forms of classification of occurrences that are very different from the ones we use in daily life—a stone falling, a man jumping out the window are two very different events in daily life, having very different values; yet they are two specimens of the same class of process in physics—bodies subjected to gravitational pull.

The Coachman Fly Illusion

One could say that the criticism of inductive generalization is inconsistent with an incontrovertible datum: the huge amount of regularities that inductive procedures of empirical investigation have enabled us to detect for the last five decades and even more.

Actually, my criticism of inductive generalization does not contradict this datum—rather, it entails a different interpretation of it from the one provided by mainstream psychology.

My thesis is that such regularities are not, as inductive logic implicitly assumes, the way psychological processes show their invariant way of functioning; rather they reflect the stability of culturally defined forms of life. This thesis is based on the recognition of the fact that the inductive aggregation of cases in terms of their empirical similarity entails—usually implicitly—the commonsensical interpretation of its content. Indeed, the fact that certain occurrences are treated as endowed with a self-evident meaning does not reflect the fact that such meaning is inherent to the occurrence, but the fact that it is deeply embedded in the normativity of commonsensical canons and, consequently, the process of its interpretation is an instantaneous, prereflexive operation of presentification (Salvatore, 2012, 2014) that escapes consciousness. This is evident in the fact that we have the experience of directly perceiving words, rather than sounds, actions (e.g., speaking), rather than behaviors (e.g., moving the mouth and the tongue with certain types of sound as a result).

To ground the construction of data on common sense hides an important issue, which represents a real fallacy when it concerns psychological empirical analysis. Indeed, insofar as one assumes that the psychological dynamic consists of sensemaking (Salvatore & Venuleo, 2013; Valsiner, 2002) one has to take into account that sensemaking consists of linkages among meanings. Therefore, once a certain occurrence is interpreted according to common sense, what one has done is not only to provide an occurrence with a significance (e.g. this is a form of drop-out), but also to activate a normative network of linkages between this occurrence and many others (e.g., drop-out is a critical violation of canon; as such it has to be caused by an undesirable factor). In other words, the interpretation of one occurrence is at the same time the instantiation of a whole frame of understanding.

As Smedslund (1995) clearly showed almost 30 years ago, in the case of a cultural dynamic the relation between meanings is given beforehand, as part of common sense. Thus, when the cultural analysis works in this way it functions as the mere descriptor of the implicit linkages that are already active within common sense. In other words, the analysis does not model the cultural dynamic and its determinants but is enacted by the latter.

Smedslund (1995) defined this form of confusion between *explanans* and *explanandum* as pseudoempiricism. As result of pseudoempiricism, the cultural analysis falls into the subtle trap of what I propose to call *the coachman fly effect*. As we all know, the fable of the coachman fly tells the story of a fly buzzing around the head of the horse, and due to this position, has the illusion of guiding the horse. The illusion, we know, lies in this: being over the horse's head was the effect, rather than the cause of the horse's movement. Similarly, the psychologist-fly ends up being driven by the cultural dynamic-horse, rather than (epistemically) driving it.

For instance, very many studies have found that males and females show differences as to social behavior. Here the issue is not to negate such findings. Rather, the point is to interpret them: do they reflect an inherent property of the sexual condition or do they detect the sociocultural system of meaning regulating gender identity? Still, consider the huge number of studies that have detected the association between the efficacy of psychotherapy and therapeutic alliance. Do these findings show that an external, independent factor (alliance) affects the outcome of psychotherapy or do they tell us what we already know as members of our society, namely, that according to our cultural canons any professional exchange where the interpersonal relationship plays a major role requires reciprocal trust and willingness as well as a certain agreement on the aims? One would not need to perform empirical analyses on the "educational alliance" to extend the same findings to the learning-teaching exchange: we already know that the greater the educational alliance, the higher the quality of the learning-teaching; and we know this simply because we are members of our cultural environment where such a linkage is a canon defining normatively that kind of life.

In the final analysis, the role of common sense can be detected by means of a very simple criterion, that can be implemented by means of the following question: would a naïve, yet clever observer regard as plausible the meaning given to data? This is what I propose to call the *journalist criterion* (Salvatore & Scotto di Carlo, 2005)—and if the answer is yes, then one has to conclude that common sense works as the tacit, more or less latent background knowledge according to which the dataset of the analysis is constituted.

ABDUCTION

Abductive generalization is the candidate to replace inductive generalization (Salvatore & Valsiner, 2010; Salvatore, 2014). Abduction consists of inference of the phenomenon through the empirical occurrences available. Peirce provides the following definitions of abduction (among others)

> there are but three elementary kinds of reasoning. The first, which I call abduction ... consists in examining a mass of facts and in allowing these facts to suggest a theory. In this way we gain new ideas; but there is no force in the reasoning.... The second kind of reasoning is deduction, or necessary reasoning. It is applicable only to an ideal state of things, or to a state of things in so far as it may conform to an ideal. It merely gives a new aspect to the premises.... The third way of reasoning is induction, or experimental research. (Peirce, 1905/1958, CP 8.209)

> It must be remembered that abduction, although it is very little hampered by logical rules, nevertheless is logical inference, asserting its conclusion only problematically or conjecturally. It is true, but nevertheless having a perfect definite logical form.

> The form of inference, therefore, is this
> The surprising fact, C, is observed;
> But if A were true, C would be a matter of course,
> Hence, there is reason to suspect that A is true. (Peirce, 1902/1932, CP 5.188-189)

Thus, abduction is aimed at identifying the most plausible event/entity (A) whose (past or current) presence would make the occurrence of the fact

(C) meaningful; namely, the event/entity is reconstructed due to the fact that it works as the grounds of the plausibility of the occurrence.

Take the policeman, who realizes that there are pieces of glasses on the floor, under a broken window, and footprints spread around the room. These co-occurring elements are mute, meaningless, part of the same background where infinite other elements co-occur (e.g., the color of the wall, the temperature of the room...). As soon as the policemen abducts a phenomenon working as the scenario of the clues—"someone must have broken the window to get inside"—the clues enter a gestalt, acquiring plausibility, then sense. Insofar as this happens, the reconstruction comes to be a meaningful inference as well.

Three aspects of abduction are worth mentioning here.

First, the knowledge produced by abductive generalization is *local* and *contingent*: it concerns the situated set of occurrences comprising the case —namely, the understanding of C in terms of the contingent event/entity according to which C ceases to be surprising (i.e., it is understood).

Second, as the example of the policemen shows, such understanding implies three intertwined epistemic operations:

- Making the salient occurrences pertinent, and backgrounding the others;
- Patterning the salient occurrences, namely, establishing a network of connections among them;
- Reconstructing their occurrence in terms of retrieving the causative event.

These three operations are strictly intertwined: they are components of the same dynamic gestalt action of sensemaking—each of them is performed by means of the performance of the others. To come back to the example of the policeman, it can be seen that the identification of the clues (pertinentization), their interconnection (patterning) as components of the same past event (reconstruction) are faces of the same dice.

Third, the three operations require a background system of knowledge to be performed. Such a system provides the semantics and syntax that frame, constrain and channel the inference.

Thus, it can be concluded that *abductive generalization is a form of knowledge building aimed at producing a local model of the phenomenon at stake (here, the case) starting from the empirical occurrences and grounded on a general system of knowledge.*

The latter statement helps to highlight the difference between abductive and inductive generalization. Induction and abduction start from the same departure point, yet they follow a different path to arrive at a different form of knowledge. As said above, inductive generalization addresses occurrences in terms of their redundancies (local rule), used for the sake of identifying the regularity (general rule). Unlike inductive inference, abduction does not pursue the general rule, namely, the definition of regularities through the generalization of redundancies; it uses the general rule (i.e., the background system of knowledge) in order to interpret the occurrences by reconstructing the phenomenon in terms of which the occurrences acquire meaning. In sum, induction is aimed at producing the general rule, while abduction tries to understand the case.

Abduction Grounds the Abstractive Generalization

My thesis is that abduction works as a more powerful and reliable grounds for empirical analyses than that provided by conceiving the investigation in terms of inductive generalization. This is so for two basic reasons. On the one hand, a "hygienic" function, namely, the chance of avoiding a trap associated with the inductive approach. I refer to the chance of making explicit—therefore subject to analysis, revision, and development —the framework of the analysis (i.e., the general rule), and in so doing facing up to the tendency of the theorization of human affairs to trip up on common sense (Salvatore, in press). On the other hand, a "promotional" function—namely, the possibility of grounding the knowledge building on the dialectics between local understanding and universal rule. This dialectics entails an old-fashioned innovative paradigm of investigation that rescues the complementarity between idiographic and nomothetic dimensions, namely, the mode of *generalizing by means of particular*, rather than in spite of it.

In the final analysis, abduction provides a way of making psychology - and in particular the psychology that takes sensemaking as its object - *the science of the contingent* (Salvatore, 2014), namely, the science of what happens within a spatial-temporal environment, as the particular, unrepeatable instantiation of a universal, a-temporal and a-spatial dynamic (as to the distinction between dynamic, process and phenomenon, see Introduction and Chapter 8). This is so because from the logic of abductive inference one can draw a specific form of generalization, which I propose to call: *abstractive generalization*. In what follows the distinctive characteristics of abstractive generalization are outlined.

First, it is worth repeating that abductive generalization starts from data and produces as output the understanding of the event under investigation, namely, the comprehension of how/why it works the way it works; in other words, abduction is aimed at building a local model of the particular, contingent phenomenon. The central point to underline here is the *local* nature of the model—it means that the understanding is idiosyncratic, focused of the peculiar quality of the event; it is the way of making sense of the combination of the occurrences that makes the event unique, contingent, different from any other. This is where the basic difference lies compared to inductive generalization. Being focused on the detection of redundancy, induction seeks what the occurrences have in common both amongst themselves and with supposedly equivalent events. In contrast, abduction focuses on the difference between the occurrences, in order to infer/model the reason (i.e., C) making this difference "a matter of course", to use Peirce's expression. From this derives a peculiar role played by the general theory. The local model is grounded on the general theory—as observed above, any understanding of the local event requires a background knowledge for the sake of performing the operation of pertinentization, patterning and reconstruction comprising abductive inference. And yet the general theory does not have a *predicative function* on the event; rather it performs an *interpretative function*; that is, it anchors but does not sustain the understanding of the local event. In other words, there is not a direct projection of general knowledge on the local phenomenon as a result of the fact that the occurrences of the latter have been categorized as specimens of the general class. In still other words, the abductive use of the theory is different from the direct application of the theory's content to the local event—where application means something like: given that occurrence *a* is part of class *A*, then *a* is/holds/has "*A-ness*", consequently all the *A-ness'* properties and conditions can be used (applied) to *a*. In the case of abduction, the general theory grounds the operation of modeling the particular, idiosyncratic pattern of co-occurrences and of reconstructing the mechanism enabling such a pattern to acquire meaning. It does so by working as background knowledge channeling the three operations that make up abductive inference (pertinentization, patterning, reconstructing). This is what the interpretative function consists of.

The interpretative role of general theory implies that in order to be used for abduction, the conceptual content of the general theory must not speak directly about the empirical content of the event. Rather, the theory is required to comprise concepts that are placed at a more abstract level than the one detecting the empirical content of the event. This is so for both logical and methodological reasons. From a logical standpoint, the very fact that contingent occurrences have to be understood implies that such an occurrence may not be the content of the theory, otherwise the occurrence would not be contingent and unique. From a methodological standpoint, the understanding of the event is a matter of identification of the local web of interconnections between the occurrences, as it is instantiated in the field contingency. As we have said, this means that occurrences have no invariant psychological meaning, since their meaning is defined by the local field pattern of which they are part and help to constitute. As a result, in order to understand the contingent pattern, a theory is required that does not define the meaning of the occurrence once and for all, but is able to ground the exploration of the different potential meanings that the occurrence may acquire locally.[3]

The empiricist view of contemporary psychology has led to the dominance of data-driven theories, consisting of the mere generalization of the relations among variables, as detected by means of empirical investigation. For instance, the theory that states the relevance of the therapeutic alliance in psychotherapy is the output of a series of empirical analyses that have found a systematic association between the level of therapeutic alliance between therapist and patient and the effectiveness of the psychotherapy (Salvatore, 2011). In sum, data-driven theory is a form of acceptance of what has been found by the empirical investigation; as such, it cannot but have the same content as the empirical investigation from which it derives. On the other hand, if one takes into account that the empirical demonstration of the core notion of the theory of relativity—the dependency of time on speed—arrived several decades after the theory, then one realizes that the data-driven construction of theories is not the only way of proceeding.

Indeed, psychology has not always been empiricist. Consider for instance the Piagetian notions of assimilation and accommodation. They are very generalized concepts that cannot be considered derived from empirical analyses. Rather, these super-ordered concepts sustain an abstract, comprehensive developmental theory that enables analysts to interpret infinite contingencies, in any psychological and sociopsychological domain. Thus, Piagetian developmental theory does not directly concern any empirical occurrence—that is, no occurrence is an instance of assimilation or accommodation in itself. Instead, Piagetian notions lend themselves to being used for the sake of interpreting very many phenomenical occurrence in terms of the role they play in the epigenetic dynamic modeled by the theory. Accordingly, the Piagetian theory works as an interpretative framework grounding abductively the understanding of the case as well as the generalization of such understanding even over different domains of investigation: the notions of assimilation/accommodation are nowadays used as a unified theoretical framework working over several domains: developmental processes, psychotherapy process, social and organizational innovation, and so forth (for an interpretation of some Piagetian empirical studies as instances of abductive reasoning, see Salvatore & Valsiner, 2011).

Cultural psychology provides several examples of this theory-driven mode of conceptualization. Consider notions like *mediation, sign, field, sensemaking*—none of them has a specific, invariant empirical content and that is precisely why they can be used for grounding the interpretation of an infinite set of phenomena. The very notion of culture cannot but be considered in this way. Culture is not an empirical object, namely, a word referring to a piece of the world whose qualities, once described by means of empirical investigation, are translated into a theory. This is evident due to the very fact of the large amount of definitions the concept has been subjected. Indeed, culture is an interpretative, theoretical concept, thanks to which a huge amount of phenomenical occurrences can be interpreted in their interconnections and therefore acquire their contingent scientific meaning. Therefore, the competition among the different definitions is not to be played in terms to their correspondence with the "real thing" they refer to, but in terms of the definitions' capacity of empowering the understanding of human affairs.

This leads to recognizing the profile of what I mean by abstractive generalization. Notions like Piagetian concepts, as well as *mediation, sensemaking, culture* and the like, are generalized categories. Yet, as should be clear, they are not so in the sense that the classes that they denote are highly extended because they hold a great many specimens. Rather, they are generalized concepts in the sense that they are very abstract, highly intensional concepts: they model a very selective theoretical focus according to and in terms of which any empirical occurrence is abstracted—namely, the aspect of the phenomenon that the theory considers pertinent is foregrounded while the rest of it is put in the background (as to the notion of abstraction in terms of pertinentization, see Bühler, 1934/1990). Thus, thanks to this abstractive capacity, the theory is able to transform the phenomenon into the theoretical object, providing a conceptual framework for its understanding.

It is worth highlighting how such a transformation leads the theory to carry out the same function of generalization performed by the predicative use of the theory. Yet, in the case of abstractive generalization, the theory does not provide "predicates" to the empirical occurrences, because its concepts are more abstract than the empirical occurrences and therefore they may not apply directly to the phenomena in terms of their attributes (i.e., as "predicates"). On the contrary, the abstract concept provides a way of looking at and understanding the occurrences.

The notion of system is an useful example for picturing the distinction between interpretative and predicative relation between class and specimen—*System* is a very abstract concept that enables an infinite set of occurrences to be collected as specimens. The concept, however, does not provide a set of empirical characteristics defining the property of the specimen. Rather, it provides a conceptual model—that is, structural linkages among parts and boundaries separating/connecting inner and outer environment—in accordance to which the specimens are understood.

To take a further example, consider the law of gravity. It concerns the falling of bodies. When the physicists see an apple falling and thinks that it is a body, in so doing they are not predicating the apple—that is, they are not stating that "this apple has the quality of being a falling body," as if being a falling body were one of the qualities an apple may have, like color, shape, and so forth. Indeed, the falling body is not an empirical characteristic to be predicated to certain pieces of the world. Rather, it is a way of seeing/interpreting the event (in this case, the apple falling) and in so doing, of transforming it into the conceptual object of the theory. In sum, when physicists think of an apple as a falling object, their reasoning is like the following: "insofar as one consider the apple falling just and only in its aspect of being a falling body, one can understand what is happening, because the apple is transformed into the object of physics."

To conclude, this is what abstractive generalization consists of—the theory's capacity to interpret phenomenical occurrences through the *encompassing distanciation* between theory and phenomena. Here the oxymoron highlights the only seemingly paradoxical logical and methodological tenet that states that theory has to take a step back from data in order to understand them.

In the final analysis, the peculiarity of the abductive form of generalization depends on the hermeneutic function of the general theory. Indeed, according to such a function, abductive generalization concerns the capacity of the general theory to ground the building of local models that are increasingly capable of making "surprising" "co-occurrences" a "matter of course." This means that according to abductive logic, the advance of knowledge is a matter of enabling the general theory to generate local understandings of more and more heterogeneous phenomena. It is in this sense that abductive generalization is abstractive: the progressive increase in the general theory's interpretative power, namely, the increasing capacity of the general theory to comprehend more and more heterogeneous phenomena is performed by and consist of its progressive abstraction, namely, it progressive capability of grasping the fundamental rule(s) governing the way contingencies can be transformed into theoretical objects and as such understood.

In sum, abductive, abstractive generalization outlines a view of the advancement of knowledge that follows a radically different path compared to the vision of scientific progress in terms of accumulation of evidence. The development of knowledge is a matter of reduction to the essential theory grounding the local understanding of human affairs, rather than the never-ending storage of pockets of evidence.

TWO METHODOLOGICAL TENETS FOR
ABDUCTIVE GENERALIZATION

In this paragraph I draw two methodological tenets from the discussion on abstractive generalization proposed above.

First, the nexus between the general rule-local model dialectics and the distinction between *dynamic* and *process* (cf. Introduction and Chapter 8 too) is worth highlighting. Due to its abstract form, to its being void of contingent empirical reference, the general theory cannot but concern the mapping of the *dynamic,* namely, the detection of the invariant way of working of a certain very general class of phenomena (e.g., human sensemaking), operating regardless of time and space. As such, the dynamics can be detected in terms of a few general, abstract rules (Salvatore & Venuleo, 2013). The *process* is the local, contingent way of working of the universal dynamic, resulting from the way the latter is instantiated in the contingent fields of human exchange. Therefore, while there is one dynamic, there are many processes each corresponding to the field conditions of human exchanges provided by the cultural system. Such field conditions do not modify the dynamic; rather, they set the way the latter instantiates itself in terms of a specific way of functioning, namely, in a process. Accordingly, abstractive generalization is the interpretation/modeling of the local process in terms of the dynamic, namely, as an instantiation of the latter, as defined by the general theory.

Insofar as sensemaking is considered the stuff of human affairs, it has to be seen as the dynamic shaping every event of human life, no matter when and where and whom it concerns. In sum, the very fact of talking about sensemaking in terms of basic human dynamics means attributing a universal, invariant form of functioning to it, namely, the form that makes this dynamic what it is, distinct from what it is not. Only on this condition can one compare—let's say—two processes of communication, considering them as specimens of the same class of phenomena (namely, as instantiation of the same universal dynamic). In the final analysis, the universal form of functioning is the invariant background against which differences can be detected.

Second, abduction-oriented analysis benefits from variability (both within and between events under investigation). Indeed, abductive analysis is validated in terms of its capacity to encompass *boundary variability,* namely, the datum that challenges the current theoretical assumptions, therefore forcing the investigator to accommodate the theory in order to enable to ground the local understanding (Salvatore & Valsiner, 2010). Here one can see the basic difference with the inductive approach—what the latter considers a source of noise that prevents the identification of regularities, the abductive approach sees as the main road to knowledge building.

Different dimensions of variability can be involved to make the local phenomenon under investigation a challenge to the hermeneutic capacity of the general theory. Below I focus on five main dimensions of variability (which can be interpreted in terms of both intra- and intercase variability).

The first source of variability concerns instruments and procedures of data retrieval. The more variable the types of data (interviews, behaviors in daily life settings, responses to questionnaires, and so forth), the better it is. Indeed, when a variety of data types is involved a more abstract model has to be built than the one required to understand just one type of data. This is so because, due to the contingency of the psychological phenomena, any instrument does not only gather information on the phenomenon, but shapes its format, its way of working. Consequently, only by varying the type of data is it possible to go beyond the mediational effect produced by the data retrieval format. For instance, consider an investigator that wants to analyze the relation between students and school. This can be carried out, among other ways, by interviewing students, by asking them to respond to a questionnaire, by observing them during school time, in class, and so forth. Each of these procedure provides a "slice" of the phenomenon at stake which is necessarily shaped by the format of the source used to obtain it—for example, open interviews could provide data concerning the nexus between free time and school experience, while the data sourced from the questionnaire may be more concerned with the attitude toward school. These differences are not "noise" to be eliminated; rather, they are the way the global field process (i.e., the student-school exchange) instantiates itself through the mediation of different settings of analysis, namely, in terms of different field parameters. Thus, the more the settings, the more the forms of the process, and the more the chance to abstract a meaningful model of the latter.

The second source of variability concerns the domains of investigation. Indeed, the phenomenon under investigation may be analyzed in a plurality of circumstances, concerning different micro and macro phenomenical domains. Coming back to the example proposed above, the investigator could focus on a plurality of domains, each of them providing a version of the whole gestalt consisting of the relation between school and students—for example, the interconnection between formal and informal role, the role played by the institutional setting in mediating the peer-to-peer exchange, the communication between teachers and students in formal and informal settings, the teaching-learning process and its outcome as well as the way the students use the school membership in their social exchanges outside the school, the teachers' image of the students, the way the school administration handles critical events concerning students, and so forth. The same tenet proposed above is at stake here as well: each of these phenomenical domains shapes a specific format of the global field under investigation; consequently, the greater the capacity of the analysis to encompass the plurality of the phenomenical forms of instantiation, the more powerful the abstractive modeling of the global process under-pinning all these instantiations. By contrast, if the analysis were limited to one domain, the investigator would be prevented from understanding what, in the model detected, would be worth considering a structural, in-variant component of the process and what should be considered contin-gent to that domain. In the final analysis, *abstractive generalization consists exactly of this distinction*. Through such a distinction a more abstract level of generalization can be reached—the level where a certain variability would be encompassed in a global understanding, namely, interpreting it as the expression of a unique field process. In the final analysis, this is another way of defining abstractive generalization: *the reconstruction of the invariant grounds sourcing the variability of the phenomenical occurrences*.

The third source of variability is time. The broader the temporal win-dow, the higher the chance of modeling the case in terms of develop-mental trajectories—namely, as an invariant source of continuous changes over time (cf. Chapter 11; see also Lauro-Grotto, Salvatore, Gennaro, & Gelo, 2009). Needless to say, until time is considered, it is impossible to understand if and to what extent the occurrences of the case could be fur-ther interpreted as depending on the sequential chain in which they are immersed, namely, as part and parcel of a dynamic gestalt unfolding over time (for a discussion of this aspect, focused on the analysis of the psy-chotherapy process, see Salvatore & Tschacher, 2012; for a methodology of case analysis focused on the detection of the temporal trajectories, see Sato, Yasuda, Kido, Arakawa, Mizoguchi, & Valsiner, 2007)

The forth source of variability concerns the *parameters* of the case—to use the terminology of dynamic system theory. The parameters are the contextual conditions that may affect the way the case works. To refer to the example provides above, the level of the class, the size of the class-room, the socioecological environment of the school, the quality of the logistics, are parameters shaping the field under investigation. It is worth noting that the distinction between what one can consider a contextual parameter and what has to be considered an inner aspect of the phenom-enon is not fixed. Rather, it is contingent to the aim and the conceptual framework of the analysis. For instance, the teachers' professional cultures may be considered a parameter in a certain analysis, while part of the pro-cess—that is, a domain of investigation—in another analysis. In general terms, one can consider a parameter to be a state/characteristic that reflect the steadiness of the field. Therefore, the parameter tends to be constant over the time of investigation, and/or it requires the intervention of the investigator to be varied. Thus the variability of the parameters (whether it is induced by the researcher or happens without his/her intervention) enables the analysis to extend the investigation to the boundaries of the system's functioning.

The final source is the *absence*, a strategic dimension of variability that can significantly enlarge the scope of the study. The analysis should not be confined to modeling the presence of the expected occurrences, but also their absence, as well as the presence of unexpected occurrences. In so doing, the model is compelled to be general enough to be able to explain not only why process X occurs, but also why other processes (Y, Z..) that could have occurred, did not. In other words, by considering the absent occurrences as data, the general theory is enabled to provide a generalized understanding of the case, explaining not only the process at stake, but also the fact that this particular process comes about instead of others. For instance, if the research intends to model the psychotherapy process and under what circumstances it is efficacious, the researcher would benefit from considering instances of psychotherapy process that have proved ineffective, as well as instances of human communication different from psychotherapy. Such phenomena would represent instances of absence of the expected phenomenon (the efficacious psychotherapy process); their analysis would provide food for thought, because they would challenge the model in its capacity to provide a deeper, more abstract understanding of the case, including its dark side too. The model would be asked to provide an understanding both of how the process works, but also of the conditions and mechanisms that make the difference between its possibility of operating and the impossibility of doing so. In the final analysis, any instance of human affairs should be understood not only in terms of why and how it occurs, but also in terms of why and how it has occurred instead of another instance and why and how it might not have occurred.

In sum, taken as a whole, these five sources of variability are ways of challenging the analysis to find an increasingly comprehensive understanding of the case, namely, a model that is abstract enough to detect the invariant mechanism sourcing the heterogeneous phenomenical occurrences—as well as the absence of the ones that there could have been but are not.

Abductive Generalization and Theory Construction

This leads to an interesting point: In abductive logic, theory and evidence are circularly bound—in an open-ended cycle. In particular, one can identify several types of emergence from the dynamic interactions between the phenomena, the local modeling of them and the general theory mediating them. The first type is that of *discovering*, that is, when the researcher has to elaborate *ex nihilo* a new general rule in order to model the local example. The second type is that of the *abstraction* of the already available general theory. In this case, in order to understand the phenomenon abductively, the researcher has to elaborate the theory making it more abstract and general. For instance, the researcher might have been able to model a case of psychotherapy only after having considering the process of psychotherapy as a specific specimen of human communication and thereby using the general knowledge concerning the latter as ground for modeling the case. The third type is *extension*. In this case the analysis of the exemplar leads to a broader domain of application of the general theory. Unlike abstraction, in this case the theory does not change, but is applied to new phenomena. For instance, the research could have modeled innovation in the work context in terms of a local model grounded on the Piagetian model of equilibrium between assimilation and accommodation. In so doing, the model is pushed toward a further enlargement of its boundaries of application. Finally, we have *differentiation*. In this case the study of the phenomenon highlights the limit of the present general theory to produce understanding. And this leads to a reduction of the domain of the theory's validity.

THE COMPLEMENTARITY OF IDIOGRAPHIC AND NOMOTHETIC

A relevant theoretical and methodological implication that one can draw from the discussion in the previous sections of this chapter is that abductive generalization provides a way of overcoming the traditional, ideological nomothetic-idiographic opposition (Salvatore & Valsiner, 2009, 2010; Salvatore, 2014, in press). This is so because the abductive generalization— as modeled above—is a way of interconnecting generalized knowledge and understanding of the contingent events—the former grounds the latter and the latter is used for the sake of developing the former.

A Misunderstood Notion

Historically, the idiographic approach has been associated with the recognition of the uniqueness of the object of investigation—nomothetic knowledge concerns regularities detected in terms of general laws, idiographic knowledge is the knowledge of the particular, of the single event, of what is happened, taken in its uniqueness.

the empirical sciences seek in the knowledge of reality either the general in the form of natural law or the particular in the historically determined form. They consider in one part the ever-enduring form, in the other part the unique content, determined within itself, of an actual happening. The one comprises sciences of law, the other sciences of events; the former teaches what always is, the latter what once was. If one may resort to neologisms, it can be said that scientific thought is in one case nomothetic, in the other idiographic. (Windelband, [1894]1904/1998, p. 13)

Later, and despite Windelband,[4] the notion of uniqueness has been interpreted as opposed to that of generalization, as if the idiographic knowledge were not knowledge of the unique, but a unique knowledge, namely, a form of knowledge nonentailing any form of generalization (Salvatore & Valsiner, 2009). This interpretation, that implicitly overlaps uniqueness and singleness, is rather problematic. In fact, any form of knowledge is inherently a form of generalization. Moreover, the very fact of recognizing an occurrence requires connecting it to a class—to say that something is unique entails using a criterion; any single event is recognized as unique through its conceptual linkages of similarity and difference with other objects. For instance, the battle of Waterloo can be represented—and considered a unique event—because it can be detected as a battle, since it shares some aspects with other events (the very many battles occurring in the history of humanity) and at the same time because of its being different from other battles (for a critical discussion, concerned with the use of the notion of idiographic in clinical psychology, see Thornton, 2008).

Uniqueness as Contingency

This interpretation of uniqueness as opposed to generalization has to be contextualized to the state of the scientific debate of the early 20th century. The contemporary scientific context calls for a different interpretation, that helps to avoid the pitfalls of the equation uniqueness = singleness. More specifically, as the discussion developed in the previous paragraph should have shown, the notion of field and the idea of the process as local instantiation of dynamic lead to the interpretation of the notion of uniqueness in terms of *contingency*. Accordingly, a phenomenon is unique not because of its being the specimen of a class having $N = 1$; rather it is unique in the sense that its occurrence is the local, not replicable instant event in terms of which a certain process instantiates the field dynamic. Thus, the interpretation of uniqueness in terms of contingency does not negate the singleness of the occurrence. Yet it enlarges the view, moving the focus of attention from the comparison of the empirical content of the occurrence to the field dynamic from which it emerges. In sum, the basic issue shifts from the question: "in which terms and to what extent is this empirical occurrence similar and can be assimilated to other comparable empirical occurrences?" to the question: "of which field dynamic is this occurrence the clue?"

Take for example an occurrence of bullying. According to the approach proposed here, the issue is not in which category of bullying to place the occurrence, but to model the field process that can help to understand the occurrence as the local emergence of the field process characterizing the human context under analysis (i.e. the class, the school, the peer group)— namely, to understand the occurrence as the contingent event of the field.

This leads to the conclusion that abductive generalization is possibly the distinctive quality of idiographic knowledge (Salvatore & Valsiner, 2009, 2010). According to our proposal, idiographic knowledge is not a form of knowledge that refuses generalization (an oxymoron, as I said above). Rather, it is a form of knowledge building that is committed to abduction as the way of generalizing through the particular.

In sum, once uniqueness is interpreted in terms of contingency and therefore recognized as the inherent quality of the psychological phenomena, due to the field nature of the latter, then the idiographic approach (i.e., the study of the unique event) can no longer be considered the opposite of nomothetic (i.e., the search for generalized rules)—Rather, idiography is the abductive way by means of which the unique event is studied for the sake of building nomothetic knowledge.

Thus, the recognition of the need for an idiographic, abductive way of analyzing psychological phenomena does not mean giving up generalization. Generalization is at the core of scientific knowledge. What is renounced is the priority of *inductive* generalization, in order to leave room for the abductive model of generalization. In abductive methodology theory and data are circularly connected and the construction of general knowledge is pursued through the model of the local phenomena.

In sum, what is proposed here is a mutually inclusive vision of the idiographic-nomothetic dichotomy (Valsiner, 2007). They are not in competition: idiography is the way of pursuing generalized knowledge (Salvatore & Valsiner, 2009, 2010) by means of the analysis of contingent events in their field. In the final analysis, abductive logic does not generalize the particular; rather it generalizes through the particular.

Conclusive Remarks

In what follows some implications of the view of the idiographic-nomothetic duality proposed above are highlighted.

First, the idiographic orientation is a methodological stance—it does not have a specific object of investigation. The idiographic approach can address any kind of psychological object (Salvatore & Valsiner, 2009; Valsiner & Salvatore, 2011; Valsiner, Salvatore, & Gennaro, 2010).

Second, the traditional idiographic/nomothetic dichotomy does not concern any of the opposition characterizing the psychology debate (quantitative versus qualitative, emic versus ethic, hermeneutic versus positivist; individualism versus collectivism, etc.). One can perform an idiographic strategy of research by adopting both quantitative and qualitative methods of analysis (Salvatore, Gennaro, & Valsiner, 2012, 2014; Salvatore, Valsiner, Gennaro & Travers Simon, 2011; Salvatore, Valsiner, Strout, & Clegg, 2009a, 2009b). And one can adopt a hermeneutic intensive analysis of a single case and nevertheless conduct a study inconsistent with the idiographic assumptions proposed in this chapter.

A final remark. The idea of the nomothetic study as the way of producing universal, validated knowledge is a myth. Because of this myth psychological science has decreased its capability of developing knowledge, rather than increasing it. And if one goes beyond the myth, it is evident that the model of psychological science based on induction is a self-referential process, a game were one finds what one looks for. Peirce conceptualizes it as "the formation of a habit." Falsificationism is the fig-leaf covering this game. How many articles are published that conclude with the acceptance of the null hypothesis? How many theories have been abandoned as consequence of the results of an experiment?

On the other hand, abduction entails a specific logic of validation that is inherently interwoven with the process of construction of knowledge itself. In the case of abduction, the validation of general knowledge is itself a possible part of further processes of knowledge construction. In fact, abduction works in terms of modeling a single case and generalizing from it. Thus, this process can go on insofar as the model elaborated fits the further case analyzed—that is, it is consistent with the model emerging from the new case. If this consistence is not given, the researcher is compelled to revise the model and/or to revise the theoretical framework grounding it. In the final analysis—the idiographic imperative moves research from the logic of confirmation to the logic of the construction of knowledge.

CONCLUSION

In this chapter I have proposed abstractive generalization grounded on abductive inference as an alternative to inductive, extensional generalization to provide the methodological framework for the psychological empirical investigation of sensemaking.

The basic issue is that psychosocial phenomenical occurrences are field dynamic, which means they are contingent to the conditions of their unfolding. This means that their empirical content does not have an unvarying psychological meaning. Instead, it depends on the way the oc-currences combine with each other in the spatial-temporal local field: two elements that are empirically similar (e.g., two episodes of school drop-out) may have two very different psychological meanings just as two very dissimilar elements may have the same psychological meaning, according to the contingency of their field co-occurrence (Toomela, 2007, 2008). Consequently, to conceive of psychological analysis in terms of inductive inferences means scotomizing the field dependency of the psychological occurrences. Inductive generalization addresses occurrences in terms of their redundancies, used for the sake of identifying the regularity (general rule). According to the terminology used by Pierce (1897/1932), induc-tion is "the formation of a habit." And this means that within the frame of induction, the occurrences are interpreted and aggregated according to their factual, commonsensical canonical meaning. Therefore, the abduc-tion is still at stake (because the occurrences are still interpreted in the light of a general rule); yet the abduction involved is that which uses com-mon sense as the grounds of understanding.

As discussed above, abstractive generalization is aimed at generalizing the theory's capacity to produce a local model of data. Thus, the occur-rences constituting the event under investigation are treated as events that call for a contingent understanding. The relevant term here is *contingent*, as opposed to *universal*. In the case of inductive generalization, the under-standing consists of the projection of the set of occurrences upon a certain class of similar occurrences, thanks to which the set is given the meaning (the predicates, in the terms adopted above) of the class. In contrast, ab-stractive generalization fosters a form of understanding consisting of the definition of a contingent class encompassing the set of occurrences (as well as the set of absent occurrences) in a whole gestalt that makes sense, namely, that enables us to understand the co-presence and co-absence of occurrences. This contingent class is not a universal. Rather, it is a model of the pattern of co-occurrences that is unique, specific, contingent to the case. On the other hand, it can be defined only on the grounds of the background universal knowledge provided by the general theory, which is validated in this very capacity to operate at the service of local under-standing.

I have drawn two methodological tenets from such a view. On the one hand, I have retrieved the distinction between dynamic and process, in order to clarify how the bridge between general theory and local model of contingency can be constructed. On the other hand, I have underlined the centrality, for abductive investigation, of focusing on variability. Variabil-ity challenges the theory to find abstract, comprehensive understanding, in so doing compelling it to develop in order to acquire more and more heuristic capacity.

Taken as a whole, my proposal lends itself to be seen as a way of giving back the primacy to theory in the psychology domain, yet not against data. Rather, the empirical investigation is a lever in the process of knowledge building. Data cannot substitute theory, but theory needs data to grow.

Before concluding, two last remarks are worth making. The abductive approach calls for a strategy (and a culture) of empirical investigation in a certain sense the opposite of the mainstream one, based on induction. The abductive development of theory outlined above requires the heuristic capacity of theory to be challenged. Consequently, the choice of phenomena is oriented to the search of the marginal event, of the divergent and surprising occurrence, the one that is able to bring the consolidated understanding into question, compelling the student to further elaborate, to increase the abstractness of the theory. In sum, marginal occurrences that inductive logic considers noise preventing the search for regularities, come to be valorized by abduction as the primary source of knowledge.

Finally, abductive logic makes it clear that for psychology it is useful to achieve modes of formalization of scientific knowledge. As discussed, abductive generalization works in terms of progressive abstraction of the model. Therefore, formal languages represent a useful tool for the development of psychology.

NOTES

1. It is worth underlining that the term "psychological" is used here to denote the conceptual meaning of phenomena according to and for the sake of psychological science. Therefore, it does not concern the content of the subjective experience. This use of the term "psychological" is thus similar to the use of the term "physical" in reference to the objects of physics, rather than as used in the phrase "physical activity."
2. Molenaar and Valsiner (2009) considers psychological phenomena as nonergodic—this property defines the field dependency of psychological phenomena in mathematical terms.
3. For instance, consider the case characterized by the occurrences: $a, b, b, a, b,$ b, b, a, b, b, b, b, a. The empirical content of such a process is unique, thus it could not be generalized if such content were taken as the object of analysis. In contrast, the pattern characterizing the relationship a–b could be analysed beyond (but not independently from) its empirical content—that is, in terms of the tendency of the second element of the dyad (b) to increase its incidence through time. Now, this model represents an abstract map of the case, a representation of it devoid of empirical content. On the other hand, "giving up" the reference to the empirical makes it possible to develop a generalization among different cases through abstraction—for instance it could be argued that a case highlighting the pattern $m, n, n, m, n, n, n, m, n,$

n, n, n, m, in spite of the different empirical content, follows the same model as the former case.

4. Windelband's contrast was build on classical philosophical grounds—as Plato focused on the general immutable character of phenomena, Aristotle sought the same—generality—in the purposefully developing individual being (Windelband, [1894]1904/1998, p. 12). Thus both nomothetic and idiographic perspectives—in their different ways—strive towards gaining generalized knowledge. The fragmentation of contemporary psychological science (Toomela, 2008; Yurevich, 2009) has led what were originally seen as two constitutive dimensions of scientific knowledge to be transformed into two diametrically opposed and incommensurable credos. On one hand, mainstream psychology that uncritically interprets its findings concerning samples as indicative of universal law (for a criticism of this interpretation in the field of theory of personality, see Lamiell, 1998, 2003) and, on the other hand, students that adopt the idiographic idea as if it meant asserting the invalidity of any kind of generalized knowledge in the case of human affairs.

CHAPTER 10

THE MODELING
OF SENSEMAKING

This chapter is devoted to an in-depth examination of two further core implications, deriving from the recognition of the field nature of sensemaking. First, the focus is on the need to re-think the subject of the analysis in accordance with the field and semiotic nature of the psychological phenomena, going beyond the reified notion of the individual. Second, the issue of the aim of the analysis is addressed. Consistently with the SDMS, the view of the analysis as aimed at mapping the semiotic landscape is proposed.

THE SUBJECT OF THE ANALYSIS

The Situativeness of Sensemaking and Its Consequence

According to the SDMS, meaning is inherently local, consisting of the ongoing shape of the trajectory of signs—more precisely, of the ongoing backward transformation of the semiotic landscape produced by the incoming sign (Chapters 1–4). Thus, sensemaking is situated not only because it can occur only in a local circumstance of communication—and this would be obvious—but above all because it consists of the instant by instant transformation of such local circumstance.

Now, given that signs are not a matter of a single individual, a situated view of the subject has to be adopted as well. Any subject's condition is

Psychology in Black and White: The Project of a Theory-Driven Science, pp. 201–228
Copyright © 2016 by Information Age Publishing

not a self-contained state, but it is the precipitate of the local combination of sensemakers' acts. In this sense, *subjectivity is inherently constituted of the other's answer*: The meaning is what follows in the gaze of the other (cf. Chapter 5). An interpretation of this kind leads to a *definitive decoupling of subject and individual*—the subject is extended and concerns the constitutive work of the otherness in sensemaking (i.e., otherness is what follows and interprets, precisely because it is not the same of what it is interpreted). In sum, the subject emerges from the field—and this is another way of highlighting the recursive linkage between presubjectivity and intersubjectivity of sensemaking (cf. Chapter 6).

One major methodological implication is worth drawing here from the recognition of the situativeness of sensemaking. Meaning can be understood only by taking into account the sensemakers' project. Any meaning is inherently performative (Salvatore, Davanzati, Potì, & Ruggiero, 2009)—it is not only a representation of a certain state, but an act performed through that representation, as such endowed with a certain form of addressivity (Linell, 2009; Salvatore & Gennaro, 2012).

Bauer and Gaskell (1999) grasped this aspect, when they underlined that the understanding of social representations requires the understanding of the project it is at the service of. However, one point has to be added. According to the considerations proposed above, the project is not only a matter of functional tasks of adjustment/purpose to pursue. Above all, it is a project of semiotic constitution and reproduction of the subject: the actor becomes subject through the enactment of meaning (cf. Chapter 5). It is through becoming part of sensemaking that the humanization of bodies occurs.

One Individual, Many Subjects

This raises the important issue of the way of conceiving the participants in empirical studies as the source of the meaning to map. Many studies define the subjects involved as participants in terms of their membership of a certain group (e.g., students, workers, French people) and/or of membership of a certain sociodemographic class (e.g., adolescents, males). This definition is then used as the ground on which data are collected and the results are interpreted and generalized. In the final analysis, grounding subjectivity on membership leads to the idea that the fact that data (broadly speaking, interviews, answers to questionnaire, behaviors) have come *from* a given subject, means that such data are *of* that subject, reflecting its characteristics. On this basis subjects can be aggregated and the data thus collected can be assumed as informative of the class of membership about which the aggregation has been carried out (see Chapter 9). Thus,

N individuals may be selected because of being members of the category X (students, immigrants, soccer supporters and so forth) and the data thus obtained (for instance the transcripts of interviews or answers to a questionnaire) are aggregated because they are assumed to concern X. Moreover, the redundancies and variety within data are interpreted as similarities and differences within X (i.e., in terms of the comparison among subclasses X_1, X_2...). Finally, interpretations are generalized to the whole population X. For instance, Scheidegger and Tuscher (2011) have showed how students' social representations of the economic system are affected by their subjective knowledge in economics and academic majors. They arrived at this result by adopting the following research design: students (X) were segmented in subclasses defined by the academic major they attended (X_1 vs X_2) and such subclasses were used as independent variable in a regression analysis with social representation as dependent variable.

Now, the recognition of the situativeness of sensemaking leads to question the "independence" of the subject towards the system of meaning. Consider the following excerpt of the interview of Sultana, a 21 year girl, Muslim, daughter of Indian parent, living in California, student. The interview was carried out in the context of a study on the culture of Muslim Indian immigrants in California (Sriram, 2014).

> As you grow older, it becomes your own responsibility to take on and learn about your religion, I've been doing that, reading books, going for lectures, things like that. I got involved in my responsibilities to learn about my religion as I grew older. A group of students for learning religion—in masjid [mosque], Sunday school, talks about various topics. [I] Went a lot in elementary, middle and high school; both me and brother. He is also a practicing Muslim, is very involved in the practice of Islam. He influenced me in my choice of joining MSA [Muslim Students Association]. (pp. 227–228)

We have a speaker—Sultana—but so many pieces of membership—so, who is the subject that is speaking? In how many studies could Sultana be involved—studies sampling girls, Californian people, immigrants, Muslims, students, and so forth. The fact is that such pieces of membership (and of the self) do not form a cumulative composite picture. Rather, they interact dynamically and form a nonstationary balance in, through and because of the local dynamic of sensemaking. In SDMS terms, Sultana's subjectivity is a matter of field.

As result, a reversion of the terms is worth considering. Instead of assuming the content of the subjectivity as an a priori defined by membership, one should start from the meaning and use it as the frame for understanding the subject. In other words, instead of asking: "what is the system of meaning of group X_1 and in what respects does it vary from that of group X_2?" one should ask: "in what respects does the system of meaning vary and how does such variation lead forms of subjectivity to emerge?"

An example of a study adopting this logic of analysis is provided by Guidi and Salvatore (2014), aimed at analyzing how students' parents represented the school system. To this end, the authors administered a questionnaire to a sample of parents of several Italian schools. The questionnaire concerned: aspects of the micro- and macrosocial environment (e.g., evaluation of social structure and institutional reliability); representations of the (local and national) school system (e.g., opinions about main school functions and goals; problems with the school system…); representation of the teacher role and function (e.g., teachers' mission; teaching aims; characteristics of the "good teacher"…); school service satisfaction models (e.g., exploring the feeling/judgement about school service and teacher qualification according to different criteria, such as: school environment, equipment and supplies). In addition, sociodemographic information about parents (e.g., gender, age, profession) as well as role characteristics (namely, characteristics of the parents' relation with the school, for example, number of children in the school, years of contact with school, distance home-school) were collected. The responses were analyzed through a multidimensional procedure (multiple correspondence analysis and cluster analysis), aimed at detecting patterns of response modalities among respondents. Each pattern was interpreted as the indication of a corresponding model of representation of the school system and participants were clustered according to their responses. Finally, the cultural segments were described (in their similarities and differences) in terms of the sociodemographic and role markers. In so doing, three complementary results were obtained: (a) the identification of a limited number of models of representation of the school system and a map of the content and structure of the culture of the parents in terms of these models and their reciprocal linkages (see next paragraph); (b) the cultural segmentation of participants in terms of such models; (c) the description of the cultural segments in terms of the sociodemographic and role markers. What is important to highlight here is that this study proposed a reversion—before the differences in the system of meaning were mapped (in terms of models of representation), and then used for the sake of interpreting the psychosocial value of the characteristics of micro and macro social membership. This approach seems to be more consistent with the assumption that the content of the subjectivity—in this case, "parentness"—is not something that exists from outside and autonomously from the dynamic of sensemaking within which it is addressed. Rather, the subjectivity emerges through and in terms of situated positioning within the semiotic dynamic.

Before concluding, a further specification is required: this last statement raises a methodological issue. Insofar as studies aimed at mapping dynamics of sensemaking have to start from the meaning, rather than from a ready-made social category of membership, the problem of defining the universe of investigation comes into play. This is so because in most cases the universe of investigation needs to be described in terms of a collective of individuals. For instance, in Guidi and Salvatore's (2014) study, the universe comprised students' parents, that is, individuals identified by means and in terms of their membership of a social category ("parentness"). So, one could be led to conclude that the reversion proposed is only apparent and the ontologization of the subject pushed it out the door only to let it back in through the window. Yet this is not necessarily so if the definitional anchorage of the universe is conceived of in terms of participation in a system of activity, rather than in terms of membership of a social category. This methodological tenet lies on the idea of the situativeness of the dynamic of sensemaking, and therefore on the recursive linkage between the presubjective and intersubjective nature of such dynamics (cf. Chapter 5). Accordingly, any system of meaning is embedded and at the same time emerges from a lived context of interaction addressing a certain more or less explicit object. Given this, the universe of meaning (i.e., the identification of the individual involved in that dynamic of sensemaking) has to be defined in terms of the common condition of relating to this object. This condition is often[1] depicted in terms of a social category (e.g., parents, students, immigrants). Yet the overlap is only apparent, because there are major differences between using the category membership as the definition of the universe and using it to interpret differences of meaning within the universe. First, according to the former use, membership of the category is not the marker of a state (being a parent), endowed with its own psychosocial characteristics, but of a situated process (to be engaged in the activity of addressing a certain object). Second, and consequently, when the category is used in defining the universe, it works as *explanandum*—that is, what has to be understood—while when it is used to interpret the variability of the system of meaning it assumes the logical position of *explanans*—that is, what is used to understand. Needless to say, this distinction is quite subtle, and often it may not be expressed in terms of an empirical difference. Rather, it is a matter of theoretical interpretation of the conceptual framework of the research design.[2]

For instance, consider the interesting study on the emerging process of social representation of the aircraft tragedy of Smolaresk (Dryjanska, 2011). The author compares two subsamples, Polish and Italian people respectively. Thus, as it seems, such categorical difference is used as an explicative factor of the variability of the meaning. Yet, one could consider the categorical distinction not as an explicative factor, but as a definitional criterion—namely, the Polish people as the marker of the condition of being involving in the system of activity consisting in addressing the suddenly emergent object of the dramatic rupture of the socioinstitutional horizon. Accordingly, the Italian subsample could be interpreted as a methodological challenge of the definition of the universe, aimed at testing the validity of the definition of universe.[3]

MODELING SENSEMAKING: THE AIM OF THE ANALYSIS

In order to model sensemaking one has to define what aspect of it has to be modeled: what it is relevant to know about it. Needless to say, the answer to this basic issue depends on the theoretical framework adopted.

The SDMS leads to the following general answer: *the aim of the analysis of sensemaking is the modeling of the phase space of the trajectory of signs, as it is shaped by the dynamic of the SIA.* In other words, analyzing sensemaking means understanding the SIA that grounds the production of signs, their capacity to interpret—and be interpreted by—other signs, therefore making up feelings, thoughts and acts.

It is worth highlighting the peculiarity of the methodological approach proposed above. According to this approach, the scientific investigation of a semiotic phenomenon does not consist only of the collection/description of its representational elements (themes, symbol, images, and the like). Rather, the investigation has to be aimed at *modeling the semiotic landscape* (in SDMS terms, the SIA) working as the *condition of interpretability* of those representational elements. Needless to say the description of the representational elements is an essential operation, yet it is not the final aim of the analysis. The final aim is to understand the latent dynamic frame (i.e., the landscape, the set of SIAs) that enable the enactment of the representational elements as acts of meaning.

The representational elements occur in terms of how they are interpreted within the population—therefore, their meaning is not the output of the scientific analysis, but its starting point. This can be said in terms of the map-territory distinction: to understand the actors' interpretation of a certain object is not the map of the territory but the territory to map. The map of such territory is the semiotic structure that makes that interpretation possible and meaningful for the interpreters. In the final analysis, the difference between the commonsensical activity of interpretation and the scientific investigation of such activity is based on the distinction between the meaning that any sign denotes and connotes (the meaning signified by the sign according to the commonsensical frame) and the meaning—what I have referred to in terms of SIA, landscape, scenarios, domain of sense— that grounds the commonsensical valence of signs. The first is the currency of common sense; the second is the semiotic field shaping the common-sensical interpretative activity that psychological science is asked to model.

The relevance of that second aspect can be found in cultural psychology's focus on the microgenesis of experience (Salvatore, 2012; Valsiner, 2007). From a complementary perspective, it is central to the debate about social representations too, where it has been underlined that the analysis of the meaning has to go beyond the mere depiction of representations and explain the sociocognitive mechanisms grounding and shaping representations (e.g., Bauer & Gaskell, 1999; Molinari & Emiliani, 1996; Moscovici, 1961/1976).

The Analysis of the Semiotic Landscape: An Example

The analysis of the Maltese immigrants' representation of Maltese people, carried out by Sammutt, Tsirogianni, and Wagoner (2012) provide a fine example of an analysis that goes beyond the representational content for the sake of understanding it. The authors adopt a different framework and terminology from the SDMS; yet their approach shows some convergence with the SDMS. Their starting point is a puzzling fact—unlike what happens in other countries, there is not a Maltese community in Britain. In order to understand the system of values and meaning that can ground such specificity, they interviewed Maltese immigrants living in Britain. And what they found was an ambivalent position—on the one hand the Maltese immigrants in Britain seem to assume a form of assimilationist acculturation, where the immigrants tend to identify with the host community and to give up their previous identity; on the other hand, Maltese immigrants are committed to the preservation of linkages with their country of origin (e.g., they cultivate relationships with family and friends living in Malta, they go back to their country, and so forth). This ambivalence is associated with a bipolar social representation of Maltese identity—on the one hand they are proud of being Maltese and of Malta, while on the other hand they avoid involvement with their compatriots in Britain, considering them negatively (as closed-minded, devoted to illegal affairs...). According to the authors, this ambivalent attitude is the way the Maltese immigrants strive to take their distance from the negative self-representation of the Maltese immigrants in order to preserve their position within the British community.

What is interesting here is the authors' way of understanding such negative self-representation. In particular, two aspects are worth pointing out. First, the study depicts the content of the social representation (i.e., the way of viewing Malta and being Maltese) and its inner structure—(i.e., ambivalence). Moreover, once this representation is analyzed, it is used as the *a quo* term for understanding the action—namely, as the factor according to which the ambivalent assimilationist form of acculturation is understood. In terms of the SDMS, this part of the study constitutes the analysis of the SIP. However, the study is not confined to this part. Rather, its focus is on the understanding of the social representation at stake, which, in this way, shifts from the logical position of *explanans* (what explains/ interprets) to the position of *explanandum* (what has to be explained/interpreted). Second, the way the authors interpret the social representation at stake has significant similarities with the idea of SIA and its analysis—so that it lends itself to be read as an instance of analysis of semiotic landscape. More specifically, the Maltese self-representation is interpreted as inscribed in a generalized system of values working as the core of social representation. Such a system of value consists of the merging of connotations of autonomy, security, economic wellbeing, with the commitment to follow foreign rules. Authors reconstruct the historical evolution of this system, dating it back to the medieval age, when, mediated by the value of chivalric love, the choice of concubinage with foreign rulers made by many young Maltese women acquired a meaning of holiness. And yet due to its peripheral position, the latter element (holiness) ended up being lost and this transformed the system of values into the mere merging between security and involvement in the sex industry (yet, as authors note, only with foreign people connoted as conveying resources useful for the Maltese's survival needs). This social representation has come down through the years, grounding different attitudes of Maltese people, due to the historical circumstances—in particular, the author shows that the evolution of the social representation defines the scenario according to which acquire sense historical phenomena such as: the development of a flourishing sex industry after World War II, when Malta was a settlement of Anglo-American troops; the exportation of such kind of business in London in the sixties and seventies; till the bivalent attitude of contemporary Maltese immigrants in Britain.

Some differences between the analytic approach adopted by Sammut and colleagues (2012) and the SDMS have to be recognized—for example, the SDMS privileges a microanalytic, subsymbolic, generalized level of meaning and the focus on the microprocess of communication, rather than patterns depictable in terms of values qualifying entire historical ages. However, despite these differences, the system of values which authors recognize as the ground of the way Maltese immigrants speak and act has two relevant convergences with the concept of SIA as proposed by the SDMS. First, as is highlighted by the authors' reference to Bartlett, the system of value is not conceived of as a superorder, self-contained meaning; rather it is conceptualized as a background of dynamic experiences ("active developing patterns") working as the ground of interpretation (see also

Salvatore & Freda, 2011). On the other hand, this view is consistent with a semiotic theory of the relation between meanings—namely, the idea that relations among meanings (namely, among thought, feelings and acts) are semiotic relationships rather than cause-effect linkages. Consequently, a generalized meaning does not "cause" a specific representational output (a SIP); rather, the former works as the condition of interpretability grounding a certain process of representation and therefore its output (Salvatore & Zittoun, 2011a). Second, the analysis of the system of values grounding the social representation is performed through a process of abductive reconstruction (that authors call a "deconstructive effort that maps the evolutionary trajectory of the representation" p. 500). Such a process entails searching for the variability/rupture of the expected datum as the source of the knowledge building. Unlike the inductive strategy, aimed at accumulating homogeneities and redundancies, the abductive logic seeks for differences and "emptiness" that requires an interpretative, conjectural model to be filled (cf. Chapter 9). Sammut and colleagues work on three sources of difference: (a) the specificity of the form of acculturation that Maltese immigrants in Britain enact towards the other country; (b) the ambivalent, contradictory attitude regarding their compatriots (avoiding the ones in Britain; seeking the ones in Malta); (c) the historical transformations of the attitude of Maltese people towards foreigners. The abductive interpretation of such difference leads authors to reconstruct the system of value—and its evolution—that enables to close the gestalt, what Peirce proposed as the "unification of the predicates" (see Chapter 9).

SEMANTIC AND SEMIOTIC

Underlined above is the need to move the analysis of sensemaking beyond the SIP, and to grasp the semiotic landscape working as the condition of interpretability of the former. This point leads to distinguishing between semantic and semiotic levels of analysis. At the semantic level, signs are assumed to be endowed with an elementary semantic content, representing the minimal units of significance working as the building blocks of the system of meaning, which in turn organizes the semantic contents. Needless to say, such building blocks are not necessarily conceived of as having a fixed meaning. Rather, insofar as the analysis is able to project them onto a salient context they can be interpreted in accordance to it. And this is the point at which one can recognize the merits of strategies like pattern and transition analysis (see Chapter 11). Yet, building blocks are assumed to have content in themselves, rather than acquiring it instantly, through the dynamic of their situated displacement. For instance, the patterns of words identified by Salvatore, Gennaro, Auletta, Tonti, and Nitti (2012) are interpreted on the basis of the assumption that each word has own semantic content and that the content of the pattern resulted from the combination of those elementary contents.

Lahlou and Abric (2011) provide a thoughtful discussion about this compositional way of considering meaning (in their theoretical orientation, the focus is on social representations, but their considerations can be generalized). They start from the recognition of how social representations are conceived in molecular terms, as combination of basic elements.

> In practice, most current descriptive theories of SR tend to be molecular, explicitly or implicitly. They search for specific nodes, or elements, usually in discourse or word associations, through qualitative analysis or statistical investigation. Then they describe the representation as a compound of these elements, and therefore can be seen as variations on the molecular model formalized by Codol. In this respect they follow, as most other psychological theories, the natural slope of symbolic modelling, which tends to describe anything as a combination of basic elements. (p. 20.4)

The authors discuss how to consider the elements, in relation to Codol's (1969) notion of *cogneme*, intended as the smallest cognitive units. And they efficaciously show all the limits of such way of thinking.

> The idea that the world would be decomposable in a finite set of discrete elements, which dates back at least to classic Greek philosophy and has influenced in its time many sciences (Physics, Genetics and Linguistics being the most prominent examples) has proven to be a dead-end. (p. 20.5)

This is so because—as Lalhou and Abric (2011) underline—elements are not fact, states of the world; they have no ontological status—rather, they are forms of description whose validity depends on the scale and purpose of the observation.

> If we want to track down representations into elementary units, at some point they will dissolve into neural networks. To take again the example of maps, at some level in scale, the very notion of "contour" of the object vanishes. The contour of "the coast" at the scale of 1:1 map becomes difficult to describe (should we trace the contour of sand grains and small rocks?) because "the coast" is a descriptive concept valid at a larger scale only. Models are valid only at a given scale. Not only is this true for individual representations, but it is even truer for SRs, which, as they are statistical constructs referring to a population, can afford no clear-cut definition. (p. 20.5)

Such considerations lead authors to recognize the epistemological limits of the molecular approach, namely, the necessity of considering cognemes as a way of describing the social representation, rather than a way of defining its ontological constitution. And this is so because, as they state, even though

> it is tricky to use cognemes to describe representations, *we have no other choice* because this is the way humans make descriptions: with signs, elements referring to other objects. (p 20.7)

Now, while the previous considerations are fully acceptable, the conclusion is not: it is worth seeking a different possibility. The fact that humans describe in a molecular way does not necessarily mean that the elements used as a scientific model and the elements constituting the object to describe must have the same epistemological quality. Just to give a couple of examples, the language of linguistics and of economics (i.e., the semantics and the syntax of the map) is not the language of language games or of economic transactions (the language of the territory). Thus, rather than assuming the molecular approach as an ineluctable destiny, one could try to go beyond it, not in order to negate its validity, but to complement it— namely to take the sensemaking model beyond the pillars of Hercules of the scale level where it is possible to analyze the constitution of the semantic content as emerging from the local dynamic network of interactions among occurrences (Visetti & Cadiot, 2002).

According to the SDMS, semantic content is not what moves sensemaking, but the product of the latter. More specifically, it is the generalization of the instant meaning emerging from the dynamic of sensemaking: a sort of pertinentization of the most frequent values that a certain sign acquires over the way it is used. This can be illustrated through the topological distinction between sense and meaning, proposed by Vygotsky (1934). According to him, "sense" is the "totality of the psychological events aroused in our consciousness by the word," while "meaning" as "only one of the zones of sense that the word acquires in the context of some kind of speaking" (p. 305, as translated by Valsiner, 2001, p. 89). So, the semantic content can be intended as the zones of sense corresponding to a redundant use of the word, as emerging over a plurality of contexts of speaking. This is what the shift from semantics to semiosis consists of—not the negation of semantics, but the enlargement of the analysis to the level of sensemaking where the dynamic of interconnection among occurrences (i.e., the context of speaking, in Vygotsky's terms) makes the latter emerge as a sign with its own content. With an analogy, the enlargement from semantic to semiotic is the equivalent, in psychology, of the passage from classic to quantum physics. The latter does not cancel the first, but enables it to be considered a special case at a specific scale of observation.

Needless to say, as in the case of classic physics, the level of observation of the sensemaking can be left in the background, as a methodological

5888

8888888

888888888888888

decision, whose validity depends on the purpose of the analysis. Yet, the background must not be forgotten, because if it is, the semantic content cannot but end up being seen as a state of fact, an inherent property of signs.

AN INSTANCE OF SEMIOTIC ANALYSIS: GAMBLING AS AN ACT OF MEANING

In what follows, a further example of the analysis of the semiotic landscape is provided. In this case the analysis is specifically grounded on the SDMS. Thus, it can be considered an instance of how the SDMS grounds a specific way of understanding a given phenomenon in a semiotic key. The phenomenon involved is gambling.

The Phenomenology of Gambling

It would be hard to conceive of the widespread involvement in gambling as the consequence of the malfunctioning of any mental mechanism and/or personality trait (e.g., control of impulses, self-aggression, masochism) in gamblers. Even if one accepted that in certain circumstances gambling could be a form of psychopathology, this cannot be a generalized interpretation, unless we are to regard most of the population (e.g., 80% of Italians gamble) as being affected by mental malfunctioning.

This leads to a shift of focus to the phenomenological standpoint, namely to gamblers' subjectivity, the world of meaning that feeds their self-representation of the experience—what punters feel and believe about their action, coming together with the action and interpreting it. Needless to say, the contents of the gambler's experience are idiosyncratic, varying from case to case. Nevertheless, keeping to a generalized level of analysis —namely, that concerning the cultural script grounding the experience of gambling—one can see some recurrent aspects—*faith, immediacy,* and *continuity*—which I examine briefly below.

Faith. Everyone who has direct or indirect experience of gambling knows that this experience is an intense, pleasant, even inebriating feeling, sustaining the sense of absolute faith in one's own ability to win, to be superior to the world—the latter being presented in the form of Chance and/or other punters. The gambler places bets trusting in the benign face of chance. Because of this faith, people may conceive of gambling as a way of coping with economic difficulties, despite the disadvantageous payoff that, though not highlighted in social communication and advertisement, is easy to recognize. The growth of gambling in times of crisis is a marker of such faith, not justified from a mere economic or functionalist point of view (for a reading of economic behavior in psychological terms, see Salvatore, Forges Davanzati, Potì, & Ruggieri, 2009; Forges Davanzati & Salvatore, 2012), nevertheless essential in the experience of the gambler —the gambler punts to win, not to lose money. It is worth noting that what has just been said does not mean that the objective pursued is to obtain an advantage associated with the win. As Dostoevsky (1866/1945) has shown magisterially, the punter is somehow insensitive to the material consequences of the act of betting. The gambler's faith in winning does not concern the material advantage associated with betting, but the local connection between this act and its positive fulfilment—one could say that is *a matter of happiness with the act, rather than with its functionality.*

Immediacy. A significant aspect of the phenomenology of gambling is that the pleasantness of gambling is associated not only or not mainly with the amount won, but with the temporal closeness between the moment of betting and its outcome. The more immediate the outcome the more appealing it is to punt. It is more exciting to place a bet of a few Euros when the result is immediate than to wait for several weeks before the result of the lottery is revealed. This aspect can be found in the recent evolution of the gambling market—there is a constant tendency to offer forms of gambling where the betting-result linkage is closer and closer and a parallel decline of forms where this linkage takes longer. For instance, the traditional Italian lotteries whose results were known periodically (e.g., weekly, even yearly) have been supplanted by "immediate" lotteries, working through 10-minute cycles.

Continuity. The gambler does not consider gambling as a discrete action with a starting point and an end. Gambling is felt and acted as an uninterrupted flow—each bet is just one step of a single, continuous process where any outcome is the triggering event for the following bet. In other words, any punting is not a self-contained act mediating between the subject (the gambler) and the object (the gambling at stake) but a whole, all-consuming world which the gambler inhabits.

The mechanism of the jackpot—that is, the transformation of the unassigned prize into the prize of the next draw—shows the reciprocal influence of the gambler's feeling of continuity and the structure of gambling—thanks to the jackpot the prize of the single draw is no longer defined within the circumscribed event, but comes to be defined in terms of the participation of the single lottery in the chain of lotteries preceding it. In sum, the jackpot makes the individual lottery a transient moment in a single flow, in which the gambler is immersed. Incidentally, it is worth noting that the jackpot mirrors and assimilates the gambler's feeling of continuity, yet does not invent this feeling. The feeling of continuity is linked to the gambling that took place long before the creation of the jackpot—take, for instance, the many specialized journals that are designed to help punters study statistics associated to lotteries (e.g., to calculate the "late" numbers), so as to make a better choice of the number to bet on in view of its behavior in the previous draws. In sum, the gambler considers the single lottery just a local battle of a perennial struggle. For him/her, any battle, whether lost or won, is just a stage in the preparation of the next one. Punting has an infinite outcome, and thus it has no outcome.

A Puzzling Issue: The Intertwining of Desire and Frustration in the Experience of Gambling

The phenomenological picture presented above is not complete. It has to be integrated with a look at the role played by the experience of *loss*, the experience gamblers have every time the outcome does not fulfil their expectation. In this perspective, it is important to recognize that both from a qualitative and quantitative standpoint, *losing is a constitutive part of the action of punting*. From a quantitative standpoint, regardless of how far chance may be on their side, gamblers cannot help experiencing frequent defeats. On the other hand, the experience of losing is structurally part of gambling—one of the contents of the possible outcome. The subjective value of winning is such because of the way it is connected with the opposite outcome—losing. In other words, the gambler's experience is drawn by the oppositional tension between the desired state and what-is-other-and-has-to-be-avoided. In sum, losing is not merely within the bounds of the act of gambling, as one of its possible results, but is part of the very definition of winning; the latter acquires subjective value only if placed in dialectic opposition to losing.

The constitutive nature of losing in gambling is an important characteristic of this field of experience, distinguishing it from other forms of practice. For instance, consider the situation in which, thanks to a strong commitment, one attains a longed-for prize for a certain merit. Also in that case the person has the experience of obtaining something of value, strongly desired, thanks to commitment. Yet it is not the same feeling as in gambling, because the win is not associated with the risk of losing—winning does not have the sense of: |not losing|. From a complementary point of view, consider the circumstances in which the search for the gratifying state is associated with a risk of negative collateral effects—for example, addiction, smoking, unsafe conduct. What distinguishes such practices from gambling is the fact that in the former cases the negative effects are a by-product of the act, not an inherent part of it. For instance, driving dangerously may lead to a crash; yet, in itself, the crash is not an outcome of the action of driving, but a result of its failure. Again, one can see a difference between gambling and those experiences directly aimed at the negative event/state, experienced as the source and the content of pleasure—for example, watching a horror film or jumping from a high bridge.

The constitutive nature of losing in the experience of gambling raises a puzzling issue. On the one hand, the gambler appears to be a person experiencing and acting out a powerful desire. The faith in winning, the search for the immediacy of the outcome, as well as the feeling of gambling as a totalizing whole are all indications of a form of subjectivity intensively projected onto the conquest of the *Valuable Object* (I use this term in the psychodynamic way, namely, to indicate the dimension of otherness constructed by desire, Klein, 1967; see also Muller, 1996; Salvatore & Zittoun, 2011a), felt as being necessarily one's own. On the other hand, gambling is a source of systematic, inherent frustration and disappointment, a symbolic place where people cannot but encounter loss in their pursuit of the win.

In sum, the phenomenological content of the punter's experience is a crucible—in variable proportions—of positive feelings (expectation, desire, explosive joy, excitement), but also negative ones (disappointment, pain, shame, anger, anxiety). And the co-presence of such oppositional elements is the source of what discriminates between those who dislike gambling, regarding it as a circumstance leading to unpleasant events, and the *player*—the one whose motivation seems to be fed, not reduced, by the experience of loss. A clue to this paradox can be found in the commonsensical image of the gambler as someone heading for disaster—an Italian proverb says: "I am not concerned about the fact that you have lost, but the fact that you want to recuperate".

How to understand such a puzzling form of experience—where the pleasure of pursuing a desire is made up, intertwined and fed by its frustration? How can two such apparently contradictory aspects sit together?

A Semiotic View of Gambling: Some Premises

To find an answer to the puzzling issue one has to go beyond the phenomenological standpoint, encompassing it in a more comprehensive, semiotic vision. The interpretation I propose below moves in this direction. It is based on two assumptions.

The first assumption is the idea that gambling is a semiotic phenomenon, namely a dynamic of sensemaking, and as such has to be interpreted. This involves regarding video-poker, betting, spending money on lotteries not merely as a behavior resulting from a certain state of the mind (a feeling, a motive, a computation, a belief) that triggers it, but as an *act of meaning*, namely, a dynamic gestalt within which action and states of mind co-participate in producing sense. More specifically, gambling is an instance of sensemaking through which the person shapes experience, construing a world charged with sense (Salvatore & Freda, 2011). Accordingly, the act of gambling lends itself to be seen as a *field sign* (Valsiner, 2007), namely as a generalized meaning that can transform experience by triggering further generalized meanings (e.g., the benign nature of chance; challenge; the ability to endure bad luck; endless *next-ness...*). Gambling, in this view, works like very many other performative acts of meaning (Austin, 1962)—for example, avoiding taxation, bullying, honoring parents, and so forth—whose generalizing symbolic force enables them to make up a world of sense, far beyond their specific content and local displacement/ target (Salvatore, 2012).

An important consequence of this semiotic view—gambling as a semiotic totality of action, language and states of mind—is that gamblers' phenomenological experience must not be considered the external cause of their conduct; rather, the gambler's experience is intertwined with the action, both (experience and action) being part of the whole field of sense that gambling comprises.

The second assumption concerns the bivalent nature of sensemaking, as modeled by the SDMS. According to this idea, signs have both an *in praesentia* and *in absentia* side (Chapter 2). The phenomenological content of the gambler's self-representation constitutes the *in praesentia* side of meaning (i.e., the SIP)—the aspect of sensemaking directly experienced by the interpreter (in this case: the gambler). At the same time, the *in praesentia* side can be experienced only in terms of a more generalized semiotic landscape—the *in absentia* side of the sign (i.e., the SIA)—in accordance to which it acquires its sense.

From Gambler to Gambling

The two assumptions explained above lead to a peculiar hermeneutic strategy that can be summarized in two basic shifts. First, one has to ask what is the meaning of gambling, rather than what causes it. Second, one has to consider this meaning not only in terms of its *in praesentia* side— that is, the phenomenological content of the gambler's experience—but in terms of the *semiotic landscape* (i.e., the *in absentia* side of the sign) that works as the context of meaning, in so doing making such experience a subjective and intersubjective matter endowed with sense—namely, a piece of existence that can be constituted as such, therefore recognized, represented, negotiated; in sum: inhabited by the subject.

Incidentally, it is worth highlighting the theoretical significance of this second shift. It entails moving from the meaning of *gambler* to that of *gambling*. In the former case, the meaning is the inner semantic and lived content of experience (feeling, representation, scripts, and so forth) through which gamblers understand and orient their participation in the reality of the game. Conceived thus, the subjective meaning is the way of adjusting (in a more or less autonomous and creative mode, not relevant here) to the preexisting and independent reality of the game. In the latter case, the meaning is what emerges from the act of gambling, namely the totality of the lived experience of the act (*in praesentia* side) together with the further generalized context of meaning (*in absentia* side) which must be added in order to make the lived experience interpretable.

In the final analysis, the focus on the act of gambling means that the semiotic analysis does not seek to "discover" the meaning hidden below/inside the gambler and as such "pushing" her to act; rather, it seeks to understand the meaning as *what is produced* by such an act. And what is produced is the context of sense the interpreter (whether it be the gambler and/or the researcher) has to add in order to semiotize the experience. In sum, the semiotic analysis focuses on the performative actualization of a world (i.e., the semiotic landscape) working as the symbolic background of the experience. It is only in relation of such a background that experience is able to acquire sense (Salvatore & Freda, 2011). Such a view is consistent with Ricoeur's (1981) idea that the interpretation has to recognize the meaning unfolding from the text, rather than searching for the author's intention. According to this, the fundamental question that must be posed is not: what does the gambler think/feel that leads him/her to gamble, but: what generalized meaning must be taken as the ground of the gambler's experience—that is, what context of sense must be constructed around this experience in order to make it interpretable?[4]

Gambling as Instantiation of the World-as-"Otherlessness"

Due to what generalized meaning does the constitutive intertwinement between winning and losing underlying the phenomenology of gambling acquire consistency and interpretability? In other words, which context of sense works as the grounds for the gambler's otherwise puzzling experience?

The Omnipotent Desire for the Absolute Object
The answer I propose is the following. The gambler's experience is grounded on the latent, generalized assumption (i.e., the *in absentia* side of the experience—its semiotic landscape) of the *Absolute (availability of the) Object*, as such always able to be attained by the subject's desire.

From a psychodynamic point of view, such a generalized meaning is rooted in the embodied early infantile feeling of omnipotence. The new-born is immersed in the narcissistic illusion that it is its own desire that creates the object (Winnicott, 1975). This illusion is important, because it ensures the constancy of the relation with the object, thus avoiding an otherwise overwhelming experience of frustration that the child's premature psychic apparatus would be unable to support.

The illusion is not the mere product of the hallucinatory capability of the child. Rather, in the early phase of life, it reflects the mother's ability to fulfil readily the demands of the newborn infant. In so doing, the mother allows the infant to feel the object as if it were there at the child's complete disposal, to perfectly fulfil its demand. The infant, therefore, *may feel fully able to instantiate the object through the act of desiring it.* Such a state of initial omnipotence is gradually overcome, as a result of the progressive experience of the absence of the object. The mother, in fact, is not totally good, but good *enough* (Winnicott, 1975)—that is, she is able to satisfy the child's desire with a certain degree of efficacy, though it may not be complete. Thus the child progressively experiences the object as an unstable duality of presence and absence—where the latter works as the condition of the development of thought, that is, of symbolic activity (Bion, 1967; Lacan, 1978). As Winnicott (1975) wrote

> We allow the infant this madness, and only gradually ask for a clear distinguishing between the subjective and that which is capable of objective or scientific proof. We adults use the arts and religion for the off-moments which we all need in the course of reality-testing and reality-acceptance. (p. 224)

Thus, the adult has recognized the unsustainability—the "madness"—of the omnipotent feeling of being capable of creating the Object; yet she/he does not totally give it up—keeping some "off-moments" as symbolic places for the pleasant experience, dense with sense, of the perfect relation with the Object.

According to my thesis, such symbolic places are not only to be found in the arts and religion, but also in other forms of mundane practices, and in particular—as at stake here—in gambling.

The Semiotic Machine of Desire: The Transformation of Loss Into Lack

Once one conceives of the absoluteness of the Object as the gambler's semiotic landscape, his/her experience stops being puzzling and can be recomposed in a consistent, meaningful picture. Take the gambler's faith in winning. It is something more than, and different from, the hope to get an advantage. The gambler's faith is the view of winning as taken for granted, as the only horizon of the gambling act. In other words, winning is the way of shaping experience, the only semiotic category available. Needless to say, this does not mean that the gambler does not perceive the loss; rather, it means that such a perception is semiotized through the certainty of winning[5]—consequently it does not arrive to become a fully experienced event, a fact endowed with value of life (Salvatore & Freda, 2011). Rather, it is experienced as a contingent step on the route towards conjunction with the Object. In other words, *in the world of absolute availability of the Object there is no room for loss—what it is possible to experience is the contingent lack of being fulfilled by it.*

A way of understanding the semiotization of loss in terms of lack is to recognize the action of such a process in other practices. For instance, consider a silence in a conversation. It is not felt as a loss of connection; rather, it is interpreted as a marker of regulation of the turn taking. Thus, the moment of silence is semiotized as being part of a more general totality of fullness (i.e., the conversation). The gambler's loss works as the silence that enables the conversation to go ahead.

The semiotization of loss in terms of lack provides a way of understanding the gambler's commitment to gambling. From a purely phenomenological standpoint, this aspect is quite hard to explain—the gambler commits to betting despite the fact that this act tends to be negatively reinforced. Besides, the more negative the experience, the greater the commitment to repeat it (recall the Italian proverb quoted above). On the contrary, from the semiotic standpoint adopted here, the triggering power of the loss lends itself to be understood—insofar as the loss is experienced as a lack, where the lack is the place/condition of the object's fulfilling (Lacan, 1978), the outcome of the gambling acquires the meaning of the presence of the desired object. In other words, the loss-as-it-were-lack acquires the status of the sign of the fulfilling object—*it stands for the desired object*. Thus, just as the silence triggers the conversation, the negative experience of losing feeds the desire to punt again and again.

In the final analysis, this means that the loss does not work as a frustrating experience constraining/contrasting the desire to gamble—the gambler can never be sated, because he/she always experiences a lack to be satisfied. Instead, the loss works as the inner trigger of the dynamic's reproduction, making gambling a self-feeding flow. In sum, the act of gambling is a semiotic dynamic made up by a peculiar recursive circuit: the loss experienced as a lack is the sign of the desired object that in turn feeds the subject's desire, in turn signified in the performative terms of the commitment to punting. The outcome of such a semiotic chain does not make it end. Whether the outcome of the bet is positive (and this is more consistent with common sense) or negative, it is experienced as the sign of the fulfilling object, and therefore it works as the trigger of the desire. And thus, the circuit goes on.

The Gambler, Scarlett O'Hara, King Midas, and Gloves

As observed above, the object the gambler engages in is not defined by the single bet. Rather, it is the circuit in itself which is experienced as the lived field of the relation with the Absolute Object. Thanks to such a transformation, the act of gambling is able to work as a constant source of the Object's availability. Any instance of punting is void of value in itself, it is only the local, contingent manifestation of the state of the relationship with the whole Object, whose presence is however assured. The search for immediacy and the feeling of continuity characterizing the gambler's phenomenology can be interpreted in the light of this basic semiotic transformation. It can be considered the outcome of a mechanism of abstractive generalization—the single event of betting is devoid of any value other than its being a local specimen instantiating the generalized class of relationship with the Object. In the final analysis, one can say that the gambler does not experience the punter; rather, he/she is engaged in the ongoing process of *"puntingness."*

According to this perspective, the gambler can be compared to the frustrated lover that subjects herself to the perennial torture of searching for the loved object and finding rejection—where such rejection is just lived as the instant experience of a lack, the not-yet moment, to be fulfilled through a continued search. In so doing, the lover, like the gambler, puts loss in place of the experience of the Object—even if at the cost of transforming it from a specific experience to the flow of engagements experienced as a single totality. The magic quality of such a transformation lies in the fact that nothing can interrupt it—it rewrites the otherness so that instead of working as the source of constraint, it works as the device of reproduction of the flow. In the final analysis, this means that through gambling the desire acquires the semiotic status of a sign that is able to satisfy itself. What is gratifying in gambling is not the quality of its outcome—rather, it is the act of desiring per se, since this act can contain the trace of the presence of its object, can instantiate it. This capacity is such regardless of the destiny of the act, that is, the mundane answer to it in terms of win or loss.

In sum, in gambling the desire is enabled to satisfy itself.[6] In this sense, *gambling can be viewed as a semiotic performative machine transforming the absence of the object (the loss) into the sign of its presence (the lack/not-yet moment).* When Scarlett O' Hara (Fleming, 1939) views her husband, Rhett Butler, turning away from her, her reaction is to state that she will recapture him —there is not loss, but only a contingent lack, which will be fulfilled in the next moment of the infinite flow of time ("tomorrow is another day"). The loss object (Rhett) is transformed into an instantaneous absence ready to be overcome (tomorrow). Scarlett has had a negative outcome, and this makes her ready for the next bet.

Seen in this way, the grounded generalized meaning instantiated by the act of gambling can be paralleled to the myth of King Midas. According to the interpretative key proposed above, the myth of King Midas is the dramatized image of the absolute power of desire to generate its object through the act of desiring it—what is desired (gold) comes into being *because of the very fact of being desired*. Yet, the absolutization of the power of desire defines the condition of its destruction—King Midas cannot but experience objects in terms of the singular quality of their being the Object of his desire—namely, as gold. And this is the same as saying that King Midas does not meet objects, whose charge of otherness make them suitable to be engaged in a contingent, constrained (and, because of that, meaningful) relationship; rather he is able and at the same time condemned to meet only and always the Object-ness: *"goldness."* This is the *tragedy of absolute desire*—its full realization is *ipso facto* its total negation. The complete saturation of desire is the death of desire.

As we have said above, the gambler shares with King Midas the same ground—the sense of the absolute availability of the Object. On the other hand, it can be considered a form of escaping from the tragedy narrated by King Midas' destiny. *The loss experienced by the gambler provides such a way of escaping, introducing the local failure of desire*. This failure plays a bivalent semiotic role: it inserts a vivifying distance between the desire and the object and at the same time signifies it as its overcoming. If you like, the gambler is a sort of King Midas in gloves—the bearer of an absolute desire contingently unable to be fulfilled and thus able to be kept alive.

The Sweet Pain of Loss

The considerations above lead us to picture gambling in terms of a peculiar dynamics of desire. The act of gambling is the performative semiotic transformation of loss into a lack and the lack into the Object fulfilling it. This transformation consists of a chain of signs, namely a connection through time of generalized meaning each of them standing for the one that follows.

According to this interpretative perspective, it can be concluded that gambling is a *powerful ritual of liquidation of otherness*, namely of the capability of the object to produce its own absence for the subject. Thus, the semiotic outcome of gambling is the *world-as-otherlessness*, the transformation of distance into absolute closeness.

Needless to say, such a ritual can have high costs—it is sufficient to think of how many people are ruined because of gambling. Yet, such costs are the "side effects" of the omnipotent transformation of the outcome into the trigger of the act. These mundane, existential costs enable the powerful semiotic mechanism to work and produce the psychological experience of the unconstrained availability of the object—which is the same as saying: *the cancellation of death,* since death is the paradigmatic, radical form of otherness.

An important consequence of such semiotic dynamics is the moving into the background—in psychoanalytic terms: the scotomization—of the outcome of the action of gambling, namely the mundane consequence of it. The gambler punts and the outcome of its action is freed of its mundane, functional meaning (e.g., the alienation of resource), and therefore able to be seen as a sign standing for the Object.

This semiotic dynamic is not a peculiar trait of gambling. Daily life is the source of many circumstances in which this kind of dynamic is involved. For instance, take the case of drinking Coca-Cola or any other sugary drink. One knows that after drinking Coca-Cola the thirst increases, rather than decreases. However, this negative outcome (i.e., the failure of the point of drinking) is not removed—rather it is pushed into the background, neutralized as an element entering the regulation of the act. And this is so because what is made pertinent in drinking coca-cola is the actual embodied experience of drinking an iced liquid in itself, as the lived instantiation of the fulfilment of the desire to be refreshed. And it is worth noting that the neutralization of the consequence of such drinking —an even more intense thirst—is not only the condition for experiencing drinking as the desired fulfilment; it is also the trigger of the further desire to drink, which in turn can be addressed with more Coca-Cola, in a circuit that tends to the perennial. In sum, drinking Coca-Cola is like gambling—a cycle of desire enacted through its recursive local frustration.

This peculiar form of scotomization of the outcome of the act can help to interpret an otherwise puzzling aspect of the gambler's phenomenology —the one recalled above in terms of immediacy and feeling of continuity. Gamblers experience loss—they are not insensible to frustration. Yet such frustration does not produce learning—rather, it seems to motivate them to gamble further. A popular way of explaining this aspect is to consider it as the effect of a deficit, namely in terms of a shortage in the functioning of any mechanism (e.g., impulse control; ability to appreciate the consequence of one's actions...) or as the product of a self-destructive motivation. By contrast, the view proposed here leads us to interpret the gambler's experience of loss as a feeling experienced as local, contingent, but projected on—and so felt in terms of—the conjunction with the fulfilling Object it stands for. Accordingly, the gambler's negative feelings associated with the loss are experienced as the sign of the object being reached. Thus, the gambler can appreciate the content of reality of the loss—and thanks to this, implement strategies and choices to avoid it— and at the same time consider the feelings associated with it as part of the pleasant experience of gambling. Somehow this gives the impression that he/she is indifferent, anesthetized to it—or even running towards it.

Recursivity as Scotomization of Otherness

As proposed above, the Absolute Object is a semiotic landscape (a SIA), rather than a representational content (a SIP). Due to its affective, hyper-generalized value (Salvatore & Zittoun, 2011a; Valsiner, 2007), it is hard to describe analytically. It grounds language, rather than being held by it. Thus, a way of depicting it is to gather a set of clues of it from a plurality of domains.[7]

From a phenomenological point of view, the feeling of being involved in the Absolute Object characterizes crucial moments, charged with emotional activation—think of the experience of falling in love. In circumstances like that, one feels that one's boundaries expand till they encompass the world and are encompassed by it—belonging is felt as totality: inner and outer merge in a single whole. Again from a phenomenological point of view, psychological marginal states of consciousness, as well as basic forms of rupture of the sense of identity (depersonalization) are experienced in terms that recall the experience of diffusion of the self as if it were a liquid dissolving within the whole.

A form of absolutization of the object is that which is enacted in terms of the activation of recursive loops. In these cases, recursivity is at the service of the negation of constraints/otherness. Insofar as the recursive loop leads to the reintroduction/incorporation of the outcome into the process which produced it, it allows the process to go on as if it were a self-contained mechanism. The outcome loses its value as an instance of the world, as such working as constraints of the desire. Rather, it is transformed into the trigger for a further desire. A clear example of this powerful semiotic mechanism is provided by the movement of the stock market over the last years—thanks to the introduction of financial derivatives, the stock market has become a world where choice is separable from its outcome. It is freed from constraint: it can develop even through its failure—everything it produces is able to feed its reproduction. In the final analysis, the fact that choice is freed from its content of otherness—that is, the meaning of the outcome which does not depend on choice and therefore constrains it (in this case, the real economic values of the financial product)—has made it possible for the market to become its own object. Needless to say, this does not actually cancel the constraints of the reality ad infinitum, yet it moves it ahead, thus producing *the sense* of unconstrained reality.[8] In so doing the stock market has become the world of the *as-if-there-is-no-world-outside*—an instance of the perfect relation with the Absolute Object.

A similar semiotic use of recursivity as a source of wholeness can also be found in obsessive symptoms—here too, recursivity creates a network of self-referential linkages of the self with the self-obsessives does not check many times that the door is closed, rather they check that they have been able to check that the door is closed and so on—allowing them somehow to saturate the relation with the world through the substitution of the latter with a self transformed into the self's object.

Conclusive Remarks

In this section I have reported a semiotic interpretation of gambling. My central thesis is that gambling is a ritual of semiotic neutralization of death. I have based this interpretation on the subjective experience of gambling, yet going beyond it. I have considered meaning to be what the act of gambling produces, rather than what triggers/motivates such an act. According to this perspective, I have proposed that gambling enacts a basic semiotic mechanism—the transformation of the absence into the presence of the Absolute Object. Thanks to such a semiotic mechanism, desire is enabled to satisfy itself—in a hallucinatory way.

It is worth highlighting some aspects that characterize my proposal both at the theoretical and methodological level.

First, my thesis shows what kind of understanding can be attained by integrating semiotic and psychodynamic views (Neuman, 2009, 2010; Neuman & Tamir, 2009; Salvatore & Zittoun, 2011a) provided by the DSMS. As it seems to me, such integration provides a rather innovative, promising way of looking at the dynamic of sensemaking.

Second, it is worth noticing the specific hermeneutic model adopted above. It starts from the content of the phenomenological experience, but goes beyond it, in order to model the semiotic dynamic producing the conditions of such experience (i.e., the semiotic landscape). This methodological choice is mirrored in the refusal to consider what the gambler experiences as the motive for his/her action. A phenomenological assumption like this raises a major theoretical issue—it means reifying the phenomenon to be explained, transforming what has to be understood— the self-representation of experience—into an explicative entity (for a similar argument concerning emotion, see Barrett, 2006). This can be said also from a complementary point of view: the gambler's commitment to betting is made up of the prefigured belief that luck will be kind; yet, if one considered such phenomenological content as the explanation of the act of gambling, one would fall into pseudoempiricism (Smedslund, 1988), namely into the fallacy of considering the semiotic linkage among signs to be part of the same semiotic dynamic totality (i.e., acts and linguistic descriptions) as if it were a causal connection (cf. Introduction and Chapter 9).

Third, further analyses are required in order to validate the interpretation of gambling offered above. However, one important aspect of conceptual validity can be picked up from the previous discussion—the fact that the theory can allow *abductive generalization*. By this term I mean a twofold pathway of knowledge-building (cf. Figure 10.1). On the one hand, the analysis of the psychological phenomenon was performed in terms of hierarchical steps of abstractive modeling. In the case of the analysis carried out above, this methodological strategy works in the following way: the empirical contents (e.g., the gambler's subjective feeling) were connected, as it were, *vertically*, namely by abductively encompassing them in a more abstract theoretical model (e.g., the psychoanalytic notion of Absolute Object). On the other hand, this theoretical model grounded a horizontal form of generalization—the gambling has thus become a specimen of a general class of phenomena and signs (e.g., the stock market, Scarlett O'Hara, drinking Coca-Cola) interpreted through the same interpretative model. In so doing, gambling has been seen both in its local, specific historical content and as the instance of (and a door for) a universal form of relation with the world, crossing time and space.

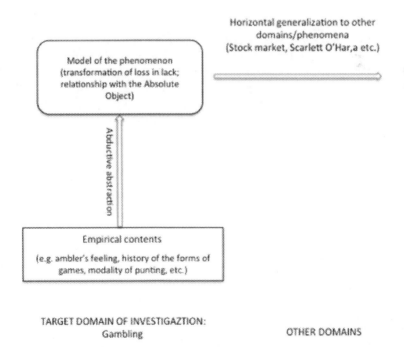

Figure 10.1. A schematic representation of the abductive pathway of knowledge building.

CONCLUSION

In this chapter, I have highlighted the need of a semiotic level of analysis of sensemaking, which has to integrate and complete the semantic one. Such a level is aimed at mapping the semiotic landscape working as the condition of interpretability of the representational content. As I argued, the same definition of participants is contingent to such a level of analysis.

In conclusion, a theoretical caution has to be taken, in order to avoid a misleading interpretation of the relation between semiotic and semantic levels of analysis, and more in general of the meaning-sensemaking relationship. According to the SDMS such distinction has to be conceived of in terms of *frames of observation*, rather than as indicating two different substances. To this conclusion one arrives insofar as one assumes the lack of ontological distinction between meaning and sensemaking. As discussed above, meaning is not a thing, a state or a property of an entity. Rather, it is an event, better a combination of events through time. Thus, meaning and sensemaking are not two different things, but two different ways of seeing the same dynamic, namely, semiosis. Accordingly, we could say meaning is the format of sensemaking extracted when a single snapshot is taken.

Given that, it is theoretically consistent to assume that *what one maps is always sensemaking*. When sensemaking is mapped in terms of instant format, then one "sees" meaning. To make an analogy with the notion of instant speed, meaning is instant sensemaking. To say this in terms of the content-process clash—a longstanding debated in social representations theory (e.g., Lahlou & Abric, 2011)[9]—the content of the representation is not a separate entity from the process of representing, but the instant depiction of the latter. What is always modeled is the process, through the content.

An analogy may help to illustrate this point. Take the representation of movement—for example, a dance, a football match, the clouds moving across the sky- in terms of a single photo. What the photo shows is not something different from the dynamic whole that is photographed. Rather, it is this dynamic whole as it reveals itself through the frame of observation chosen (in this case defined by parameters like the camera's focus and exposure time, the film's light sensitivity); it is the process as it produces an effect on the observer, limited to the observer's frame. Accordingly, any frame of observation can be conceived of as a specific model of disposition to be "effected" by the process. In the final analysis, strictly speaking one should consider the photo a representation *by*, rather than *of* movement.

The analogy proposed above raises the relevant epistemological issue of the language required for representing sensemaking. What is involved here is the need to distinguish the map from the territory: insofar as one assumes that meaning is instant sensemaking, the representation of the sensemaking is of a higher logical order than the meaning of sensemaking. In other words, the phenomenon of representation (i.e., sensemaking) is different from the representation of such a phenomenon (i.e., the scientific map of the sensemaking). The difficulty of retaining this distinction depends on the fact that, in the case of semiotic phenomena, the territory is a map itself. But this makes it even more necessary to separate the semantics and syntax of the scientific mapping from the semantics and syntax of the phenomenon to be mapped. In the final analysis, this means that the psychological inquiry of common sense (i.e., the daily life dynamic of sensemaking) requires a language that is quite independent from common sense (Salvatore, 2006; Salvatore & Valsiner, 2006; Valsiner & Salvatore, 2012). This is so because common sense by definition is blind to itself. When we think and talk daily, we experience meaning. Such meaning, for us, is the world we inhabit. This is so because we are embedded within sensemaking, which works as the dynamic environment through which we experience the world. Therefore, the meaning produced by common sense cannot represent the commonsensical production of such meaning.

NOTES

1. Yet it is not always so. For instance, in studies implementing procedures of text mining the universe is defined in terms of mass-medial agencies. For instance, in order to analyse the representations of nanothecnology in the Spanish mass-media, Veltri (2013) collected articles from a sample of newspapers, assumed to be representative of the universe of the mass-media of that country.

2. This does not mean that it may not undergo empirical testing. Indeed, one can image that the categorical definition of the universe is challenged by involving sources of data from the outside of the universe so defined. On this ground one can use the definitional category as a dependent variable mapped in terms of the variability of the system of meaning of the "enlarged" universe. The more the difference at the categorical level can be projected on the variability of the system of meaning, the more the category is a valid definition of the universe of a system of activity, given that it corresponds to a specific subsystem of meaning. In the final analysis, such a procedure would allow an answer to the preliminary question: is this actually a universethat because of the specific system of activity defining it, has its own, local system of meaning worth investigating as such?

3. On the other hand, this interpretation would mean a different design— namely to start from the map of the universe's system of meaning and to use the variability thus mapped as the ground of the understanding of the sociocultural and pragmatic characteristics of the participants involved in the study.

4. An interesting connection can be found between this way of interpreting human experience and activity and the interpretation of an artistic work in terms of the iconological context governing how the iconographic signs implemented by the work acquire sense—namely can be felt and thought as part of a consistent totality (Panofsky, 1939/1962). In the final analysis, in both kinds of text—human experience and artistic work—the interpreter has to construct a world—in the former case a local context of sense, in the latter case the cultural background of the work—which has to work as the semiotic environment in accordance to which textual elements are put in relation with each other and in so doing acquire the status of signs concurring to the constitution of meaning.

5. To be precise, one cannot talk about certainty, because it still entails the possibility of a difference, even if void of probability. Winning as a goal means just that—it is the absolute assumption within and in terms of which events are experienced.

6. "desire's raison d'être is not to realize its goal, to find full satisfaction, but to reproduce itself as desire" (Žižek, 1997, p. 39).

7. On the other hand, such a meaning is not restricted to daily life experiences. One can also find it in philosophical thought. For instance, take the Hegelian ideal of absolute knowledge as the terminal stage of the Spirit that comes progressively back to itself through dialectically incorporating what is other than itself. Consider, furthermore, the phenomenological notion of belonging as the preexisting linkage that any person cannot but participate in.

8. As we have learnt through the repeated economic clashes of recent years, the stock market represents reality's constraints only in terms of catastrophic rupture of its own self-referentiality. The recent Martin Scorsese (2013) film *The Wolf of Wall Street* provides a clear representation of such a dynamic of desire.

9. We distinguished between two perspectives which, in our opinion, summarize the theoretical and methodological foundations of social representations theory. The first perspective is content-oriented and it is located at the crossroads of several scientific disciplines, in particular sociology, anthropology and social psychology. In this perspective, social representations are considered a sort of "map of contents" on a topic which is particularly relevant to the groups of subjects interviewed. In the second perspective, which we call sociodynamic, social representations are instead located at the core of the internal debate of social psychology on the ways in which individuals arrange and merge the knowledge of their own world. In this view, social representations are not mere descriptions of contents of knowledge, but modes of sociocognitive functioning (Doise, 1990), which start from the assumption that the individual is a socially inserted actor and that such interactions (Bevous, Monteil, & Trognon, 1991) determine the psychosocial specificity of the notion" (Molinari & Emiliani, 1996, p. 42).

CHAPTER 11

MODELS AND STRATEGIES OF EMPIRICAL INVESTIGATION

The field nature of sensemaking is a methodological challenge for psychology and calls for the introduction of a major innovation in methodology (Valsiner, Molenaar, Lyra, & Chaudhary, 2009; Salvatore & Tschacher, 2012). This chapter is devoted to presenting some ideas in this perspective, grounded on the SDMS and designed to contribute to the development of the methodology of empirical analysis of sensemaking. To this end, two complementary dimensions—structural and dynamic analysis—are distinguished first of all. Second, a methodological strategy and its conceptual framework are presented for each dimension. Finally, some procedures and criteria of analysis are presented; this has the twofold purpose of providing an exemplification of the strategies as well as operative indications of how to carry them out.

DYNAMIC AND STRUCTURAL ANALYSIS OF SENSEMAKING

As discussed in the previous chapters, the field dependency of sensemaking highlighted by the SDMS consists of the fact that the meaning of any sign is a matter of the way it combines with other signs, namely, in which synchronic and diachronic pattern of co-occurrence it enters into. The twofold dimensionality of the pattern—namely, its being both synchronic and diachronic—leads one to recognize the need of two complementary foci of analysis: one devoted to depicting the structure of meaning,

Psychology in Black and White: The Project of a Theory-Driven Science, pp. 229–263
Copyright © 2016 by Information Age Publishing
All rights of reproduction in any form reserved.

namely, the synchronic co-occurrence of signs—and the other to mapping its dynamic, namely, the diachronic combination of signs over time. Incidentally, the distinction proposed here can be related to the distinction between syntagmatic and paradigmatic axes presented in Chapter 2. The structural analysis concerns the foreground/background differentiation that any sign produces over the paradigmatic axis—namely, the fact that any patter of signs occurring in a certain instant of time is at the same time a specific pertinentization of a zone of the paradigmatic axis, therefore a specific connection between SIP and SIA. The dynamic analysis concerns the trajectory of signs over the syntagmatic axis, namely, over time.

Needless to say, these foci must not to be considered as two different objects: their differentiation is a matter of frame of observation (Chapter 10)—the structure is what one sees of the dynamic when time is not considered.

Structural Analysis

In order to specify the task of structural analysis, it is worth coming back to the distinction between SIP and SIA, so as to see the structure of meaning in more detail.

As the SDMS shows, meaning is not a thing within the sign, but a field of potentiality (Visetti & Cadiot, 2002), which is actuated in and through the local circumstances of sensemaking. As we have said, this leads to an inversion of the relations between meaning and sensemaking, namely, to look at meaning as the *product* rather than as the *origin* of sensemaking.

This change in the definition of the relationship between meaning and sensemaking allows us to think of the multidimensionality and situativeness of meaning as an inherent and constitutive component of how semiosis works, rather than an accident, a noise that should be put in brackets for the sake of the development of a rigorous model. According to Peirce (1897/1932) the sign stands for the object just *in reference to a specific aspect* (the ground; cf. Chapter 1)—hence, the interpretation performed by the sign-to-come (i.e., the interpretant) concerns the identification of such an aspect. Therefore, it is thanks to *what comes after*—that is, the concrete contingent circumstances of discourse—that the sign is able to signify, namely, to stand for something else, to a specific capacity or aspect, as opposed to all the others that are possible. *Multidimensionality and situativeness is not the problem, it is the solution.*

Let us to see in more detail how multidimensionality and situativeness do their job. Consider the following simple utterance:

You are a girl

What does it mean? It may mean that the reference (presumably a person, but not necessarily...) is an exemplar of the female sexual genre; or that she is young, or that she is a human being, or that she is not a baby anymore, and so forth. And the matter becomes even more complex if one does not stop at the level of utterance, but takes into account the uttering too, namely, the act of producing the utterance: this sentence as a speech act can have infinite meanings, depending on who, when, to whom it is performed (Freda & Pagliaro, 2012).

If one carefully considers how a sentence like that produces meaning, it must be concluded that it happens *both for what the sentence says and what it does not say*. In other words, the meaning of the sentence depends on the fact that the very statement that "something is ...." ("S is x") is at the same time the statement that "something is not something else" ("S is not '*non-x*'"). And this is another way of recognizing that meaning is a matter of the interconnection between SIP and SIA. The paradigmatic axis denotes the set of signs that can occupy the position of the sign x within the syntagma (i.e., within the sequence of signs). In the previous example, the paradigmatic axis indicates the set of signs (x_1, x_2, x_3,...) that can assume the position x in "you are x."

Yet, the notion of paradigmatic axis needs to be further elaborated in two directions, in order to be helpful for the sake of our discussion. First, one has to take the oppositional nature of meaning into account: the meaningfulness of stating "x" consists of the fact that in so doing "S is not *non-x*" is stated as well. For example, consider a discursive circumstance in which stating "you are a girl" acquires the meaning of making pertinent the gender of the subject the term "you" refers to. In such a case, the meaning is both |being a girl|, and |not being a boy|. In order to represent the oppositional nature of the paradigmatic axis, it could be useful to think of it in terms of a circumference (cf. Figure 11.1a). If one assumes that each point of the circumference is a sign, it can be concluded that every other sign lying on the circumference is different from x (i.e., is "*non-x*"); moreover, each sign x has a sign that is diametrically opposed to it: it is the one most distant from it along the circumference; for this reason, here it is indicated with the notation *anti-x*. It is worth noting that, unlike any *not-x*, any *anti-x* has one x as its own *anti-x*. And this is the same as saying that once x is defined, an *anti-x* is defined as well.

Second, as shown in the previous section, it must be considered that the meaning of x varies through the circumstances, in reason of the scenario at stake (Chapters 2–4)—being a girl can mean not being a boy (*anti-x_1*) in one case, yet not being a child or not being a woman (*anti-x_2*) in another case. This means that any x is embedded in a multiplicity of oppositional linkages, each of them having a certain *anti-x*. Thus, one is led to move from the idea of paradigmatic axis, to that of *paradigmatic circumflex*. As

Figure 11.1b illustrates, the paradigmatic plane of *x* consists of an array of circumferences P; each of them represents a given subset of paradigmatic variability in terms of the complementarity between a sign *x* and its oppositional sign *anti-x*. The circumflex S represents the set of oppositional signs, in terms of which the sign *x* can be interpreted. It is worth underlining that any circumference—therefore any opposition *x/anti-x*—of the circumflex corresponds to a scenario in SDMS terms (cf. chapter 2). Accordingly, the view of the meaning of the sign *x* as a function of the particular region of the S represents a geometrical illustration of how the meaning of the SIP is contingent to the SIA.

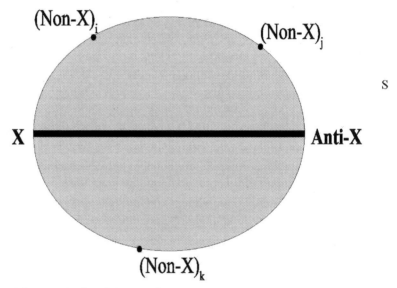

Source: Salvatore, Tonti, and Gennaro (in press).

Figure 11.1a.   The oppositional nature of the meaning (a) and the paradigmatic circumflex (b).

Thus, in conclusion, the final aim of the structural analysis concerns the modelling of the relationship between the SIP and the SIA. It follows that the structural analysis has to address two complementary tasks. First, to map the pattern in terms of which the SIPs are combined with each other within the event under investigation—namely, which SIPs tend to be used together, therefore making up specific patterns of co-occurrence comprising the syntagma comprising the event.[1] As such, a pattern of this kind represents a specific instantiation of the paradigmatic axis. Consequently, it can be interpreted as the clue of a corresponding meaning—namely, a theme, a discursive nucleon (inter alia, see Lancia, 2002, 2005). For example, if

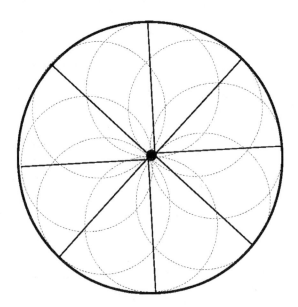

Figure 11.1b. The oppositional nature of the meaning (a) and the paradigmatic circumflex (b).

one finds that words (SIPs) like "freedom," "identity," "family," "Country," "Nation," "danger," "democracy," "membership," "identity," tend to co-occur within a certain discourse, then one can conclude that such a pattern could mark a thematic nucleon concerning |the Nation as value and grounds of identity|.

Yet the identification of the pattern of SIPs is not sufficient in order to deeply understand the structure of a text. This is so because, as SDMS emphasizes, meaning is given by the interplay between SIP and SIA, namely, by the fact that a given SIP a activated on the syntagmatic axis, circumscribes its semiotic value due to the pertinentization of a certain oppositional sign ("*anti-a*") among the infinite possible on the paradigmatic circumflex. For instance, take the SIP a, given by the discursive nucleon |the Nation as value and source of identity|. Imagine now that it is opposed to the oppositional sign |Arabs as absolute evil| (*anti-a$_1$*), or to the oppositional sign |the rights deriving from being member of a State | (*anti-a$_2$*). It is apparent that a acquires a very different meaning in the two cases—in the first case the Nation as value acquires the sense of a guarantee of survival, something that has to be defended from the attack of the persecutory foreigner; in the second case the discursive nucleon would seem to be charged with the global meaning of a super-ordered value constraining/opposing the individual rights/needs—the Nation to serve. This is the second task the structural analysis addresses—mapping the oppositional linkages sustaining the paradigmatic structure in function of which the SIP acquires its field value.

It is worth adding that while the first task of the structural analysis is essentially descriptive, this second task means to go beyond the empirical content of the occurrence (i.e., the SIP), and interpreting it in terms of the latent organization it is embedded in, namely, in terms of the semiotic landscape it is part of.[2] The extrapolation of the pattern of SIPs from the phenomenon is a matter of making relationships of contiguity and redundancy pertinent—namely, of foregrounding patterns of signs whose combination (contiguity) occurs several times through the phenomenon (redundancy). In this sense, it is focused on the similarity-closeness among signs. By contrast, the interpretation of the latent semiotic organization consists of understanding the relation between what "there is"—that is the combinations of the SIPs—and what is *structurally* absent—namely, not any absence, but exactly the one associated with the presence: the *anti-x* which results from the fact that a given pattern of signs instantiates the position *x* instead.

Dynamic Analysis

The structural analysis of the text allows the global organization of signs guiding and constraining the flow of signs to be understood. Yet it does not provide direct access to how such use leads to the emergence of meaning within the concrete circumstances of discourse (Gastaldi, Longobardi, Pasta, & Sclavo, 2010). In general terms, this is not an absolute constraint. Consider anatomy: it concerns the structure of the body, the conditions and the constraints of its functioning; the knowledge of the anatomic structures indirectly allows one to draw hypotheses on the body's way of functioning (i.e., on its dynamic) as well.

Dynamic analysis, as opposed to structural analysis, is however the direct way of addressing the issue of the emergence of meaning—a purpose that requires the focus to be shifted from the *products* of sensemaking to the *process* itself of producing them; that is, to focus on the chain of signs that are combined through the unfolding of the communication.

The defining characteristic qualifying a phenomenon as dynamic is dependence on time. This means that a phenomenon is dynamic if, in order to understand it, one has to take the temporal dimension into account. To clarify a possible point of misunderstanding: it is obvious that any phenomenon, by definition, unfolds in time. Yet, not all phenomena are dynamic, because not all phenomena require reference to their temporality in order to have their functioning understood. Obviously, a lever needs to be moved, yet we need not refer to time in describing (and foreseeing) the extent of the force we have to implement in order to raise a certain weight. Therefore, the movement of a lever is not a dynamic phenomenon. Many models treat their objects as nondynamic phenomena. For instance, Matte Blanco's bi-logic model of unconscious (Matte Blanco, 1975; cf. Chapter 7) does not entail reference to time.

According to SDMS, which is a dynamic model of sensemaking, time is not only the container (the mere "time axis", so to speak) within which signs unfold, but it has a constitutive role (Lauro-Grotto, Salvatore, Gennaro & Gelo, 2009). On this point, SDMS shares the view of several other psychological models, that recognize the dynamicity of meaning. For instance, the psychoanalytic principle of free association is grounded on the tenet that the associative chain created by the temporal contiguity among signs is a major vector conveying unconscious meaning (e.g., Salvatore & Venuleo, 2010). The dynamicity of meaning is evident at the phenomenological level too: it is easy to see how meaning depends not only on what is said, and not only on how it is said, but also by means of *when* it is said—that is, before and after what. Consider the following two statements:

X = I totally disagree with you, but I am your friend

Y = I am your friend, but I totally disagree with you

X and Y are made up of the same subset of words, but, due to the fact that their order is different, they have a different meaning: X focuses on the bond and the need to defend it from the threat posed by the disagreement. Y gives a sense of someone that makes the disagreement pertinent, despite the friendship. In X the friendship is in the foreground and it works as the value magnified by the act of communication. In Y the disagreement is in the foreground and the friendship acquires the valence of a virtual constraint on the autonomy of the actors engaged in negotiating their own divergent positions. In sum, sensemaking is carried out not only by means of *what* is said, and not only by *how* it is said, but also by means of *when* what is said is said—before and after what.

Incidentally, it is worth pointing out that time-dependency is a different characteristic from the historicalness of meaning. Historicalness concerns the fact that the meaning *evolves over time*; whereas time-dependency concerns the idea that time is a constitutive condition of meaning—

accordingly, meaning *works by means* of time. This means that the longitudinal approach, aimed at mapping the historicalness of meaning, is a necessary (see Bauer & Gaskell, 1999; Sammut, Tsirogianni, & Wagoner, 2012) but not sufficient methodological tenet. It has to be complemented by the dynamic approach, aimed at mapping time-dependency, namely, at modeling the emergence of meaning from the local transition between signs over the syntagmatic axis.

Theory of Dynamic Systems (TDS)

TDS is a network of mathematical concepts aimed at modelling phenomena once their time-dependency is recognized. TDS sees the phenomenon under investigation in terms of dynamic system. A dynamic system is a mathematical model of the phenomenon. The phenomenon is defined as the response to an external input, which depends both on the input itself and on the inner state of the system. Accordingly, a set of equations formally maps the behavior over time of the system, as a function of the temporal evolution of its inner state and of the input, both depending on time. This function, once assigned to the state of the system at an initial moment t_0, allows the state of the system to be determined at any subsequent instant of time.[3]

It is worth adding that the mathematical description of the evolution of the system can also be depicted in terms of a geometrical representation, by drawing the system's evolutive trajectory in the phase space. This is a "shaped" space spanned by the degrees of freedom of the system as dimensions (i.e., coordinate axes): the points of phase space comprise all possible states of the system.

There are different models of dynamic systems. Following Lauro-Grotto and colleagues (2009) and Salvatore and Tschacher (2012) here I focus on four types, the ones I consider the most useful for mapping sensemaking. For details, see the works mentioned above.

Periodicity

Periodic behavior is the first type of dynamic system of interest to our discussion. The perpetual motion of a pendulum (in the frictionless case) is the classical instance of this kind of dynamic. The position and velocity of the pendulum change with time, therefore it is a dynamic system. In addition, this change follows a cycle that remains constant on a larger time scale. The time evolution of a periodic system can be represented by a closed orbit in the phase space, with every point representing the position of the system at a given instant. Therefore, the system changes positions at every instant, and returns to identical positions after a certain period. This characteristic of the periodic behavior makes it a linear and stationary system, that is, a system whose dependence on time is stable and does not change as the system evolves. The interesting property of the periodic trajectory is that it shows a kind of behavior that appears to change with time—that is, the velocity of the pendulum changes instant by instant,—yet is globally stable, in the sense that the system will return to the same point of (unstable) equilibrium.

The *bootstrapping mechanism* envisaged by the SDMS with its working through two stages—a stage of *propagation* and a stage of *reduction*—lends itself to be seen as approximating a periodic dynamic. More in general, periodicity characterizes many aspects of living systems (e.g., the sleep-waking cycle, the metabolism, the seasonal trends of many biological parameters). Examples of periodic behavior are known in the clinical psychology realm as well—the bipolar syndrome may be taken as prototypical. Periodicity is also found in psychotherapy process research. For instance, as regards the therapeutic alliance, the initial assumption of a linear linkage between this construct and the clinical effectiveness of psychotherapy has currently been overtaken by the more sophisticated vision that views the therapeutic alliance as a cyclic process of ruptures and repairing (Safran & Murray, 2000). According to this vision, what is clinically significant is not the absolute trend of the alliance, but the capacity of the therapeutic dyad to systematically cooperate in order to repair the inevitable micro-ruptures of their bond—that is to say the capacity of the therapeutic dyad to produce a virtuous cycle of separation and closeness. Accordingly, therapeutic alliance is better understood and studied in its clinical impact insofar as it is mapped as a periodic dynamic, which alternates between positive and negative poles.

Nonlinearity

In its basic meaning, nonlinearity concerns the fact that the change of the state of the system does not follow a regular trend over time: in certain moments of time it is faster than in others.

This characteristic should be considered the rule rather than the exception of psychological phenomena. As to the clinical realm, Hayes, Laurenceau, Feldman, Straus, and Cardaciotto (2007) have highlighted several instances of nonlinearity. For example, various studies have documented that, following dramatic and traumatic events, the life trajectory does not evolve in coherence with the local effect of the trauma, namely, in terms of the onset of pathological conditions (so called post-traumatic stress disorders). In various cases, people have shown they are able to regain their pre-traumatic condition. In further cases the traumatic event is shown to be the premise and the means for reaching an even better psychological condition (the so called post-traumatic growth). Other studies have shown that people with clinical problems—for example, with problems of substance abuse—can fundamentally change their condition as the result of a sudden, rapid and global transition. Moreover, such changes are often preceded by periods of worsening of the clinical condition. Other clinicians have shown that the clinical improvement can follow a threshold mechanism, as a consequence of the accumulation of a set of eliciting conditions, yet none of them sufficient to be effective alone. Finally, Barkham, Stiles, and Shapiro (1993) assumed, as appears reasonable from a clinician's perspective, that progress in psychotherapy is never constant, passing through sudden accelerations followed by moments of stasis. Consequently, they hypothesized that the trend of patients' relevant clinical problems (as assessed by patients themselves) in the course of psychotherapy followed a U-shaped trajectory, best modelled by a quadratic function. Their findings supported the hypothesis even though they underline that other nonlinear curves (cubic or of higher order) may have been equally appropriate.

Chaotic Behavior

Chaos appears in the nonlinear dynamic when certain specific conditions occur. As a result of these conditions, the system enters a state of apparent randomness. Chaos can therefore be understood as this specific form of erratic, disordered behavior, resulting from deterministic rules— the ones defined by the set of equations. Chaos theory aims to represent apparent disorder by showing its inner regularity.

The chaotic dynamic has two main properties. The first is *sensitivity to initial conditions*. According to this property, even a very small change in initial condition may create large consequences over time, like the metaphor of the movement of the butterfly's wings in Cape Town causing—after a while—a tornado in New York (from that, the sensitivity property became popular as "butterfly effect"). This characteristic of chaotic dynamic is responsible for the intrinsic unpredictability of the system after a long enough period. Even tiny differences in the measurement of the initial condition—and no measure can be absolutely precise—will lead to a marked divergence of the trajectories.

The second characteristic property of a chaotic dynamic is the *density of the periodic orbit*. The trajectory of a chaotic system stays inside a circumscribed portion of the phase space (i.e., strange attractor). This means that the system does not assume all possible values represented by the infinite number of points of phase space; to the contrary, it reduces its variability in the course of time (for this reason it is called a *dissipative system*). Nevertheless, the chaotic system is not periodic: the system will never present the same state twice. In geometrical terms, the system never passes through the same point of phase space twice. This means that however small the subregion of phase space to which the orbit of the chaotic system is confined, one will find infinitely many points, each of these representing the state of the system in a generic instant t. The presence of strange attractors leads to the recognition that even if chaotic behavior seems random, this is actually the expression of a different, more complicated order. A chaotic trajectory shows a *quasi-periodic* course: over time it reproduces cyclic behavior that is similar yet always different to a certain extent. Therefore, a chaotic system can be predicted, if one assumes a conception of prediction aimed at identifying the region of the phase space where the dynamic is constrained within a temporal range, rather than its point-like position in a given instant t.

Chaos theory is a popular notion and a source of fashionable metaphors. However, several methodological and technical issues lead one to be cautious as to the possibility of using it as a suitable source of computational devices for the analysis of sensemaking (for a discussion, see Laura-Grotto et al., 2009; Salvatore & Tschacher, 2012). On the other hand, its greatest merit lies in the possibility to recognize how phenomena that show a disordered, erratic behavior at the descriptive level, may yet turn out to be the product of deterministic rules—that is, a more sophisticated form of order, which may then be addressed. More in particular, one has to recognize that both properties of chaotic behavior find a certain correspondence with characteristics of sensemaking. Indeed, as discussed in Chapter 6, sensemaking is sensitive to the local condition: slight differences associated with the sensemaker's idiosyncratic biography are able to antagonize the normativity of the cultural ground, triggering even important differences in the semiotic trajectories, which, for this reason, are unpredictable. On the other hand, this is a common experience: a little nuance in the how and the what of the communication, like the movement of the butterfly's wings, can have a very impressive effect on the exchange. From a complementary point of view, as discussed in chapter 6, despite its inherent unpredictability, the semiotic trajectory tends to be sensitive to cultural normativity. Accordingly, it lends itself to be seen in terms of the second property of chaotic behavior: the strange attractor—namely, as a behavior always new and at the same time whose evolution is confined within a limited domain of meaning (in formal terms, in a region of the phase space). This means that the cultural normativity makes sensemaking lose its freedom to assume every state theoretically available. Yet, at the same time, sensemaking keeps its inherent local unpredictability, namely, the chance of entering infinite, always new states over irreversible time.[4]

Self-Organization

The self-organizating system is characterized by a huge amount of interacting microelements—for example, the neurons in a neural network—that can behave either in a deterministic or in a stochastic (noisy) way. The self-organizing system is capable of creating forms of persistent order spontaneously, "by themselves," in terms of a sharp reduction of the variability of the behavior of the systems' elements. The elements of the system, which until a critical moment have acted independently of each other, suddenly start to act as if in a linkage of close reciprocal dependence. Such a pattern formation is reflected as the emergence of a structure of order (i.e., an organization) at the macroscopic, phenomenal level. Thus, reduction of variability and emergence are the two main markers of self-organization: the order emerges from within the system, rather than being imported from outside—and consists of the structure of reciprocal dependence among the elements of the system.

An example of how the notion of self-organization can be used for framing empirical investigation is provided by Salvatore, Tebaldi, and Potì's (2006/2009) analysis of the verbal interaction between therapist and patient of a 123-session good-outcome psychotherapy (cf. the study is presented in Chapter 12). The study assumes that sensemaking—and therefore sensemaking within psychotherapy—works as a *self-organizing system* because it emerges *from within* the dialogical dynamic, as a product of the discourse's own functioning, rather than as a consequence of an external intervention (i.e., not as a consequence of "metastipulation" among the actors in the discourse about a set of assertions, fixing the semiotic ground of the relationship).

A similar approach and consistent findings were obtained by Tschacher, Ramseyer, and Grawe (2007), who showed that self-organization emerged at the level of nonverbal communication between therapist and patient.

STRATEGIES OF STRUCTURAL ANALYSIS

Descriptive Level of Analysis: Pattern Detection

As discussed in the previous paragraph, the descriptive, semantic level of the structural analysis is aimed at detecting the patterns of co-occurring signs. In Chapter 2, I proposed considering sensemaking in terms of trajectory of sign. Yet, such a view has to be recognized as a simplification. Indeed, the syntagmatic axis on which the trajectory unfolds is hyper-dimensional like the paradigmatic one. This means that in any instant of time a set of co-occurring signs are made pertinent on the paradigmatic axis, rather than a single element. Thus, what is relevant is not the occurrence of the sign in itself, but the relationship among signs: what other signs come together with the sign. Accordingly, sensemaking is a system: the whole network of relations among the elements is different from their additive composition. Meanings are like chemical elements: the same elements can produce very different entities precisely as a result of a slight variation in the way they combine with each other. Freud (1900/1953) had already highlighted this point, when he warned about the risk of giving simplistic interpretations of dream symbols, in terms of one-to-one correspondence with explicit meanings (e.g., the cigar meaning the penis).

This is the reason for proposing to see the analysis of meaning in terms of pattern detection. Indeed, according to the logic of pattern detection, what is significant, endowed with informative power, is not the single element (e.g., a certain sign, a given word or behavior, a certain value of an index), but the co-occurrence of several elements whose interpretation reflects their way of combining with each other. In this there is the difference between a pattern and an aggregation of elements: the elements of an aggregation have a meaning before their coming together, the elements of a pattern acquire their value due to their being part of the pattern.

The recent study on the genesis of the representation of the aircraft crash at Smolensk, where on April 2010 the main members of the Polish government and institutions lost their lives (Dryjanska, 2011; see Chapter 9), provides instances of both approaches (pattern detection and analysis of aggregate). On the one hand, the author compares the frequency distribution of answers to questions concerning the event (e.g., the description of the event, the immediate reaction) between a Polish and an Italian sample. This distribution represents an instance of aggregation of elements, as defined above—the set of answers, the content of some of which is seen as having its own already established meaning and can therefore be analyzed separately from the others. The answers concerning a certain topic can then be computed, cumulated, and so forth, in search of redundancies as well as differences among (sub)groups. On the other hand, the author provides field descriptions obtained through participant observation. In this case, what they focus on is co-occurring items, which depict a global scenario. Consider for instance the following excerpt

> On April 11, 2010 (Sunday) it was observed that the church next to the Presidential Palace was very crowded, and the presence of more people in front of the Presidential Palace was recorded. There were already candles placed in front of the Presidential Palace, and the participants would stop and place flowers and more candles. There was a presence of boy scouts for about an hour each, who took care of arranging the flowers and candles. Two thirds of the participants who stopped would not speak and children were instructed to be quiet. (pp. 13–14)

The author interprets the scenario as the manifestation of a shared feeling of "united in silence," fed by a longstanding social representation of death, in its turn grounded on the Polish ethnic and religious feeling. Now, regardless of the content of the interpretation, it is evident that it is the result neither of the accumulation of information contained in the elements nor of the extraction of redundancy from them. This is so because no element among the ones reported (candles, flowers, boy scouts, children asked of being quiet) has its own fixed meaning—all of them, taken in themselves, could be interpreted in very many ways. Thus, what is informative and leads to the interpretation is the co-occurrence of the elements, namely, the dynamic gestalt that such co-occurrence produces.

Methods of automated textual analysis provide examples of pattern detection. Traditionally, textual analysis has been based on the computation of the frequency of content and/or lexical units. For instance, Holzer, Mergenthaler, Pokorny, Kachele, and Luborsky (1996) computed the amount of shared vocabulary between therapist and patient, taken as a marker of the therapist's ability to be attuned to the patient, which is in turn seen as a factor of psychotherapy efficacy. Reyes Aristegui, Krause, Strasser, and colleagues (2008) counted the combinations between the first person and the present tense, taking this index as a marker of psychological change. In the last two decades, however, more sophisticated approaches have been developed, aimed at taking into account the contextuality of lexical and semantic units (Chartier & Meunier, 2011; Lahlou, 1996; Lancia, 2007, 2012; Salvatore, Gennaro, Auletta, Tonti, & Nitti, 2012; Veltri & Suerdem, 2011). Regardless of methodological and theoretical differences, such developments can be viewed as many instances of pattern detection. In the words of Chartier and Meunier (2011), the basic idea grounding such approaches, is that "the meaning of a word is measured by the set of works that co-occur within it in a given context of enunciation, usually a window of a few words, a sentence or a paragraph" (p. 5).

From a computational standpoint, the detection of the patterns of co-occurring words may be carried out through procedures of clustering analysis, applied on a data matrix with context units as rows, lexical units (e.g., words, lemmas) as columns and presence/absence values in cells. The clusters thus obtained are interpreted as sets of statements that, given their similarity to the words they share, can be seen as having a common semantic core. Thus, the contextuality of the meaning is taken into account in its intratextual component—the textual surrounding within which the combination of the words with others words makes them be acquiring their situated meaning. Needless to say, the anchorage to the intra-textual dimension of context is only a partial reconstruction of the multidimensionality of the meaning. Paralinguistic, pragmatics and performative components of meaning are not considered. Nevertheless, even if only partial, the anchorage to the context has proved to improve the heuristic power of analysis. Salvatore and colleagues (Salvatore, Gennaro, Auletta, Tonti, & Nitti, 2012) subjected an automated procedure of thematic analysis, focused on the detection of word co-occurrences within sentences, to a Turing-like test—namely, to a comparison with parallel analyses performed by expert researchers. To this end a textual corpus (the transcript of a psychotherapy) was subjected to automated analysis. At the same time, three skilled analysts were asked to perform the same tasks of semantic analysis (on the same textual data)—namely, comparison of the semantic similarity among context units and their classifications in semantic classes. The main result was that the differences among researchers were even greater than the differences between the automated method's output and the researchers' outputs; accordingly, it was not possible to distinguish two such kinds of output.

The Abductive Reconstruction of the Semiotic Landscape

According to the discussion as far, the mapping of the semiotic landscape, being a latent field dynamic, has to be performed in terms of inferential reconstruction based on the abductive logic of interpretation of the relationship among units of analysis.

Abductive reconstruction requires a set of clues to start from. This means that abductive inference is not the first step of an empirical investigation, but the conclusive phase that comes after a previous process of investigation aimed at identifying/selecting/constructing the pertinent clues from the empirical field.[5] In an analogy with police work, the first step of the investigation is the study of the scene of the crime, in order to retrieve the right clues that can lead to the discovery of the murderer.

Below, I briefly present a strategy of analysis aimed at constructing an empirical basis for the abductive reconstruction of the semiotic landscape. It is based on the assumption of the oppositional structure of the SIA (see above, first paragraph this chapter). Any oppositional dimension corresponds to a component of the sense, a scenario in the terms of the SDMS. The more generalized this component is, the more polarized its structure (Salvatore & Freda, 2011). Accordingly, the basic state of affective activations can be conceived of as polarized highly generalized embodied patterns of meaning—positive versus negative—providing the basic semiotic differentiation of experience (cf. Chapter 7; see also Salvatore & Zittoun, 2011a).

On the grounds of the assumption of the oppositional structure of the SIA, it is possible to conceive the semiotic landscape in terms of an array of oppositional dimensions of sense, each of them mapping a specific scenario, from the most generalized embodied affective ones to those concerning specific areas of sense (as to the notion of scenario, see Chapter 2). Given this, the semiotic landscape lends itself to be mapped in terms of a multidimensional procedure of data analysis (in particular, correspondence analysis, CA), applied on a matrix composed of the units of analysis (rows) x SIP (columns) and presence/absence values in cells.[6] CA breaks down and reorganizes the relationship occurring among signs in terms of a multidimensional structure of opposed factorial polarities; where each polarity is characterized by a set of signs that tend to co-occur and do not occur in the event of the occurrence of an opposite set. Accordingly, this structure can be interpreted as *the operationalization of the phase space of the sensemaking* (on the notion of phase space of the sensemaking, see Chapter 2), with any factorial dimension to be seen as an indication of a *latent component of sense* that is active in the dynamic of sensemaking. Thus the output of the CA provides the empirical basis for the abductive reconstruction of the semiotic landscape (for details, see the study we refer to below).

Needless to say, also the factorial dimensions are depicted in terms of elements that, in the final analysis, can be used as clues insofar as a semantic content is attributed to them (for instance, a factorial polarity may be described in terms of a pattern of co-occurring words). Yet this is not the same as saying that the factorial dimensions *have* semantic content. This is so for two reasons. First, from a conceptual standpoint, the main factorial dimensions are conceived of, and interpreted as, indications of generalized, embodied components of sense[7] (Guidi & Salvatore, 2014; Mossi & Salvatore, 2011; Venuleo, Mossi, & Salvatore, 2014); as such they are a-semantic—they ground any enactment of signs, but cannot be fully grasped by any of them (Chartier & Meunier, 2011). Second, from a methodological standpoint, any component of sense is abductively reconstructed as the gestalt grounding the opposition between the two polarities. Due to this, by definition it is not obtained by means of composing the information held in each polarity; rather, it is interpreted in terms of the information provided by the combination of the *in presentia* relationship (i.e. the pattern of co-occurring sings mapped by a single polarity) and *in absentia* relationship (i.e., the oppositional bond with the pattern mapped by the opposed polarity). In the information provided by this combination lies the specificity of the semiotic level of analysis: the factorial dimension is interpreted not in terms of the content of the pattern of co-occurring signs (i.e., the pattern placed on the polarity), but in terms of which component of sense corresponds to the fact that the enactment of that pattern of signs is the instantiation of a specific network of *in absentia* relationship among signs (i.e. the enactment of a SIA). For instance take the pattern "1, 2, 3, 4". Despite its invariant content, its sense is different if it is opposed to the pattern "4, 3, 2, 1" or to the pattern "A, B, C, D". In the former case its sense is: |an increasing sequence|, in the latter: |numbers|. These are two different spheres of sense, each of them magnifying an area of the semantic content of the pattern. Thus, *the content needs to be projected on the semiotic network of in absentia linkages among signs to be fully interpreted*.

It is worth insisting on the latter point a little more. The map of the semiotic landscape provides a further level of interpretation of the content of signs. In particular, we focus here on the possibility of integrating the semantic interpretation of the co-occurring signs that pattern analysis is able to identify as well as of the characteristics of the participants marking their subjectivity (see Chapter 10). The central point here is that the CA allows for the representation of any further variable on the factorial dimensions extracted from the data matrix. Such further variables are called *illustrative*, because they do not contribute to the definition of the multidimensional semiotic phase space, but are associated with the factor dimensions once they are defined. Thus, the patterns of co-occurring signs interpreted as indicative of thematic nuclei may work as illustrative variables in the CA. The same can be done for the characteristics of the participants. In so doing, topics and subjects (as well as any other aspect researchers are interested in analyzing) may be interpreted in reference to the semiotic landscape, namely, they may be mapped in terms of their position on the semiotic phase space.

Sometimes the interpretation of the patterns of signs in accordance to the semiotic context may provide quite interesting and counterintuitive insights. This is so because it allows access to a level of analysis where it is possible somehow to put into brackets the semantic contents of the topics, in order to interpret them in terms of their semiotic relationship, namely, their positions on the semiotic landscape. Accordingly, this level of analysis can be seen as a way of modelling the semiotic genesis of the topics. For instance, the study of Guidi and Salvatore (2014) I have already mentioned (cf. Chapter 10), in their analysis of parents' model of representation of the school system, showed that a model expressing an idealization of the school had a similar position on the phase space of two other models whose contents were very different from the former (i.e., parents expressing reactive and negative attitudes to school). All three of these models proved to be positioned on the polarity labelled "Familistic relation with the context" and interpreted as the marker of an anomic conception of the social environment, connoted in terms of in-group membership as opposed to a persecutory representation of otherness. Accordingly, the authors concluded that the three models, so different in terms of content, shared the same semiotic root, a generalized meaning (a generalized SIA, in SDMS terms) that allows positive relations with the environment only if the social system is experienced as part of the in-group niche, while it leads to sharp negative connotations when the social system is experienced as other than the primary niche.

In another study, Mossi and Salvatore (2011) analyzed the self-representations of Italian students before and after the passage between two levels of school (from the level of middle school to the secondary level—a passage that in the Italian system occurs when students are 13–14 years old, representing a relevant moment in the students' career). They found that while at the level of the content of the representation there was a clear transition—students' topics changed—the semiotic landscape remained the same. They interpreted this result as the basis for rethinking the notion of transition from a psychological standpoint, suggesting the need to distinguish between changes at the experiential level—which is sensitive to the contingency of the context—and actual transition—which requires a transformation of the deep structures of meaning (i.e., the semiotic landscape, in the SDMS terms) grounding the experience.

The position within the phase space of meaning may be of interest also for modeling the subject of meaning (see Chapter 10) from a semiotic point of view. Venuleo and Salvatore (2006) analyzed the transcripts of the five official political debates occurring during the electoral campaign for the 2006 Italian political elections. Each statement was associated with the subject that uttered it. And subjects were marked in accordance to the role performed in that context—in particular: the journalists that asked questions, the politicians that answered, the host that moderated the communication and supervised the respect for the rules of the debate. In order to fully understand this structure of events, one has to consider that five such debates—each involving a politician representing the left wing and a politician representing the right-wing—were subject to strict rules in order to ensure that participants had the maximum level of equal conditions. The textual analysis of transcripts, based on the procedure of CA described above, led to the identification of some sets of co-occurring words that lent themselves to be interpreted in terms of a corresponding number of topics. Moreover, the association of such topics with the politicians' orientation proved to be obvious as well. Less obvious was the position of the topics as well as that of the journalists within the semiotic phase space. The topics proved to be very close to one another, placed on the same polarity and opposed to another topic concerning the co-occurrence of signs referring to the regulation of the here and now communication. Moreover, while the journalists gave no indication of being associated to a particular topic, their position on the phase space proved to be very close to that of the right-wing politicians. Thus, this twofold level of analysis (semantic and semiotic) allowed the authors to arrive at the following interpretation as to the dynamic of sensemaking characterizing the debates (and supposedly their impact on public opinion): (a) the symbolic relevance of the equality of the conditions was so strongly salient that it worked as the fundamental semiotic organizer of the communication—somehow the basic sense of the debates was to respect the rules of the debates; (b) the salience of the here and now concerns about the rules of communication had obscured the differences among the political positions; (c) quite ironically, despite the attention to the rules of communication, the journalists' questions (also the ones asked by journalists with a left-wing political orientation) were more consistent with the semiotic structure of the right-wing politicians' discourse.

Chartier, and Meunier (2011) described the rationale of the method of textual analysis elaborated by Lalhou (1996), aimed at the identification of thematic nuclei through a computational procedure of clustering. They recognize that such a method can analyze the content of social representations but not map its structure. The integration of the semiotic level of analysis could help to make it possible to address this further level/task in the challenging enterprise of understanding the meaning of meaning.

CONSTRAINTS AND STRATEGIES FOR THE DYNAMIC ANALYSIS

I present below some criteria for the dynamic analysis of psychological processes. In doing so, I will both highlight some precautions that are worth taking into account and propose methodological tactics to help grasp the situativeness of psychological phenomena. Needless to say, they are just some of the many one could adopt—they are proposed here as examples to clarify the theoretical statements about the dynamic analysis discussed above (first section of this chapter) as well as to show how the methodological discussion on the dynamic nature of the sensemaking can be translated into concrete practices of empirical investigation.[8]

Analyzing Nonindependent Data

In many longitudinal studies researchers use procedures of data analysis (ANOVA, parametric coefficient of correlation) entailing the assumption of independence of the observations, that is, the casual distribution of the values. Nevertheless, the sequence of values of a dynamic process unfolding through time is by definition dependent on time. This means that the sequential observations of a temporal trajectory can hardly be considered as belonging to a distribution of a single population of observations. Here the point at stake is not the fitness of the data for the assumption of normal distribution. The issue is indeed more radical, and it concerns the notion of distribution. The statistical concept of distribution by definition means that the distributed observations are equivalent, which means that they are considered to belong to or be extracted from a single population.

It is only on this condition that variability between observations can be considered the effect of random fluctuation and consequently any high difference between observations with a low probability of occurring can be assumed as being due to the intervention of a cause rather than being an expression of chance (Maruyiama, 1999).[9]

Yet, in the case of a dynamic process, any subsequent observation is the product of the previous history of the system by definition—this is equivalent to saying that the process is time dependent. Consequently, every observation has, as its own object, an event that is produced according to conditions—the previous chains of events—that are very specific— which is a different way of saying that dynamic phenomena concern the irreversibility of time. In other words, in the case of a dynamic system, event a depicted by the observation xa in time ta works as the immediate environment of the following event (b, xb, tb) that in its turn works as the immediate environment for the following event (c, xc tc). Now, affirming the dependence on time means that the three events in the case of a dynamic system are by definition different. Therefore, in the case of a dynamic system every event is the product of a different immediate environment, "incorporating" the previous history of the system. That is to say that in the case of a dynamic system events are not equivalent, each of them being the population of itself (see Chapter 9 for the criticism of the notion of population as the methodological grounds of contemporary psychology empirical analyses). Thus, one is led to recognize that the nonindependence of observations is the norm rather than the exception in the case of within-subject data, depicting temporal trajectories.

A way of dealing with this kind of data set is provided by procedures based on bootstrapping methodology. The rationale of this approach is well illustrated by a paper (Borckardt, Mash, Murphy, Moore, Shaw, & O'Neil, 2008) dealing with the issue of the way of measuring individual psychotherapeutic change. The authors' starting point is the underlining of the nonindependence of the data retrieved from the same subject through time. This recognition is even obvious from a developmental as well as clinical point of view. Let us imagine a patient whose level on a clinically significant index is measured n times in the course of the psychotherapy, say, the level of severity of symptomatology at the end of every session through the course of a 30-session psychotherapy treatment. Now, let us imagine that at the end of a certain session x the patient feels very depressed and anxious. It is evident that this state will tend somehow to persist, therefore to affect the further trajectory. And if the level of severity at the time x affects the level of the severity at time $x + 1$ (and even decreasingly also at the level $x + 2$, $x + 3$,...), this means that the observations are associated to each other. In the final analysis, nonindependence is involved when the knowledge of the state of the variable at time $x + 1$

makes the probability of the state of the variable at the following temporal moment different from chance. In statistical terms this phenomenon is defined in terms of autocorrelation: a variable correlated with itself (that is, with its state at a given temporal lag).

> Conventional parametric and nonparametric statistics assume that observations are independent. For instance, the result of a coin toss on Trial 1 does not influence the result on Trials 2 and 3, and so on. No matter how many times in a row "tails" is obtained, the probability that the next toss will be "heads" is unimpeachably still 50%. Hence, each observation (i.e., result of a coin toss) is independent. Similarly, in group designs, Subject 1's height is independent of Subject 2's height. Whether coin toss or height, one observation does not influence another. However, single case time-series observations, … are in principle not independent…. These data are in fact autocorrelated. Simply put, a series of observations … is said to be autocorrelated if the value of one observation depends (at least in part) on the value of one or more of the immediately preceding observations. Later observations are explained by earlier ones. Weather is autocorrelated. What the noon temperature will be on Wednesday is predicted by what the noon temperature was on Tuesday, and to a lesser extent what the noon temperature was on Monday or Sunday. Although the weather is certainly variable, how it changes from hour to hour, day to day, and season to season is to a degree lawful and structured, in a way that is not true when moving from one coin toss to the next…. Indeed, autocorrelation is an inevitable aspect of the periodicity, trending, and gradualism that one encounters regularly when tracking change over time in a single individual (weight loss, heart rate, tissue or psychological repair) or system (corporate earnings, birth rate). (Borckardt et al., 2008, p. 82)

As Borckardt and colleagues (2008) underline, autocorrelation is the norm rather than the exception in clinical research (and one can add: in any psychological research dealing with dynamic trajectories). Moreover, the authors highlight that calculating the difference of the scores and/or monitoring the slope of the index through time, without taking into account the autocorrelation of the values leads to overestimating the effect size (i.e., the difference through time). And this happens whether the autocorrelation is significant or not. For instance, a calculated autocorrelation of 0,10 can inflate the statistical values of the effect size by more than 100%. Affection gets 200% when autocorrelation is at 0,6. In accordance with these considerations, Borckardt and colleagues present a procedure of analysis— SMA (simulation model analysis)—which, unlike the conventional statistical tools, is able to take into account the autocorrelational effect. To put it simply, the procedure entails the following rationale. First, a huge number of casual data sets are randomly generated, with some *parameters* of the real data set assumed as constraints. For instance—the authors use as example a data set obtained by measuring the blood pressure 28 times—14 before the treatment (as baseline) and 14 during the treatment. This data set is defined according to four parameters: the number of observations comprised in each phase as well as the rates of autocorrelation for each phase. Then they randomly produced 1.000 virtual data sets, all of them sharing these four parameters. Second, for each virtual data set the statistical indicator depicting the relevant information is calculated. In the case example authors calculate the effect size of the treatment in terms of the correlation between the indicator (blood pressure) and the phase of the treatment. It is worth noticing that because of the random generation of the population of data sets, the distribution of the chosen statistical indicator is null. In other words, for each of the 1.000 data sets the effect size of the treatment is calculated. And the mean of the 1.000 effect sizes is 0. Third, the latter operation allows the statistical meaning of the real value of the statistical indicator (i.e. in the example: the effect size) to be calculated in terms of the probability associated to it in the distribution of virtual data sets.

In sum, this kind of method adopts the strategy of randomly generating a population of virtual data sets comparable with the real data set and then calculating the probability that from such a random distribution one can extract a data set showing an effect equivalent or higher than the real data set's. If this probability is lower than the alfa value, then the effect can be considered statistically significant.

From Comparison to Transitions

The post- and predifference is unsuitable for studying dynamic processes (Laurenceau, Hayes, & Feldman, 2007). In fact the difference is meaningful only when the evolution of the dimension under investigation is assumed to be linear and constant. Figure 11.2 shows how two very different trends can have the same post- and predifference. Consequently, focusing on the difference means losing one of the most interesting aspect of the phenomenon. At the same time, one can easily imagine processes having very similar shapes, yet presenting very different post- and predifference. More in general, conditions like quasi-periodical trends, dissipative trajectories, sensitive dependence to the initial conditions, phenomena of order emergence (see above, first section of this chapter), and the like, clearly make the post- and predifference a quite misleading device.

An alternative approach, more consistent with the time dependency of sensemaking is to adopt sequential analysis (Bakeman & Gottman, 1997) and focusing on the transition between sign. This strategy has been implemented in a recent study by Salvatore, Gennaro, Auletta, Grassi, Rocco, and Gelo (2011), focused on the patient-therapist communication. Authors computed the probabilities of transition between thematic contents, considering such probabilities the marker of the dialogical dynamic between the patient and her therapist. To this end, firstly the set of thematic nuclei characterizing the communicational process in question was identified. After that, the probability of transition $[PT(j_{t+1}i_t)]$ of each thematic nucleus toward every other thematic nucleus (including itself) was computed. The calculations were made separately for each session of psychotherapy. The $PT(j_{t+1}i_t)$ is the probability that—given a sequence S of a finite set of states M, with states M_i, $i=1,\ldots, n$, the state i-th occurring in the temporal unit t is followed by the state j-th in the subsequent temporal unit $(t+1)$.

$PT(j_{t+1}i_t)$ was calculated as the relative frequency of the sequence—namely: $PT(j_{t+1}\, i_t)_S = k/p$, where k is the frequency of the occurrences of the states i_t-j_{t+1} in the sequence of states S and p is the number of states i in the same sequence. In this case S is the sequence of units of analysis in which the transcript of the single psychotherapeutic session was segmented and the states M are thematic nuclei.[10]

The most interesting result of the study was that, while the frequency of Patterns of content taken in themselves did not discriminate between clinically good and nongood sessions (as evaluated by independent blind clinical judges), some probabilities of transition between patterns of contents were associated with the positive (or negative) clinical efficacy of the session.

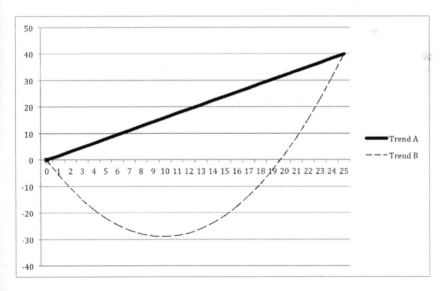

Figure 11.2. Same pre- and postdifference, different trends.

The Limit of the Assumption of the Invariance of the Process

In most cases, the analyzes assume that the phenomenon under investigation always follows the same way of working throughout the temporal window of the study. According to this assumption, the researchers strive to identify the law governing the functioning of the phenomenon. Now, this assumption is acceptable only insofar as one has to deal with a stationary dynamic (see above, first section of this chapter). However, if the process under investigation shows a nonstationary trajectory—because of the presence of phase transitions and/or the emergence of patterns of self-organization—the assumption of invariance becomes highly confusing. For example, let us consider a psychotherapy process in which the researcher wants to study the relationship between the patient's symptomatology and the patient's commitment to clinical work.

From a clinical point of view this relationship may actually change, moving from the first phase of the therapy to the second. In fact, in the first phase symptomatology and commitment can be proportional to each other (see Mahoney, 1991): the more the symptoms, the more the patient hopes the therapy will bring an improvement, then the greater the potentiality for improvement (Lambert, 2004), therefore the greater the commitment. In a complementary way, the greater the commitment, the more willing the patient will be to deal with his/her problems, therefore the more conflict she/he is willing to tolerate, and the more the symptoms are mobilised. In a subsequent phase, the relationship may be dramatically reversed: the more the symptoms, the less the patient hopes for improvement, therefore the less the commitment. At the same time, the less the commitment, the less the therapeutic work can support the patient to revise her/his consolidated strategy of adjustment, therefore the greater the defensive recourse to the symptomatology. In a case like this, if one does not consider the first and the second phases separately, what may happen is that no relation is found between commitment and symptomatology.

A subcategory of the issue at stake is the assumption that the variables are symmetrical. Researchers generally assume that the incidence of a given variable is invariant (in absolute terms) regardless of its direction. Referring to the previous example, the assumption of symmetry leads one to think that an increase in symptomatology produces the same kind of effects on commitment—though in inverse terms—as a decrease. Yet this assumption is often clearly an oversimplification. In fact, the increasing level/presence and the decreasing level/absence of a certain dimension can be two different phenomena rather than two states of the same linear variable. For instance, organizational psychology shows that there is not a single relationship between the so called "hygienic factors" (work load, safety conditions, quality of air and lighting....) and motivation on the job: the absence or the low level of these factors is associated with low motivation, yet the presence or the high level of these factors is not associated with high motivation (Herzberg, Mausner, & Snyderman, 1959).

Modeling

The dynamic system theory (DST) leads a central meaning to be attributed to the description of the temporal trajectory characterizing the processes. This means that in studying a phenomenon, the shape of the process is relevant, maybe in certain cases more than the measure/comparison of specific states in given instants.

This is evident in some phenomena where the relevant aspect is not the mere variability of the values through time, but the structure of the trend involved, as one can grasp by considering the process as a whole. One could speak in this case of *metatrend*. An example of this kind of phenomena is the trend that can be expected to characterise *insight*. As a matter of fact, in a psychoanalytically oriented therapy insight does not have a constant linear development. This is because, as the theory conceptualizes the construct, insight is a sudden recombination of meaning and creation of new connections among the cognitive and affective elements of the mental scenario (it being individual or intersubjective depending on the theoretical preference of the authors; for example, see Langs, 1974; Hoffman, 1998). This means that insight occurs only rarely, as a discrete and circumscribed moment of rupture of the normal process of sensemaking. This does not necessarily mean that the strength of insight—that is, its power to recombine and create semiotic novelty—is constant. On the contrary, one is justified in thinking that during a clinically efficacious psychotherapy treatment, the strength of insight increases.

In Figure 11.3 the trend of Activity during a 124-session psychotherapy treatment is plotted. Activity is one of the parameters of the DFA (*discursive flow analysis*). DFA is a method describing the psychotherapy process in terms of the structure and the dynamic of the discursive exchange between patient and therapist (Salvatore et al., 2010; cf. Chapter 12). It depicts the semiopoietic power of the discourse—that is, the capability of increasing its meaning variability through time. Accordingly, in the first approximation, Activity can be seen as a marker of insight. It is calculated as the ratio between the role in the dialogue of two types of meanings: generative meaning—whose occurrence in the flow of communication enlarges the variability of the subsequent dialogue—and absorbing meaning—whose occurrence in the flow of communication narrows the subsequent semiotic variability. Figure 11.3 shows how Activity proceeds by fits and starts, with sharp peaks coming out from an almost flat basic trend. What is interesting to note here is that the level of the Activity peaks follows a rather clear reversed U-shaped trend. It increases almost constantly throughout the first two out of three parts of the psychotherapy, to then decrease in the third (last) phase. This is quite consistent with the model of insight referred to before. According to this model, the psychotherapy at stake seems to have led to increasing "bursts" of insight; in particular, this seems to be happened in at least two out of three parts of its progress; the beginning of the downward phase would introduce the conclusive phase of the clinical work. However, regardless of the interpretation one gives to the figure, here it is worth noticing that what is meaningful is not the first order trend, that of Activity, but the second order trend—the metatrend, to use the terms proposed above—concerning the temporal trajectory of the intensity of the peaks.

A simple but conceptually relevant kind of metatrend that is worth considering is the *mobile difference*. In several circumstances, the psychological meaning of a given state is not provided by its inherent characteristics but by how and how much it is different from the previous state. The relevance of this difference is a common experience of daily life. Think of driving a vehicle; after having adjusted to a certain speed, the driver experiences the variations of speed, not the speed itself. In clinical fields, variables such as the therapeutic alliance, defense mechanisms, reflective functioning, and so forth may work and are perceived in terms of their variations, rather than of their absolute levels. Nitti and colleagues (Nitti, Ciavolino, Salvatore, & Gennaro, 2010) have discussed the empirical relevance such mobile differences may have. They applied DFA (*discourse flow analysis;* see above and Chapter 12) to the case of Lisa [for further analysis of Lisa's case, see Angus, Goldman, & Mergenthaler, 2008]. DFA depicts each session as a set of parameters describing the structural and functional characteristics of verbal exchange between patient and therapist (e.g., level of connectivity among the meanings exchanged between patient and therapist). In addition to the absolute levels of these parameters, the mobile differences (i.e., the variation of the level of the parameter at session $x + 1$ with respect to session x) were calculated. Taking into account the two sets of values (absolute levels and mobile differences) as discriminative variables, the authors were able to distinguish the good-outcome sessions with a 100% rate of success (this was impossible when either absolute levels or mobile differences alone were taken into account as discriminative variables).

Interestingly, a similar result was reported about 25 years ago by Greenberg and Pinsof (1986):

The experience of the Vanderbilt group is particularly illuminating in this regard. Suh et al. (this volume) found that when they examined frequencies of process variables in the first three sessions they found no relationship to outcome, but when they examined the pattern of change in the variables over the first three sessions, process-outcome links began to emerge. Increase in therapist warmth and exploration, and in patient participation over the initial sessions were highly correlated with outcome. (p. 15)

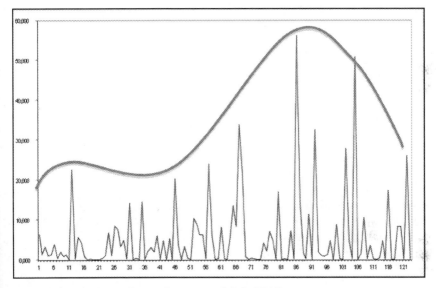

Source: Salvatore, Laura-Grotto, Gennaro, and Gelo (2009).

Figure 11.3 The metatrend of the semiopoietic power (Activity) of the clinic exchange.

Trajectory in the Phase Space

The dynamic of a system can be depicted in terms of its trajectory in the phase space (see Chapter 2). In this way, the focus is on the shape of the trajectory and its behavior though time rather than on the study of individual points. On the other hand, only in a minority of cases can the trajectories be described in an analytic way. More often the dynamic is too complicated to be analytically studied by means of a formal representation. In latter cases a qualitative inspection is performed, aimed at identifying the kind of dynamic phenomenon (i.e., the presence and the nature of peaks and attractors, types of trends...) characterising the trajectory.

This qualitative approach leads to move the focus from the amount of the state of a given variable or of the relationship among variables (which can be contingent to the context), to the way the phenomenon as a whole develops. One can find an example of this attitude by referring to Barkham, Stiles, and Shapiro (1993). In their study, authors did not deal with the measurement of their main variables—that is, the relevance of the clinical problems brought into psychotherapy. Rather, they focus on the modelling of the trajectory shaping the trend of the variable under investigation through the psychotherapy process. It is worth noticing that they test the fitness of a specific model formally defined by means of a second order equation. In this way they are able to test the hypothesis of the U-shaped trend in the psychotherapy process.

Similarly, Salvatore and colleagues (Salvatore et al., 2010) conceptualise the psychotherapy process according to their two stage semiotic model (TSSM) (details in Chapter 12), asserting, among other statements, the U-shaped trend of the Super-Order Meanings active in clinically efficacious psychotherapy. Like Barkham, Stiles, and Shapiro (1993), their attention was not on the absolute value of the variables, but on the global shape of the trajectory depicting the course of psychotherapy.

It is to be underlined that the interest in the global form of the trend is not a second choice due to the difficulty of a more analytic investigation. Rather, it concerns and is aimed at developing the clinical theory of psychotherapy. In the case in question, the U-shapes trend of the Super-Order Meanings exchanged within the therapist-patient communication has important theoretical implications. In particular: (a) it means underlining the role played by this kind of semiotic device in psychotherapy; (b) it helps to go beyond a technical and a-contextual approach to the clinic practice, grounded on the assumption that a given kind of intervention —for example, psychoanalytic interpretation—is always useful and always in the same way, always having the same effects. On the contrary, the alternation of deconstructive and constructive phases in the psychotherapy process means that cogent clinic interventions can vary according to the history of the process: such interventions can also have different effects, whose clinical significance depends on the time too.

From a more general point of view, it is evident that focusing on the shape of the trajectory helps decisively to collect the knowledge produced by intensive studies of single cases, thus reflecting the idea of an idiographic science as a process of accumulation of knowledge while at the same time being the product of the systematic empirical investigation of single, unique phenomena (see Chapter 9; see also Molenaar & Valsiner, 2006/2009; Salvatore & Valsiner, 2010).

Before concluding, it is worth noticing that in the recent years some statistical devices consistent with the aim of modeling the processes have been developed. In particular, the growth mixture model (Laurenceau et al., 2007) is aimed at formalizing the temporal evolution of single cases, in order to use the identified parameter of the formalization as the criteria for comparing the cases to one another. Thus, the interest of this statistical technique lies in its aim of integrating the within-subject and between-subject levels of analysis, without confusing them. Moreover, it is worth mentioning Hartmann, van der Kooij, and Zeeck (2009) that presented a regression method with categorical variables assuming nonlinear relationships among variables. However, while on the one hand these types of procedures are able to take nonlinear dynamic of phenomena into account, they are valid as long as stationary trends are analyzed. They are inappropriate, however, for the class of nonlinear processes characterized by phenomena of dissipative dynamic and/or emergence of order (Laurenceau et al., 2007).

Depicting the Dynamic of Emergence

The methodological discussion developed so far concerns some ways of taking into account the nonlinearity of psychological phenomena. Yet, such ways are not consistent with the subset of dynamic processes characterized by self-organization and emergence of order. Self-organization processes introduce a fundamental change in the way of functioning of the system. The fact that a structure of order emerges means that the system considerably modifies its behavior model. Some indications about how to deal with this kind of phenomena are proposed by Tschacher, Schiepek, and Brummer (1992), in their application of the synergetic to clinical psychology. Here I will simply to mention some other general issues (further details in Salvatore, Tebaldi, & Potì, 2009; Salvatore & Tschacher, 2012). First, at the operational level, emergence, and therefore self-organization (emergence being the distinctive trait of self-organization; cf. first section of this chapter) can be defined in terms of the following four criteria:

1. a considerable change in the state of the system consisting of a significant reduction of the variability of the system;
2. occurring suddenly;
3. carried out in a limited period of time;
4. lasting—that is, not disappearing after a short while

The analysis of the psychotherapy process performed by Salvatore and colleagues (2009) is an example of the use of such criteria for the sake of detecting a dynamic of emergence. According to the tenet of the self-organizational nature of the psychotherapy process, the authors have hypothesized that some close relation between major aspects of the process is created in the course of the psychotherapy (Criterion 1). Moreover, to be considered a phenomenon of emergence, this change is sudden (Criterion 2), rapid (Criterion 3), and lasting (Criterion 4). In order to deal with this hypothesis authors analyzed the relation between two of the major DFA (*discourse flow analysis*, see Chapter 12) indexes—Activity and Super-Order Meanings—through time. This was due to the fact that they assumed that these two parameters depict two very different aspects of the discursive exchange: the former is an index concerning the dynamic of the discursive network; the latter an index concerning the structure and the content of the network. The analysis of the relationship between the two parameters was carried out in the terms of an adapted version of the univariate method of trend analysis proposed by Molenaar and Valsiner (2006/2009). They defined a set of 5- session blocks with n as starting session and $n + 4$ as ending session, obtained by stepwise varying the cutting point n between $n = 1$ and $n = 11$. (They choose a 5-session range in order to obtain the highest number of blocks to be compared, yet without compromising the calculation of the correlations within each block). The coefficients of correlation between Activity and Super-order Meaning obtained for each window were compared. As Figure 11.4 shows, after the first window, the correlation dramatically increases and then remains almost constant till the second last window. The authors claimed that this result was quite consistent with their hypothesis stating that in the case of a clinically efficacious psychotherapy process the discourse between patient and therapist has to be thought of as a self-organizational system, characterized by an early nonlinear emergence of a structure of order.

An Example of Analysis: The Modeling of the Psychotherapy Process as Field Dynamic

In what follows, as an exemplificative illustration of the methodological look outlined in this chapter, I present a strategy of analysis of a specific phenomenon,—the psychotherapy process—based on, and integrating in a unique approach, several of the criteria discussed above.

This strategy of analysis is based on the interpretation of the psychotherapy in terms of communicative process (see Chapter 8) and the latter in terms of field dynamic. Accordingly, the communicative field represents a higher-order level of functioning. This high-order level has to be interpreted in epistemological, rather than ontological, terms. In other words, the communicative field is not considered a separate reality; but an observational level, which allows a structure of order to be recognized in the behavior of the specific components of the clinical exchange and

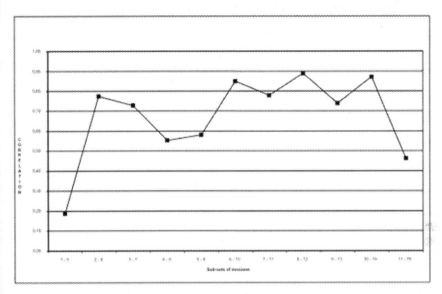

Source: Salvatore, Laura-Grotto, Gennaro, and Gelo (2009).

Figure 11.4. Correlations between Activity and Super-Order Meanings within subset of five sessions.

in their interaction. This brings into the foreground the methodological issue of how to model this structure of order. The abductive, theory driven strategy of analysis (see Chapter 10) is a way of addressing such an issue. It works in two steps.

Step 1: Intensive Analysis of a Set of Cases
Each case is analyzed in terms of the following phases

1. *Local analysis of a set of relevant components of the clinical exchange* (e.g., level/model of patient mentalization; content of narratives) and their interaction (i.e., mentalization/narratives). This means modelling the trend over time of such elements in order to identify markers of field effects (e.g., auto-regression, nonlinearity, bifurcations, attractors, dissipative dynamic). Accordingly, the aim is to identify those areas of the clinical exchange on which to focus the subsequent analysis—since they have been showed to be more influenced by the field dynamic. Moreover, the results of this phase have to allow the elaboration of hypotheses about the global dynamic depicting the clinical exchange (i.e., periodic trajectories, nonlinear dynamic, self-organization), that can guide the subsequent choice of the mathematical model to adopt

for the mapping of the global communicative field (e.g., quadratic or third order models).

2. *Individual case analyzes in terms of patterns of functioning.* This phase has to be carried out through the following two substeps: *i)* multidimensional breakdown of the molar characteristics of the therapeutic process, *ii)* their bottom-up re-aggregation in terms of stable patterns identified in the multidimensional space (phase space) obtained by the previous breakdown.

3. *Description of the evolution over time of the identified pattern.* This operation involves the qualitative-quantitative description and the formal modelling of the trajectories that patterns display in the phase space (e.g., in terms of stability, peaks, metatrends).

4. *Interpretation of the role played by identified patterns.* Patterns will be considered as II order latent constructs, working as mediator/moderator in the relationship between important clinical aspects of the process and their clinical effects.

5. *Analysis of field conditions determining pattern evolution.* This operation calls for the identification of states of the clinical exchange (i.e., control parameters, in terms of the dynamic system theory) associated with major variation points in the field dynamic (e.g., the characteristics of therapist intervention just preceding a peak in the trajectory of the communicative field).

Step 2. Generalization of the Explicative Models

The output of Step 1 is expected to determine the mapping of each case, thus the definition of a pool of explicative models of the dynamic of clinical change. This means that there is expected to be not a single model that explains change, but a limited set of trajectories, each one associated to specific relevant characteristics of the clinical exchange. Explicative models can be validated in terms of their ability to depict the dynamic of change in new cases (at the operational level, by means of the estimation of the goodness of fit).

CONCLUSION

In this chapter I have proposed some methodological implications drawn from the acknowledgement of the field nature of psychological phenomena, once they are seen through the semiotic and dynamic lens of the SDMS. Such implications have a twofold valence. On the one hand, they have a normative side—the field nature of the sensemaking reduces the validity of some largely used procedures of analysis. On the other hand, the discussion above should have envisaged how the new approach to sensemaking opens the way to methodological innovation, calling for a new deal in the way of approaching the empirical investigation of psychological phenomena, more consistent with the field dependency of such phenomena, therefore more rigorous and valid in their assumptions.

It is worth underlining that the field nature of the psychological phenomena can be acknowledged merely in a metaphorical way, with no production of methodological innovation. This may have its uses, yet it means giving up the most interesting opportunity of theoretical and methodological development. This does not mean ignoring the difficulty of such an endeavour of methodological innovation. The building of a field-methodology is a hard task. To be sure, it requires new sets of competences and technical skills—as, for example, the reference to the theory of dynamic system shows. However, I do not see this as an absolute obstacle—the history of empirical psychology shows that much research has been using more and more sophisticated procedures of analysis. Rather, the hardest aspect of developing a methodology of analysis consistent with the dynamic nature of sensemaking lies in the change of epistemological approach that the field logic requires. Indeed, to think of psychological phenomena in terms of field dynamic means putting aside the inductive, data-driven philosophy of investigation that grounds most of contemporary empirical psychology. The field approach requires us to go beyond the view of empirical analysis as a way of gathering data with a self-contained meaning, namely, as if they were facts. On the contrary, the field logics asks the researcher to model phenomena. This means a turnaround in the relationship between theory and data, with the former being preeminent. Needless to say, this does not mean that data are not relevant—on the contrary, this chapter has been devoted to outlining an array of strategies and modalities of *data analysis*. Yet, the methodological approach proposed in this chapter—and more in general in the III part of the book—sees data analysis at the service of and framed within the theory. Even if one is not willing to agree with the student who claims that "if results are not consistent with theory, consider them invalid" (claim attributed to an anonymous reviewer, cited from Barrow, 2011), one can refer to physics to find many examples of empirical findings that are driven and validated by theory development, rather than the opposite. And this happens not in the lands of angels, but in the area of scientific development that, thanks to its feedback into technology, has a tremendous impact on concrete daily life.

NOTES

1. Here I adopt the generic term "event." It may denote a speech (e.g., an interview) and/or a written text (e.g., a newspaper article), and/or an action and the like.
2. One can see here how the two tasks can be put in correspondence to the distinction between semantic and semiotic level of analysis, discussed in

Chapter 10. Semantic level of analysis corresponds to the descriptive focus on the SIP, where the analysis of the latent semiotic organization is a matter of semiotic analysis.

3. When the system's behavior can be mapped in terms of sequences of discrete states, in its simplest version the model assumes the following form:

$$X_{t+1} = r\, X_t$$

This equation expresses how the state of the system at a given moment of time X_{t+1} depends, by a function r, on the state of the system at the previous moment of time X_t. When the system's behavior is continuous, it is mapped in terms of the following equation:

$$dX(t)/dt = f(X(t), x_0, u(t), t)$$

where $X(t)$ is state of the system at the time t; $dX(t)/dt$ is its variation with respect to time, x_0 provides its initial conditions, and the vector $u(t)$ is the input of the system at time t. Thus, the equation maps the variation of the state of the system as a function f of the state of the system at time t, of the input at time t and of the initial conditions.

4. Venuleo, Salvatore, Mossi, Grassi, and Ruggieri's (2007) analysis of the discursive exchange occurring between high school students and teacher provides an illustration of sensemaking's sensitivity to local conditions. The analysis shows how the affective intersubjective regulation of the participants' reciprocal positioning is carried out by means of subtle discursive devices (e.g., by means of the use of worlds like "guys," "want" "somebody" in an utterance like this: "Well, guys, now I want to examine somebody," as compared with a sentence like: "Well, students, we must have a test now"). This fine tuning is very hard to recognize in real time, but at the same time is very powerful in creating the emotional sense of the social bond (Salvatore & Venuleo, 2009).

5. Incidentally, this process of collection is guided by the general theory. This is why abductive inference is theory driven, rather than data driven, the way induction is (see Chapter 10; see also Salvatore & Valsiner, 2010; Salvatore, 2014).

6. Due to its flexibility, the CA can be applied to various kinds and formats of data and mixes among them as well (e.g., answers to questionnaires, textual data, data describing behavior).

7. The factorial dimensions extracted by the CA are associated with progressively lower amounts of variability. This leads to conclude that the first dimensions—that are associated with the highest amount of variability—are the ones associated with generalized components of sense. This is so because the more generalised a component is, the more it spreads to the field of experience and therefore is able to affect (to polarize) the whole set of signs involved. For instance, when one feels very happy everything seems rosy, even things that have nothing to do with the circumstances that have triggered such happiness. Mannarini Nitti, Ciavolino, and Salvatore (2012) have provided a source of evidence of this tenet, showing how the representations of different objects share a generalized a-semantic ground of meaning, which

binds representations of objects that have no semantic relation with each other (see Chapter 12 for details on this study).

8. The majority of the examples reported below are sourced from the domain of psychotherapy research and more generally of clinical psychology. This is not because this domain is more concerned with dynamicity than others, but just because—for contingent and idiosyncratic reasons—I have focused most of my activity of empirical investigation in that domain.

9. The assumption of the singleness of the population is more than an implicit assumption grounding the inferential statistic: it is an explicit central concept of it, directly expressed by the null hypothesis that the study has to decide whether or not to accept. In fact, the null hypothesis statement that the two (sets of) observations compared are equivalent corresponds to the claim that they belong to the same population—since their difference is due to the casual variability within the population. On the other hand, the alternative hypothesis statement of a significant difference between the observations compared corresponds to the claim that they belong to different populations—that is the population not affected by the effect of the independent variable and the population affected by it.

10. For instance, consider that the sequence $i - j$ is Pattern A – Pattern B. Consider also that Pattern A occurs 10 times in the session under analysis and Pattern B occurs 4 times after that - namely, P $= i = 10; k = i\text{-}j = 4$. Thus, $PT(AtBt+1) = k/p = 4/10 = 0.4$.

CHAPTER 12

STUDIES OF SENSEMAKING

In this chapter I report briefly some instances of empirical analysis concerning phenomena of sensemaking. In so doing, I intend to show how the strategies and the criteria outlined in the previous chapters of the third part of the volume can be implemented in concrete research practices. The instances illustrated below are selected among the ones carried out over the last decade by myself, with others, and pursue different purposes. Some of them (first, second, third and fifth sections) are aimed at modeling basic aspects of the sensemaking dynamic; in other cases (fourth, sixth and seventh sections) their purpose is to detect the local meaning emerging from this dynamic and characterizing the psychosocial phenomenon investigated. Moreover, some of them (second, third, fourth, fifth, and sixth sections) adopt a structural strategy of analysis, while others are instances of dynamic analysis (seventh section); one of them (the first) combines both approaches (on the distinction between structural and dynamic analysis, see Chapter 11).

THE DETECTION OF EMERGENCE IN TERMS OF DIMENSIONALITY OF THE PHASE SPACE

Salvatore, Tebaldi, and Potì (2006/2009) is an example of a combined structural and dynamic analysis of sensemaking in terms of the dimensionality of the phase space, aimed at modeling sensemaking in terms of emergence.

Psychology in Black and White: The Project of a Theory-Driven Science, pp. 265–294
Copyright © 2016 by Information Age Publishing
All rights of reproduction in any form reserved.

Framework

Authors assumed that meaning can be modeled as constraints that communication places on the virtually infinite possibilities of combination of signs—namely, as the SIA shaping the semiotic landscape. According to this general assumption, at the very first moment (t_0)—in communication among complete strangers[1]— the communication can be seen as a system with the maximum extent of entropy, that is, characterized by the absence of any constraint on the freedom of signs to combine with each other. This condition is equivalent to saying that in the instant t_0 there is no meaning grounding communication, namely, there is the maximum communicational uncertainty.

In order to model communication empirically according to this assumption, the authors analyzed the communicational exchange between a patient and her therapist, chosen as an instance of social interaction whose development can be easily described through all its course, in this case by recording the verbal communication. The central hypothesis was that in the first moments of the interaction a shared landscape emerges and starts to work as the attractor of the further communication. This phenomenon can be viewed as a dynamic of emergence—and therefore the communication has to be seen as a self-organizational system—because it is not the product of a specific agreement between the participants (which would entail subjects being able to import ready-made meaning from outside); rather, it happens from within the system, as a consequence of its functioning.

Method

In order to depict the dynamic of emergence empirically, the authors analyzed the transcripts of a 124-session psychotherapy process. More particularly, they performed 4 Lexical Correspondence Analyses (LCAs), each of them applied to the subset of the whole matrix *sentences x words*, corresponding to a segment of the whole text (blocks 1, 2, 3, 4), therefore to a temporal window of the psychotherapy. The analysis focuses on the phase space dimensionality produced by the LCAs. For this purpose the authors calculated the distribution of inertia associated to the factorial components.

Findings

As Figure 12.1 shows, after the initial sessions (block 1) the phase space reduces its dimensionality. In other words, the lexical variability explained (*inertia*) tends to be concentrated on the first hundred factorial dimensions. This means that, for instance, in comparison with the first LCA, the other 3 LCAs (concerning blocks 2, 3, 4) need a lower number of factorial dimensions to explain the same amount of inertia. Moreover, it is worth noticing that the reduction of the dimensionality does not follow an incremental course. Rather, it seems more like a single jump that happens just once (between block 1 and block 2)—and then remains constant across blocks 2, 3 and 4.

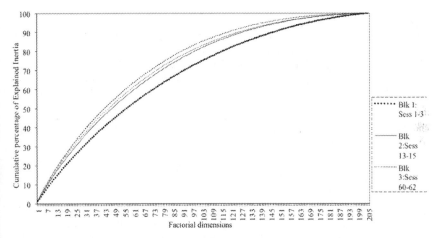

Source: Adapted from Salvatore, Tebaldi, and Potì (2006/2009).

Figure 12.1. Cumulative percentage of explained inertia by factorial dimensions.

The authors interpret this finding as evidence consistent with the hypothesis of the emergent behavior of the sensemaking dynamic. In the final analysis the reduction of the phase space dimensionality means that after a while a constraint on the possibility of sign combination emerges from within the dialogue. Once this happens, each sign loses some degree of freedom, being allowed to associate only with a subset of other signs. In other words, after the first moment of discursive interaction, the communication places constraints on the possibility of combination among words, preventing some combinations, making other improbable, and others more frequent.

It is worth noticing that this phenomenon of emergence of a structure of order seems to be specific to interpersonal exchange. In fact, the study compared the verbatim transcription of the psychotherapy process with the text of a novel. In the latter case, the phase space dimensionality increases —rather than decreasing—after the first moment, to remain constant over the rest of the text. Authors interpreted this finding by highlighting that while in the case of interaction among people the participants can create a shared frame of sense by means of their dialogue, an already shared system of meaning between author and reader is required in order to make the novel readable. Once the text is approached, it can work as a source of novelty, allowing for multiple paths of sensemaking—therefore creating an increase in semiotic variability.

THE HOMOGENIZING POWER OF EMOTION

The study by Tonti and Salvatore (in press) is a further example of structural analysis based on a geometrical approach to meaning— namely, on the study of the dimensionality of the phase space. In this case the geometrical approach grounds a method—the *homogenization of classification functions measurement (HOCFUN)*—designed for analyzing emotional arousal in terms of the tendency to homogenize ratings based on the semantically independent evaluation dimensions (i.e., classification functions) of Relevance and Pleasantness (on the view of emotional arousal in terms of homogenization, see Chapters 2 and 7).

Framework

The homogenization of the classificatory functions consists of that: people tend to use characteristics (i.e., classificatory functions) that have the same affective valence in the same way, regardless of their semantic differences. For instance, classification functions like "good," "smart," "honest," "emphatic" are used as if they were the same as each other and in so doing merged in a single generalized set which has no justification from the semantic standpoint. The homogenization of classification functions is already present in Plato, who based part of his philosophy on the assumption that what is beautiful cannot but be good and vice-versa. The Greek philosopher himself therefore brought together and homogenized two classificatory functions in a single word, the ancient Greek term *Kalokagathia* (= "beautiful and good").

Many signs of the homogenization of classification functions (in the terms described above) can be found in everyday life, particularly in the case of circumstances of emotional activation. Take the emotional reaction one may have when approached by an unknown man who looks dirty and badly dressed—one is easily led to consider him dishonest and also possibly dangerous. This can be seen as due to the fact that classification functions (CFs) are homogenized:— x is CF_1 (badly dressed) and therefore also CF_2 (dishonest), CF_3 (dangerous) and so forth.

HOCFUN is based on the assumption that there is a direct positive linkage between the intensity of emotional arousal and the degree of homogenization: the greater the former the greater the latter. Accordingly, the level of the homogenization is considered a marker of emotional arousal.

Method

HOCFUN consists of a rating task. To this end, HOCFUN adopts two classification functions that, due to their being related to two basic affective, connotative dimensions (Barrett, 2006; Osgood, Suci, & Tannenbaum, 1957), are expected to be quite subject to the homogenizing effect of emotional arousal. The rating scales show classification functions—Unpleasant-Pleasant (henceforth: *Pleasantness*) and Irrelevant-Relevant (henceforth: *Relevancy*). Participants are asked to rate each object of a series of images on these two continuous bipolar dimensions. Target objects are pictures of common elements one can meet in daily life (e.g., a newsstand, a train). The current version of the test uses 38 objects.

HOCFUN is implemented as a fully computer-based test, thanks to an ad-hoc software (Tonti, 2009). The participant is asked to rate the 38 objects—one object at a time—as to how unpleasant-pleasant as well as how irrelevant-relevant it is. Each rating is performed analogically, namely, through the selection of a point on the continuous axes representing the bipolar dimension—the position of the point compared to the polarities marking the extremes of the dimension defines the score of the rating. The system records, for every object, the participant's ratings and the time (in milliseconds) from the appearance of the image to the click on the "confirm" button.

HOCFUN measures the homogenization of the classification function in terms of the amount of within-subject association of the two bipolar dimensions on which the objects are rated. The association between the two bipolar rating dimensions is measured in terms of the coefficient of determination (R), namely, the amount of shared variance between the two rating dimensions. More specifically, for each participant, the Pearson's product-moment correlation coefficient between Pleasantness and Relevancy scales is performed on the intra-subject ratings matrix—that is, the matrix composed of the ratings of the 38 objects on each of the two bipolar dimensions. Then, the Pearson's r is squared so as to calculate the coefficient of determination $(R = r^2)$. In so doing, the measure of the association is made independent from the direction of the association. In the context of the HOCFUN, in order to highlight its conceptual meaning, the extent of the homogenization of the classification function is labeled with the Greek letter k (in accordance to the *Kalokagathia* effect).

Findings

In order to test the construct validity of the HOCFUN, the association of the k index with three further indexes was analyzed. Consistently with the hypotheses, the k index proved to be associated, even if weakly and nonlinearly, with (a) a marker of the homogenization of classificatory functions derived from a separate rating task—a differential semantic concerning with the objects "My Self" "Future," "This situation" and "Immigrants" (Analysis 1); (b) two indirect indicators of emotional activation—the speed of performance on the HOCFUN task (Analysis 2); (c) an index of the intensity of mood—that is, the polarization of semantic differential ratings the participant gave to the object "Myself" (Analysis 3).

As to Analysis 1, a second order regression model showed a nonlinear, positive association between k as predictor variable and the other index of homogenization of classificatory function. This is consistent with the interpretation of k as a measure of the homogenization of the classificatory functions, albeit after recognizing a threshold effect—namely, the fact that the association between the two indexes becomes high and significant only above a certain level of k (i.e., above the median). As to Analysis 2 a positive correlation was found between the speed of the performance on the HOCFUN task and the k index. This provided support to the interpretation of k as a marker of emotional arousal. Indeed, insofar as the speed of performance is taken as an index of emotional activation, it can be concluded that the k index is sensitive to emotional activation—it increases as the emotional activation increases and vice-versa. Interesting enough, the correlation was quite low ($r = .292$), though significant. Also in this case, the low level was attributed to the nonlinearity of the association. Indeed, a threshold effect appeared: if one focuses on the sub-sample with higher k value (i.e., above the median) the correlation was quite a bit higher ($r = .420$). The results of Analysis 3 were also consistent with the interpretation of k as a marker of emotional arousal. As expected, the first order regression model showed a positive association between k as predictor variable and Intensity of mood as criterion: the higher the k scores the higher the intensity of mood. Moreover, the threshold effect is present also in this case: the strength of the association does not spread over the whole distribution, being rather a matter of k scores being above the median.

Taken as a whole, such findings show that evaluations can highlight a linkage among actions that have no semantic bond (i.e., the homogenization of classificatory functions) and this linkage lends itself to be considered an indirect marker of the salience of the affective activation in thinking processes discussed in Chapter 7.

THE AFFECTIVE GROUNDS OF SENSEMEANING

The study by Mannarini, Nitti, Ciavolino, and Salvatore (2012) is an example of structural analysis aimed at detecting the affective grounds of meaning. It is based on the same conceptual framework as the HOCFUN method (Tonti & Salvatore, in press), namely, on the tendency of the affect to homogenize, that is to construct linkages between elements that have no semantic connections. In this case, however, this view is used for the sake of detecting the role played by affect in the sociosymbolic process, namely, in the way people construct the representation of objects of their social life.

Framework

The study focused on the generalized meanings that—regardless the specific meaning of the objects of the social worlds, channel the way individuals make sense of such objects. More specifically, the aim of the study was to test a model showing the relevance of these generalized meanings and their relation to object-specific meanings. Such a model is based on the view of the affect as a hypergeneralized, embodied meaning (i.e., a scenario, as defined in Chapters 2 and 7) in terms of which people connote the field of experience, and therefore ground and channel the semantic elaboration of the objects of the experience.

Method

In order to develop such a framework, a model of the relation between the affective generalized meanings and the semantic, object-specific meanings was defined and this model was given its first empirical test. The model was hierarchical: it encompasses first order factors (i.e., semantic meanings concerning discrete objects) and second order factors (i.e., affective generalized meaning concerning the whole field of experience in which the objects are embedded).

To test the model, a secondary analysis on a dataset resulting from a survey involving freshmen in the undergraduate psychology program at the University of Salento, in Italy (Venuleo, Mossi, & Salvatore, 2014) was performed. The original questionnaire, composed of 135 items, was designed to map the students' semantic meanings (enacted in terms of opinions, judgments, evaluations) associated with four objects: (a) $\xi 1$, *Commitment to the university* (motivations, expectations), (b) $\xi 2$, *Trustworthiness of the social system* (reliability of social structures, e.g., local administration and services), (c) $\xi 3$, *Psychology profession* (functions of psychologists and psychological knowledge); and (d) $\xi 4$, *General values* (morality, respect for rules, etc.). All variables were measured with a 4-point Likert-like scale, either in the format of agreement (from "fully disagree" to "fully agree") or intensity (from "not at all" to "very much"). For the current study, a subset of 19 items was selected, also called *manifest variables*, based upon the results of an item analysis performed on the whole dataset. Items were selected according to the strength of the contribution they provided to the measurement of the semantic meanings attributed to the four objects upon which the questionnaire was focused.

To test the model, a procedure of analysis based on PLS path modeling with high order constructs was implemented. Due to its ability to estimate complex models, Partial Least Square path modeling can be used to investigate models at a high level of abstraction (Esposito Vinzi, Chin, Henseler, & Wang, 2010). The procedure can be thought of as the analysis of two conceptually different models: (a) A structural (or inner) model that specifies the causal relationships among Latent Variables (LVs), as posited by a given theory; (b) A measurement (or outer) model that specifies the relationship of the Manifest Variables (MV—for example, *commitment to the university, trustworthiness of the social systems, psychology profession, general values*) with their (hypothesized) underlying LVs. In our case, the latent constructs are the semantic (I order) and affective (II order) level of meanings.[2]

According to the theoretical model, the LVs $\xi 1$ (UNIVERSITY[3]), $\xi 2$ (SOCIETY), $\xi 3$ (PSYCHO), $\xi 4$ (VALUES) were considered as independent first order constructs. This assumption of independence was made because these constructs concern separate objects that lack semantic linkage between them. Consequently, in the first-order model, no causative relation was considered. The second-order construct ($\xi 5$) introduced, named IMAGE, was a dimension assumed to underlie the first order LVs, and causatively linked with all of them. It is worth noting that the second-order factor was modeled by means of the full set of items measured as part of it. This means that the second factor was defined as a construct pertaining to the meaning of the experience, yet independent from its specific semantic content (since it is the set of items *taken as a whole* that measured the construct, regardless of the fact that items pertained to different semantic domains/objects—that is, *commitment to the university, trustworthiness of the social systems, psychology profession, general values*). Thus, this way of measuring the second order factor legitimized the conceptualization of it as *affective meaning*—namely, as the global connotation of the whole field of experience not dependent on/constrained by the semantic specificity of the discrete objects in which the field is articulated.

Figure 12.2 shows the path diagram of the theoretical model.

Findings

The empirical test provided data that were consistent with the theoretical model proposed. Both models (i.e., inner and outer) proved to have an acceptable goodness of fit. Taken together, these results provided evidence

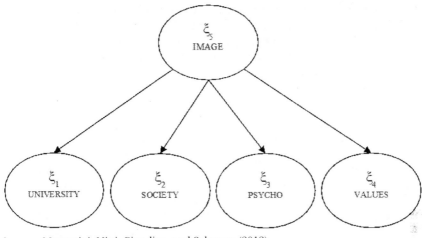

Source: Mannarini, Nitti, Ciavolino, and Salvatore (2012).

Figure 12.2.   Path diagram of the model of relations among constructs.

supporting the hypothesis that the semantic representation of different objects is grounded in a generalized affective meaning (i.e., a scenario) shaping the connotation of the whole field of experience. This common affective ground enables one to make sense of an aspect that would otherwise be counterintuitive: the fact that the ways people represent the objects under analysis—that is, the objects detected by the first order constructs—were associated among them (in particular, people's representations of the society, the university and the system of values were somewhat similar). If one conceives of sensemaking in a one-dimensional way—namely, only as a matter of semantic elaboration—these associations are hard to understand, given that there are no semantic similarities/connections among the involved objects. However, the model provides a way of understanding such associations: indeed they can be interpreted as indirectly reflecting the salience of the generalized affective meaning. In other words, what the first order constructs have in common is not their semantic content, but their being embedded in the same generalized affective meaning shaping the field of experience as a whole.

THE STUDY OF THE BOUNDARIES

Ciavolino, Salvatore, and Calcagnì (2013) have developed a particular interpretation of the strategic approach in order to establish a new method of analysis of the interrater agreement among judges.

Framework

In the field of psychology, and in the social sciences generally, rating scales and coding systems are widely used. Such measures are generally based on evaluations performed by independent competent raters, whose reliability is generally esteemed in terms of interrater agreement. The rationale of this way of esteeming the reliability is grounded in the classic theory of measurement: any instance of measurement is composed of the true depiction of the measured object plus an error component; the former component is invariant across instances, and the limitation on the latter is directly proportional to the similarity of the instances of the output. This leads to the conclusion that the level of interrater agreement is an estimate of the incidence of the true depiction of the object.

Despite its widespread adoption, this rationale possesses a logical flaw that cannot but have important consequences on the interpretation of interrater agreement as a measurement of reliability. To put it in general terms, if two instances of the measurement (of the same object) had no error component, then they would produce the same output. Yet the converse is not necessarily true: the fact that two outputs are identical does not mean that there is no error component. And the same can be said in the case of disagreement among raters: it does not necessarily mean that the error component is high. In sum, a high interrater agreement is neither a necessary nor a sufficient condition for considering a measure to be reliable, and neither is a low interrater agreement a necessary or sufficient condition for considering a measure to be unreliable.

Based on that premise, the authors provided a method of appraisal of the quality of rater judgment aimed at integrating the use of inter-rater agreement as a measure of reliability. According to this method, the quality of the rater's judgment, is conceptualized in terms of (rater's) *marginal sensitivity* (MS). The greater this capability, the more information the rater is expected to be able to take into account, hence the greater the precision of the evaluation. Accordingly, MS lends itself to be conceptualized as reflecting the rater's autonomy by implicit higher ordered assumptions (i.e., generalized meanings) channelling and constraining the judgements. This is so for the following reasoning.

First, consider a set of items concerning a certain dimension D of a certain object O to be measured. Then consider the rater's global, generalized representation—say H_0—of the object. In other words, H_{DO} is the higher-ordered meaning of the object O as a whole, regardless its specific dimensions.

Second, in the light of the above, one can define two basic, opposite heuristics as the ground of the rating. On the one hand, the *top-down approach*. According to such a way, the ratings are guided by H_0. This is the same as saying that a (generally implicit) higher ordered assumption concerning O-as-a-whole tends to guide the ratings of any single dimension D. On the other hand, the *bottom-up approach*. In this case any item is rated in accordance with its own specific content; such ratings being independent of H_0. Daily life thinking is based mainly on the top-down approach. Only in specific and limited circumstances do persons retrieve a global representation by a systematic computation of its components. On the other hand, such a heuristic reduces the marginal sensitivity, therefore the quality of the rater's judgment, because the elements tend to be homogenized by reason of their common membership in the higher-ordered class.

The Method

The authors provided a method for appraising the quality of the rater's judgment in terms of esteeming of the rater's marginal sensibility. Such a method adopts a computational model based on *fuzzy set theory* and focused on the analysis of the profile of the individual rater's performance. Very briefly, fuzzy set theory models sets that are characterized in terms of continuous membership function. For instance, considers the two sets of rich and poor people. Such sets have a fuzzy boundary, namely, the distinction among them is not defined in terms of a sharp cut-off point; accordingly, the higher the income of the person, the higher the fitness of the membership to the set of the rich, the less the fitness of the membership to the set of poor people. Thus, the membership of fuzzy sets is not mutually exclusive—they are described by values of membership being more or less high, whose global amount is equal to 1.

Schematically, marginal sensitivity can be esteemed in terms of fuzziness, namely, in terms of the extent of the fuzzy value associated with the individual rater's performance. Indeed, the more the fuzzy value, the less prototypical is the rater's judgment on a certain item, namely, the less such judgment reflects the global representation of the object as a whole (i.e., the H_0). Accordingly, a high fuzzy value can be interpreted as indicative of high marginal sensitivity, namely, of a bottom-up way of judging, while a low fuzzy value as a top-down way, characterized by the fact that the response reflects the salience of the generalized representation of the object (H_0), rather than the specific content of the item.

Findings

In order to provide an exemplificative application of the method, as well as to subject it to a preliminary test of validity, it was applied so as to esteem the quality of 6 raters' judgments applying the PQS[4] on the verbatim transcripts of a set of sessions from a single psychotherapy. Esteems of the rater quality provided by the method were then compared with a further index of rater competence, based on the classical modality of esteeming the rater's reliability. To this end, for each rater, the rater competence was calculated as the mean of the interrater agreement with the other five raters. The two measures—that is, that based on the within-rater esteem of marginal sensitivity and that based on the classical interrater agreement were correlated, though weakly. This result led authors to conclude that the esteem of the marginal sensitivity based on the fuzzy set theory is a promising procedure to integrate the esteems of the judgment's reliability based on the inter- subject agreement by means of a within-subject measurement, aimed at detecting the heuristic mechanism of the judgment.

AN AUTOMATED PROCEDURE OF CONTENT ANALYSIS

This section reports a study (Salvatore, Gennaro, Auletta, Tonti, & Nitti, 2012) presenting an automated method of content analysis (ACASM—automated co-occurrence analysis for semantic mapping) based on the criterion of pattern detection that informs the structural approach. (The method has been studied within the domain of the psychotherapy research. However, it can be used in other research domains as well)

Framework

ACASM is a bottom up method of textual analysis. This is so because it does not start with a preestablished repertoire of thematic contents in accordance with which the units of analysis are classified. Rather, the repertoire of thematic contents working as a coding system is produced by the analysis itself.

ACASM focuses on the co-occurrence of words—that is, the way the words combine with each other within the same unit of analysis into which the text is segmented (generally, the unit of analysis consists of an utterance or a group of a few utterances). The co-occurrence of words is taken as a criterion of similarity for clustering the units of text, namely, the units of analysis are clustered in accordance with the words co-occurring within them: units of text containing the same co-occurring words are considered similar and therefore grouped. The rationale is that a set of co-occurring words marks a specific thematic content (also called thematic nucleon). Therefore, units having a certain set of co-occurring words in common share the thematic content marked by such a set. In this way, the procedure of semantic analysis is able to provide a fine level of semantic representation, coding each unit of analysis in terms of a specific content—namely, the one marked by the set of co-occurring words according to which the unit has been clustered.

From a conceptual point of view, the reference to co-occurrence of words within the same unit of analysis can be considered a way of taking into account the linguistic level of the contextuality of meaning, namely, the level consisting of the way the words are combined within the text (cf. Chapter 11).

Method

ACASM is aimed at extrapolating thematic contents (i.e., semantic meanings) active in the text. Each thematic content is characterized by a cluster of words which tend to *co-occur* (i.e., to be associated with each other) throughout the text. Such sets of co-occurring words are identified by means of invariant but context-sensitive computational rules implemented automatically by an ad-hoc software. Due to these characteristics, ACASM procedures are: (a) implementable through automated routines carried out by computer; (b) reproducible reliably across analyzes and analyzers; (c) able to produce a valid representation of the textual data.

ACASM procedure is based on five steps. First, the textual corpus is automatically segmented into elementary context units (ECUs). This is carried out according to the following criteria: (1) Each ECU begins just after the end of the previous ECU; (2) Each ECU ends with the first punctuation mark ("." or "!," or "?") occurring after the threshold of 250 characters from the first character; (3) If an ECU is longer than 500 characters, it ends with the last word found within such a length, even if there is no punctuation mark.

Second, a dictionary for the text-analysis is constructed. In order to do this, each lexical form present in the textual corpus is categorized into the lemma it belongs to, thus producing a list of lemmas present in the textual corpus analyzed. Thereafter, the first x% (usually, x = 5) of the most frequent lemmas are excluded; this is done since very high-frequency lemmas (such as "to," "and," "of," etc.) tend to co-occur in too many different ECUs, thus reducing their ability to discriminate among different patterns of co-occurrence. Then, y% (usually y = 10) of the most frequent lemmas of the remaining list is selected, in order to reduce the variability of the dataset.

Third, the textual corpus is digitally represented in terms of a matrix displaying ECUs in rows and lemmas in columns; the cell x_{ij} receives the value "1" if the jth lemma is contained in the ith ECU, the value "0" otherwise.

Fourth, a combined multiple lexical correspondence analysis and cluster analysis is applied to the matrix in order to group the ECUs of the textual corpus into clusters, using the co-occurrence of lemmas among the ECUs as criterion of similarity—in this way, each cluster could be considered a thematic content active in the textual corpus, since it contained groups of utterances (i.e., ECUs) sharing a similar pattern of co-occurring lemmas, therefore a semantic content.

Finally, each of these clusters is interpreted and labelled in accordance to the utterance and words comprising it.

In the case of the study reported here, ACASM was applied to the verbatim transcripts of a good-outcome Italian speaking 124-session psychotherapy. As result of ACASM, 14 clusters—corresponding to thematic nuclei—were identified.

Findings

Salvatore and colleagues (2012) analyzed the validity of ACASM in terms of a Turning-like criterion. According to this criterion, ACASM could be considered a valid method of content analysis if and only if the analysis it produces cannot be distinguished from that produced by expert human coders.

More specifically, the comparison between ACASM and human raters was focused on two basic operations grounding the semantic analysis of any utterance comprising a text: the evaluation of their similarity and their classification in terms of the class of meanings.

In order to compare the evaluations of similarity, a group of human raters were asked to esteem the similarity among a selection of utterances ($n = 70$) of the textual corpus. These estimates were then compared with the corresponding ACASM values of similarity among the same utterances[5]. As to the comparison concerning the classification of utterances, further raters were asked to classify the same 70 utterances used for the previous analysis into 14 semantic classes, namely, in the same number of classes extrapolated by the preliminary application of ACASM to the textual corpus. Then, the four classifications—that is, the three performed by human raters and the one performed by ACASM—where compared in terms of interrater agreement.

The results were consistent with the turning-like criterion: (a) ACASM's estimates of semantic similarity were consistent with the corresponding estimates provided by human coders; (b) coders' agreement and coder-ACASM agreement on the task of semantic classification had the same magnitude, which led to conclude that the classification of the utterances performed by ACASM was undistinguishable from that carried out by the human raters.

A METHOD BASED ON PATTERN DETECTION

The GMI (Auletta, Salvatore, Metrangolo, Monteforte, Pace, & Puglisi, 2012) is a method of analysis of the psychotherapy process, specifically devoted to the detection of the therapeutic interventions—more specifically, of the subclass of interventions defined as "interpretation." I present it here because it is an example of a strategy based on pattern detection.

Framework

The GMI is aimed at analyzing the interpretive work performed by therapists of different therapy orientations. It is based on the view that in order to examine the qualitative variations of interpretations across different therapy orientations, interpretive interventions should be understood in terms of *patterns* changing across contexts, rather than in terms of predefined, fixed macrotypologies (e.g., interpretation of transference, interpretation of the defence mechanisms). This means focusing (1) on the constitutive categories of interpretation, and (2) on the possible combinations among such categories. This way of studying interpretations—based on the logic of pattern detection—can be applied to a variety of theoretical contexts and therapy orientations, and would allow the personal styles and/or theory-guided pattern of interpretation displayed by therapists to be analyzed.

Method

The GMI is a molecular method for evaluating psychotherapy transcripts. The basic evaluation unit of the GMI is the therapist's speaking turn (unlike the "molar" or "global" methods, which examine therapist techniques across an entire segment or session). However, the concept of interpretation, and the specific definition used in this study, imply that knowledge of both patient and therapist talk is necessary for a correct application of the coding system. Accordingly, judges must be provided with information as to what has gone on previously in therapy and are required to read the whole session transcript carefully to be aware of the patient-therapist context generating the interpretation.

The GMI-based evaluation of psychotherapy transcripts involves two steps: first, the judge selects the therapist's speaking turn where interpretation occurs according to the GMI's operative definition of interpretation; then he or she applies the GMI's dimensions which describe interpretation.

The GMI provides the following operative definition of interpretation: "Interpretation is a therapist statement where an innovative meaning is suggested as regards the patient's current framework." Patient's framework is intended as the system of assumptions on his or her own self and the world, grounding, constraining and channelling the speaker's way of thinking. Thus, to consider a therapist intervention as an interpretation, it is not sufficient for the therapist to restate, paraphrase, or simply contradict what has been explicitly or implicitly stated by the patient. Rather, the therapist has to go beyond the system of assumptions grounding the patient's discourse.

The GMI code system encompasses five dimensions, each of them consisting of a set of mutually exclusive categories. Each category is depicted on a nominal (categorical) scale. On the whole, GMI encompasses 17 categories (cf. Table 12.1).

The dimension of "Content" pertains to the focus of the interpretation. It is articulated in six mutually exclusive categories—*Representation, Defense, Motive, General functioning, Drive, Affect*. Such categories do not provide information about whether the content concerns the self or the therapist, or other people, pertains to the past or the present moment—such aspects being described through further dimensions.

The dichotomous dimension of "Domain" distinguishes whether the interpretation concerns the patient's interpersonal or the intrapsychic life.

The "Time Orientation" dimension pertains to the temporal reference of the therapist's interpretation. Four mutually exclusive categories are distinguished within Time Orientation: two categories concern discrete temporal references (Past, Present), and two categories concern the directions of their connection (Past-to-Present and Present-to-Past).

The dichotomous dimension "Space Frame" distinguishes two general kinds of interpretive focus, regardless of their temporal reference— that is, patient' experience concerning the therapeutic situation (internal) or the experience outside therapy (external).

The dimension of "Style" refers to the therapist's modalities of delivering the interpretation, examining whether the therapist is neutral, self-disclosing, and so forth. The Style dimension includes three mutually exclusive categories, representing the epistemic status the therapist attributes to his or her own acts: specifically, interpretations can be presented as descriptions of facts, as his or her own personal beliefs, or as something that must be demonstrated.

Table 12.1.   GMI Code System

Dimension	Category	Description	Example
Content	Representation	Interpretation focuses on patient's ideas, mental schemas or fantasies.	"You conveyed to me that you regularly feel as being put aside, in your relations with your mother, your partner, maybe …"
	Defence	Interpretation focuses on the patient's tendency to protect him/herself from painful, unacceptable external situations or inner experiences	"That's interesting, because if you ignore her, or you don't think of it as a rejection, well you can ignore your feeling of being deserted."
	Motive	Interpretation focuses on patient's mental schemas, behaviours or attitudes that have a purpose, like getting something from someone, changing an inner state or interpersonal situation	"Maybe you were intended to go to Milan just to stay alone with dad …"
	Gen. Functioning	Interpretation focuses on patient's general ways to act or behave with respect to self or others	"At the beginning of the therapy, I had the feeling that here, by coming to therapy, you're attempting to imitating the relationship with your father … you're playing the role of the child."
	Drive	Interpretation focuses on drives, wishes, and instincts	"I think you always felt compelled to stay alone with dad …"
	Affect	Interpretation focuses on patient's emotional or affective states like fear, love, rage	"Now you are facing all of this by yourself … the examinations, the divorce … I think you're getting frightened for that."
Domain	Intrapsychic	Interpretation focuses on contents pertaining the patient's self	"You're feeling overwhelmed and you must run away. It's like you're fearing your own reactions."

(Table continues on next page)

Table 12.1.   (Continued)

Dimension	Category	Description	Example
Domain	Interpersonal	Interpretation focuses on contents pertaining the others	"And this is expressing all your helplessness …. Maybe with you father too, you had this kind of competition".
Time orientation	Present	Interpretation focuses on the present moments of patient's life	"I think you're afraid of your rage, somehow, so you're afraid it goes out, this is such an inner fight …"
	Present-to-Past	Interpretation links events belonging to present with past issues	"What you're feeling now, with me, it is far similar to what you experienced as a child, when you left home for the first time."
	Past	Interpretation focuses on the past moments of patient's life	"And I guess, at times, this episode made you look for some loneliness."
	Past-to-Present	Interpretation links events belonging to past with present issues	"It was last session, you told me you were sorry for me, for what happened … I think even now you're afraid you're not good, for what you are, for how you look …"
Space frame	Internal	Interpretation focuses on what happens during the therapy sessions	"Even with me, sometimes you're feeling you can't, you've no hope, but sometimes you feel very strong … it's the same with your work plans."
	External	Interpretation focuses on what happens outside the session	"Maybe he reminded so much of your father, his character, his constant control, almost anxious."
Style	Factual	Interpretations is provided by the therapist as something that he/she considers sure and certain – a fact.	"So this is attracting for you, since it reminds of your need to turn everything upside down."

(Table continues on next page)

Table 12.1.   (Continued)

Dimension	Category	Description	Example
Style	*Subjective*	Interpretation is delivered with a degree of uncertainty: the therapist may communicate his/her own point of view, state caution or present interpretation to patient as something needing to be tested.	"I don't know if I understand: I think you're on the look out, in every new relation. Isn't it?"
	Demonstrating	Interpretation is delivered by explaining how he/she attained it, making examples, and/or reporting anecdotes	"And if we try to remember, this happens everytime you must start to do something. The first time you went here, you told that you were reluctant to enter in therapy… and yesterday you presented your curriculum and were waiting for a call…".

Source: Auletta, Salvatore, Metrangolo, Monteforte, Pace, and Puglisi (2012).

The GMI is implemented by means of a bottom-up procedure, aimed at depicting the local way—namely, the case-specific mode—the categories combine with each other in meaningful patterns.

To this end, first each session transcript under analysis is divided into therapist's and patient's speaking turns (ST). Second, the rater selects the therapist's STs that are consistent with the definition of interpretation given above. Third, focusing on the therapist STs selected, the rater codes them according to the five GMI dimensions. Fourth, in order to map the way categories combine with each other, a procedure of multidimensional analysis integrating multiple correspondence analysis (MCA) and cluster analysis (CA) is performed. In so doing, interpretations are grouped according to their similarities, namely, in subsets, each of them characterized by a peculiar pattern of co-occurring categories across the five dimensions. Finally, each subset is understood as a specific model of interpretation, due to the pattern of co-occurring categories characterized it.

Findings

In order to provide an example of the method, the GMI was applied to four cases (two psychodynamic and two cognitive-oriented psychotherapies).

Five models of interpretation (MI) were identified, all of them endowed with a clear clinical meaning.

- MI 1—*Interpretation of outside-session mental schemas*. Interpretations focus on patient's thoughts and ideas pertaining to his or her (current or past) experience, outside therapy (example: "You conveyed to me that you regularly feel like you are being put aside, in your relations with your mother, your partner, maybe …").
- MI 2—*Interpretation of transference*. The interpretation, proposed in a factual style, concerns the patient's here-and-now representations of the relation with the therapist ("Even with me. Sometimes I reminded you of your father, his constant control … sometimes you feel you are caught in a trap").
- MI 3—*Interpretation of patient's behaviors and actions*. Patient's way of functioning outside the session is interpreted in a factual style ("I think that you're attempting to imitate the relationship with your father … you're playing the role of the child").
- MI 4—*Subjective interpretation*. Therapist conveys his or her own point of view, states caution, or presents his or her statements as something needing to be tested ("I don't know if I understand: I think you're on the lookout, in every new relation. Is that it?").
- MI 5—*Interpretation with connections*. Therapist makes links between issues belonging to different temporal planes or between different events of the treatment by means of examples, anecdotes, explanations, and so forth ("And if we try to remember, this happens every time you must start to do something. The first time you came here, you said that you were reluctant to enter therapy … then yesterday you presented your curriculum and were waiting for a call …").

Moreover, two of the five models of interpretations ("interpretation of outside-session mental schemas" and "interpretation of transference") were able to differentiate treatments according to their orientation (i.e., cognitive vs. psychodynamic).

Consistently with such findings, authors concluded that GMI proved helpful in analyzing interpretations in terms of case-specific and distinctive patterns.

DISCOURSE NETWORK OF THE CLINICAL EXCHANGE

The discourse flow analysis (DFA; Salvatore et al., 2010; Nitti, Ciavolino, Salvatore, & Gennaro, 2010) is a method aimed at detecting the therapist-patient exchange in terms of its capacity of producing semiotic innovation, where such capacity is taken as a marker of the clinical quality of the psychotherapy. The DFA is of interest here, because it is an example of the analysis of the communication in terms of nonlinear semiotic dynamic[6]

Framework

DFA is based on the view of the psychotherapy process as an intersubjective dynamic of co-construction of meaning producing semiotic novelty. According to such a view, psychotherapy can be seen as a transformative dialog, where new meanings are elaborated, new categories are developed, and patient's assumptions are transformed within and through an intersubjective context.

Such an intersubjective view of psychotherapy led to the definition of the *two-stage semiotic model* (TSSM; cf. Gennaro et al., 2010; Gennaro, Salvatore, Rocco, & Auletta, in press; Salvatore et al., 2010; Salvatore & Gennaro, 2014): a model of a clinically efficacious psychotherapeutic process, upon which DFA is based. According to the TSSM, the psychotherapy process can be depicted through the formal analysis of the global structural qualities of the patient-therapist's verbal exchange. The TSSM is based on the following two assumptions.

Assumption 1. Two-stage articulation. Human beings are meaning-generating systems. Psychotherapy can thus be considered as an emerging context that promotes the continuous revision and elaboration of new meanings over time. The psychotherapeutic process is seen as the "development of co-evolving languages of coordinated exchanges" between patient and therapist (Goolishian & Anderson, 1987, p. 533). The motivation leading the patient to seek therapy and the clinical goal of such human activity make the clinical exchange a quite unique form of intersubjective sensemaking. The clinical exchange is not only a co-construction of meaning like every other form of sensemaking. Rather, it represents a dialogical dynamic aimed at changing the patient's affective and cognitive modality of interpreting his/her experience. In other words, the clinical exchange is not only a negotiation between the patient's and the therapist's systems of interpreting the world, but a negotiation by means of which the patient's system is expected to change. The patient arrives at psychotherapy with a predefined, more or less rigid system of declarative and procedural assumptions (e.g., concepts of self and others, affective schemata, metacognitive modalities, relational and attachment strategies, unconscious plans, etc.), which are taken for granted and work as embodied generalized meanings regulating the interpretation of experience (Zittoun, 2011). This system of assumptions is therefore the source of the patient's psychological problems: symptoms, at the intrapsychic as well as at the relational level, can be understood as sustained by and/or the consequence of such high-ordered generalized meanings. One of the main therapeutic activities consists therefore of triggering the reorganization of the patient's super-ordered generalized meanings.

On the ground of the framework outlined above, it is thus possible to claim that the change process in the communicational system made up of the patient-therapist interaction has two stages. In the first stage the patient-therapist exchange works mainly as an external source of limitation on the patient's system of assumptions. The first stage is therefore fundamentally a *deconstructive* process, with therapeutic dialog aimed at placing constraints on the regulative activity of the patient's problematic generalized meanings. The weakening of the patient's critical generalized meaning opens the way for the emergence of new super-ordered meanings. This is what happens in the second, *constructive* stage, when the patient-therapist dialog favors the emergence of new super-ordered meanings, replacing the previous ones Obviously, the two stages are not totally distinct and mutually exclusive. Both of them are present throughout the whole psychotherapy, within every session, though to different extents. Moreover, the two stages may tend to alternate with each other over the course of the psychotherapy. However, the two-stage assumption asserts that, at the macroanalytical level, it is possible to discriminate, in a clinically efficacious psychotherapy process, between sessions where deconstructive sensemaking is dominant, and a second one where the dynamic of sensemaking acquires a prevalent constructive function. Following this postulate it is expected that the incidence of the generalized super-ordered meanings that are active within the therapeutic dialog will decrease in the deconstructive stage and then increase in the constructive stage.

Assumption 2. Nonlinearity of the psychotherapy process. Assumption 1 suggests that the clinical exchange performs different functions in the two stages—respectively a deconstructive and a constructive one. If this assumption is true, it follows that the system comprised by the patient-therapist verbal exchange must present a peculiar and different mode of working in each stage. Consequently, sensemaking does not follow a linear way of functioning over the course of the psychotherapy, but instead, at a certain point, it has to deal with a reorganization of its functioning.

Following this assumption, the TSSM assumes that the deconstructive and constructive sessions will be characterized by different patterns of relationships among those features of the therapeutic dialog which contribute to sensemaking, esteemed by the DFA indexes (see below, Method section).

DFA analyzes patient-therapist dialog in *formal* terms—that is, by depicting the structural global qualities of the communicational exchange—rather than merely in terms of the semantic contents exchanged within their dialog. In so doing, DFA enables a dynamic analysis of the patient-therapist communication, focusing on temporal patterns of meanings, rather than on the survey of discrete contents. More in particular, DFA maps the verbatim transcript of psychotherapy dialog in terms of the associations for adjacency between semantic contents occurring within the clinical exchange. Thus, DFA focuses on a specific dimension of the sense-making, namely, that implemented by sequential combinations of meanings (i.e., associations for adjacency) over time. In order to operate in this way, DFA refers to the concept of "discourse network." A discourse network is made of semantic nodes, each of which represents one of the units of semantic contents active in the communicational exchange between patient and therapist (the choice of not distinguishing patient and therapist contents reflects the DFA dialogical model; DFA can however be applied to patient or to therapist contents too, in order to deepen the observations relating to each participant). The directional linkage between two given semantic nodes shows the association by adjacency between the corresponding contents—namely, what content follows what content.

Method

DFA works in three steps. In the first step, ACASM is implemented (see Section 5) in order to identify the semantic contents active in the text and to categorize it in terms of them.

DFA's second step uses the output of the previous step in order to model the clinical exchange in terms of *discourse network*—each thematic content identified by ACASM is considered to be a *node* of the discourse network (henceforth: semantic node). To do this, a Markovian sequence analysis is applied to the sequence of the semantic nodes identified previously in order to calculate the probability associated with the linkage for adjacency between each pair of semantic nodes. In other words, for each thematic content, DFA calculates its probability of coming straight after every other thematic content (see Figure 12.3 for an example of discourse network extracted from a psychotherapy session).

The third step is aimed at analyzing the *structural* and *dynamic characteristics* of the discourse network, insofar as they are considered indicative of relevant aspects and qualities of the sensemaking process. It is carried out by means of descriptive (*Connectivity, Heterogeneity*) and interpretative (*Activity and Super-Ordered Nodes*) indexes

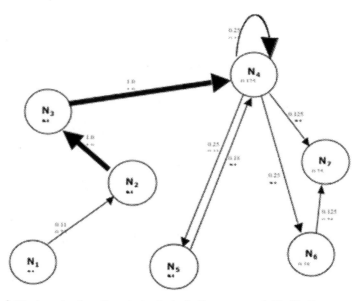

Each node Ni represents a thematic content active in the discourse network (N_1: "feeling/expression of impotence"; N_2: "feeling/fear of being abandoned"; N_3: "desire to indulge own selfish—N_4: "temporal and spatial constraints"; N_5: "autonomy-dependence"; N_6: "self-appreciation"; N_7: "schedules in life and in therapy"). The directional linkage between two given nodes shows the association for adjacency between the corresponding contents. The thickness of the line is proportional to the strength of the association (measured in terms of probability, expressed by the coefficient close to each line). This discourse network indicates that the thematic content N_1 (corresponding to Cluster 4 of the output) is followed by the thematic content N_2 (Cluster 20) in the 11% ($p = 0.11$) of the cases. In turn, this last thematic content always ($p = 1.0$) precedes N_3 (Cluster 22). N_4 (Cluster 23) is followed by N_5 (Cluster 15) and N_6 (Cluster 16) and itself in equal proportion (25% of cases) and by N_7 (Cluster 2) in 12.5% of cases; and so on. (Note that the probability of the connections outgoing from the singular node does not get systematically get 1.00 because the Figure shows just a partial area of the discourse network. The whole discourse network of the first session encompasses 19 nodes.)

Source: Salvatore, Gelo, Gennaro, Manzo, and Al-Radaideh (2010).

Figure 12.3. A selected area of the discourse network of the Lisa psychotherapy's first session.

1. *Connectivity*: This index measures the network's density of associations, that is, the relative amount of connections among the semantic nodes. It is calculated as the ratio between the active connections present in the network (as identified through the Markovian analysis) and the network's maximum theoretical amount of possible connections. This maximum is n^2, where n is the number of semantic nodes present in the discourse network. This is because theoretically each node can be connected with every other node, including itself.

Therefore, every node can theoretically have n connections - and the whole network $n \times n$ connections. For instance, the discourse network depicted in Figure 12.3 has a connectivity of 0.163 (Number of connections: 8; Maximum theoretical amount of possible connections: 49—as a result of the fact that there are 7 semantic nodes; Connectivity = 8/49). Figure 12.3 can be interpreted as follows: the discourse network of figure 19 has 16.3% of the possible connections among its nodes active.

2. *Heterogeneity*: This index depicts how the connections are distributed among the nodes. It is calculated as the standard deviation of the distribution of the amount of connections starting from and arriving at every semantic node. The higher the level of this index, the higher the variability of the connection distribution among nodes (i.e.,, some nodes have many connections and others very few). With reference to figure 19, the discourse network has a Heterogeneity of 1.069. This value represents the standard deviation of the distribution of the number of the ongoing (o) and incoming (i) connections of the 7 nodes (N_1: $o = 1, i = 0$; N_2: $0 = 1, i = 1$; N_3: $0 = 1, i = 1$; N_4: $0 = 4, i = 3$; N_5: $o = 1, i = 1$; N_6: $0 = 1, i = 1$; N_7: $0 = 0, i = 2$).

3. *Activity* (A): This is a global parameter depicting the network's capability of enlarging meaning variability (previously defined as the spectrum of associations for adjacency among the semantic nodes) through time. Therefore, a high Activity level indicates that the discourse, as it evolves, progressively tends to increase the variability of the connection between meanings—that is, the number of other nodes that follow adjacently each node. In metaphorical terms, a high Activity level depicts a discourse dynamic capable of enlarging the paths of sensemaking, by enriching the possibilities of combination among the meanings making up these paths. Activity is calculated as the ratio between the *Generative Power* and *Absorbing Power* of the network. These two parameters concern the capability of the discourse network to, respectively increase and decrease the meaning variability (i.e., the spectrum of associations for adjacency among the nodes) through time. The estimate of *Generative Power* and *Absorbing Power* is based on the measure of each single node's contribution to the variability of discourse meaning (henceforth: *Contribution*). The Contribution of each single node is calculated as the product of the absolute difference between the amount of outgoing (o) and incoming (i) connections of the node considered, and the ratio of the frequency of connections from/to that node (o + i) to the number of its theoretically possible connections (n; where n is the number of semantic nodes present in the discourse network). Calculating it in this way allows the absolute difference between incoming and outgoing

connections not only to be taken into account, but also to be weighted according to the importance of the node (i.e., the amount of linkages between the node considered and the others). For instance, in the discourse network depicted in Figure 12.3, the Contribution of N_4 is 1.00 [($o = 4$; $i = 3$; $n = 7$; (4–3)*(4+3)/7)]; while the Contribution of N_7 is 0.574 [($o = 0$; $i = 2$; $n = 7$; (0–2)*(0+2)/7]. According to such a parameter, a node can be classified as a "generative," "relay," or "absorbing" node. A node is generative when it has more outgoing than incoming connections; relay when it has the same number of incoming and outgoing connections; absorbing when the incoming connections exceed the outgoing ones. Referring to Figure 12.3, it can be seen that node N_4 is a generative one, because it has more outgoing (4) than incoming connections (3); N_5 is a relay node, because it has the same number of connections both entering and going out (1); N_7 is an absorbing node because it has fewer outgoing (0) than incoming connections (2). According to this operational definition, a generative node helps to increase the meaning variability of the discourse, because it activates more semantic nodes than it is activated by. Instead, an absorbing node reduces the discourse meaning variability, because the outgoing spectrum of thematic contents is narrower than the incoming one. A relay node reproduces the variability. Lastly, the network's *Generative Power* and *Absorbing Power* are calculated as the average contribution of the generative nodes and of the absorbing nodes respectively.

4. *Super-Ordered Nodes*: A Super-Ordered Node is a node carrying out a function of super-ordered meaning regulating the sensemaking process. In other words, a Super-Ordered Node represents thematic content activating further meanings—a promoting sign (Valsiner, 2007). DFA assumes the high frequency of occurrence (i.e., the number of tokens) of a node and its strong associability with the other nodes as the markers of the super-ordered regulative function. Accordingly, the index is calculated as the percentage of nodes of the network having both high frequency and high associability. DFA defines a highly frequent node as a node having a frequency higher than 1.5 time the average frequency of tokens. A node is moreover defined as having high associability if it has outgoing and/or incoming connections with more than 33% of the nodes in the network. For instance, consider the discourse network depicted in Figure 12.3: it was obtained from a text with the following occurrences (token) for each kind of thematic content (type): $N_1 = 10$ (that is, the thematic content N_1 occurs 10 times in the text), $N_2 = 28$, $N_3 = 20$, $N_4 = 50$, $N_5 = 43$, $N_6 = 44$, and $N_7 = 5$. This means it is a text with 200 tokens corresponding to seven types—therefore 28.57

as token/type average ratio. Consequently, the threshold for defining a node as highly frequent in this discourse network is 42.85 (i.e., 1.5 * 28.57). As regards associability, node N_4 is the one with associability above the threshold (i.e., linkage with more than 33% of the nodes of the network—since there are seven nodes, the threshold is 2.31). Therefore, N_4 is the only node that has both high frequency and high associability—thus fulfilling the criteria for being defined a Super-Ordered Node.

It is worth noting that DFA also provides a qualitative level of analysis of the discourse network, grounded on the clinical interpretation of the meaning of the nodes. To this end, a group of trained judges analyses the content of the semantic nodes in order to interpret them. However, this level of analysis is not discussed here, where the focus is only on the formal-quantitative level of analysis.

DFA interpretative indexes (*Activity and Super-Ordered Nodes*) are expected to detect important clinical features of the therapeutic process under analysis. However, DFA hypothesizes a nonlinear relationship between each of these indexes and between them and the clinical quality of the process. Therefore it is not expected that, for instance, an increase in Super-Ordered Nodes will always bring an improvement in the clinical quality of the psychotherapy process. This tenet is a consequence of the field contingency of sensemaking—accordingly, what is relevant is not the trend of the indexes taken singly, but the synchronic and diachronic patterns of their combination, characterizing the organization of the discourse network as a whole.

Findings

Salvatore and colleagues (2010) applied the DFA to the Lisa's case (15-session psychotherapy). First, they found that the trend of Super-Ordered Nodes fundamentally fits a U-shape, as hypothesized in accordance with TSSM assumption 1 (two-stage articulation). The proportion of sessions fitting the quadratic curve described by the Super-Ordered Nodes is significantly different by chance; moreover, the observed trend is consistent with the quadratic fitted curve within a confidence interval between 95% and 99% (cf. Figure 12.4). On the basis of these results, one can describe the patient-therapist verbal exchange as divided into two stages. The first (deconstructive) stage, where the Super-Ordered Nodes decrease (session 1–10), and the second (constructive) one, where they increase (Session 11–15). These results suggest that the system of assumptions (operationally marked by the Super-Ordered Nodes) regulating the therapeutic dialog enters first a "destabilization" process, were the existing assumptions are weakened (Session 1–10). This may be seen as creating the conditions for triggering a change process, which leads to—and at the same time is comprised of—the emergence of new assumptions (Session 11–15). Incidentally, this interpretation of the course of Lisa's psychotherapy was consistent with the results of two other empirical studies which investigated the same case using different methods (Nicolò et al., 2008; Carcione et al., 2008). Second, consistently with TSSM assumption 2, the comparison of the correlations among the DFA indexes (Heterogeneity, Activity, Super-Order Nodes) between the two stages led to identify a shift from the deconstructive stage (Session 1–10) to the constructive one (Session 11–15) in the relationships between the variables used to depict the verbal exchange. This shift detected a major change in the dynamic underlying the therapeutic discourse from the first to the second stage.

Thus, this result supports the view that psychotherapy has to be conceived in terms of interacting patterns of reciprocal modifications, rather than as an additive and cumulative collection of independent single effects. According to this view, change in psychotherapy is a matter of pattern modification (Greenberg, 1994) which is hard to grasp in terms of variation of isolated variables.

Taking these findings as a whole, and together with the other data previously discussed, one sees two different ways in which the Lisa-therapist discourse functions, each of them characterizing one stage of the psychotherapy. In the first stage the discourse dynamic works in terms of a decrease in the incidence of the super-ordered regulative meanings, which runs alongside a broad reduction of the connections among all the network's meanings. In other words, in the first stage the constraints upon regulative meaning are the result of a more *global* tendency of the communication between Lisa and her therapist to place constraints upon all the connections active in the discourse exchange. In contrast, in the second stage the increase in super-ordered regulative meanings seems to depend on the creation of connections more specifically concerning the regulative meaning itself. It could be said that whereas the first deconstructive stage works, from a linguistic perspective, in a generalized way over the whole spectrum of associations of the entire discursive exchange, the constructive stage operates in a specialized way, focusing on the regulative meanings.

CONCLUSION

In this chapter I have illustrated some instances of empirical investigation of sensemaking phenomena. Studies presented are characterized by different content, strategies and aims. They concern a plurality of phenomenological

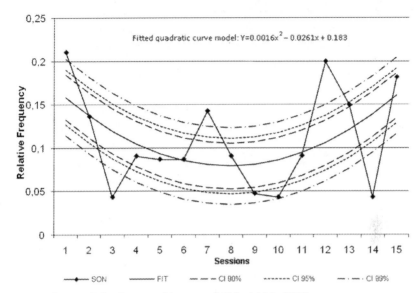

Source: Salvatore, Gelo, Gennaro, Manzo, and Al-Radaideh (2010).

Figure 2.4. Fitted Quadratic curve (FIT) of Super-Ordered Nodes (SON) over the sessions with correspondent Confidence Intervals (CI).

domains: psychotherapy process, social behavior, rating task. In some cases, a structural approach was adopted, while in others the study took the time dependency into account (dynamic analysis). Some studies were aimed at modeling basic aspects of the dynamic of sensemaking through the analysis of the contingent phenomenon, while in other cases the understanding of the phenomenon was foregrounded, with the general model used as the frame of the interpretation.

Despite such diversities, or rather, thanks to them, the studies should have shown a basic constant, reflecting the methodological philosophy they express, namely, the abductive logic underlying them. This logic is evident in a fundamental characteristic of all empirical analyses, which can be considered their marker—studies do not "extract" the knowledge from data, as if the latter were ready-to-use packets of information to be collected and assembled. Rather, data acquire meaning according to the theory and, in the final analysis, this is what the knowledge-building carried out consists of. In sum, data are not used for "fulfilling" the theory, but as open potentialities that the theory transforms into events.

A general methodological consideration can be drawn from this—the studies presented call for us to go beyond the ideological opposition between qualitative and quantitative. They are not examples of integration between the two approaches (a perspective that many scholars have been endorsing for the last few years; for example, Gelo, Braakmann, & Benetka, 2008); rather, they are instances of a methodological attitude where the very distinction between qualitative and quantitative dissolve in the view of a single process of knowledge building, putting the *qualification* (namely, the interpretation of data grounding their understanding) at the service of the *quantification* (namely, the computation of the relation between data), which in turn is at the service of the *qualification* (the interpretation of the interpretation as the path of generalization).

But that is a matter for another book...

NOTES

1. Needless to say, this is only a virtual condition, because a cultural linkage —regardless of its salience—is however present as the ground of any communication.
2. The two models' equations are as follows:

   $$\xi_{(m,1)}=B_{(m,m)}\cdot\xi_{(m,1)}+\tau_{(m,1)}$$

   $$x_{(p,1)}=\Lambda_{(p,m)}\cdot\xi_{(m,1)}+\delta_{(p,1)}$$

   where the subscripts m and p are the number of latent and manifest variables in the model, while ξ represents the LV's vector and x the vector of MVs. Path coefficients linking the LVs are indicated by the matrix B, while factor loadings linking MVs to LVs are represented by the matrix Λ. Finally, the τ and δ vectors indicate error terms of the structural and measurement model respectively.
3. Caps indicate latent constructs and italics the corresponding objects
4. The PQS is a method widely used in the field of psychotherapy process research (Ablon & Jones, 1998), aiming at depicting the global quality and characteristics of the therapist-patient relationship. It is made up of 100 items concerning three areas of investigation: (a) the patient's attitude toward and experience of the therapy; (b) the therapist's actions and attitude; (c) the nature of the interaction and the climate of the encounter between the therapist and the patient. For each session, the rater is asked to sort 100 items on 9 ordinal categories on the continuum from absolutely not so (score 1) to absolutely so (score 9).
5. To this end, for each couple of utterances, the Euclidean distance between the two points was used, each of them defining the position of one utterance on the factorial space resulting from the multidimensional lexical correspondence analysis performed by ACASM (see method section).

EPILOGUE

The reader who has had the patience to go through the pages of the book will have found an array of conjectures and proposals that are indebted to several streams of thought—semiotic cultural psychology, psychoanalysis, embodied cognition—integrated within the framework provided by the foundational assumption of psychological object as field dynamic. The intertwining of such streams, as it seems to me, is able to draw fascinating theoretical perspectives. On it I have built five general ideas. First, a semiotic, processual ontology, according to which the mind is not an entity, but a recursive dynamic—namely, an ongoing flow whose emerging instant outputs are part and parcel of the flow as well. Second, the idea that such a recursive dynamic lends itself to be modelled in terms of semiosis—namely, as an infinite movement of connections of signs through time. A sign is something that stands for something else. Thus, a semiotic dynamic is a process of combination among elements that do not have an inherent substance but acquire their value thanks to combination—that is, thanks to their capacity to refer to "something else." As I have suggested, the meaning is the sign that follows. Third, the idea that the semiotic dynamic is not in the person's skull; rather, it is distributed, it is inherently inter-subjective —namely, it is prior to, and the grounds of, the very distinction between subject and object, inner and outer. To paraphrase the Bible: *in the beginning was the sensemaking*. The subject, and with it the object as its own inherent limit, emerge from sensemaking as its fundamental product in the ongoing recursive autopoietic circle through which semiosis builds the condition of its own reproduction. Fourth, signs are states of the body. Having the format of image, letter, digital symbol, and the like, in the

Psychology in Black and White: The Project of a Theory-Driven Science, pp. 295–298

final analysis a sign is a modification of the body that stands for a further modification of the body. No sign has content—it acquires meaning by means of the infinite game of referring to something else, thanks to which the body is constituted as mind. Finally, such a process of emergence of the mind from sensemaking is possible because of the inherent affective nature of the latter. According to my proposal, affective activation is not one possible consequence of sensemaking, or a valence that qualifies some forms of meanings. Rather, it is the basic component of its dynamic, that which makes it a hyperdimensional field whose reduction of dimensionality lets meaning emerge.

Taken as a whole, these ideas envisage a peculiar way of looking at psychology. This attitude does not consist only and mainly of a set of different answers to questions at the core of the current scientific debate; rather, it is the proposal of a new agenda of theoretical and methodological aims emerging from a profound change in the very definition of the object and the mission for the science of the psyche. Through the volume I have tried to highlight some of these basic challenging issues. Three, in particular. First, the constitution of experience, namely the emergence of the symbolic order intended as the capacity for living a certain body modification as experience-of-the-reality, i.e. as a representation endowed with value of life. Second, the overcoming of the dichotomies that are the grounds of the reifying semantics of common sense: subject *vs.* object; inner *vs.* outer; micro *vs.* macro; singular *vs.* universal. Here the point is not to find a new solution to these conceptual problems, but to deconstruct them, namely to recognize how these dichotomies are not primitive, but instances of the commonsensical semantics that demand to be analyzed, rather than taken as self-evident. Third, the development of an old-fashioned new logic of knowledge building, aimed at modeling phenomena for the sake both of understanding them in their contingency and of developing general laws concerning the universal dynamic of the psychological object. In the final analysis, these issues outline a project of psychology that intends to go *beyond* experience, for the sake of understanding it more deeply, in its way of constituting the subjective life.

People live their lives thanks to and through the basic, generalized assumption of having their own mind comprising a network of feeling and thoughts, and of taking a position in the world due to this. Everyone believes that when they make a decision, or perform a certain act, or produce a certain judgment, they do so because of a certain motivation or feeling and/or on the basis of a certain idea, and/or for the sake of a certain purpose. Thus, the experience of being in the world—what is perceived, felt, imagined, thought, projected, desired, enacted—is constitutive of the subject: it is what makes the individual feel her/himself a human being, a person endowed with a mind. Psychology seems to share the same taken-for-granted assumption. It has taken the mind and its phenomenological contents (perceptions, feelings, thoughts) as a self-evident starting point, namely the primitive bricks to be studied in their way of interacting in associative and/or causative linkages, in order to understand how they shape subjective life and channel behavior. The phenomenological subject has become the measure of everything; and in so doing the science that was that of James, Freud, Wertheimer, Baldwin, Piaget, Vygotsky, Werner has been transformed into the empire of empiria. In so doing, contemporary psychology seems to have forgotten several streams of thought (psychoanalysis, Gestalt theory, behaviorism, Kantianism, phenomenology) which, in different ways, have highlighted the unsuitability of the foundational vision of subjectivity. What such streams of thought teach is that the phenomenical experience does not lend itself to work as the primitive grounds for understanding human life; rather, subjectivity is what has to be understood. This insight represents the idea of Psychology as the science of the *explanandum* that I have presented throughout the pages of the book. According to this view, phenomena of subjectivity (e.g. emotions, motivations, thoughts, and so forth) acquire the status of object of psychology insofar as they are modeled in terms of theoretical categories (e.g., sign, semiotic hyperspace, bootstrapping mechanism, SIP/SIA, scenario and so forth).

What has been said above should have made it clear in what sense and why the project of a psychology that shifts experience from the *explanans* to the *explanandum* cannot but be a theory-driven science, namely a science that defines its own language independently of the language of experience. *In what sense*: a theory-driven science is a science that uses its own categories, grounded in the theoretical framework, as the way in which phenomena (i.e., subjectivity as it is phenomenologically manifested in lived experience) can be modelled. In the final analysis, this is the same as calling for a psychology that strives to go beyond the pillars of Hercules of the self-evident meanings of things, in so doing following the route of sciences like physics and chemistry that have empowered their capacity to understand their target phenomena when their languages are separated from the commonsensical languages of the phenomena. *Why:* Insofar as one considers the understanding of the semantics of experience as the core task of psychology, the need for an autonomous language is evident: common sense cannot be studied by means of itself (i.e., by means of categories embedded in the semantics of daily life experience), because in so doing the difference between the enactment of common sense and its understanding would not be possible. In sum, the project of a theory-driven psychology is the perspective of a psychology that builds from within itself its own categories, in so doing freeing itself from common sense, in order to understand the latter as a psychological dynamic, namely as the semiotic dynamic through which the body constitutes itself as mind.

   Life is in color, but black and white is more realistic.

REFERENCES

Abbey, E., & Valsiner, J. (2005). Emergence of meanings through ambivalence. *Forum Qualitative Sozialforschung/Forum: Qualitative Social Research*, *6*(1), 58.

Ablon, J., & Jones, E. (1998). How expert clinicians' prototypes of an ideal treatment correlate with outcome in psychodynamic and cognitive-behavioral therapy. *Psychotherapy Research*, *8*(1), 71–83.

Acemoglu, D. (2009). *Introduction to modern economic growth*. Princeton, NJ: Princeton University Press.

Albertazzi, L., Jacquette, D., & Poli, R. (2001). Meinong in his and our times. In L. Albertazzi, D. Jacquette, & R. Poli (Eds.), *The school of Alexius Meinong* (pp. 3–48). Aldershot, England: Ashgate.

Allen, M., & Williams, G. (2011). Consciousness, plasticity, and connectomics: The role of intersubjectivity in human cognition. *Frontiers in Psychology*, *2* (Article 20), 1–20. doi:10. 3389/fpsyg.2011.00020

Ancona, L. (2002). Pragmatica clinica del gruppo mediano e grande [Clinical pragmatics of median and large group]. In F. Di Maria, & G. LoVerso (Eds.), *Gruppi. Metodi e strumenti* (pp. 235–251). Milano: Raffaello Cortina.

Andersen, P. B., Emmeche, C., Finnemann, N. O., & Christiansen, P. V. (Eds.). (2000). *Downward causation*. Aarhus, DK: Aarhus University Press.

Andersen, S. (2001). the emergence of meaning: generating symbols from random sounds: A factor analytic model. *Journal of Quantitative Linguistics*, *8*(2), 101–136.

Angus, L. E., & McLeod, J. (Eds.). (2004). *The handbook of narrative and psychotherapy: Practice, theory and research*. London, England: Sage.

Angus, L. E., Goldman, R., & Mergenthaler, E. (Eds.). (2008). The case of Lisa. *Psychotherapy Research* [Special Section], *19*(6), 629–682.

Auletta, A., Salvatore, S., Metrangolo, R., Monteforte, G., Pace, V., & Puglisi, M. (2012). The study of therapist's interpretive activity: The grid of the models of interpretations (GMI). A trans-theoretical method. *Journal of Psychotherapy Integration*, *22*(2), 61–84.

Austin, J. (1962). *How to do things with words*. Oxford, England: Oxford University Press.

Bakeman, R., & Gottman, J. M. (1997). *Observing interaction: An introduction to sequential analysis* (2nd ed.). Cambridge, England: Cambribge University Press.

Barkham, M., Stiles, W. B., & Shapiro, D. A. (1993). The shape of change in psychotherapy: Longitudinal assessment of personal problems. *Journal of Consulting and Clinical Psychology, 61,* 667–677.

Barrett, F. L. (2006). Solving the emotion paradox: Categorization and the experience of emotion. *Personality and Social Psychology Review, 10,* 20–46.

Barrow, J. (2011). *The book of universes: Exploring the limits of the cosmos.* New York, NY: W. W. Norton.

Bartlett, F. C. (1932). *Remembering: A study in experimental and social psychology.* Cambridge, England: Cambridge University Press.

Bateson, G. (1972). *Steps to an ecology of mind: Collected essays in anthropology, psychiatry, evolution, and epistemology.* Chicago, IL: University of Chicago Press.

Bauer, M. W., & Gaskell, G. (1999). Towards a paradigm for research on social representations. *Journal for the Theory of Social Behaviour, 29*(2), 163–186.

Benzecri, J.-P. (1980). *L'analyse des données tome 2: L'analyse des correspondances* [Data anaysis. Volume 2. Analysis of correspondence]. Paris, France: Bordas.

Bickhard, M. H. (2009). Interactivism: A manifesto. *New Ideas in Psychology, 27,* 85–89.

Billig, M. (1999). *Freudian repression: Conversation creating the unconscious.* Cambridge, MA: Harvard University Press.

Billig, M. (2003). Studying repression in a changing world. *European Journal of School Psychology, 1*(1), 37–42.

Bion, W. R. (1961a). *Experience in groups and other papers.* London, England: Tavistock.

Bion, W. R. (1962b). *Learning from experience.* London, England: William Heinemann.

Bion, W. R. (1967). Notes on memory and desire: *The Psychoanalytic Forum, 2,* 272–273 and 279–290.

Bion, W. R. (1967). *Second thoughts.* London, England: Maresfield Library.

Borckardt, J. J., Mash, M., Murphy, M. D., Moore, M., Shaw, D., & O'Neil, P. (2008). Clinical practice as natural laboratory for psychotherapy research. A guide to case based time analysis. *American Psychologist, 63,* 77–95.

Bowlby, J. (1961). Process of mourning. *International Journal of Psycho-Analysis, 42,* 317–340.

Bowlby, J. (1969). *Attachment and loss: Attachment* (Vol. I). London, England: Hogarth.

Brakel, L. A, Shevrin, H., & Villa, K. K. (2002). The priority of primary process categorizing: experimental evidence supporting a psychoanalytic developmental hypothesis. *Journal of American Psychoanalytic Association, 50*(2), 483–505.

Brenner, C. (1973). *An elementary textbook of psychoanalysis.* New York, NY: International Universities Press.

Brenner, C. (2002). Conflict, compromise formation, and structural theory. *The Psychoanalytic Quarterly, 71*(3), 397–417.

Breuer, J., & Freud, S. (1955). On the psychical mechanism of hysterical phenomena: Preliminary communication. In J. Strachey (Ed. and Trans.), *The standard edition of the complete psychological works of Sigmund Freud* (Vol. 2, pp. 1–18).

London, England: The Hogarth Press and the Institute of Psycho-analysis. (Original work published 1893)

Bruner, J. (1990). *Acts of meaning*. Cambridge MA: Harvard University Press.

Bucci, W. (1997). *Psychoanalysis and cognitive science*. New York, NY: Guildford Press.

Bühler, K. (1990). *Theory of language: The representational function of language*. Amsterdam/Philadelphia, PA: John Benjamins Publishing. (Original work published 1934)

Busch, F. (1993). "In the Neighborhood": Aspects of a good interpretation and a "developmental lag" in ego psychology. *The Journal of the American Psychoanalytic Association, 41*, 151–177.

Cabell, K. R. (2010) Mediators, regulators, and catalyzers: A context–inclusive model of trajectory development. *Psychology, & Society, 3*. Retrieved January 3, 2012, from http://www. psychologyandsociety.ppsis.cam.ac.uk

Cabell, K. R. (2011) Catalysis: Cultural constructions and the conditions for change. *Journal of Integrated Social Sciences, 2*(1), 1–12 .

Cabell K., & Valsiner, J. (2011). Self–making through syntesis: extending dialogical self theory. In H. Hermans, & T. Gieser (Eds.), *Handbook of dialogical self* (pp. 82–97). Cambridge, England: Cambridge University Press.

Carcione, A., Dimaggio, G., Fiore, D., Nicolò, G., Procacci, M., Semerari, A., & Pedone, R. (2008). An intensive case analysis of client metacognition in a good-outcome psychotherapy: Lisa's case. *Psychotherapy Research, 18*, 667–676.

Carli, R. (1987). L'analisi della domanda [The analysis of demand]. *Rivista di Psicologia Clinica, 1*(1), 38–53.

Carli, R. (1996). Psicoanalisi, mandato sociale e formazione [Psychoanalysis, social demand and professional training]. *Psicologia Clinica, 2*(1), 5–24.

Carli, R. (2002). Appunti di viaggio di uno psicologo scolastico [Travel notes of a school psychologist]. *Psicologia Scolastica, 2*(1), 5–21.

Carli, R. (2007). Pulcinello or "on ambiguity". *Rivista di psicologia clinica/Journal of Clinical Psychology* [Online Journal], *3*. Retrieved September 20, 2009, from http://www.rivistadipsicologiaclinica.it/english/number3_07/Carli.htm

Carli, R., & Giovagnoli, F. (2011). A cultural approach to clinical psychology. Psychoanalysis and analysis of the demand. In S. Salvatore, & T. Zittoun (Eds.), *Cultural psychology and psychoanalysis: Pathways to synthesis* (pp. 117–150). Charlotte, NC: Information Age Publishing.

Carli, R., & Paniccia, R. M. (1999). *Psicologia della formazione* [Psychology of the training]. Bologna, IT: Il Mulino.

Carli, R., & Paniccia, R. M. (2002). *L'Analisi emozionale del testo: Uno strumento psicologico per leggere testi e discorsi* [The emotional textual analysis: A psychological tool for reading texts and discourses]. Milano, IT: Franco Angeli.

Carli., R., & Paniccia, R. M. (2003). *Analisi della domanda: Teoria e tecnica dell'intervento in psicologia clinica* [Analysis of demand: Theory and technique of the intervention in clinical psychology]. Bologna, IT: Il Mulino.

Carli, R., & Salvatore, S. (2001), *L'immagine dello psicologo* [The image of the psychologist]. Rome, Italy: Kappa Editore.

Carvalho, R., Ginzburg, A., Lombardi, R., & Sanchez-Cardenas, M. (2009). *Matte Blanco: une autre pensée psychanalytique. L'inconscient (a)logique* [Matte Blanco: A different psychoanalytic thought. The (un)logic unconscious]. Paris: L'Harmattan.

Chartier, J.-F., & Meunier, J. G. (2011). Text mining methods for social representation analysis. *Papers on Social Representations, 20,* 37.1–37.46.

Christopher, J. C., & Bickhard, M. (2007). Culture, self and identity: Interactivist contributions to a metatheory for cultural psychology. *Culture & Psychology, 13*(3), 259–295.

Chryssides, A., Dashtipour, P., Keshet, S., Righi, C., Sammut, G., & Sartawi, M. (2009). We don't share! The social representation approach: Enactivism and the fundamental incompatibilities between the two. *Culture & Psychology, 15,* 83–95.

Ciavolino, E., Salvatore, S., & Calcagnì, A. (2013). A fuzzy set theory based computational model to represent the quality of inter-rater agreemen. *Quality and Quantity, 48,* 2225–2240. doi:10.1007/s11135-013-9888-3.

Codol, J.-P. (1969). Note terminologique sur l'emploi de quelques expressions concernant les activités et processus cognitifs en psychologie sociale [Terminological note on the usage of some terms concerning the cognitive processes and activities in social psychology]. *Bulletin de psychologie, 2*(1–3), 280, 63–71.

Cole, M. (1996). *Cultural psychology: A once and future discipline.* Cambridge, MA: Harvard University Press.

Corballis, M. C. (2011). *The recursive mind: The origins of human language, thought, and civilization.* Princeton, NJ: Princeton University Press.

Cousins, S. D. (2012). A semiotic approach to mind and culture. *Culture & Psychology, 18*(2), 149–166.

Croom, A. M. (2012). Aesthetic concepts, perceptual learning, and linguistic enculturation: Considerations from Wittgenstein, language, and music. *Integrative Psychological and Behavioral Science, 6*(1), 90–117. doi:10.1007/s12124-011-9184-5.

Damasio, A. R. (1999). *The feeling of what happens: Body and emotion in the making of consciousness.* Orlando, FL: Harcourt.

De Leo, D. (2009). Intersubjectivity as co–phenomenology: From the holism of meaning to the being-in-the-world-with-others. *Integrative Psychological and Behavioral Science, 43*(1), 78–83.

Doise, W. (1986). *Levels of explanation in social psychology.* Cambridge: Cambridge University Press.

Doise, W. (1990). Les représentations sociales [Social representations]. In R. Ghiglione, C. Bonnet, & J. F. Richard (Eds.), *Traité de Psychologie cognitive.* Paris, France: Dunod.

Dostoevsky, F. (1945). The gambler. In C. Garnett (Trans. and Ed.) *The short novels of Dostoevsky.* New York, NY: Dial. (Original work published 1866)

Dryjanska, L. (2011). Social representations of Smolensk April 10, 2010, in Poland and in Italy. *Papers on Social Representations, 20*(2), 41.1–41.35.

Eco, U. (1975). *A theory of semiotic.* Bloomington, IN: Indiana University Press.

Eco, U. (2009). On the ontology of finctional charachters: A semiotic approach. *Sign Systes Studies, 37*(1/2), 82–98.

Eagle, M. N. (1987). The psychoanalytic and the cognitive unconscious. In R. Stern (Ed.), *Theories of the unconscious and theories of the self* (pp. 155–189). Hillsdale, NJ: The Analytic Press.

Ekman, P., & Rosenberg, E. L. (2005). *What the face reveals: Basic and applied studies of spontaneous expression using the Facial Action Coding System (FACS)* (2nd ed.). New York, NY: Oxford University Press.

Ellenberger, H. F. (1970), *The discovery of the unconscious. The history and evolution of dynamic psychiatry.* New York, NY: Basic Books.

Epstein, S. (1998). Cognitive-experiential self–theory: A dual-process personality theory with implication for diagnosis and psychotherapy. In R. F. Bornstein, & J. M. Masling (Eds.), *Empirical perspectives on the pschoanalytic unconscious* (pp. 99–140). Washington, DC: American Psychological Associaton.

Erdelyi, M. H. (1985). *Psychoanalysis: Freud's cognitive psychology.* New York, NY: Freeman and Company.

Esposito Vinzi, V., Chin, W. W., Henseler, J., & Wang, H. (2010). *Handbook of partial least squares: Concepts, methods and applications.* New York, NY: Springer Handbooks of Computational Statistics.

Eysenck, H. J. (1952). The effects of psychotherapy: An evaluation. *Journal of Consulting Psychology, 16*(5), 319–324.

Faccio, E., Centomo, C., & Mininni, G. (2011). "Measuring up to measure". Dysmorphophobia as a language game. *Integrative Psychological and Behavioral Science, 43*(3), 350–354.

Fini V., Guidi M., & Salvatore, S. (2012). La visione della pianificazione quale dinamica di significazione [The social planning as sensemaking]. In D. De Leo, & V. Fini (Eds.), *Attualità dello sviluppo. Riflessioni in pratica per costruire progetti locali di qualità* (pp. 158–171). Milano, IT: Franco Angeli.

Fodor, J. A. (1983). *The modulary of mind: An essay on faculty psychology.* Cambridge, MA The MIT Press.

Forges Davanzati, G., & Salvatore, S. (2012) Institutions and job flexibility: A psychological approach. *Dialettica e filosofia* [On to Group Analytic Psychotherapy Line Journal], *4*(1). Retrieved April 20, 2013, from http://www.dialetticaefilosofia.it/scheda-filosofia-saggi. asp?id=46

Fornari, F. (1979). *I fondamenti di una teoria psicoanalitica del linguaggio* [Foundations for a psychoanalytic theory of the language]. Torino, IT: Boringhieri.

Fornari, F. (1981). *Il codice vivente* [The living code]. Torino, IT: Bollati Boringhieri.

Fornari, F. (1983). *La lezione Freudiana* [Freud's lesson]. Milano: Feltrinelli.

Foulkes, S. H. (1983). *Introduction: Studies in the social integration of individuals and groups.* London: Karnac (Original work published in 1948 by William Heineman Medical Books Ltd, London)

Freda, M. F. (2008). *Narrazione e intervento in psicologia clinica* [Narration and intervention in clinic psychology]. Napoli, IT: Liguori.

Freda, M. F., & Pagliaro, F. M. (2014). Narration and discourse in the clinical dialogue. In S. Salvatore, A. Gennaro, & J. Valsiner (Eds.), *Making sense of infinite uniqueness: The emerging system of idiographic science* (*Yearbook of Idiographic Science, Vol, 4,* pp. 175–203). Charlotte, NC: Information Age Publishing.

Frege, G. (1980). On sense and reference (3rd ed.). (M. Black, Trans.). In P. Geach, & M. Black (Eds. and Trans.), *Translations from the philosophical writings of*

Gottlob Frege (pp. 56–78). Oxford, England: Blackwell. (Original work published 1892)

Freud, S. (1950). Project for a scientific psychology. In J. Strachey (Ed. and Trans.), *The standard edition of the complete psychological works of Sigmund Freud* (Vol. 1, pp. 281–391). London, England: The Hogarth Press and the Institute of Psycho-analysis. (Original work published 1895)

Freud, S. (1953). the interpretation of dreams. In J. Strachey (Ed. and Trans.), *The standard edition of the complete psychological works of Sigmund Freud* (Vol. 4–5). London, England: The Hogarth Press and the Institute of Psycho-analysis. (Original work published 1900)

Freud, S. (1953). Psycho-analytic procedure. In J. Strachey (Ed. and Trans.), *The standard edition of the complete psychological works of Sigmund Freud* (Vol. 7, pp. 247–254). London, England: The Hogarth Press and the Institute of Psychoanalysis. (Original work published 1904 [1903])

Freud, S. (1957). Instincts and their vicissitudes. In J. Strachey (Ed. and Trans.), *The standard edition of the complete psychological works of Sigmund Freud* (Vol. 14, pp. 109–140). London: The Hogarth Press and the Institute of Psychoanalysis. (Original work published 1915)

Freud, S. (1959). Inhibitions, symptoms and anxiety. In J. Strachey (Ed. and Trans.), *The standard edition of the complete psychological works of Sigmund Freud* (Vol. 20, pp. 75–176). London, England: The Hogarth Press and the Institute of Psychoanalysis. (Original work published 1926)

Freud, S. (1926). The question of lay analysis. In J. Strachey (Ed. and Trans.), *The standard edition of the complete psychological works of Sigmund Freud* (Vol. 20, pp. 177–258). London, England: The Hogarth Press and the Institute of Psycho-Analysis. (Original work published 1926[1925])

Freud, S. (1964). New introductory lectures on psycho-analysis. In J. Strachey (Ed. and Trans.), *The standard edition of the complete psychological works of Sigmund Freud* (Vol. 22, pp. 1–182). London, England: The Hogarth Press and the Institute of Psychoanalysis. (Original work published 1933[1932])

Friedman, R. C., & Downey, J. I. (1998). Psychoanalysis and the model of homosexuality as psychopathology: a historical overview. *The American Journal of Psychoanalysis, 58*(3), 249–270.

Fronterotta, F., & Salvatore, S. (in press). Processual monism. A fresh look at the mind-body problem.

Gastaldi, F. G. M., Longobardi, C., Pasta, T., & Sclavo, E. (2010). The reflexive training setting and the trajectory equifinality model: Investigating psychic function in a socio–cultural light. In S. Salvatore, J. Valsiner, J. B. Traves Simon, & A. Gennaro (Eds.), *Yearbook of Idiographic Science* (Vol. 3, pp. 117–128). Rome, Italy: Firera Publishing Group.

Gelo, O., Braakmann, D., & Benetka, G. (2008). Quantitative and qualitative tesearch: Beyond the debate. *Integrative Psychological and Behavioural Science, 42*(3), 266–290.

Gennaro, A. (2011). The building of models as pathway to understand the therapeutic process. *Integrative Psychological and Behavioral Science, 43*(3), 355–365.

Gennaro, A., Al–Radaideh, A., Gelo, O., Manzo, S., Nitti, M., & Salvatore, S. (2010). Modelling psychotherapy process as sense-making dynamic: The two stage semiotic model (TSSM) and the discourse flow analyzer (DFA). In S. Salvatore, J. Valsiner, A. Gennaro, & J. B. Traves Simon (Eds.), *Yearbook of Idiographic Science* (Vol. 2, pp. 131–170). Rome, Italy: Firera Publishing Group.

Gergen, K. J. (1991). *The saturated self: Dilemmas of identity in contemporary life*. New York, NY: Basic Books.

Gergen, K. J. (1999). *An invitation to social construction*. London, England: Sage.

Giannakoulas, A. (1984). I Fondamenti di una Teoria Psicoanalitica del linguaggio. Turin: Boringhieri. 1980, pp. 392 [review]. *International Journal of Psycho-Analysis, 65*, 218–221.

Gibson (1979). *The ecological approach to visual perception*. Boston, MA: Houghton Mifflin.

Gigerenzer, G. (2008). Why heuristics work. *Perspective in Psychological Science, 3*(1), 20–29.

Gigerenzer, G., & Todd, P. (Eds.). (1999). *Simple heuristic that make us smart*. Oxford, England: Oxford University Press.

Gill, M. (1994). *Psychoanalysis in transition*. Hillsdale, NJ: The Analytic Press.

Gillespie, A. (2010). The intersubjective nature of symbols. In B. Wagoner (Ed), *Symbolic transformation:. The mind in movement through culture and society* (pp. 23–37). London, England: Routledge.

Goolishian, H. A., & Anderson, H. (1987). Language systems and therapy: An evolving idea. *Psychotherapy: Theory, Research, Practice, Training, 24*, 529–538.

Grasso, M., & Stampa, P. (2011). Psychological normality, psychopathology and evidence-based psychotherapy: are we so sure "we're not in Kansas anymore"? In S. Salvatore, & T. Zittoun (Eds.), *Cultural psychology and psychoanalysis: Pathways to synthesis* (pp. 225–278). Charlotte NC: Information Age Publishing.

Green, A. (1973). *Le discours vivant: La conception psychanalytique de l'affect* [Living discourse: The psychoanalytic conception of affects]. Paris, France: Presses Universitaires de France.

Green, A. (2005). *Key ideas for a contemporary psychoanalysis: Misrecognition and recognition of the unconscious* (Andrew Weller, Trans.). London, England: Routledge. (Original work published 2002)

Greenberg, J. R., & Mitchell, S. A. (1983). *Object relations in psychoanalytic theory*. Cambridge, MA: Harvard University Press.

Greenberg, L. S. (1994). The investigation of change: Its measurement and explanation. In R. L. Russell (Ed.), *Reassessing psychotherapy research* (pp. 114–143). New York, NY: Guilford Press.

Greenberg, L. S., & Pinsof, W. M. (Eds.). (1986). *The psychotherapeutic process: A research handbook*. New York, NY: The Guilford Press.

Grossen, M. (2009). Interaction analysis and psychology: A dialogical perspective. *Integrative Psychological and Behavioral Science, 44*(1), 1–22.

Guidi, M., & Salvatore, S. (2014). Parents' images of their children's school system. In A. Iannaccone, K. Komatsu, & P. Marsico (Eds), *Crossing boundaries: Intercontextual dynamics between family and school* (pp. 271–300) Charlotte, NC: Information Age Publishing.

Harré, R., & Gillett, G. (1994). *The discursive mind*. London, England: Sage.

Hartmann, A., van der Kooij, A. J., & Zeeck, A. (2009). Exploring nonlinear relations: models of clinical decision making by regression with optimal scaling. *Psychotherapy Research, 19,* 482–492.

Hartmann, D. (2014). *Economic complexity and human development: How economic diversification and social networks affect human agency and welfare.* New York, NY: Routledge.

Hayes, A. M., Laurenceau, J. P., Feldman, G., Strauss, J. L., & Cardaciotto, L. A. (2007). Change is not always linear: The study of nonlinear and discontinuous patterns of change in psychotherapy. *Clinical Psychological Review, 27,* 715–723.

Hermans, H. J. M., & Dimaggio, G. (Eds.). (2004). *The dialogical self in psychotherapy.* New York, NY: Brunner-Routledge.

Hermans, H. J. M., & Hermans-Konopka, A. (2010). *Dialogical self theory: Positioning and counter-positioning in a globalizing society.* Cambridge, England: Cambridge University Press.

Herzberg, F., Mausner, B., & Snyderman, B. B. (1959). *the motivation to work* (2nd ed.). New York, NY: John Wiley & Sons.

Hill, C. E., & Lambert, M. J. (2004). methodological issues in studying psychotherapy process and outcome. In J. M., Lambert (Ed.), *Bergin and Garfield's handbook of psychotherapy and behavior change* (5th ed., pp. 84–135). New York, NY: Wiley and Sons.

Hoffman, I. Z. (1998). *Ritual and spontaneity in the psychoanalytic process.* Hillsdale, NJ: The Analytic Press.

Holzer, M., Mergenthaler, E., Pokorny, D., Kachele, H., & Luborsky, L. (1996). Vocabulary measures for the evaluation of therapy outcome: Re-studying transcripts from the Penn Psychotherapy Project. *Psychotherapy Research, 6,* 95–108.

House, R. (2003) *Therapy beyond modernity: Deconstructing and transcending profession–centred therapy.* London, England: Karnac.

Jakobson, R. (1956). Two aspects of language and two types of aphasic disturbances. In R. Jakobson, & M. Halle (Eds). *Fundamentals of language* (Revised edition 1971, pp. 67–96). The Hague, NL: Mouton.

Johnson–Laird, P. N. (1983). *Mental models: Towards a cognitive science of language, inference, and consciousness.* Cambridge, MA: Harvard University Press.

Kahneman, D. (2003). A perspective on judgment and choice: Mapping bounded rationality. *American Psychologist, 58,* 697–720.

Kanizsa, G (1955) Margini quasi-percettivi in campi con stimolazione omogenea [quasi–perceptual contours in homogeneously stimulated field]. *Rivista di Psicologia, 49*(1), 7–30.

Kharlamov, N. A. (2010). Theory strikes back: Performativity and the messy empirical in human sciences. In S. Salvatore, J. Valsiner, J. T. Simon, & A. Gennaro (Eds.), *Yearbook of Idiographic Science* (Vol. 3, pp. 49–63). Rome, Italy: Firera & Liuzzo.

Kernberg, O. F. (1990). New perspectives in psychoanalytic affect theory. In R. Plutchik, & H. Kellerman (Eds.), *Emotion: Theory, research, and experience* (pp. 115–131). New York, NY: Academic Press.

Kim, J. (2000). Making sense of downward causality. In P. B. Andersen, C. Emmeche, N. O. Finnemann, & P. V. Christiansen (Eds.), *Downward causation* (pp. 305–321). Aarhus, DK: Aarhus University Press.

Kintsch, W. (1988). The use of knowledge in discourse processing: A construction–integration model. *Psychological Review, 95,* 163–182.

Kirshner, L., A. (2010). Between Winnicott and Lacan: Reclaiming the subject of psychoanalysis. *American Imago, 67,* 331–351.

Klein, G. S. (1976), *Psychoanalytic theory: An exploration of essentials* (M. M. Gill, & L. Goldberger, Eds.) New York, NY: International Universities Press.

Klein, M. (1967). *Contribution to psychoanalysis, 1921–1945.* New York, NY: Mac Graw-Hill.

Klein, M., Heimann, P., & Money-Kyrle, R. (Eds.). (1955). *New direction in psychoanalysis.* London, England: Tavistock.

Klein, N. (1999), *No logo: Taking aim at the brand bullies,* New York, NY: Picador.

Lacan, J. (1978). *The four fundamental concepts of psychoanalysis.* New York, NY: Norton & Company.

Lahlou, S. (1996). The propagation of social representations. *Journal for the Theory of Social Behaviour, 26*(2), 157–175.

Lahlou, S., & Abric, J. C. (2011). What are the "elements" of a representation? *Papers on Social Representations, 20,* 20.1–20.10.

Lakoff, G., & Johnson, M. (1980). *Metaphors we live by.* Chicago, IL: The University of Chicago Press.

Lambert, M. J. (Ed) (2004). *Bergin and Garfield's handbook of psychotherapy and behavior change* (5th ed.). New York, NY: Wiley and Sons.

Lamiell, J. T. (1998). "Nomothetic" and "idiographic": Contrasting Windelband's understanding with contemporary usage. *Theory & Psychology, 8*(1), 23–38.

Lamiell, J. T. (2003). *Beyond individual and group differences.* Thousand Oaks, CA: Sage.

Lancia, F. (2002). *The logic of a textscope.* Retrieved August 18, 2007, from http://www.tlab. it/en/bibliography.php

Lancia, F. (2005) *Word co-occurrence and theory of meaning.* Retrieved August 18, 2007, from http://www. mytlab. com/wctheory.pdf.

Lancia, F. (2007). *Word co-occurrence and similarity in meaning.* Retrieved September 22, 2010, from http://www. tlab. it/en/ bibliography.php

Lancia, F. (2012). *The logic of T–LAB Tools explained.* Retrieved from September 12, 2013, from http://www.tlab.it/en/toolsexplained.php

Landauer, T. K., & Dumais, S. (1997). A solution to Plato's problem: The latent semantic analysis theory of acquisition, induction and representation of knowledge. *Psychological Review, 104,* 211–240.

Langs, R. (1974). *The technique of psychoanalytic psychotherapy.* New York, NY: Jason Aronson.

Laurenceau, J. P., Hayes, A. M., & Feldman, G. C. (2007) Statistical and methodological issues in the study of change in psychotherapy. *Clinical Psychology Review, 27,* 715–723.

Lauro–Grotto R. P., Salvatore, S., Gennaro A., & Gelo O. (2009). The unbearable dynamicity of psychological processes: Highlights of the psychodynamic theories. In J. Valsiner, P. C. M. Molenaar, M. C. D. P. Lyra, & N. Chaudhary (Eds.), *Dynamic process methodology in the social and developmental sciences* (pp. 1–30). New York, NY: Springer.

Lazarus R. S. (1991). Cognition and motivation in emotion. *American Psychologist, 46*(4) 352–267.

LeDoux, J. E. (1996). *The emotional brain.* New York, NY: Simon, & Schuster.

Leiman, M. (2000). Ogden's matrix of transference and the concept of sign. *British Journal of Medical Psychology, 73,* 385–397.

Lepper, G. (2012). Taking a pragmatic approach to dialogical science. *International Journal of Dialogical Science, 6*(1), 149–159.

Libet, B. (1999). Do we have free will? *Journal of Consciousness Studies, 6*(8–9), 47–57.

Lichtenberg, J. D. (1989). *Psychoanalysis and motivation.* Hillsdale, NJ: Analytic Press.

Linell, P. (2009). *Rethinking language, mind and world dialogically: Interactional and contextual theories of sense-making.* Charlotte, NC: Information Age Publishing.

Luborsky, L., Singer, B., & Luborsky, L. (1975). Comparative studies of psychotherapies. Is it true that "Everyone has won and all must have a prize?" *Archives of General Psychiatry, 32,* 995–1008.

Luhmann, N., & De Giorgi, R. (1992). *Teoria della società* [Theory of society]. Milano: Franco Angeli.

Mahoney, M. J. (1991). *Human change processes. The scientific foundations of psychotherapy.* New York, NY: Basic Books.

Mannarini, T. M., Nitti, M., Ciavolino, E., & Salvatore, S. (2012). The role of affects in culture-based interventions: Implications for practice. *Psychology, 3,* 569–577 doi:10.4236/psych.2012.38085.

Manzotti, R. (2006). A Process oriented view of conscious perception. *Journal of Consciousness Studies, 13,* 7–41.

Manzotti, R. (2009) No time, no wholes: A temporal and causal-oriented approach to the ontology of wholes. *Axiomathes, 19,* 193–214.

Manzotti, R. (2010). There are no Images (to be seen) or the fallacy of the intermediate entity. *APA Newsletter on Philosophy and Computers, 9,* 59–66.

Manzotti, R. (2011). The spread mind: Is consciousness situated? *Theorema, 30*(2), 55–78.

Marr, D. (1982). *Vision: A computational investigation into the human representation and processing of visual information.* New York, NY: Freeman.

Martirani, G. (1985). *La geografia come educazione allo sviluppo e alla pace* [Geography as education for development and peace]. Neaples, IT: Edizioni Dehoniane.

Martsin, M. (2014). Self-regulation by signs: A social semiotic approach to identity. In S. Salvatore, A. Gennaro, & J. Valsiner (Eds.), *Multicentric identities in a globalizing world (Yearbook of Idiographic Science, Vol. 5,* pp. ix–xx). Charlotte, NC: Information Age Publishing.

Maruyiama, M. (1999). Heterogram analysis: Where the assumption of normal distribution is illogical. *Human Systems Management, 18,* 53–60.

Matte-Blanco, I. (1975). *The unconscious as infinite sets: An essays in bi-logic.* London, England: Gerald Duckworth and Company.

Matte-Blanco, I. (1988). *Thinking, feeling, and being: Clinical reflections on the fundamental antinomy of human beings and world* (New Library of Psychoanalysis, 5, 1–336). London and New York: Tavistock/Routledge.

Matte Bon, F. (1999). Lingua, analisi della lingua e bi-logica [Language, analysis of language and bi-logic]. In P. Bria & F. Oneroso (Eds.), *L'inconscio antinomico. Sviluppi e prospettive dell'opera di Matte Blanco* (pp. 88–132). Milano: Franco Angeli.

Maturana, M. R., & Varela, J. F. (1980). *Autopoiesis and cognition: The realization of the living*. Dordrecht, NL: Reidel.

Matusov, E. (1996). Intersubjectivity without agreement. *Mind, Culture, and Activity, 3*(1), 25–45.

Migone, P. (2011). Vanno pagate le sedute di psicoterapia non effettuate? [Have missing sessions to be paid?]. *Il Ruolo Terapeutico, 117,* 71–82.

Mitchell, S. A. (1988). *Relational concepts in psychoanalysis: An integration*. Cambridge, MA: Harvard University Press.

Mitchell, S. A., & Aron, L. (Eds.). (1999). *Relational psychoanalysis: The emergence of a tradition*. Hillsdale, NJ: The Analytic Press.

Modell, A. H. (1984). *Psychoanalysis in a new context*. New York, NY: International Universities Press.

Molenaar, P. C. M., & Valsiner, J. (2009). How generalization works through the single case: A simple idiographic process analysis of an individual psychotherapy. In S. Salvatore, J. Valsiner, S. Strout, & J. Clegg (Eds.), *Yearbook of Idiographic Science 2008* (Vol. 1, pp. 23–38). Rome, Italy: Firera Publishing. (First published 2006, in *International Journal of Idiographic Science* [Online Journal], Article 1. Retrieved August 28, 2007, from http://www.valsiner.com/articles/)

Molinari, L., & Emiliani, F. (1996). More on the structure of social representations: central core and social dynamics. *Papers on Social Representation* [Online Journal], *5*(1), 41–49 .

Moscovici, S. (1976). *La psychanalyse son image et son public. Etude sur la répresentation sociale de la psychanalyse*. Paris, France: Presses Universitaires de France [English edition by G. Duveen (2008), *Psychoanalysis. Its Image and Its Public*. Cambridge: Polity Press]. (Original work published 1961)

Mossi, P. G., & Salvatore, S. (2011). Psychological transition from meaning to sense. *European Journal of Education and Psychology, 4*(2), 153–169.

Muller, J. P. (1996). *Beyond the psychoanalytic Dyad: Developmental semiotics in Freud, Peirce and Lacan*. London, England: Routledge.

Neisser, U. (Ed.). (1987). *Concepts and conceptual development: Ecological and intellectual factors in categorization*. Cambridge, England: Cambridge University Press.

Neuman, Y. (2009). On love, hate and knowledge. *The International Journal of Psychoanalysis, 90,* 697–712.

Neuman, Y. (2010). Penultimate interpretation. *The International Journal of Psychoanalysis, 91,* 1043–1054.

Neuman, Y., & Tamir, B. (2009). On meaning, consciousness and quantum physics. *Journal of Cosmology, 3,* 540–547.

Niedenthal, P. M., Halberstadt, J. B., & Innes-Ker, Å. H. (1999). Emotional response categorization. *Psychological Review, 106*(2), 337–361. doi:10.1037//0033-295X.106.2.337

Nicolò, G., Dimaggio, G., Procacci, M., Semerari, A., Carcione, A., & Pedone, R. (2008). How states of mind change in psychotherapy: An intensive case analysis of Lisa's case using the Grid of Problematic States. *Psychotherapy Research, 18*, 645–656.

Nightgale, D. J., & Cromby, J. (Eds.). (1999). *Social constructionist psychology: A critical analysis of theory and practice*. Buckingham, England: Open University Press.

Nitti M., Ciavolino E., Salvatore, S., & Gennaro, A. (2010). Analyzing psychotherapy process as intersubjective sensemaking. An approach based on discourse analysis and neural network. *Psychotherapy Research, 20*(5), 546–563.

Nisbett, R. E., & De Camp Wilson, T. (1977). Telling more then we can know: Verbal reports on mental processes. *Psychological Review, 84*(3), 231–257.

Odgen, T. H. (2004). The analytic third: Implications for psychoanalytic theory and technique. *The Psychoanalytic Quarterly, 73*(1), 167–194.

Osgood, C. E., Suci, G. J., & Tannenbaum, P. H. (1957). *The measurement of meaning*. Chicago, ILL: University of Illinois Press.

Paniccia, R. M. (2003). The school client as an unknown friend: a stranger. *European Journal of School Psychology, 1*(2), 247–285.

Panksepp, J. (1998). Affective neuroscience: The foundations of human and animal emotion. Oxford, England: Oxford University Press.

Panofsky, E. (1962). *Studies in iconology* (2nd ed.). New York, NY: Harper & Row. (Original work published 1939)

Peirce, C. S. (1932). On sign: In C. Hartshorne, & P. Weiss (Eds.), *Collected papers of Charles Sanders Peirce* (Vol. II). Cambridge, MA: Harvard University Press. (Original work published 1897)

Peirce, C. S. (1932). Harvard lecture on pragmatism. In C. Hartshorne & P. Weiss (Eds.), *Collected papers of Charles Sanders Peirce* (Vol. II). Cambridge, MA: Harvard University Press. (Original work published 1902)

Peirce, C. S. (1958). Letter draft to Mario Calderoni. In A. W. Burks (Eds.), *Collected papers of Charles Sanders Peirce* (Vol. VIII). Cambridge, MA: Harvard University Press. (Original work published 1905)

Perret Clermont, A. N. (1993). What is it develops? *Cognition and Instruction, 11*(3–4), 197–205.

Perret–Clermont, A.-N., Pontecorvo, C., Resnick, L. B., Zittoun, T., & Burge, B. (Eds.). (2004). *Joining society: Social interaction and learning in adolescence and youth*. Cambridge, England: Cambridge University Press.

Pine, F. (1988). The Four psychologies of psychoanalysis and their place in clinical work. *The Journal of the American Psychoanalytic Association, 36*, 571–596.

Pizarroso, N., & Valsiner, J. (2009, April). *Why developmental psychology is not developmental: Moving towards abductive methodology*. Paper presented at the Society of Research in Child Development, Denver, CO.

Puget, J., Bernard, M., Games Chaves, G., & Romano, E. (1982). *El grupo y sus configuraciones* [The group and its configurations]. Buenos Aires, ARG: Lugar.

Rapaport, D. (1960). *The structure of psychoanalytic theory: A systematizing attempt*. New York, NY: International Universities Press.

Ratner, C. (2008). Cultural psychology and qualitative methodology: Scientific and political considerations. *Culture & Psychology, 14*(3), 259–288.

Rayner, E. (1995). *Unconscious logic: An introduction to Matte Blanco's bi-logic and its uses.* Hove and New York: Brunner-Routledge Taylor and Francis Group.

Reyes, L., Aristegui, R., Krause, M., Strasser, K., Tomicic, A., Valdes, N., et al. (2008). Language and therapeutic change: A speech acts analysis. *Psychotherapy Research, 18,* 355–362.

Ribeiro, A., Gonçalves, M., & Santos, A. (2012). Innovative moments in psychotherapy: From the narrative outputs to the semiotic-dialogical processes. In S. Salvatore, A. Gennaro, & J. Valsiner (Eds.). *Making sense of infinite uniqueness: The emerging system of idiographic science (Yearbook of Idiographic Science, Vol. 4,* pp. 149–176). Charlotte, NC: Information Age Publishing.

Ricoeur, P. (1981). *Hermeneutics, & human sciences* (J. B. Thompson Ed. and Trans.) Cambridge, England: Cambridge University Press.

Rommetveit, R. (1992). Outlines of a dialogically based social-cognitive approach to human cognition and communication. In A. H. Wold (Ed.), *The dialogical alternative towards a theory of language and mind* (pp. 19–44). Oslo, N: Scandinavian University Press.

Rosa, A. (2007). Act of psyche. In J. Valsiner, & A. Rosa (Eds.), *The cambridge handbook of sociocultural psychology* (pp. 205–237). Cambridge, England: Cambridge University Press.

Rudolph, L. (2006a). The fullness of time. *Culture and Psychology, 12*(2), 157–186.

Rudolph, L. (2006b). Mathematics, models and metaphors. *Culture and Psychology, 12*(2), 245–265.

Rumelhart, D. E., & McClelland, J. L. (1986). *Parallel distributed processing: Exploration in the microstructure of cognition. Volume I: Foundation; Volume II: Psychological and biological models.* Cambridge, MA: The MIT Press.

Russell, R. L. (Ed.). (1994). *Reassessing psychotherapy research.* New York, NY: Guilford Press.

Safran, J. D., & Muran, J. C. (2000). *Negotiating the therapeutic alliance. A relational treatment guide.* New York, NY: Guildford Press.

Salgado, J., & Clegg, J. W. (2011). Dialogism and the psyche: Bakhtin and contemporary psychology. *Culture & Psychology, 17*(4), 421–440.

Salgado, J., & Cunha, C. (2012). Positioning microanalysis: The development of a dialogical–based method for idiographic psychology. In S. Salvatore, A. Gennaro, & J. Valsiner (Eds.), *Making sense of infinite uniqueness: The emerging system of idiographic science (Yearbook of Idiographic Science, Vol. 4,* pp. 95–123). Charlotte, NC: Information Age Publishing.

Salvatore, S. (2003). Note per un modello della formazione alla competenza psicologica: Il caso della psicologia per la scuola [Notes on the model of the training of psychological competence: The case of the psychology for the school]. *Psicologia Scolastica, 2*(2), 161–181.

Salvatore, S. (2006). Models of knowledge and psychological action. *Rivista di Psicologia Clinica, 1*(2–3). Retrieved June 21, 2008, from http://www.rivistadipsicologiaclinica. it/english/number2/Salvatore.htm

Salvatore, S. (2011). Psychotherapy research needs theory: Outline for an epistemology of the clinical exchange. *Integrative Psychological and Behavioural Science, 45*(3), 366–388.

Salvatore, S. (2012). Social life of the sign: sensemaking in society. In J. Valsiner (Ed.), *The Oxford handbook of culture and psychology* (pp. 241–254). Oxford, England: Oxford Press.

Salvatore, S. (2013). The reciprocal inherency of self and context. Outline for a semiotic model of constitution of experience. *Interacções, 24*(9), 20–50. Retrieved June 3, 2013, from http://www.eses.pt/interaccoes

Salvatore, S. (2014). The mountain of cultural psychology and the mouse of empirical studies. Methodological considerations for birth control. *Culture & Psychology, 20*(4), 477–500. doi:10.1177/1354067X14551299

Salvatore, S. (in press). The contingent nature of psychological intervention. From blind spot to basic resource of psychological science. In G. Sammut, G. Foster, R. Ruggieri, U. Flick, & S. Salvatore (Eds.). *Methods of psychological intervention (The Yearbook of Idiographic Science, Vol. 7)*. Charlotte, NC: Information Age Publishing.

Salvatore, S., Forges Davanzati, G., Potì, S., & Ruggieri, R. (2009), Mainstream Economics and sensemaking. *Integrative Psychological and Behavioral Science, 43(2)*, 158–177.

Salvatore, S., & Freda, M. F. (2011). Affect Unconscious and Sensemaking. A Psychodynamic Semiotic and Dialogic Model. *New Ideas in Psychology, 29*, 119–135.

Salvatore, S., Gelo, O., Gennaro, A., Manzo, S., & Al-Radaideh, A. (2010). Looking at the psychotherapy process as an intersubjective dynamic of meaning–making. A case study with discourse flow analysis. *Journal of Constructivist Psychology, 23*, 195–230.

Salvatore, S., & Gennaro, A. (2012). The inherent dialogicality of the clinical exchange. Introduction to the special issue. *International Journal for Dialogical Science, 6*(1), 1–14 .

Salvatore, S., & Gennaro A. (2014). The clinical exchange as communicational field: Outlines of a general Semiotic and Dynamic theory of the psychotherapy process. In O. C. G. Gelo, A. Pritz, & B. Reiken (Eds.), *Psychotherapy research: Foundations, process, and outcome*. Berlin, Germany: Springer.

Salvatore, S., Gennaro A., Auletta A., Grassi R., Rocco, D., & Gelo, O. (2011). Dynamic Mapping of the Structures of Content in Clinical Settings (DMSC). A new coding system for analysing the patient's narratives. *Psychology and Psychotherapy: Theory, Research and Practice. 85*(4), 391–423. doi:10.1111/j.2044-8341.2011.02038.x

Salvatore, S., Gennaro, A., Auletta, A., Tonti, M., & Nitti, M. (2012). Automated method of content analysis. A device for psychotherapy process research. *Psychotherapy Research, 22(3)*, 256–273.

Salvatore, S., Gennaro, A., & Valsiner, J. (Eds.). (2012). *Making sense of infinite uniqueness: The emerging system of idiographic science (Yearbook of Idiographic Science, Vol. 4)*. Charlotte, NC: Information Age Publishing.

Salvatore, S., Gennaro, A. & Valsiner, J. (Eds.). (2014). *Multicentric Identities in a Globalizing World (Yearbook of Idiographic Science, Volume 5)*. Charlotte, NC: Information Age Publishing.

Salvatore, S., Lauro–Grotto, R., Gennaro, A., & Gelo, O. (2009). Attempts to grasp the dynamicity of intersubjectivity. In J. Valsiner, P. C. M. Molenaar, M. C.

D. P. Lyra, & N. Chaudhary (Ed.), *Dynamic process methodology in the social and developmental sciences* (pp. 171–190). New York, NY: Springer.

Salvatore, S., & Scotto di Carlo, M. (2005). *L'intervento psicologico per la scuola* [Psychological intervention for the school]. Rome, Italy: Edizioni Carlo Amore.

Salvatore, S., Tebaldi, C., & Potì, S. (2009). The discursive dynamics of sensemaking. In S. Salvatore, J. Valsiner, S. Strout, & J. Clegg (Eds.), *Yearbook of Idiographic Science–Volume 1* (pp. 39–72). Rome: Firera Publishing. (First published 2006, in *International Journal of Idiographic Science [Online Journal]*, Article 3. Retrieved June 28 2007, from http://www.valsiner.com/articles/salvatore.htm).

Salvatore, S., Tonti, M., & Gennaro, A. (in press). How to model sensemaking. A contribution for the development of a methodological framework for the analysis of meaning. In M. Han (Ed.), *The subjectified and subjectifying mind*. Charlotte, NC: Information Age Publishing.

Salvatore, S., & Tschacher, W. (2012). Time dependency of psychotherapeutic exchanges: The contribution of the theory of dynamic systems in analyzing process. *Frontiers in Psychology, 3,* 253. doi:10.3389/fpsyg.2012.00253

Salvatore, S., & Valsiner, J. (2006). Am I really a psychologist? Making sense of a super–human social role. *European Journal of School Psychology, 4*(2), 127–149.

Salvatore, S., & Valsiner, J. (2009). Idiographic science on its way: Towards making sense of psychology. In S. Salvatore, J. Valsiner, S. Strout, & J. Clegg (Eds.), *Yearbook of Idiographic Science* (Vol. 2, pp. 9–19). Rome, Italy: Firera Publishing Group.

Salvatore, S., & Valsiner, J, (2010). Between the General and the Unique: Overcoming the nomothetic *versus* idiographic opposition, *Theory & Psychology, 20*(6), 817–833.

Salvatore, S., & Valsiner, J. (2011). Idiographic science as a non–existing object: The importance of the reality of the dynamic system. In S. Salvatore, J. Valsiner, A. Gennaro, & J. B. Traves Simon (Eds.), *Yearbook of Idiographic Science* (Vol. 3, pp. 7–26). Rome, Italy: Firera Publihing Group.

Salvatore, S., & Valsiner, J. (2014). Outline of a general psychological theory of the psychological intervention. *Theory & Psychology, 24,* 217–232. doi:10.1177/0959354314524295.

Salvatore, S., Valsiner, J. Gennaro, A., & Traves Simon, J. B. (Eds.). (2011). *Yearbook of Idiographic Science* (Vol. 3). Rome, Italy: Firera Publishing Group.

Salvatore, S., Valsiner, J., Strout, S., & Clegg, J. (Eds.). (2009a). *Yearbook of Idiographic Science* (Vol. 1). Rome, Italy: Firera Publishing Group.

Salvatore, S., Valsiner, J., Strout, S., Clegg, J. (Eds.). (2009b). *Yearbook of Idiographic Science* (Vol. 2). Rome, Italy: Firera Publishing Group.

Salvatore, S., & Venuleo, C. (2008). Understanding the role of emotion in sensemakingL A semiotic psychoanalytic oriented. *Integrative Psychological and Behavioral Science, 42*(1), 32–46.

Salvatore, S., & Venuleo, C. (2010). The unconscious as source of sense: A psychodynamic approach to meaning. In B. Wagoner (Ed.), *Symbolic transformation: The mind in movement through culture and society* (pp. 59–74). London, England: Routledge.

Salvatore, S., & Venuleo, C. (2013). Field dependency and contingency in the modelling of sensemaking. *Papers on Social Representation* [Online Journal], *22*(2), 21.1–21.41.

Salvatore, S., & Zittoun, T. (Eds.). (2011a). Outlines of a psychoanalytically informed cultural psychology. In S. Salvatore, & T. Zittoun (Eds). *Cultural psychology and psychoanalysis in dialogue: Issues for constructive theoretical and methodological synergies* (pp. 3–46). Charlotte, NC: Information Age Publishing.

Salvatore, S., & Zittoun, T. (Eds.). (2011b). *Cultural psychology and psychoanalysis in dialogue: Issues for constructive theoretical and methodological synergies.* Charlotte, NC: Information Age Publishing.

Sammutt, G., Daanen, P., & Sartawi, M. (2010). Interobjectivity: Representations and cultural artifacts in cultural psychology. *Culture & Psychology, 16*(4), 451–463.

Sammut, G., Tsirogianni, S., & Wagoner, B. (2012). Representations from the past: social relations and the devolution of social representations. *Integrative Psychological and Behavioral Science, 46*(4), 493–511.

Sanchez–Cardenas, M. (2011). Matte Blanco's thought and epistemological pluralism in psychoanalysis. *The International journal of psycho-analysis, 92*(4), 811–831. doi:10.1111/j.1745–8315.2011.00381.x

Dreher, A. U., & Sandler, J. (1996). *What do psychoanalysts want? The problem of aims in psychoanalytic therapy.* London, England: Routledge.

Sandler, J., & Sandler, A.–M. (1978). On the development of object reletionships and affects. *International Journal of Psycho-Analysis, 59,* 285–296.

Sanford, A. J. (1987). *The mind of man: Models of human understanding.* London, England: Harvester Wheatsheaf.

Sasso, G. (2011). *La nascita della coscienza* [The birth of consciousness]. Rome, Italy: Astrolabio.

Sato, T. (2011). Minding money: How understanding of value is culturally promoted. *Integrative Psychological and Behavioral Science, 45*(1), 116–131.

Sato, T., Yasuda, Y., Kido, A., Arakawa, A., Mizoguchi, H., & Valsiner, J. (2007). Sampling reconsidered: Idiographic science and the analyses of personal life trajectories. In J. Valsiner, & A. Rosa (Eds.), *Cambridge handbook of sociocultural psychology* (pp. 82–106). Cambridge, England: Cambridge University Press.

de Saussure, F. (1977) *Course in general linguistics* (W. Baskin, Trans.). Glasgow, Emgland: Fontana/Collins. (Original work published 1916)

Schachter, S., & Singer, J. (1962). Cognitive, social, and physiological determinants of emotional state. *Psychological Review, 69*(5), 379–399.

Scheidegger, R., & Tuscher, T. (2011). Who is responsible for the crisis? Perceived self–efficacy in politics and economics and attitudes towards the market economy. *Revue internationale de psychologie sociale, 4*(24), 5–21.

Schenellenberg, E. G. (1996). Expectancy in melody: Tests of the implication-realization model. *Cognition, 58,* 75–125.

Scorsese, M. (Director). (2013). *The Wolf of Wall Street* [Motion Picture]. United States: Paramount Pictures.

Simon, H. A. (1957). *Models of man: Social and rational.* New York, NY: Wiley and Sons.

Singer, J. L. (1998). Daydreams, the stream of consciousness, and self-representation. In R. F. Bornstein, & J. M. Masling (Eds.), *Empirical perspectives on the psychoanalytic unconscious* (pp. 141–186). Washington, DC: American Psychological Association.

Sloane, R. B., Staples, F. R., Cristol, A. H., Yorkston, N. J., & Whipple, K. (1975). *Psychotherapy versus Behavior Therapy*. Cambridge, MA Harward University Press.

Smedslund, J. (1982). Commons sense as psychosocial reality. A reply to Sjöberg. *Scandinavian Journal of Psychology, 23*(1), 79–82.

Smedslund, J. (1988a). *Psycho-logic*. Heidelberg: Springer-Verlag.

Smedslund, J. (1988b). What is measured by a psychological measure? *Scandinavian Journal of Psychology, 29*, 148–151.

Smedslund, J. (1992). Are Frijda's "laws of emotion" empirical?. *Cognition & Emotion, 6*, 435–456.

Smedslund, J. (1995). Psychologic: Common sense and the pseudoempirical. In A. Smith, R. Harré, & L. V. Langenhove (Ed.), *Rethinking psychology* (pp. 196–206). London, England: Sage.

Smith, M. L., Glass, G. V., & Miller, T. I. (1980). *The benefit of psychotherapy*. Baltimore, MD: John Hopkins Hospital University Press.

Sovran, T. (1992). Between similarity and sameness. *Journal of Pragmatics, 18*, 329–344.

Sriram, S. (2014). Negotiating identity in immigrant families: Indian Muslim youth in the United States of America. In S. Salvatore, A. Gennaro, & J. Valsiner (Eds.), *Multicentric Identities in a Globalizing World (Yearbook of Idiographic Science, Vol. 5*, pp. 219–249). Charlotte NC: Information Age Publishing.

Stein, R. (1991). *Psychoanalytic theories of affect*. London, England: Karnac Books.

Stern, D. N. (1985). *The interpersonal world of the infant*. New York, NY: Basic Books.

Stern, D. N. (2004). *The present moment in psychotherapy and everyday life*. New York, NY: W. W. Norton & Company.

Stiles, W. B., & Shapiro, D. A. (1989). Abuse of the drug metaphor in psychotherapy process-outcome research. *Clinical Psychology Review, 9* (4), 521–543.

Stolorow, R. D., Atwood, G. E., & Brandchaft, B. (1994). *The intersubjective perspective*. Hillsdale, NJ: Jason Aronson.

Stolorow, R. D., Orange, D. M., & Atwood, G. E. (2001). World horizons: A post-Cartesian alternative to the Freudian unconscious. *Contemporary Psychoanalysis, 37*(1), 43–61. (Republished in A. M. Cooper (Eds.). (2006). *Contemporary Psychoanalysis in America. Leading Analysts Present their Work* (pp. 671–699). Washington, DC: American Psychiatric Publishing).

Strupp, H. H., & Hadley, S. W. (1979). Specific *versus* non specific factors in psychotherapy. *Archives of General Psychiatry, 36*, 1125–1136.

Sullivan, H. S. (1953). *The interpersonal theory of psychiatry*. New York, NY: W. W. Norton & Company.

Tarsi, P. P., & Salvatore, S. (2013). From minimal self to self as hyper-generalized sign: Notes for an integrated model of subjectivity. *Rivista Internazionale di Filosofia e Psicologia, 4*(1), 11–21.

Teo, T. (2005). *The critique of psychology: From Kant to postcolonial theory*. New York, NY: Springer.

Thornton, T. (2008), Should comprehensive diagnosis include idiographic understanding? *Medical Health Care and Philosophy*, *11*, 293–302.

Tomkins, S. S. (1970). Affect as the primary motivational system. In M. B. Arnold (Ed.), *Feelings and emotions* (pp. 101–110). New York, NY: Academic Press.

Tonti, M. (2009). *EgoProbe* [Ad–hoc software].

Tonti, M., & Salvatore, S. (in press). The homogenization of classification functions measurement (HOCFUN): A method for measuring the salience of emotional arousal in thinking.

Toomela, A. (2007). Culture of science: Strange history of the methodological thinking in psychology. *Integrative Psychological and Behavioral Science*, *41*(1), 6–20.

Toomela, A. (2008). Variables in psychology: A critique of quantitative psychology. *Integrative Psychological and Behavioral Science*, *42*(3), 245–265.

Toomela, A., &. J. Valsiner (2010). *Methodological thinking in psychology: 60 years gone astray?* Charlotte, NC: Information Age Publishing.

Tronick, E. (2010). *Multilevel meaning making and dyadic expansion of consciousness theory: The emotional and the polymorphic polysemic flow of meaning.* In D. Fosha, D. J. Siegel, & M. Solomon (Eds.), *The healing power of emotion* (pp. 86–111). New York, NY: W. W. Norton & Company.

Tronick, E., & Beeghly, M. (2011). Infants' meaning-making and the development of mental health problems. *American Psychologist*, *6*(2), 107–119.

Tschacher, W., Ramseyer, F., & Grawe, K. (2007). Der Ordnungseffekt im Psychotherapieprozess Replikation einer systemtheoretischen Vorhersage und Zusammenhang mit dem Therapieerfolg [The order effect in the psychotherapeutic process: Replication of a dynamic systems-related prediction and relationship with the outcome]. *Zeitschrift für Klinische Psychologie und Psychotherapie*, *36*, 18–25.

Tschacher, W., Schiepek, G., & Brummer, E. J. (Eds.). (1992). *Self-organization and clinical psychology: Empirical approaches to synergetics in psychology.* Berlin, Germany: Springer Verlag.

Tversky, A., & Kahneman, D. (1981). The framing of decision and the psychology of choice. *Science*, *211*, 453–458. doi:10.1126/science.7455683

Uexküll, J., von (1926). *Theoretical biology* (D. L. MacKinnon, Trans.). New York, NY: Harcourt, Brace & Company. (Original work published 1920)

Valsiner, J. (2001). Processes structure of semiotic mediaton in human development. *Human Development*, *44*, 84–97.

Valsiner, J. (2002). Forms of dialogical relations and semiotic autoregulation within the self. *Theory & Psychology*, *12*, 251–265.

Valsiner, J. (2006, June). *The overwhelming world: Functions of pleromatization in creating diversity in cultural and natural constructions.* Keynote lecture at International School of Semiotic and Structural Studies, Imatra, Finland.

Valsiner, J. (2007). *Culture in minds and societies: Foundations of cultural psychology.* New Delhi, India: Sage.

Valsiner, J. (2009a). Integrating psychology within the globalizing world: A requiem to the post-modernist experiment with Wissenschaft. *Integrative Psychological and Behavioral Science*, *43*(1), 1–21.

Valsiner, J (2009b). Between finction and reality: Transforming the semiotic object. *Sign Systes Studies, 37*(1/2), 99–113.

Valsiner, J. (Ed.). (2012). *The Oxford handbook of culture and psychology.* New York, NY: Oxford University Press.

Valsiner, J. (2013). Creating sign hierarchies: Sociale representation In *Its Dynamic Context. Papers on Social Representation*[Online Journal], *22*(2), 16.1–16.32 .

Valsiner, J. (2014). *An invitation to cultural psychology.* London, England: Sage.

Valsiner, J., Molenaar, P. C. M., Lyra, C. D. P., & Chaudhary, N. (Eds). (2009). *Dynamic process methodology in the social and developmental sciences.* New York, NY: Springer.

Valsiner, J., & Rosa, A. (Eds.). (2007). *The Cambridge handbook of sociocultural psychology.* Cambridge, England: Cambridge University Press.

Valsiner, J., & Salvatore, S. (2012). How idiographic science could create its terminology? In S. Salvatore, J. Valsiner, & A. Gennaro (Eds.), *Making sense of infinite uniqueness: The emerging system of Idiographic Science (Yearbook of Idiographic Science, Vol. 4,* pp. 3–20). Charlotte, NC: Information Age Publishing.

Valsiner, J., Salvatore, S., Gennaro, A., & Traves Simon, J. B. (2010). Generalized realities of the particulars. In S. Salvatore, J. Valsiner, A. Gennaro, & J. B. Traves Simon (Eds.), *Yearbook of Idiographic Science* (Vol. 2, pp. 7–10). Rome, Italy: Firera Publihing Group.

Veblen, T. (1975). *The theory of the leisure class: An economic study of institution* (John Kenneth Galbraith, Ed.). Boston, MA: Houghton Mifflin. (Original work published 1899)

Veltri, G. A. (2013). Viva la Nano–Revolución! A semantic analysis of the Spanish national press. *Science Communication, 35*(2), 143–167.

Veltri, G. A., & Suerdem, A. (2011). Worldviews and discursive construction of GMO–related risk perceptions in Turkey. *Public Understanding of Science, 15,* 1–18.

Venuleo, C., Mossi, P. G., & Salvatore, S. (2014). Socio-symbolic models and retention study at university. A case study. *Studies in Higher Education.*

Venuleo C., & Salvatore, S. (2006). Linguaggi e dispositivi comunicativi. I Faccia a Faccia televisivi [Communicative languages and devices. The Face-to-Face TV debates]. In S. Cristante, & P. Mele (Eds.), *Da Vendola a Prodi. I media nelle campagne elettorali 2005–2006* (pp. 151–189). Nardò, IT: Besa Editrice.

Venuleo, C., Salvatore, S., Mossi, P. G., Grassi, R., & Ruggieri, R. (2007). The teaching relationship in the changing world. Outlines for a theory of the reframing setting. *European Journal of School Psychology, 5*(2), 151–180.

Venza, G. (Ed.). (2006). *Psicologia e psicodinamica dell'immersione subacquea* [Psychology and psychodynamics of diving]. Milano: Franco Angeli.

Verheggen, T., & Baerveldt, C. B. (2007). "We Don't Share!" Exploring the theoretical ground for social and cultural psychology: The social representation approach versus an enactivism framework. *Culture & Psychology, 13*(1), 5–27.

Verheggen, T., & Baerveldt, C. B. (2012). Mixed up perspectives: Reply to Chryssides et al. and Daanen and their critique of enactive cultural psychology. *Culture & Psychology, 18*(2), 272–284.

Visetti, Y. M., & Cadiot, P. (2002). Instability and theory of semantic forms. Starting from the case of prepositions. In S. Feigenbaum, & D. Kurzon (Eds.), *Preposi-*

tions in their syntactic, semantic and pragmatic context (pp. 9–39). Amsterdam: John Benjamins.

Vygotsky, L. S. (1986). *Thought and language* (A. Kozulin, Rev. ed.). Cambridge, MA: MIT Press. (Original work published 1934)

Wagner, W. (2011). Researching the offbeat: A metaphor. *Papers on Social Representation* [Online Journal], *20*, 10.1–10.7.

Wallerstein, R. S. (2000). Psychoanalytic research: where do we disagree?. In J. S. Sandler, & A.-M. Davies (Eds.), *Clinical and observational psychoanalytic research: Roots of a controversy* (pp. 28–31). Madison, CT: International Universities Press.

Wampold, B. (2001). *The great psychotherapy debate: Models, methods, and findings.* Mahwah, NJ: Erelbaum.

Weiss J., Sampson H., & Mount Zion Psychotherapy Research Group. (1986). *The psychoanalytic process: Theory, clinical observations, and empirical research.* New York, NY: The Guilford Press.

Wenders, W. (Director). (1982/1983). *Der stand der dinge* [The state of things] [Film]. West Germany/Portugal/USA.

Westen, D., Morrison, K., & Thompson-Brenner, H. (2004). The empirical status of empirically supported psychotherapies: assumptions, findings, and reporting in controlled clinical trials. *Psychological Bulletin, 130*, 631–663.

Windelband, W. (1998). History and natural science. *Theory & Psychology, 8*(1), 5–22. (Original speech 1894. German published version 1904)

Winnicott, D. W. (1975). Psychoses and child care. In D. W. Winnicott (Ed.), *Through pediatrics to psychoanalysis: Collected papers* (pp. 219–228). New York, NY: Basic Books.

Winnicott, D. W. (1960). The theory of the parent–infant relationship. *International Journal of Psycho-Analysis, 41*, 585–595.

Wittgenstein, L. (1958). *Philosophical Investigations.* Oxford, England: Basil Blackwell. (Original work published 1953)

Yurevich, A. V. (2009). Cognitive frames in psychology: Demarcations and ruptures. *Integrative Psychological and Behavioral Science, 43*, 89–103.

Ziemke, T., Zlatev, J., & Frank, R. R. (Ed.). (2007). *Body, language and mind: Volume 1: Embodiment.* Berlin, Germay: Mounton De Gruyte.

Zittoun, T. (2006). *Transitions.* Charlotte, NC: Information Age Publishing.

Zittoun, T. (2011). Meaning and change in psychotherapy. *Integrative Psychological and Behavioral Science, 43*(3), 325–334.

Žižek, S. (1997). *The plague of fantasies.* London, England: Verso.

ABOUT THE AUTHOR

Sergio Salvatore is Full Professor of Dynamic Psychology. His scientific interests regard the psychodynamic and semiotic theorization of mental phenomena and the methodology of analysis of psychological processes as field dependent dynamics. He also takes an interest in theory and the analysis of psychological intervention in clinical, scholastic, organizational, and social fields. On these issues he has designed and managed various scientific projects and published more than 200 volumes and papers (e-mail: sergio.salvatore@unisalento.it) articles in Italian and international journals).

Printed in the United States
By Bookmasters